Racial Uncertainties

AMERICAN CROSSROADS

*Edited by Earl Lewis, George Lipsitz, George Sánchez,
Dana Takagi, Laura Briggs, and Nikhil Pal Singh*

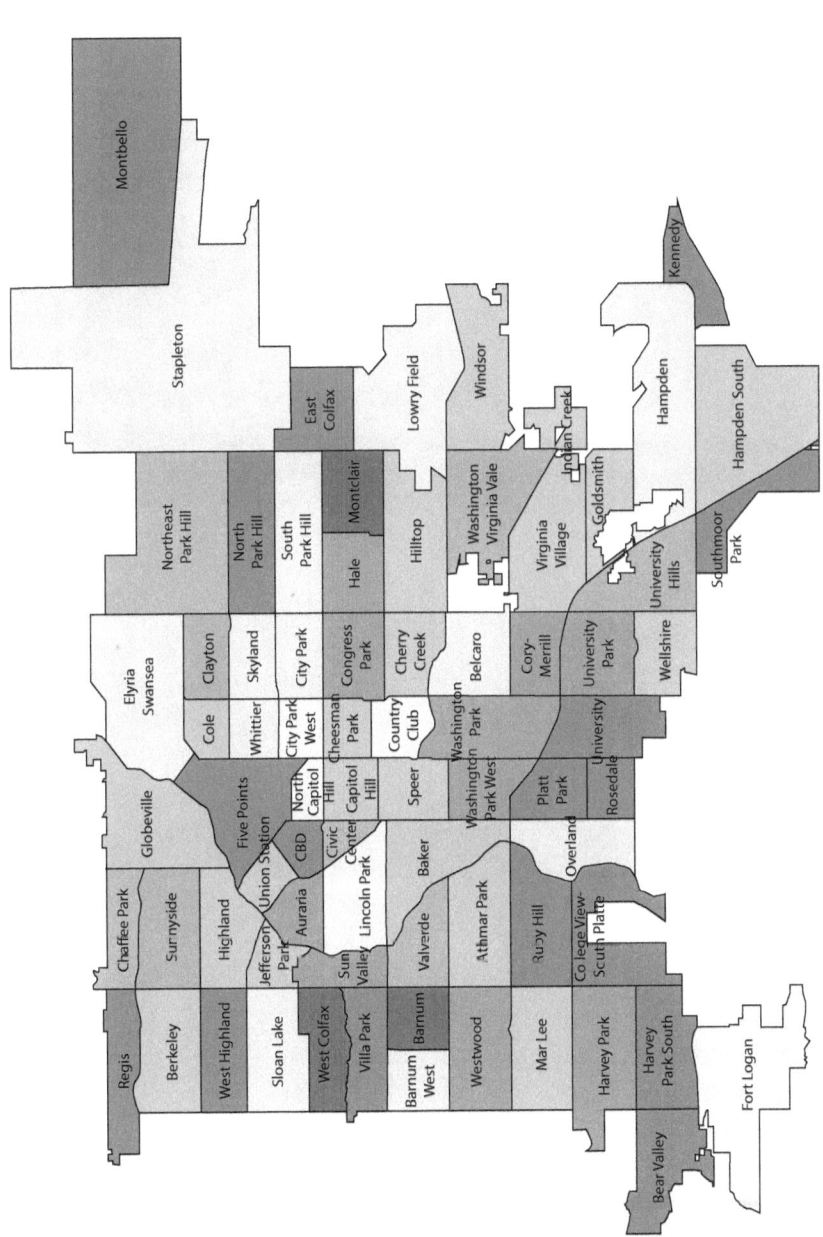

MAP 1. Denver neighborhoods, 1960s and 1970s. *Source:* Adapted from a map created by Justin Bruce Sorensen.

Racial Uncertainties

MEXICAN AMERICANS, SCHOOL DESEGREGATION,
AND THE MAKING OF RACE IN
POST–CIVIL RIGHTS AMERICA

Danielle R. Olden

UNIVERSITY OF CALIFORNIA PRESS

University of California Press
Oakland, California

© 2022 by Danielle R. Olden

Library of Congress Cataloging-in-Publication Data

Names: Olden, Danielle R., 1983– author.
Title: Racial uncertainties : Mexican Americans, school desegregation, and the making of race in post-civil rights America / Danielle R. Olden.
Other titles: American crossroads ; 68.
Description: Oakland, California : University of California Press, [2022] | Series: American crossroads ; 68 | Includes bibliographical references and index.
Identifiers: LCCN 2022011407 (print) | LCCN 2022011408 (ebook) | ISBN 9780520343344 (cloth) | ISBN 9780520343351 (paperback) | ISBN 9780520974746 (epub)
Subjects: LCSH: Segregation in education—Colorado—enver. | Mexican Americans—Education—Colorado—Denver. | Racism in education—Colorado—Denver. | Mexican Americans—Civil rights—Colorado—Denver. | Racism—Colorado—Denver.
Classification: LCC LC212.523.D46 O54 2022 (print) | LCC LC212.523.D46 (ebook) | DDC 379.2/630978883—dc23/eng/20220521
LC record available at https://lccn.loc.gov/2022011407
LC ebook record available at https://lccn.loc.gov/2022011408

31 30 29 28 27 26 25 24 23 22
10   9   8   7   6   5   4   3   2   1

For my family

CONTENTS

Acknowledgments xi

Introduction 1

1 . (Un)making Mexican American Racial Identity, 1848–1964 27

2 . Racial Migrations: The Mile High City
in Transition, 1945–1969 49

3 . Public Schools in Denver's Racialized Urban Geography 68

4 . Becoming Minority under the Law 85

5 . "Not White, Yet Not, in the Old-Style Parlance, 'Colored'" 113

6 . "American," Not "Minority": Mexican Americans
and Colorblindness 145

Conclusion 188

Notes 193
Bibliography 243
Index 265

ACKNOWLEDGMENTS

This book evolved into something I could not imagine when I first began research for it a decade ago. It took years of research, writing, thinking, workshopping, and rewriting to produce the text before you, a journey that has been humbling and, at times, frustrating. Learning how to manage a complex, book-length project was not easy for me, and at times I doubted whether I could complete it. Its publication represents a major milestone in my career as a scholar and in my life. There are many people to thank.

First and foremost, I want to acknowledge my family members, who have always provided a foundation of love and support. This book is dedicated to you. Mom, your early guidance shaped me into who I am today. Your sacrifices and hard work enabled me to thrive. Thank you for being you, a strong, independent woman who would do anything for her daughters. I don't know where I would be without you. My sisters, Laura Leigh and Whitney, helped keep me grounded when grown-up life got to be a little too much. Together, we have navigated some difficult moments. I am grateful for their commitment to our family and for my nieces and nephew, whom I adore. My grandparents, Thomas and Ruth Gonzales, were a source of strength and inspiration. Growing up, I spent just as much time in their home as I did in my own. Most of my memories of family consist of time spent there, watching movies with my cousins, cooking delicious food, and laughing together. When I think of home now, I return to that place and smile. My grandparents' early support of my educational goals made my decision to pursue graduate school and a career in higher education easier. My grandma's work supporting the education of Mexican American youth in the 1950s, 1960s, and 1970s partly inspired this project. I wish she had made it to see the book finally published, but I know she would be so proud. Both she and my grandpa would brag to all their friends about their *doctor* granddaughter, who just published a book. If you have grandparents like I did, you know what I mean. I truly miss them. Arthur, you are my rock. Thank you for building a life with me, writing with me, co-parenting dogs with me, and making this journey easier. It means so much that you are always willing to take on more home responsibilities so that I can concentrate on writing and meeting deadlines. You are a true partner.

From the early stages of my dissertation research at Ohio State University through my time as an assistant professor at the University of Utah, there have been many people who mentored me, workshopped my writing, and offered their collegiality and friendship. My graduate adviser, Kevin Boyle, was outstanding from day one. His teaching and advising were integral to my development as a scholar. Lilia Fernández and Judy Wu also shaped my trajectory in important ways. Combined, they helped me become a better thinker and writer. They became my biggest advocates, writing countless letters of recommendation for fellowships, grants, and jobs. After I graduated and left Ohio State, they continued to support my scholarship and career.

At the University of Utah, my colleagues in the History Department embraced me and my work and welcomed me into the department as an equal. Making the transition from graduate student to assistant professor can be challenging and intimidating, but having the right peers can make all the difference. I am grateful to have landed in a department that values my contributions and helps ensure my success. Several people deserve my special thanks. Beth Clement, Susie Porter, Janet Theiss, Nadja Durbach, and Matt Basso read drafts, helped me craft fellowship applications, wrote recommendation letters, and took the time to mentor me as I navigated life as an assistant professor. Eric Hinderaker, Becky Horn, Paul Reeve, Greg Smoak, Ben Cohen, and Ray Gunn served on my review committees for formal reviews, where they read and evaluated my scholarship and teaching. University of Utah Tanner Humanities Center (THC) director Bob Goldberg and my fellow THC fellows workshopped a part of the manuscript, while peers in other departments, including Annie Fukushima and Hokulani Aikau, read an early version of my introduction and provided much-needed feedback. In ways big and small, my U colleagues helped make the publication of this book possible.

People further away from home also contributed. I value tremendously these individuals for their willingness to support me and my scholarship. Ed Muñoz, Adrian Burgos, and Andrew Sandoval-Strausz stepped in at critical moments to write letters of recommendation for various fellowships. Workshops at the Clements Center for Southwest Studies at Southern Methodist University and the Center for Great Plains Studies at the University of Nebraska-Lincoln gave me the opportunity to discuss some of the central ideas in the book and helped me produce one of the chapters. Katrina Jagodinsky and Pablo Mitchell coedited a volume that resulted from these workshops. Their leadership on that project, *Beyond the Borders of the Law: Critical Legal Histories of the North American West*, is much appreciated. Working together on that volume has been one of the highlights of my career. Other contributors read and commented on drafts of my essay, which became part of chapter 6. In addition to Katrina and Pablo, I especially want to thank Tom Romero, Kelly Lytle Hernández, Dana Weiner, and Allison Powers Useche for their useful and generative remarks that no doubt influenced the final text you see here. Tom's expertise on Denver and the *Keyes* case, moreover, was tremendously helpful. His willingness to meet with me, send me resources, and connect me to other people, as well as his wonderful scholarship, aided me throughout this project.

Researching and writing a book often is a solitary process, but having people to write with and be accountable to makes it more community-oriented and, at times, fun. Sonya Alemán reached out and invited me to join her writing group when I first got to the University of Utah. I completed my first dissertation revisions with that group of women, sitting in Salt Lake Roasting Company on a weekly basis. When Noël Voltz arrived on campus, she became a good friend and a favorite writing buddy. The University of Utah women of color writing group and annual writing retreat provided a space to write, as well as to talk about the joys and pains of writing. Back in Columbus, Eva Pietri, Yalidy Matos, and Delia Fernández were my regular writing comrades. We spent hours in Apropos, drinking coffee, diet Coke, and sometimes wine, crafting our dissertations in solidarity. Along the way, we became best friends.

Eva, Yalidy, and Delia, along with Tiffany Bourgeois and Mei-Ling Rivera-Cerezo, also helped me to relax, cut loose on the dance floor, and laugh until my stomach hurt. They made graduate school one of the most memorable parts of my life by becoming my confidants, advisors, cheerleaders, and motivators. Our nights out, recovering from the weekly grind that was the graduate experience, were epic. Our Halloween costumes were unforgettable. Our careers took us to different parts of the country, but they still hold a special place in my heart. Now, many job moves, weddings, and children later, we still celebrate each other's victories and major milestones. Ladies, thank you for your friendship.

This book would not have been possible without the financial support of numerous entities. At Ohio State University, I received research support from the Department of History, the College of Arts and Sciences, the Graduate School, the Office of Diversity and Inclusion, and the Diversity and Identity Studies Collective at OSU (DISCO). During the early stages of my dissertation research, I received support from the Coca-Cola Critical Difference for Women research program, and as I neared completion, I received a year-long Presidential Fellowship from the Ohio State Graduate School that allowed me to finish and defend my dissertation. At the University of Utah, I was awarded fellowships from the THC and the University Research Council. A research grant from the Charles Redd Center for Western Studies at Brigham Young University provided crucial funding that enabled me to visit archival collections I had not used in my dissertation. As I finalized my revisions, a yearlong National Endowment for the Humanities Fellowship allowed me time away from teaching to focus on the book.

Finally, I want to thank the amazing librarians and archivists who assisted me through years of research. David Hayes at the University of Colorado at Boulder was particularly helpful. He volunteered to take me to lunch during my first visit so that he could learn more about my project and recommend primary and secondary sources. His intimate knowledge of UC-Boulder's collections and his expertise in regional history proved invaluable. Library and archives professionals at the Denver Public Library Western History Collection, the Blair-Caldwell African American Research Library, History Colorado, Auraria Library Special Collections, and the National Archives and Records Administration in Denver assisted me during several archival visits over the years. This book would not be possible without their important work.

Introduction

"NOSOTROS VENCEREMOS." In English, "We shall overcome." The words were scrawled across a large poster board and carried by a high school student who sat atop the shoulders of one of his peers. Next to them another pair marched down the street, one sitting on the other's shoulders, with a sign that read "Shaffer must go."[1] (See figure 1.) They were joined by hundreds of other students from West High School and surrounding schools who, moments earlier, had walked out of their classrooms and onto the street. The march was a protest against the Denver Public Schools (DPS) that was set off by racist remarks made by social studies teacher Harry Shaffer. Students reported that he purposely mispronounced Spanish surnames and made disparaging remarks about Mexican Americans in class. As young Mexican Americans, they were fed up with teachers like Shaffer and a curriculum that ignored their group histories and contributions while celebrating US exceptionalism. They were sick of administrators who punished them more harshly than White students and a school system that tracked them into vocational courses rather than advanced academic or college preparation classes while doing nothing to address the high rate of Mexican American dropouts. On March 20, 1969, they had had enough.

The walkouts that day and the following two days were a catalyst for change for many Mexican Americans in Denver. When they walked out a second time, they were greeted by the Denver police, clad in riot gear and armed with nightsticks. They sprayed the students with mace and clubbed their bodies even though, according to many witnesses, they were peacefully assembling. The third day the clashes continued as students remained out of school, protesting in and around the area surrounding West High School. The *Denver Blade*, one of two African American newspapers in the city,

FIGURE 1. West High School student demonstration. 1969. Photo by Dick Davis. Courtesy of The Denver Public Library, Western History Collection, WH2129.

compared the incident to the nationwide urban uprisings that sprang up every summer between 1965 and 1968, its front-page headline boldly proclaiming, "Summer in March."[2] From the perspective of that paper's editors, Denver appeared on the verge of rebellion, and Mexican Americans were right in the middle of it.

Three months later, on June 19, 1969, a group of White, Black, and Mexican American parents filed a lawsuit against DPS, arguing that the district intentionally segregated Black and Mexican American pupils from White pupils. Denver school officials, they maintained, were guilty of violating the Fourteenth Amendment rights of both Mexican American and Black students.[3] *Wilfred Keyes v. School District No. 1, Denver, Colorado* went on to become the first "non-southern," or "de facto," school segregation case heard by the US Supreme Court. When the court ruled in favor of the plaintiffs in 1973, *Keyes* set a nationwide precedent that even school districts without a history of state-sanctioned segregation could be in violation of *Brown v. Board of Education of Topeka* (1954). Denver's school desegregation story, therefore, is integral to the history of desegregation in modern America. As in other school districts across the United States with large populations of Mexican Americans or other Latinas/os, school desegregation in Denver did not proceed along Black-White lines.[4] Both the litigation and the various community responses it elicited unfolded according to the multiracial formations that structured social, political, and economic life in the Mile High City and many other places.

The first story describes one of many instances in the late 1960s and 1970s when Mexican Americans protested for a more socially just public school system, one that recognized and valued Mexican Americans' historic and contemporary contributions to American society. Their struggles for bilingual and bicultural education, as well as more Mexican American teachers, counselors, and administrators, were central to the burgeoning Chicana/o movement. The second story illustrates integration advocates' commitment to desegregated schooling. For many African Americans, in particular, school integration was essential for ensuring high-quality, equal education for all students. This was not true for all African Americans in all places, but in Denver the vast majority supported the integrationist project. By connecting these two separate but interrelated histories, *Racial Uncertainties* unpacks a different history of civil rights and racial formation in the late 1960s and 1970s. Mexican Americans and African Americans in Denver had different conceptions of what educational equality entailed, although there was always some crossover. At the very moment when Mexican Americans in the city began to organize effectively for the betterment of Mexican American education, organizing that prioritized bilingual-bicultural education, integration proponents initiated what would become a precedent-setting case that many felt hindered the ability of the school district to implement bilingual-bicultural programs. Desegregation and the enactment of bilingual-bicultural education programs were not inherently contradictory, but many Mexican Americans understood them to be in conflict. From their perspective, if the school district spread Mexican American students around the district, as the *Keyes* plaintiffs sought, bilingual-bicultural programs would not be feasible. Thus, many Mexican Americans pitted desegregation against bilingual-bicultural education and believed that only one of these reforms could be realized. This was a dilemma faced all over the country, one that White politicians exploited to help break apart coalitions between African Americans, Asian Americans, and Latinas/os, and to win Asian American and Latina/o votes.[5] Adopting this strategy as governor of California, Ronald Reagan argued on multiple occasions that school desegregation would spell the end of bilingual education efforts in the state. "We have in Los Angeles," he remarked in a 1970 press conference, "the community of Americans of Mexican Descent," who desire and often require bilingual programs. He cautioned that desegregation would imperil those efforts. "I don't know how we'd meet it [desegregation] if you disperse those students out of that neighborhood and scatter them all over the Los Angeles School District."[6]

Later that year he partly justified his signing of a bill that attacked school desegregation by saying he was protecting bilingual education "in Spanish-speaking areas."[7]

Divergent visions of quality education for Mexican Americans and African Americans worked in tandem with distinct but interconnected racial projects that demonstrate how constructions of Mexican American racial identity and racial politics shifted during the late 1960s and 1970s. A racial project, according to Michael Omi and Howard Winant, is "simultaneously an interpretation, representation, or explanation of racial identities and meanings, and an effort to organize and distribute resources (economic, political, cultural) along particular racial lines." It encompasses both the ideological and material manifestations of race in any given society. Different racial projects emerge in specific times and spaces and are always a reflection of the particular historical context in which they develop.[8]

One such project involved Mexican Americans' reconceptualization of their racial identity as a resistance tactic designed to challenge White hegemony in US culture and society. As more and more Mexican Americans cast off the logics of colonialism and whiteness in favor of a politics of Chicanismo, they transformed into Chicanas/os. To be Chicana/o was to reject identification with whiteness, long a Mexican American social uplift strategy. It was to reclaim Indigenous history and ancestors. As a radical philosophy, Chicanismo meant accepting a distinct Chicana/o identity, becoming more aware of Chicanas/os' shared history of struggle and injustice, and developing a desire to work within the community for Chicana/o liberation. These politics informed Mexican American educational organizing, as well as their responses to calls for integration. For many Chicanas/os, integration with Whites would not provide the kind of education they sought for their children. These politics also shaped how Mexican American lawyers understood Mexican American racial positionality. When attorneys with the Mexican American Legal Defense and Educational Fund (MALDEF) intervened in *Keyes* on behalf of Mexican Americans, they argued that because Chicanas/os were part of a distinct, non-White/non-Black race, they had a right to representation to protect their specific interests.

While many Mexican Americans adopted Chicana/o identities and politics, still others rebuffed such thinking. Content with society as it was and their place within it, these Mexican Americans continued to embrace the long-standing practice of claiming racial whiteness. Thus, a second racial project involved the maintenance and deployment of whiteness to challenge school desegregation. Some of these individuals supported bilingual-bicultural education and worried that school desegregation would eliminate such programs. Others staunchly rejected both desegregation and bilingual-bicultural education. In both cases, these Mexican Americans either claimed a White identity or embraced the politics of whiteness in their opposition to court-ordered desegregation.

My study of Denver demonstrates that these dynamics played an important role in the reworking of Mexican American racial identity and in broader patterns of racial formation that centered Mexican American racial uncertainties. Disputes over where Mexican Americans were racially located—were they closer to whiteness or blackness—revealed important details about how people conceptualized school desegregation, race, and rights in the post–civil rights period. Conversely, how various groups and individuals organized around school desegregation illuminated much about how they racially constructed Mexican Americans.

Mexican Americans' ambiguous racial identities resulted in an array of complications that, on the one hand, provided support for Denver school officials in their attempt to prove they had not intentionally segregated Black and Mexican American students and, on the other hand, provided multiple avenues of resistance for parents who refused to accept school desegregation was the law of the land. The constant debates over whether Mexican Americans were White or non-White encouraged school officials, parents, community activists, and lawyers to racialize Mexican Americans in whatever way would benefit them. That is, all parties utilized Mexican American racial uncertainty as a weapon in their attempts to secure or challenge school desegregation. Attorneys for the *Keyes* plaintiffs positioned them as "minority" and grouped them with African Americans to prove to the courts that DPS was guilty of maintaining a dual school system that contained "majority Anglo" schools and "majority minority" schools. DPS lawyers countered that "minority" was never a category utilized by school officials and, moreover, "Hispanos," as Mexican Americans were called in Denver, were White. The courts' determination that Mexican Americans were minority, akin to African Americans, set off debates among Mexican Americans of various racial and political subjectivities about their individual and collective identities. While Denver had a robust Chicana/o movement, and many Mexican Americans were influenced by its racial politics, others rejected the racial and political ideology coming out of the movement and remained committed to long-standing notions of Spanish whiteness. Such understandings filtered into the contest over school desegregation and helped some Mexican American opponents of desegregation challenge their placement in the district court's plan. As these various groups fought over the implementation of the court's desegregation plan, Mexican American racial uncertainty became not only a point of debate but also a useful argument against race-based civil rights remedies. The fact that people could not agree on whether Mexican Americans were White or non-White, even after the Supreme Court agreed with the plaintiffs that they were minority, raised critical questions about the meaning of race and the legality of requiring racial balance in the schools when not even Mexican Americans could agree on their own racial identities.

This history of school desegregation and Mexican American racial formation demonstrates that the race work in-between Black and White is fertile ground for examining the complexity and absurdity of race in modern America, as well as the longevity and adaptability of Mexican American whiteness. As people tried to articulate, negotiate, and adjudicate Mexican American racial identity, they brought to the surface long-standing debates over the relationship between Mexican Americans and whiteness and the role of the state in determining racial identity in the post–civil rights nation. Denver's school desegregation case and the various Mexican American responses to it challenged what had become "common sense" understandings of race, ethnicity, and culture.[9] As in other cities with multiracial student populations that included Latinas/os, their very existence in the public schools forced the courts, attorneys for both sides, school officials, and parents to grapple with the racially in-between status of Mexican Americans. The existence of such racial uncertainty and its utility as a tool of resistance to civil rights are hallmarks of the operation of race in post–civil rights America. People's inability to categorize Mexican Americans as either White or Black and subsequent debates about their location along the racial spectrum raised questions about the legitimacy of court-ordered desegregation and provided avenues for challenging it. That some Mexican Americans were among these voices only added credibility to the argument that court-ordered desegregation was not only illegal but un-American.

MEXICAN AMERICANS AND WHITENESS

The contention over Mexican American whiteness or non-whiteness in Denver was influenced by the legacies of migration from northern New Mexico and southern Colorado earlier in the twentieth century. Most Mexican Americans in Denver traced their family roots back to this region, which over centuries had developed particular social, cultural, and economic relations that were the products of "double colonization," first by the Spaniards and then by the Americans.[10] Contestations over land, water, and other resources forced the mestizo peoples who called this region home to develop new strategies of resistance and survival. As they navigated the new American social order, they came to understand themselves as "Hispanos," a culturally unique people with deep ancestral ties to the region that linked them to the Spanish settlers of the sixteenth and seventeenth centuries.[11] While memories of Spanish colonization were prominent in Mexican American identity constructions across the Southwest, they played a particularly important role in northern New Mexico and southern Colorado, an area that one scholar labeled the "Hispano Homeland."[12] In response to US colonialism and White racism, Mexican Americans in this region developed a mythology about the Spanish origins and cultural distinctiveness of Hispanos or Spanish Americans, a mythology that reinforced Spanish whiteness and helped shape civil rights politics in the post–World War II period.

Speaking in the 1960s, Dr. Daniel T. Valdes stated, "Hispano is a cultural term accurately applied to people of and from Spain, Mexico, Cuba, and any other country with a Spanish heritage.... And, of course, it identifies with the presently powerful transplanted Europeans, rather than the intelligent and highly imaginative, often non-literate, Indian peoples."[13] Valdes explained that racially, Hispanos were "biologically white Caucasians."[14] Thus, *Hispano* was an ethnic identity that denoted cultural distinctiveness and racial whiteness. It was an identity construction that held firm for many *nuevomexicanos* in the twentieth century and to the present day.

By 1969, when *Keyes* was filed, many Mexican Americans were undergoing a major shift in the way they racially identified and formed their racial politics. No longer content to identify as Hispano, these mostly young people took up the cause of the burgeoning Chicana/o movement and proclaimed themselves now to be proud "Chicanas/os." For them, the terms *Hispano* or *Spanish American* celebrated a White, European ancestry and history, which they now rejected. Instead of whiteness, they celebrated brownness, a color identity that positioned them in stark opposition to Whites and linked them more closely with their Indigenous ancestors. But these newer ideas did not influence everyone. Instead, many Mexican Americans remained committed to older notions of racial identity and political subjectivity, and they positioned themselves against the expanding Chicana/o movement. In Denver, political conflicts between these various factions of the Mexican American community were frequent, particularly once the city's most visible Chicana/o social justice organization, the Crusade for Justice, began to agitate regularly for social, economic, and political changes. The battle over school desegregation only heightened these conflicts.

While the vexing question of Mexican American whiteness had shaped ideas regarding Mexican American racial categorization for over a century, the changed social, cultural, political, and legal context of the late 1960s and 1970s breathed new life into this long-standing issue.[15] Simply, the reasons people claimed or rejected whiteness changed. This does not mean that the previous rationales for or against whiteness disappeared; rather, the list of possible rationales expanded. Throughout the 1930s, 1940s, and 1950s Mexican American civil rights efforts were centered on winning whiteness from the courts and recognition of that whiteness by individual states and local communities. If only Whites would acknowledge Mexican Americans as fellow White citizens, the argument went, they would be able to take advantage of all the privileges such whiteness conferred. When Mexican Americans in the League of United Latin American Citizens (LULAC) began their campaign against segregated "Mexican" schools in Texas, they argued that such schools were illegal because you could not segregate White children from "other White" (Mexican American) children.[16] In 1954, when the Supreme Court heard a case dealing with the civil rights of Mexican Americans for the first time, lawyers for the plaintiff argued that even though Mexican Americans were White, state officials treated them *as if they were not* White. They were, in other words, a "distinct class" of Whites.[17] Such actions, they claimed, proved that the state of Texas was guilty of violating Mexican Americans' constitutional rights. Achieving recognition of Mexican American whiteness was an important step in Mexican Americans' efforts to secure full access to the benefits of US citizenship. In a society built first on Native American dispossession and Black enslavement, then the US conquest of northern Mexico, becoming fully American meant being White.

The passage of the 1964 Civil Rights Act, which formally ended legal discrimination, and the 1965 Voting Rights Act, which outlawed racial requirements for voting, dramatically altered the terrain upon which civil rights battles were waged. Whiteness was still a prerequisite for full Americanism in the post–Jim Crow nation, but it was no longer the sole method of challenging discrimination in the courts. The civil rights movement, the Chicana/o movement, new civil rights laws, legal decisions, and Great Society programs, created largely in response to the civil rights upheavals of the previous decade, initiated a cultural shift in how Mexican Americans conceptualized their difference, organized for social change, and developed legal strategies for challenging discrimination.

By the late 1960s many Mexican American civil rights leaders and attorneys began to frame their strategies around the idea that Mexican Americans were racially distinct from both Whites and Blacks, a repositioning that allowed them to put Mexican Americans' nonwhiteness to political and legal use. They no longer were bound by the "other White" strategy adopted by Mexican American civil rights advocates in the 1930s. Yet whiteness still had great allure for some Mexican Americans. Particularly those with lighter skin color and middle-class status, but also others drawn to the privileges of whiteness, identifying as White and buying into White racial politics still held the best promise of material success, social acceptance, and political power. Efforts to categorize Mexican Americans racially as something other than White, such as the requirement to classify them as "minority" for racial balance purposes in *Keyes*, challenged the precarious White existences they had built. The Chicana/o movement, too, raised serious questions about Mexican Americans' relationship to race and racial politics, questions that forced some of them to reinforce their claims to whiteness and its benefits. They sought, in the formulation of legal scholar Cheryl Harris, to assert their property rights in whiteness, rights they had come to expect as the natural entitlements of whiteness.[18] This included the right to send their kids to school where they saw fit, regardless of what the courts said. In this way, claiming whiteness in the post–civil rights period could also, and often did, mean rejecting the social, economic, and political changes brought on by the civil rights movements of the previous decade. It meant opposition to being labeled "minority" in the new context of group rights that made possible civil rights victories like court orders for school desegregation.

The historical scholarship on Mexican American whiteness demonstrates the contingent nature of racial formation and the important ways that whiteness has operated in Mexican American communities, as both an enabler of social hierarchy and a producer of material wealth. Studies on mid-twentieth-century Mexican American civil rights politics have pointed to the ways groups like LULAC and the American G.I. Forum (AGIF) organized around the politics of whiteness. By emphasizing their status as US citizens and their whiteness, civil rights leaders in these groups espoused a moderate political ideology very much in line with the period. Historians who have documented these racial politics differ in how they interpret their meaning and in how much significance they ascribe to Mexican American claims of whiteness. One side of the debate underscores how Mexican Americans, who "walked the color line" in a place like Texas, employed anti-immigrant and anti-Black politics to secure their own whiteness and, in the process, their status as full-fledged American citizens. According to this interpretation, middle-class Mexican Americans in groups like LULAC eschewed alliances with Mexican immigrants and African Americans to prove they were worthy of whiteness and, thus, full belonging.[19] Other scholars maintain that whiteness was a strategic necessity, rather than a true representation of how Mexican Americans self-identified and thought about the world around them. In a Jim Crow society, Mexican American civil rights proponents' tactical choices were limited by the Black-White color line and its corresponding social, economic, and political structures. Rather than attack the legality of Jim Crow, they chose the much simpler and more pragmatic approach, which was to argue that they fell on the White side of the color line. Much of LULAC's work to secure Mexican American civil rights, moreover, was transnational, demonstrating a commitment to maintaining Mexican cultural, social, and political ties. While they privileged American citizens of Mexican descent, they did not always turn their backs on the Mexican immigrants among them.[20]

By focusing on Denver and the historic connection between Mexican Americans in that city and northern New Mexico/southern Colorado, *Racial Uncertainties* contributes new insights to this important scholarly conversation. By the late 1960s and 1970s, many Mexican Americans in Denver had adopted the racial politics of the Chicana/o movement, but others continued to accept earlier racial constructions that were rooted in colonial relations and a staunch acceptance of the politics of whiteness, what Daniel Martinez HoSang describes as "political whiteness." As a conceptual category, "political whiteness describes a political subjectivity rooted in white racial identity, a gaze on politics constructed by whiteness." It is a way of looking at the world and one's place in it, a roadmap for how to think, act, and vote to secure and defend the psychological and material benefits of whiteness, not merely a description of the politics of people who understand themselves to be White.[21] For Mexican Americans who identify as White, "political whiteness" operates in the same ways, but it also is adapted for the particular needs and investments of ethnic others. These individuals think, act, and vote in the name of (aspirational) whiteness, but they evoke their ethnicity both to support the bootstraps narrative of hard work and upward mobility that defines their identities and to provide cover for their support of the politics of whiteness. I argue that these politics were reinforced not only by public displays of Chicana/o pride and power, with which many Mexican Americans vehemently disagreed, but also by the court's remaking of Mexican American racial identity in the *Keyes* case. Compelled to develop a strategy for keeping their children in the neighborhood school, some Mexican Americans challenged their racialization as "minority" and insisted they were White. This 1970s claiming of whiteness was as strategic as it had been in earlier decades. Strategic choices, however, still have political consequences. In the context of the post–civil rights period, denying Mexican American nonwhiteness and allying with the burgeoning "antibusing" movement made important political statements about Mexican American efforts to secure bilingual-bicultural education and African American efforts to dismantle segregated schooling.[22] By committing to the "antibusing" cause and putting their racial uncertainty to use in the name of "political whiteness," some Mexican Americans helped reinforce antiblackness and the growing conservative movement against civil rights.

BROWN V. BOARD OF EDUCATION AND SCHOOL DESEGREGATION IN THE POSTWAR UNITED STATES

Racial Uncertainties uses the *Keyes* case, community responses to it, and organizing around it to examine Mexican Americans' shifting racial identities and political commitments, as well as broader societal processes of Mexican American racialization in a period of profound transformation. Because of the importance of school desegregation for the racial, political, and ideological changes of the post–civil rights period, *Keyes* offers a useful lens through which to examine Mexican American racial formation. At the heart of legal and social understandings of race and civil rights in the post–World War II period was the issue of school segregation and the legal decision that laid the groundwork for desegregation efforts around the nation, *Brown v. Board of Education of Topeka* (1954).

While *Brown* initiated decades of legal challenges to school segregation and led to fewer racially concentrated schools in some places, primarily in the South, these victories were fleeting. The movement of White families from the cities to the expanding suburbs had been an important feature of postwar metropolitan America and helped erect what the US Commission on Civil Rights in 1961 called a "white noose" of suburbs around the nation's increasingly non-White central cities.[23] The Charlotte-Mecklenburg school district, which encompassed both the city of Charlotte, North Carolina, and the surrounding county, was different. There was no escaping to the suburbs for many people who lived in Mecklenburg County. In 1969, a federal judge ordered the district to desegregate and said that school officials should expand the use of "busing" to accomplish more racial balance. By the time the case, *Swann v. Charlotte-Mecklenburg Board of Education*, was heard by the Supreme Court in 1970, "busing" had become a national controversy. In 1971, the court affirmed the district court's desegregation order, setting an important precedent about the constitutionality of transporting students to effect desegregation. Whereas anti-integrationists maintained that ordering transportation of students was beyond the remedial powers of the courts, the high court ruled that transportation by bus was within the courts' powers. "Busing," the court wrote, was "one tool of school desegregation" among many and, furthermore, "desegregation plans cannot be limited to the walk-in school." School officials in districts with histories of state-sanctioned segregation, that is, could not use a neighborhood school system as an excuse for not implementing a proactive desegregation plan.[24]

As Whites continued to leave urban cores in the wake of housing and school desegregation efforts in the 1970s, the "white noose" was pulled ever tighter. Consequently, city schools became increasingly non-White, making it difficult to impossible to achieve racial balance without involving majority White suburban school districts. The Supreme Court's decision in *Milliken v. Bradley* (1974), however, halted such plans and ensured that White families who wanted to avoid integration could abandon the nation's cities for the suburbs without the fear of cross-district desegregation orders.[25] Some districts already included surrounding suburbs and could not escape city-suburb desegregation. Knowing this, anti-integrationists in some metropolitan areas moved to ensure city school districts could never combine with suburban districts. In 1974, Colorado voters overwhelmingly passed the Poundstone Amendment, which effectively ended annexations to the city of Denver by requiring a majority vote of residents in the counties that would be losing land to approve such annexations. Whereas residents of surrounding communities had enthusiastically pursued annexation in the postwar period, mostly to achieve access to the city's cheaper water and other public services, including the schools, a decisive shift occurred once school desegregation came to Denver. After the Supreme Court prohibited desegregation plans that crossed district lines in *Milliken*, White, suburban support for the Poundstone Amendment skyrocketed, helping to guarantee its victory. Passage of the amendment ensured that only limited desegregation in Denver could be achieved. The school district, in fact, never secured long-term racial balance. As more and more White families fled the city, DPS came to represent an increasingly smaller percentage of metropolitan area students. By 2003, only 19 percent attended Denver schools.[26]

When the Supreme Court issued its opinions in *Keyes* and *Milliken*, the "antibusing" movement had already gained adherents across the country, who worked to reshape the narrative around school desegregation so that Whites became the victims in the courts' zeal to force racial balance via "busing," the transportation of students to schools outside their neighborhoods to create racially balanced schools. According to the "busing" narrative, Whites in northern and western cities had had nothing to do with creating segregated schools. They should not, therefore, be punished for it by being made to "bus" their children across the city. Like the courts, they refused to acknowledge how they had benefited from discriminatory social and economic policy at the expense of mostly poor, non-White inner-city communities.[27] By embracing seemingly race-neutral arguments like "freedom of choice" and "freedom of association," White parents, homeowners, and taxpayers railed against school desegregation plans as attacks on their rights as citizen consumers and individual meritocratic class accomplishments and helped develop the colorblind legal language that eventually rolled back race-conscious civil rights remedies like racial balance and affirmative action.[28] Central to this emerging colorblind racial discourse was the idea that the US Constitution required racial nonrecognition by the state. Any recognition of race was viewed by civil rights opponents as unfair, immoral, and illegal. Such arguments became powerful tools in White efforts to undo court-ordered desegregation because without the ability to racially categorize students, creating racial balance would be impossible. White resistance to school desegregation, along with the Supreme Court's refusal to recognize the history of government policies that had created segregated housing and schooling, greatly limited *Brown*'s reach. Within a matter of decades many of those schools that achieved some level of integration became resegregated, and many northern and western school districts became more and more racially segmented.[29]

Nonetheless, *Brown* laid the groundwork for racial discrimination jurisprudence in the postwar United States and ushered in many of the political conflicts that came to define the era. At the most basic level, this seminal civil rights case established that racially segregated schools were unconstitutional. But there are several aspects of the Supreme Court's decision that would go on to inform the *Keyes* case and the outcomes that are explored in this book. First, *Brown* was argued and decided on the grounds that school segregation violated the equal protection clause of the Fourteenth Amendment. Thus, the court maintained that segregated schools were "inherently unequal" and violated the Fourteenth Amendment rights guaranteed by the US Constitution. Supreme Court jurisprudence going back to the 1883 *Civil Rights Cases*, however, greatly limited the reach of the Fourteenth Amendment by declaring a distinction between state and private action. In those cases, testing the constitutionality of the Civil Rights Act of 1875, the court ruled that the Fourteenth Amendment banned only state action to enforce discrimination in public accommodations like public transportation, theaters, and inns. Congress could not, therefore, prohibit discrimination in privately owned accommodations. *Brown* applied to state-mandated segregation in public schools, schools that were understood to be de jure segregated. But there were questions about whether it applied to de facto segregated schools, or schools that were segregated not by law but by "private" actions (such as a family's individual choice of where to reside and send their children to school).[30] When the Supreme Court heard the *Keyes* case, this was one of the questions before it. Were "neighborhood schools" constitutional, even when they produced segregated schooling? This is the reason *Keyes* set such a significant precedent.

The fact that *Brown* was decided on the grounds that school segregation violated the equal protection clause of the Fourteenth Amendment also informed the racial negotiations employed by the plaintiffs in *Keyes*. Passed and ratified in the aftermath of the Civil War, the principle of equal protection clearly was meant to apply to African Americans. But there was uncertainty as to whether it applied to other racialized groups. In the case of Mexican Americans, it took decades for the courts to finally rule that it did. At the same time *Brown* was winding its way through the courts, a case dealing with the civil rights of Mexican Americans, *Hernandez v. Texas*, was doing the same. In that case, the plaintiff, Pete Hernandez, maintained that his Fourteenth Amendment right of equal protection was violated because the jury that convicted him of murder did not have any Mexican Americans on it. He had not, therefore, received a trial by a jury of his peers. His lawyers argued that in Texas Mexican Americans systemically were kept out of jury pools because of their *ethnicity*. Even though they were *racially* White, Texas officials treated them as if they were non-White. In their opinion, the judges for the Texas Court of Criminal Appeals cited a case they had heard the year before in which they pointed out that the equal protection clause of the Fourteenth Amendment applied to two groups only, Whites and Blacks. Mexican Americans, they wrote, "are not a separate race but are white people of Spanish descent, as has often been said by this court. We find no ground for discussing the question further." Irritated that this issue kept coming up in their court, the judges even remarked that "no member of the Mexican nationality challenges that statement." They seemed to mock Hernandez's lawyers for trying to argue they were a "special class" of Whites who should be granted a "special privilege": the right to a trial by jury that included people of their nationality.[31] The Supreme Court overruled this decision, stating that in Jackson County, Texas, Mexican Americans were a "distinct class," separate from Whites based on their ancestry or national origin. Thus, they were protected by the Fourteenth Amendment. The court did not, however, issue a ruling on the universal status of Mexican Americans. Instead, the justices opined that the determination must be made in each case, based on the local conditions and social relations in the community in question.[32] This remained legal doctrine in the late 1960s, when integration proponents in Denver were pushing for DPS to develop a desegregation plan and gearing up for litigation. In order to demonstrate that Denver school officials were guilty of creating majority minority and majority Anglo schools—that is, a dual school system—the plaintiffs' lawyers in *Keyes* needed to first prove that local Whites discriminated against Mexican Americans as a class. They had to show that they were, in fact, a distinct minority. This is what explains the racial categories the plaintiffs chose to employ, as well as the strategy they developed.

The second aspect of *Brown* that informed *Keyes* and the outcomes that grew out of it was the Supreme Court's decision in *Brown II* to withhold immediate relief and defer to district courts on the specifics of the remedy. Generally, when the court ruled in favor of an aggrieved party and granted relief, it ordered the immediate implementation of that relief. Not so when it came to school desegregation. In 1955 the court famously determined that school districts in violation of its decision in *Brown* must desegregate "with all deliberate speed."[33] This timeframe was purposefully vague. Because of the explosiveness of the school integration issue, many on the court felt that a unanimous decision in *Brown I* was necessary to stave off potential problems. The justices correctly believed that many White southerners would resist once the court issued its decision invalidating school segregation, and they hoped to issue an opinion that would make the transition as painless as possible. To secure unanimity, those justices who were inclined to rule in favor of the plaintiffs had to compromise on the remedy. They had to promise to implement a remedy that gave White southerners time to come to terms with the decision. Accordingly, the court concluded that "'the personal interest of the plaintiffs in admission to public schools . . . on a non-discriminatory basis' had to be balanced against 'the public interest' in desegregating 'in a systematic and effective manner.'" A desire to appease White southerners also shaped the court's decision to adopt a gradual approach to desegregation. Rather than issue concrete guidelines for developing desegregation plans, the justices determined to leave the details to the district courts. This would ensure, they reasoned, a commitment to "local conditions" and "flexibility" in the development and implementation of plans on a case-by-case basis.[34] By adopting gradualism and vagueness, the court protected the interests of White segregationists over those of African Americans, whose constitutional rights had been violated.

These choices informed decades of school desegregation litigation and enabled anti-integrationists to resist full desegregation much more effectively than if the court had issued more specific guidelines and mandated immediate relief. *Racial Uncertainties* shows that in Denver and many other northern and western cities, the long delay between the court's initial finding that school officials had violated *Brown* and the final order to desegregate system-wide (a period of almost six years) allowed anti-integrationists to develop sophisticated arguments against a more robust and fair desegregation plan. These arguments centered on colorblindness, already a powerful weapon against race-conscious civil rights remedies. During this period of delay, people opposed to the court's order for city-wide desegregation pushed colorblind arguments beyond the common freedom of choice and freedom of association claims to "reverse discrimination" claims. According to proponents of this view, requiring "busing" to achieve racial balance was reverse discrimination against White students and families. Yet it was not only Whites who took advantage of this new argument; some Mexican Americans opposed to "busing" did as well. Their commitment to this emerging form of White resistance reveals new insights into the ideological worldviews of those Mexican Americans who retained their sense of Hispano (White) identity and political subjectivity, even as other Mexican Americans refused the same.

RACE AND ANTI–CIVIL RIGHTS POLITICS IN POST–CIVIL RIGHTS AMERICA

In the most basic sense, the descriptor *post–civil rights* refers to the period after the federal government passed the 1964 Civil Rights Act, which ended legal discrimination of the Jim Crow kind, and the 1965 Voting Rights Act, which outlawed racially motivated disenfranchisement practices. These two landmark pieces of legislation, the result of massive grassroots civil rights mobilizations, were profoundly important and set the stage for decades of legal challenges to discrimination based not only on race and ethnicity, but also on gender, sexuality, class, immigration status, age, and more. For many African Americans, the elimination of Jim Crow changed the way they lived their lives and propelled some into the growing middle class. Many scholars, writers, politicians, and news commentators have hailed these civil rights victories as a "revolution." Yet the breakdown of formal, legal discrimination and elimination of some forms of racially motivated voter suppression did not end the structural workings of race that produced the most consequential outcomes for African Americans and other racialized groups. This legislation also did not end discrimination in the law. Thus, in a second sense, I define the post–civil rights period as *ideologically* and *legally* distinct from the pre-1964 period. Under Jim Crow most Americans conceived of racism as prejudice. According to this model, racism derived from individuals' own conceptions of racial superiority and inferiority. Racism, therefore, had an important psychological dimension that could be addressed—in a way, "solved"—through intercultural education and tolerance training. Once the law made prejudiced acts illegal, some people might still be racist, but the majority rejected such prejudice as no longer socially acceptable. And if public institutions did try to discriminate, the courts could step in to remedy the wrong. Many Americans concluded, in the aftermath of this victory, that the nation had finally reached the zenith of racial liberalism. The promise of "liberty and justice for all," many believed, was finally a reality.

After 1964 this understanding of racism as prejudice held, but all was not calm. Conservative intellectuals and legal scholars convinced a wide swath of the American public that racism was over. Yet civil rights activists continued to push for reforms meant to address what Kwame Ture and Charles Hamilton referred to as "institutionalized racism."[35] Widely publicized instances of urban rebellion and the expansion of neighborhood and school integration efforts to the north and west revealed the continued existence of material racial disparities. For some this was deeply confounding. For others, urban rebellions were further proof of Black depravity and violence. And continued calls for desegregation and other civil rights were evidence of Black overzealousness and selfishness. Accusations of racism were easy to dismiss because, in many cases, there was no proof of prejudice as the motive behind individual action. A White family's decisions to move to a majority White suburb and send their children to majority White schools were not racist, such thinking implied, but rather were pragmatic economic and educational choices. As Americans moved deeper into the 1960s and 1970s, they developed sophisticated arguments, steeped in the idea of colorblindness, to combat continued calls for civil rights policies and legal decisions that would redress material inequities. Having learned that racial civility was a stronger weapon than outright racial hostility in the post–civil rights nation, these anti-integrationists embraced colorblindness with wholehearted fervor. Out of this new, colorblind worldview emerged a set of assumptions that began to guide opposition to civil rights.[36] This is the context in which the *Keyes* drama unfolded.

THE SOCIAL AND LEGAL CONSTRUCTION OF RACE

At its heart, this is a history of racemaking. By linking social, cultural, and legal history, I trace the structural, discursive, and legal shifts that produced new understandings of Mexican American racial identity in the critical period after major civil rights reform in the United States. *Racial Uncertainties* is premised on the notion that race is a sociohistorical construct. Rather than a natural or biological essence, it is a system of ideas and social relationships that change over time and look different according to region, nation, city, or neighborhood. That is, race is time and place specific. By racemaking, racialization, or racial formation I mean the process whereby individuals, groups, practices, relationships, or even spaces become imbued with racial meaning. This occurs at the level of both structure and representation, as racialization is a material and discursive phenomenon. Thus, ideas about physical appearance, behavior, morality, intellectual ability, language, and culture, among other things, are attached to specific bodies as a way of making sense of and organizing a particular society. In time, these representations of race become socially ingrained, and people start to understand them as natural or inherent, the "common sense" of race. As these ideas are filtered throughout a given society they merge with other economic, cultural, and political forces to produce racialized social structures.[37] For example, in the twentieth-century United States dominant ideas about non-White students' racial undesirability and intellectual inferiority worked in tandem with real estate and banking practices and federal policy to produce systems of racially stratified schooling across the nation.

The law is an intrinsic part of how race is made in any given society. Law operates to construct and reconstruct race both by creating and enforcing legal rules that dictate human behavior (social control) and by reflecting and reinforcing the social and cultural value systems of society at all levels. Because the law is both a set of regulations for socially acceptable behavior and a set of ideas, it operates on the levels of both coercion and ideology. Some of the earliest laws in US history had to do with defining the status of unfree people: Who was free and who was enslaved? Where could enslaved people go? How could they act? Such laws helped give social meaning to both blackness and whiteness, meanings that have survived in only sightly different forms for centuries. Immigration and naturalization law similarly has shaped the ideas that inform constructions of belonging and exclusion by limiting who could enter the nation and who could become US citizens. Starting in 1790, whiteness was a prerequisite for naturalization, a law that was not eliminated completely until 1952. These notions of whiteness and blackness filtered into everyday social encounters; were reinterpreted and reinforced at the local level; and then went on to instruct legal actors and institutions in the legal production of new racial categories, identities, and definitions. In this way, the law both produces racial knowledge and is itself manufactured by the racial knowledge that filters through society. As legal scholar Ian Haney López writes, "Through law, race becomes real becomes law becomes race in a self-perpetuating pattern altered in myriad ways but never broken."[38]

Racemaking is both a top-down and a bottom-up process.[39] In the post–World War II United States, this means that the state, through its judicial, legislative, and bureaucratic arms, produced and disseminated racial ideas that played important roles in the construction of the law, the operation of state programs, and the maintenance of US geopolitical power. The state, over the course of the twentieth century, became increasingly adept at utilizing race in its state-building projects. At the same time, racemaking is an independent, grassroots process that allows people and groups to form their own racial identities that can, and often do, change over the course of a lifetime. The courts and the US Census Bureau identified Mexican Americans as White for much of the postwar period, yet by the late 1960s increasing numbers of Mexican Americans had cast off the White label and embraced identities as brown mestizos, more akin to their Indigenous ancestors than their European ancestors. Such divergent racial projects are not an anomaly; rather, contradictory racial projects are an intrinsic aspect of racial formation.[40]

Racial Uncertainties approaches Mexican American racialization from both directions (top-down and bottom-up) because each process produced oppositional racial constructions that clashed in significant ways. Starting in the late 1960s and accelerating by the early 1970s, both the courts and the federal government began to reconceptualize Mexican Americans and other Latinas/os as non-White minorities. Prior to this period the state recognized them as White. This shift did not translate across the entire federal bureaucracy—the US Census Bureau, for example, continued to understand Latinas/os as ethnically distinct but racially White—but bureaucrats working in civil rights and other agencies tasked with implementing Great Society programs understood Mexican Americans as one of several minority groups in American society.[41] Legally, federal courts came to different conclusions about the nonwhiteness of Mexican Americans, but this was finally put to rest in *Keyes*. After 1973 Mexican Americans were legally non-White minorities. One of the purposes of this book is to trace that development. I focus on the case at the district court level in order to elucidate the legal logics that went into the formation of Mexican Americans as minority after so many years of being legally White.

The story looks slightly different from the ground level. Social movement participants, members of various organizations, students, teachers, and parents, among others, had multiple, shifting perspectives on Mexican American racial identity. While the racial politics of the Chicana/o movement had a major influence on Mexican Americans' racial and cultural identities, there were also many others who vehemently disagreed with these newer ideas. Most of the time they kept their opposition silent because there was no need to bring it out into the open. For many people, identity was deeply personal, and it was nobody else's business. But sometimes these private musings entered the public debate, as when people wrote to Denver newspapers to argue for one viewpoint or another. Within the context of the post–civil rights period, ideas about race, culture, and identity were highly politicized, helping propel them into public conversations about civil rights. Writers of letters to newspapers were not motivated simply by a desire to state their identity politics in a public forum. They were compelled to stake a position on the direction of civil rights by invoking their own racial/ethnic identity. Unpacking the connections between the politics of the era and grassroots racemaking underscores the significance of politics for Mexican American racial identity formation. "Political conflict," one scholar of race argues, "is ... itself generative of racial identity."[42] Put another way, race is always caught up in politics, just as politics are always entangled with race.

Mexican American racial construction forms the core of this book, but understanding how different groups of Mexican Americans and the wider public encountered, negotiated, adopted, and discarded various strands of racial thinking requires examining their relationship to other groups of people, primarily Whites and Blacks. Because race is relational, it always exists within a web of racial identities, representations, structures, and histories. Understanding the ways that racial ideas influence each other is essential for comprehending the complex, multiracial nature of racial formation in modern America.[43] Throughout the history *Racial Uncertainties* examines, from the Spanish conquest of what would become the US Southwest to the late 1970s, Mexican Americans were always constructed in relation to whiteness *and* blackness. Where they were positioned along the racial spectrum from Black to White was dependent upon a variety of factors, including color, class, language, gender, and location. Much of the history of Mexican American civil rights making in the middle of the twentieth century is about Mexican Americans striving to achieve whiteness, particularly in the law. *Keyes* helped upend that approach by locating Mexican Americans closer to blackness than whiteness, a strategy that not all Mexican Americans found useful or appropriate.

CHAPTER OUTLINE

Chapter 1 explores the history of Mexican American racial identity in the United States. Here I lay the theoretical framework for my analysis, situating

Mexican Americans within the broader histories of Spanish settler colonialism in the US Southwest and legal efforts to establish Mexican American whiteness. By tracing the transformation of Mexican and Mexican American racial identity from the second half of the nineteenth century through the mid-twentieth century, I explain the multiple and contesting ideas that informed Mexican American individuals' own racial identification and the ways that society and the courts racialized them. I demonstrate that many Mexican Americans in postwar Colorado were deeply influenced by their familial roots in New Mexico and the colonial legacies that shaped community life, and that Mexican American legal whiteness was a significant mid-century civil rights strategy that set the stage for litigating Mexican American racial identity in the 1970s.

The local context for school desegregation leading up to *Keyes* is examined in chapter 2. This chapter describes how post–World War II migrations reshaped the city's demographics, employment, and housing patterns. These changes, which transformed Denver into a thoroughly multiracial city, led residents to reconstruct local racial knowledge. As they grappled with not one but multiple color lines, Denverites of all races revealed fractures in the myth of western racial utopianism that had long defined Whites' understanding of race in the Mountain West. Having always taken pride in the perceived egalitarian foundations of the state and its relative racial harmony compared to many cities in other regions, they struggled to understand the racial conflict that emerged in the late 1960s, which culminated in the battle over school desegregation and "busing" that brought their city into the national spotlight.

Chapter 3 traces the development of school segregation in Denver and the schooling experiences of Mexican Americans and African Americans. Based on their distinct experiences of racialization within the Denver public schools, these two groups established different perspectives on what constituted equal schooling, and they embraced different goals and tactics for pushing school officials to address their concerns. By the late 1960s both Mexican Americans and African Americans increased their demands on DPS and adopted more forceful strategies for making sure they were heard. Whereas Mexican American students walked out of their schools demanding culturally specific education to counter the poor-quality education they received, Black activists pushed school officials to integrate Denver schools, particularly in the northeast corner of the city. By 1969 integration proponents would wait no longer, and they filed a federal lawsuit against DPS for segregating Black and Mexican American students.

During the 1970 trial, race was prominent in the arguments of both the plaintiffs and the defendants, as they each sought to define the racial identity of Mexican Americans and what constituted a segregated school. These complexities are highlighted in chapter 4. Although race was supposed to be common sense, all parties quickly discovered the difficulty of litigating a school desegregation case in a multiracial school district. With few precedents available to support such a case, in a city where there had never been any law requiring segregation, the plaintiffs' attorneys were forced to develop a new approach. By constructing an Anglo/minority binary they argued that Denver school officials had purposely maintained schools that were predominantly Anglo (White) and schools that were predominantly minority. Black and Mexican American students were included in the minority category. The defendants countered by consistently challenging the plaintiffs' racial positioning of Mexican Americans. Revealing these constructions, contradictions, and negotiations highlights the ways that the post–civil rights racial regime radically altered the motivations guiding people's use of racial knowledge, as well as the stakes of Mexican American racial categorization.

Chapter 5 moves from the courtroom to the community to examine various responses to the case. Here I position Denver within the national struggles over civil rights, the Chicana/o movement, school desegregation, and "busing." As *Keyes* moved up the court circuit, it became highly politicized, polarizing the city even further along racial lines and intensifying cultural and political divisions among Mexican Americans. With so many different perspectives on race and civil rights in Denver's Mexican American community, it was difficult for Chicana/o movement activists to achieve the unity they sought. These divisions are clearer when viewed through the lens of the city's school desegregation drama. By centering Mexican Americans' diverse political subjectivities, often deeply informed by racial ideology, this chapter complicates our understanding of the Chicana/o movement and its role in shaping racial understandings in the post–civil rights period.

Chapter 6 explores the interactions between the district court, the plaintiffs, the DPS Board of Education, various community organizations, and Denver citizens. While the court struggled to define racial identities and balance interests, different community factions tried to do the same. As they sought to achieve the best possible scenario for their own children, some Denver parents used the flexibility of racial categories to claim alternative racial identities, and Mexican Americans were often at the center of such efforts. A little noticed but revealing outcome of these racial negotiations was the emergence of mixed-race activism as a tactic for upending court-ordered desegregation. By pointing out the existence of thousands of mixed-race children, many with a Mexican American parent, in the district and questioning how they would be racialized for the purpose of racial balance, they identified what could become a major hurdle for racial balance advocates. Their use of mixed-race identities as an argument against race-conscious civil rights remedies was an important step in the evolution of anti-integrationism and, in turn, a critical step in the development of colorblind racial ideology.

This chapter also brings the story through 1976, a decisive year in the implementation of the district court's desegregation plan. In March, a group of Mexican American parents filed a separate lawsuit against the Denver schools for forcing their children to be transported to another school. In an interesting twist, they actually sued school officials for implementing the court's order in *Keyes*. On the one hand, their lawsuit resulted from these parents' deep frustrations with the ways in which the courts had considered their educational needs and desires in the city's desegregation case. Many Mexican Americans had never argued for integration, believing that it would not solve the problems their children faced in the Denver schools. Rather, they advocated for bilingual education and culturally relevant courses and pedagogy. These parents' lawsuit was a final attempt to get the courts to listen to their pleas. On the other hand, in making their claims they emphasized their rejection of racial classification schemes that placed them on the minority side of the Anglo/minority binary. In so doing they dismissed both Black efforts to desegregate Denver schools and Mexican American efforts to unite around a collective approach to the debate over equal educational opportunity spawned by *Keyes*. I demonstrate that Mexican Americans like these parents, opposed to court-ordered desegregation, participated in the development of colorblind racial ideology by positioning themselves as "Americans" opposed to racial classification in the name of civil rights. By refusing to be identified as "minorities," they joined others around the nation in challenging the entire framework of racial classification in the post–civil rights period.

Throughout the text I use several different terms to describe racial groups, so it is important to clarify how I am using them and why I choose to use some terms over others. The terminology used to talk about various racial and ethnic groups is highly contested among both scholars and the general public. Moreover, because one of my goals is to expose the ambiguity of racial understandings, it is somewhat problematic to choose racial labels because I risk oversimplification. For clarity and consistency, however, I have chosen specific terms. To denote people traditionally understood as "Caucasian," or those with European ancestry, I use the term *White*. When citing from sources I often use *Anglo*, which was a common term used to designate White people in Colorado and much of the Southwest during this period. I use *Black* and *African American* interchangeably, while sometimes I use *Negro* or *colored* when I am citing the sources.

To describe people of Mexican descent, I use the term *Mexican American*. While there were some noncitizen Mexicans in Denver, the vast majority were born in the United States and migrated from other parts of the Southwest. In Denver, the most common term used to describe Mexican Americans was *Hispano*, although *Spanish*, *Spanish-American*, *Spanish-speaking*, and *Spanish-surnamed* were used as well.[44] I have chosen not to use Hispano to avoid the language of ethnicity and to focus on race, even though that was the most common term used in Colorado in the postwar period. I do, however, use Hispano when making particular references to the sources. *Chicana/o* became a commonly used term in the 1960s as a new movement for Mexican American rights gained momentum. The Chicana/o movement in Denver was central to shaping the discourse around racial identity that emerged among activists and the wider Mexican American community. I do not use Chicana/o throughout the text because it was not in wide usage until the late 1960s, and one of the central divides that ran through the Mexican American community was between those who claimed to be Hispano and those who claimed to be Chicana/o. Mexican American is a more neutral term, denoting both Americans of Mexican descent and a smaller number of Mexican nationals.

At specific times I use the term *non-White* to refer, collectively, to the groups of people historically racialized by most Whites as "other," including Mexican Americans. Although I argue that whiteness is fluid and dynamic and that grouping all people constructed as non-White into one category essentializes their experiences, it is also true that most people within certain groups have remained outside the boundaries of whiteness. I avoid using this term as much as possible, but at times I use it to refer to the large and diverse group of people who have historically experienced racial discrimination in the United States, the people who have been denied the privileges of whiteness in everyday life. I adhere to Stephanie Wildman's observation that sometimes we must be strategically essentialist in how we talk about race if we want to really expose how it operates in American society. Critical theorists have demonstrated the problems with essentialism. "But strategic essentialism," Wildman suggests, "recognizes that we have to name things in order to talk about them and that sometimes we should."[45]

ONE

(Un)making Mexican American Racial Identity, 1848–1964

DURING THE POST–WORLD WAR II PERIOD civic leaders in Denver's Mexican American community made education a major part of their outreach efforts and activism. For them, education was at the core of what it meant to be a well-adjusted, prepared, and responsible citizen. It was Mexican Americans' lack of education, they argued, that was the root of their many social and economic ills. High rates of school absenteeism and dropouts led to youth delinquency and fewer economic opportunities, which in turn contributed to their lower socioeconomic standing compared to other groups in the city and higher rates of incarceration. Members of the Latin American Educational Foundation (LAEF), founded in 1949, made it their mission to keep Mexican Americans in school and provide financial opportunities for them to attend college. Comprised of middle-class Mexican Americans, many of whom were involved in broader campaigns to aid their community, the LAEF's members set out to uplift their fellow Mexican American citizens at a time when Mexican Americans attended college at extremely low rates. Their efforts were significant not only for those they were able to assist but for their families and neighborhoods as well. Ultimately, LAEF hoped that more educated and professionally successful Mexican Americans would amount to a more stable, healthy, middle-class community.[1]

Not only did the LAEF promote education generally among Mexican Americans, it also made history education a central part of its own identity and advocacy work. Promoting Mexican Americans' own history in the region was an essential part of its mission to make the community respectable. To that end, members of the organization and others like it urged Denverites to recognize their history and their contributions to the development of the state and the surrounding area. In speeches, newspaper articles, reports, and

FIGURE 2. Latin American Education Foundation (LAEF) seal, detail of full image, inside of pamphlet entitled "Strength for America," ca. 1950s. The central image of the conquistador and the slogan celebrated Spanish conquest and suggested that the LAEF would conquer educational inequities, just as its Spanish forebears had conquered the Americas. Photo courtesy of The Denver Public Library, Western History Collection, WH1839.

other publications, they argued that as Spanish Americans they were inheritors of a great European civilization, whose ancestors first conquered the American Southwest. The LAEF's promotional tagline on its seal, "LAEF: A New Conquest in Learning," demonstrates the emphasis Mexican American leaders placed on their history as Spanish settlers (see figure 2). Driving the point home was the image that appeared in the middle of the seal: a conquistador, the archetypal image of Spanish conquest in the Americas.[2]

When Colorado governor John Love signed a proclamation naming November 14–20, 1955 Latin American Educational Foundation Week, a gambit to kick off a fundraising drive, several members of the organization dressed as conquistadors and rode on horseback through downtown city streets to the state capitol in a show of pageantry that must have provoked curiosity and surprise. But the message was clear: while Mexican Americans were deemed a "problem" by many in the larger Denver community, their history as Spanish conquerors and settlers made them essential players in the "taming" of the region, founders of many of its cities, and participants in the making of a modern metropolis. Without them, such messaging implied, the US West would look very different indeed.[3]

The strategies these Colorado activists used to write Mexican Americans into the dominant narrative of US history reveal the ways that Mexican American racial identity was shaped by the history of settler colonialism in the postwar period. As a social uplift tactic, embracing and putting to political use Spanish settler histories—a move that required they disavow or de-emphasize their Indigenous ancestors—enabled them to overcome

Mexican Americans' long-standing racial ambiguity by linking them to the European conquest of the Americas. Aligning with conquest, moreover, was a de facto alignment with whiteness. Particularly among those who traced their roots back to colonial New Mexico, as many in Denver did, the history of Spanish colonialism in what became the US Southwest was more than a point of pride; it was proof of their European ancestry and right to the privileges of whiteness, privileges withheld from Indigenous peoples and African Americans.

Identification with the Spanish settlers of centuries past was a crucial part of how many Mexican Americans in Denver identified and viewed the pressing racial issues of the postwar decades. By examining this history and linking it to postwar Denver, this chapter develops an interpretation of Mexican American history that helps recast the complicated racial and political negotiations that emerged in the period after major civil rights reform in the United States. Understanding modern Mexican American racial politics necessitates a longer historical view that extends temporally back to the colonial period and geographically to Mexico and other parts of Latin America. It also means examining how Mexican American racial identity has been litigated in the courts. Thus, the second goal of this chapter is to trace the ways that Mexican Americans were racially constructed by US law prior to the mid-1960s. During the 1930s, 1940s, and 1950s, Mexican American civil rights attorneys had come to rely on arguments that situated Mexican Americans on the White side of the Black-White color line.

As Mexican Americans at mid-century struggled to compete for access to high-quality education, decent-paying jobs, affordable housing, and equal citizenship in unwelcoming social environments, memories of Spanish colonialism played a central role in the ways they articulated their belonging. Local projects of colonial storytelling appear throughout the archives of Mexican American civic and social organizations in Denver. The LAEF's strategic adoption of a Spanish colonial identity is but one example. As community advocates worked to obtain funds for implementing much-needed social welfare programs and justified the need for continued attention to the needs of poor Mexican Americans, they relied on these stories for validation in a White settler society. "Those who first brought the Christian religion to the southwest—the first white settlers in the state and region," claimed Julian Samora in a mid-1950s foundation grant application, were those Americans of Spanish descent who made up about 10 percent of Colorado's population. These "descendants of the pioneers of the southwest" were in desperate need of an adult education program that would, over time, help mitigate high unemployment and underemployment, substandard housing, and high rates of incarceration.[4] As inheritors of Spanish civilization, such claims implied, these Mexican Americans were deserving of aid and, more than that, had a *right* to a decent standard of living. By evoking Spanish whiteness—"the first white settlers in the state and region"—Samora, perhaps unknowingly, reproduced and claimed for Mexican Americans an already deeply embedded notion: White people had a fundamental right to the things that constituted modern life, including safe, sanitary, and modern living conditions.

These kinds of arguments were also useful in encouraging a sense of pride and belonging among Mexican Americans, particularly the youth, who often lacked an understanding of their own history and place in society. A 1950 pageant, entitled Fiesta de Coronado: A Pageant of the Peoples of the Southwest, was promoted by Mexican American civic leaders for its potential to "give dignity to the people by showing that they came from a background in which a noble tradition plays an all-important part." Typical of many dramatizations in the early twentieth century that depicted Spanish settlement in the Southwest, Fiesta de Coronado celebrated the Spanish conquest and glamorized life under Spanish rule, providing a mythologized history lesson on the benefits of colonization. In California, for example, many mission plays were performed, often to reinforce racial distinctions between White Spaniards and mixed-race poor peons. During a 1915 performance of a mission play in Santa Clara, California, a young, light-skinned man dressed as a caballero proclaimed to the audience that they were about to be treated to a vision of Spanish California wherein the people were "young and gay," and so happy and free that they "used to sing and dance and laugh in the sunshine."[5] In 1950, Denver pageant organizers argued that the pageant message, that Spanish Americans not only participated in the development of the state but were in fact the original settlers, would promote strong moral development and enhanced self-confidence among Mexican American youth.[6] The authors of the pageant (see figure 3) promoted the show as a celebration of Spanish American contributions to the state of Colorado. Even the Colorado governor endorsed the pageant, noting that the state had Spanish settlers to thank for many Colorado place-names, including the name of the state itself. He maintained, moreover, that the contributions of the "descendants of the 'conquistadores'" were to be recognized and commended.[7] Claiming a settler past and present provided the framework for Mexican American inclusion efforts in the immediate postwar years and

FIGURE 3. Three of the four authors of Fiesta de Coronado: A Pageant of the Peoples of the Southwest, *Denver Post*, July 19, 1950. Left to right: Dr. Arthur Campa of the University of Denver, Bernard Valdez of the city's Recreation Department, and Bert Gallegos, Denver lawyer and president of the LAEF. Photo courtesy of the *Denver Post* via Getty Images.

demonstrates the ways that historical memory functions in racial and cultural identity formation.

Historians have long since documented the existence of "Spanish" or "Spanish American" identities among some of the Mexican American descendants of Spanish colonization. Throughout the Spanish, Mexican, and American periods, proximity to pure Spanish-ness (whiteness) helped dictate an individual's social status and material wealth in a society obsessed with racial caste. In New Mexico, these patterns contributed to the development of a particular identity linked to a Spanish settler past. As *nuevomexicanos* migrated into Colorado and Wyoming in the twentieth century, these identities also made the trip north. Connecting the history of Spanish colonialism to postwar transformations in Mexican Americans' racial-subject positions provides important insight into why some Mexican Americans rejected school desegregation efforts in the 1970s and, more broadly, why they aligned themselves with the politics of the "anti-busing" movement.

MEXICAN AMERICANS' TENUOUS WHITENESS

For Mexican Americans in Colorado, as for those around the nation, identity and understandings of race were informed by the specific historical contexts and patterns of migration that led to Mexican American community formation.[8] At mid-century many of them had familial roots in northern New Mexico or southern Colorado. Before moving to northeast Colorado, many of their families had lived in small rural communities that often were somewhat isolated from modern life in industrialized America. Many traced their lineage back centuries to the Spanish settlers who arrived in the seventeenth and eighteenth centuries. While they sometimes made reference to Indigenous ancestors, their understanding of the history of Spanish conquest and colonization in the New Mexico territory shaped how they conceptualized their own histories and identities. Just like the scholars and community activists who led local Mexican American civil rights efforts, most Mexican Americans in mid-century Colorado understood themselves to be "Spanish American" or "Hispano." When asked to explain their identity they frequently invoked this history. The president of Denver's Latin American Research and Service Agency (LARASA) argued in the mid-1960s that 90 percent of Mexican Americans in Colorado were from New Mexico or Colorado, while only 10 percent were from Mexico. The reason for many of the problems they faced in Denver was that they were from a "rural-folk background" that had not prepared them for urban life. One of his solutions for improving the socioeconomic position of Mexican Americans, which he often reiterated, was education to prepare them to "compete" in a modern industrialized society.[9] Rather than discuss Mexican American difference as racial, he emphasized culture. Cultural difference could be surmounted easily through assimilation, whereas racial difference was a more difficult challenge to overcome.

This history, whether accurate or not, even influenced how city committees and agencies understood the problems Mexican Americans faced.

Study committees frequently began their reports on Mexican Americans with a historical examination, a practice that did not transfer to their reports on African Americans. The discrimination African Americans faced did not merit explanation because it was self-evident that race was the cause. In the case of Mexican Americans, report authors needed to be able to describe the root cause of discrimination against them. "It is customary when writing of the Spanish-American in Denver," a 1950 survey conducted by the Denver Area Welfare Council began, "to introduce the subject on a historical note concerning the expeditions of Coronado and Cortez."[10] The authors then spent several pages outlining a simplistic version of Spanish colonial history in the US Southwest and explained that there were three distinct groups of Mexican Americans in Denver. The largest group consisted of "Spanish-colonial[s]" who were longtime residents of the Southwest and US citizens. The second group was made up of Mexicans who had migrated to the United States within the last couple of decades and their Mexican American children and grandchildren. Finally, the third group was composed of recent migrants from Mexico, many of whom had American-born children.[11] While there were some differences among the three groups in terms of their level of assimilation to US social and cultural norms, the biggest difference, according to the report, was between the "Spanish-colonial[s]" and everyone else. Even though the majority of Mexican Americans in the city lived under similar conditions and often faced the same levels of discrimination and segregation, the report's authors indicated that distinguishing between the three groups was important for studying the community, an indication that citizenship status, level of assimilation, and class were important divisions among the groups. As historian Tyina Steptoe argues, ideas about racial and cultural identity coexist alongside broader state efforts to racialize groups of people. Within each community exists a microcosm of racial and cultural ideas both similar to and different from broader racial formations.[12] While "Mexicans" were all the same in the eyes of many White Denverites, numerous Mexican Americans embraced racial subjectivities that evolved from their specific group histories in New Mexico and Colorado and, in particular, their understanding of those histories. By the mid-1960s it was standard for local study authors to address Spanish colonial history in their explanations of "Spanish American" life in the city. A Commission on Community Relations report from that period began with a lengthy history, starting with the 1598 arrival of Juan de Oñate in Santa Fe, New Mexico.[13]

This process of racial identity formation was influenced by centuries of colonial social relations and racial mixture. In colonial New Mexico, elites sought ever greater power through a convergence of gendered and racialized social relations that ensured lighter-skinned offspring and economic prosperity for their families. This "pigmentocracy" reproduced particular racial understandings about color and class that gave whiteness its social meaning.[14] Those with lighter complexions were more often the elites of society, while those with darker complexions were more likely to reside at the lower end of the socioeconomic spectrum. Families often tried to better their financial fortunes by whitening their heirs. Middle- to upper-class Mexican families sought European suitors for their daughters in hopes that they might gain social standing through the husbands' ability to literally reproduce whiteness by fathering lighter-skinned children.[15] By the turn of the twentieth century these strategies for achieving upward mobility and status were still implemented by families and individuals throughout the US Southwest. A desire to whiten families through European "blood" was so powerful that in 1904 a Mexican American family in Arizona sought out Euro-American orphans to adopt as their own, hoping their whiteness would lead to a higher social status and the ability to make more money for the family.[16]

Those who were successful often imagined for themselves a Spanish past that justified their current social position and ensured their future prosperity. In California, where the racial hierarchy became largely "land based," people could whiten themselves by acquiring land and becoming a ranchero. By the 1840s, the racial order operated through a confluence of property, class, and color.[17] In this way, it was the dispossession of Indigenous peoples of their land that made possible the social, economic, and political ascendancy of elite Spanish and, later, Mexican landholders. Yet this violent history of dispossession was erased in favor of a romanticized mythology that depicted life under colonialism as bucolic and pleasant, filled with beautiful señoritas and chivalrous caballeros. Through the deployment of this "Spanish fantasy heritage," in the words of Carey McWilliams, elite Mexicans (re)invented themselves as purely Spanish and celebrated Spanish colonization as a means of claiming a White, European identity.[18]

Nowhere was the acceptance of a glorified Spanish history and identity more enduring than in the "Hispano Homeland," a region that included northern New Mexico and southern Colorado. According to geographer Richard Nostrand, this area was home to a community of people who were both historically and ethnically unique. Here Hispanos, or Spanish

Americans, had lived since the late sixteenth century, often isolated and concentrated in small villages where a distinct culture, separate from the culture that existed among Mexicans and Mexican Americans in other parts of the Southwest and Mexico, developed and was sustained over the centuries. Their ancestors "came more directly from Spain," and "they reject that which is Mexican."[19] Nostrand's studies, published between 1975 and 1980, achieved scholarly legitimacy for a set of arguments that had been accepted and paraded around as historical accuracy for decades, and they set off a major controversy among scholars of New Mexican history and culture.[20] The New Mexico exceptionalism thesis, explains legal historian Laura Gómez, constructs New Mexican history as unique. While Mexicans and Mexican Americans in other southwestern states, like California and Texas, experienced a lot of loss in the wake of the Mexican-American War (1846–48), those in New Mexico survived relatively unscathed. The state could boast of a long history of Mexican American elected officials; less overt forms of anti-Mexican sentiment; and, of course, a widely accepted and powerful claim to Spanish, rather than Mexican, ancestry and identity.[21]

The debate is not really about the reality, historic or contemporary, of a Hispano or Spanish American identity among a large proportion of Spanish speakers in New Mexico and Colorado, but about how to interpret this reality. What social, political, or anthropological significance are scholars supposed to give to the existence of a people who understand themselves to be Hispano?[22] Most historians agree that the formation of a distinct Hispano identity is a process only understood through careful attention to the specific social, political, and economic conditions that gave rise to it. Hispano and Spanish American are, like other ethnic and racial categories, socially constructed.[23] It was the 1880 arrival of the railroad that prompted increasing numbers of Euro-American migrants to settle in areas of New Mexico that had been dominated by "Indians," "Mexicans," and other mestizo peoples for generations. On what Sarah Deutsch calls the "Anglo-Hispanic frontier," struggles over land, water, and other resources, as well as clashes over cultural traditions and ways of life, resulted in new strategies of accommodation, resistance, and survival.[24] In this space, Mexicans, Pueblos, Apaches, Navajos, Zunis, and Utes, as well as other Indigenous peoples, far outnumbered Euro-Americans, making it difficult for the latter to direct the territory to their liking. Euro-Americans *needed* some Mexicans to aid them in running local governments and establishing a social order in the Euro-American, colonial vision. Thus, not all Mexicans were excluded from participation in local governance and full citizenship in the territory. Elite Mexican men were given the vote and empowered to lead their communities. In return for their loyalty and acceptance of the American colonial venture, these elites became Spanish. That is, they were whitened. As Whites, they held certain rights that were withheld from the majority of people in the territory, even though both they and their Euro-American sponsors understood that their whiteness was fragile and that they were still racially inferior. Aware that their position was based on a tenuous whiteness, Mexican elites sought to prove their worth—in a sense, prove their whiteness—by creating a stark dividing line between themselves and those beneath them. Not only did they disenfranchise Pueblo Indians, but they also espoused a virulent form of anti-Black racism and proslavery sentiment.[25] Such were the requirements of belonging in a White settler society like the United States. To prove they were worthy and equal members of society, they had to accept and perpetuate White racial dominance.

Yet as time went on it was not only the elite who became Spanish. Many ordinary New Mexicans adopted Hispano or Spanish identities as well. In the context of shifting colonial relations, as New Mexico moved from US territory to US state, and as industrialization and modernization transformed the region, they did so as a way to resist complete social, political, and economic marginalization. In some places, embracing a Hispano or Spanish American identity enabled them to organize collectively in opposition to changes that negatively affected them and to challenge racist sentiments that painted them in a negative light. When Nellie Snyder, a Methodist missionary, published a newspaper article in 1901 that lamented the degraded state of the "native" New Mexican population, hundreds of Hispanos gathered in protest. Together, they composed a series of resolutions that called out the missionary's "lies" and "slander," and they challenged her depiction of them as "a dirty, ignorant and degraded people, a mixture of Indians and Iberians" who lacked the evangelical impulse. This *la junta de indignación*, or mass meeting of indignation, became a prime method of protest for New Mexicans during this period and helped many participants develop a sense of themselves as a distinct ethnic community.[26] They understood themselves in relation to Euro-Americans but also in opposition to Indians and Blacks. In defending themselves against Snyder's racist vitriol, they promoted themselves as Spanish conquerors, rightful claimants to the land and to full US citizenship. "I am Spanish American," proclaimed lawyer Eusebio Chacón to the gathered crowd, "as are those who hear me. No other blood circulates through my veins but that which was brought by Don Juan de Oñate and by the illustrious ancestors of my name. If there is any place in Spanish America or in the former Spanish colonies that has conserved the physiognomic traits of the *raza conquistadora* it is New Mexico."²⁷ Such a declaration must have resonated with the men and women who had assembled to defend their honor that day. Not only did Chacón push back against Snyder's depiction of them as a mixed-race, mongrel people, but he used science to proclaim Spanish Americans a White race, more European than any other descendants of Spanish colonialism. To possess Spanish "physiognomic traits" was not only to possess whiteness; it was to exhibit the behaviors and intellectual capacities of Whites. As a "race science," physiognomy was the study of physical appearance, particularly the face, and its relation to intellectual and ethical behavior. Like other race sciences, it was built on the idea that race was biological.²⁸ Such an argument challenged Snyder by proclaiming Spanish Americans both White and proper, virtuous citizens deserving of full belonging. Of course, local boosters and a growing tourism industry that celebrated the area's Spanish colonial past encouraged this transformation. A "Hispanophilic" cultural movement and the writing and dissemination of popular and scholarly history texts that adopted the mythology of New Mexico's Spanish heritage and history also contributed to this development.²⁹ By the end of the 1930s the myth of New Mexico's Spanish past was so engrained that it left little room for other interpretations, and a Spanish American or Hispano identity was firmly rooted among Mexican Americans in the region. A writer in *Harper's Weekly* captured the intensity of this feeling in 1914, echoing the words of the lawyer Eusebio Chacón:

> These Spanish people of New Mexico . . . are not of the mixed breed one finds south of the Rio Grande, or even in Arizona, where there is a small remnant of Spanish blood. Indeed, it is probable that there is no purer Spanish stock in Old Spain itself, unless it be in the remote mountain regions where there was little admixture with the Moorish population that remained in Spain and was finally absorbed.³⁰

Starting in the 1920s many New Mexicans who had lived their entire lives in the state began to migrate north into parts of southern and northern Colorado. Many chose Denver. As they established their homes in a new, urban environment, they continued to embrace a vision of history and identity that privileged their Spanish heritage. During the 1950s and 1960s they created new organizations to combat the negative perception many White

Denverites had of them and launched several initiatives aimed at improving the social and economic position of their Mexican American peers. In most cases their understanding of themselves as descendants of Spanish settlers informed the ways they organized and the inclusion strategies they developed. In particular, community activists in the immediate postwar period maintained two distinct but interrelated tactics in their quest for full social acceptance and economic mobility. First, they insisted on their distinction from Mexicans. Partly this was a holdover from an earlier period. During the 1910s and 1920s, increasing numbers of Mexicans fled the violence of revolutionary Mexico by crossing into the United States. While many of them settled in border cities like El Paso, others decided to try their fortunes farther north. Hank Lopez's father, who had been a soldier in Pancho Villa's army, predicted that jobs would be scarce in border cities that were flooded with new migrants, so he and his family, including young Hank, boarded a bus bound for Denver. There they settled into a community of other Mexicans and Mexican Americans but, as Lopez recalled in 1967, this was a community with deep divides. Those "who chose to call themselves Spanish-American" looked upon the new arrivals from Mexico with disdain and referred to them as *surumatos* (southerners). "These so-called Spanish-Americans claimed direct descent from the original conquistadores of Spain," and "insisted that they had *never* been Mexicans."[31] Despite the fact that both groups had similar physical appearances (though there was always variety), spoke the same language, and shared experiences of prejudice and discrimination in the majority White city, the Spanish Americans, whom the newcomers called *manitos* (little brothers), refused to be grouped with Mexicans. Consequently, tensions between them often boiled over. "So intense was this intergroup rivalry," Lopez explained, "that the bitterest 'race riots' I have ever witnessed—and engaged in—were between the look-alike, talk-alike *surumatos* and *manitos* who lived near Denver's Curtis Park."[32]

Many Mexican American leaders in the 1950s continued to deny any connection (racial, cultural, or national) to Mexico or Mexican-ness. When one of the two Denver dailies wrote that Spanish Americans were culturally, and by default racially, "Mexican," League of United Latin American Citizens (LULAC) members were incredulous. Their culture, they insisted, could be traced back to the American Southwest with "little or no impact from the culture of Mexico." They argued that anyone wanting to comprehend the socioeconomic condition of the city's Mexican American population needed to be informed about their (non-Mexican) history.[33] By linking them to Mexico instead of the Spanish settlers of centuries past, LULAC implied, the newspaper had done them a great disservice. In fact, American-born citizens of Mexican descent throughout the United States were acutely aware of how increasing migration from Mexico heightened White animosity toward them. One way to counter claims that they were not a part of this unwanted stream of Mexicans was to distance themselves, as much as possible, from any semblance of pro-immigrant sentiment and staunchly defend their status as Americans.[34] Similar dynamics played out in other parts of the Southwest, where LULACers and other Mexican American civil rights activists used their status as US citizens to argue for their civil rights, a strategy that often meant rejecting both Mexican-ness and pro-immigrant policies.[35] Even though the number of Mexican nationals in Denver was small compared to many cities in Texas and California, the ideological and strategic importance of distancing themselves was still an important part of their uplift strategy.

The second, and related, tactic for achieving their civil rights goals was to downplay the significance of race in their lives. On the extreme end this meant claiming a White identity for Hispanos or Spanish Americans, while on the other end it meant resisting claims that racial discrimination had harmed their community in any way. Many Mexican Americans in Denver fell somewhere in the middle, but a discussion of the two ends of the spectrum provides a useful way of explaining how racial knowledge and racial identity formation informed Mexican American political organizing in the postwar period. When Mexican American leaders came together in the early 1960s to organize LARASA, they explicitly argued that the problems they faced in Denver were not the same as those faced by African Americans because, unlike African Americans, they were not racially different than Whites. They resented Denver leaders who told them to use the Urban League as a vehicle of advancement because, quite simply, the Urban League was developed to deal with the race problem. "In contrast," they argued, "the Spanish-American background is less characterized by racial differences than it is by the 'rural-folk' culture of the American southwest."[36] LARASA's insistence on a separate organization to serve the needs of the city's Mexican American population was well founded. The organization needed a mechanism for raising awareness about the specific problems that troubled its community and for fighting for access to city resources, jobs, and housing. By tying the community's need for a service organization to their cultural distinctiveness, they resisted the argument that they were racially different from Whites. Culture talk, the use of culture to discuss matters that are ostensibly about race, has long been used as a racializing force when a more race-neutral tone is desired.[37] By the mid-twentieth century, culture had supplanted race as the way to conceptualize and talk about group difference in the United States. This shift from biological understandings of race to ethnicity was grounded in American social scientists' push to move away from biological determinism in the study of race and, in particular, the eugenics projects that had led to genocide in Europe. This new conceptualization of race as culture subsumed visible markers of difference and focused on more elastic categories like language and religion, aspects of identity that were chosen and changeable. Thus, different groups of people could be said to be distinct because of their culture, and their eventual assimilation was simply a matter of time because as they adapted to the dominant culture they would assimilate into it. Mexican Americans clearly were influenced by these ideas.[38]

What does it mean that Mexican American civic leaders claimed they did not experience racism? Does this tell us anything about the ways they self-identified and formed political ideologies? I argue that it does. Scholars have demonstrated the important links between racial and ethnic identity and how Mexican Americans think on a variety of political issues. David Gutiérrez's work on Mexicans, Mexican Americans, and the politics of immigration shows that as more and more Mexicans migrated into the United States and settled in existing Mexican American communities in the twentieth century, Mexican Americans were forced to grapple with their own ethnic identities and the political meanings they ascribed to those identities. Forced to determine how to maneuver in a society constantly experiencing large migrations from Mexico, Mexican American civic leaders and civil rights activists, in particular, had to first figure out who they wanted to be, how they wanted to act, and how they wanted to relate to dominate conceptions of Americanism. In short, before they could take a stance on the question of immigration, they had to make decisions about their own identities and histories.[39] Julie Dowling's investigation into why so many Mexicans and Mexican Americans claim to be White on the US Census also reveals meaningful connections between racial and ethnic identity and political perceptions. Her analysis, based on interviews, exposes the important relationship between how Mexican Americans racially identify and how they think about race in US life. Those who claim to be White are more likely to believe in the myth of colorblindness. That is, they are more likely to believe that race does not matter and that the only barriers to socioeconomic advancement are personal values and work ethic. Individuals who fall on this end of what Dowling calls the "Mexican American Racial Ideology Continuum" also are strongly motivated to deny or minimize their experiences of racial discrimination. Conversely, those who reside on the other end of the spectrum are more likely to identify as non-White—many of these people mark "other race" on the US Census, to indicate their difference from the available racial categories—and are more committed to anti-racism, a commitment that stems from their belief that racism is endemic in modern America. Many of Dowling's participants who identified as non-White revealed personal stories of discrimination and everyday racism and expressed solidarity with African Americans and other people of color.[40] While her study is based on data collected from 2002 to 2007, Dowling's analysis provides important insights for historians who are interested in understanding the identity politics and racial ideologies of Mexican Americans in the post–World War II period. Many of the social, economic, and political dynamics that shape present-day race relations and understandings of race, in fact, emerged in the postwar context. Increased migration to cities, deindustrialization, the transformation of the US welfare state, the expansion of the federal government's civil rights apparatus, the development of race-conscious civil rights policies and the subsequent backlash against them, and the growth of neoliberalism have all contributed to the maintenance of systemic racism. Colorblindness itself emerged in the critical decades following World War II and set the stage for today's racial landscape. Applying Dowling's framework to postwar racial thinking, in combination with Gutiérrez's insights and historical contextualization, allows for a new interpretation of postwar Mexican American racial politics.

Just like the Mexican Americans in Gutiérrez's history and Dowling's interviews, Mexican Americans in postwar Denver revealed much about their personal and collective sense of racial/ethnic identity and cultural belonging when they discussed their views on Mexican immigrants, civil rights, and racial politics generally. Denying racism was one way to demonstrate their collective understanding of racial dynamics in a multiracial environment. LARASA members recognized their city had a race problem; they just did not see themselves as a part of it. By relying on culture to explain their group difference they indicated Mexican American cultural assimilation was key to their eventual integration into US society. Such thinking built on and contributed to long-standing patterns of antiblackness within Mexican American communities. Antiblackness has deep roots in Mexican racial, cultural, gender, religious, and political formations, ideas that transferred easily to a more modern context.[41] Within the postwar United States the simple act of advocating for civil rights automatically linked one to African Americans, those understood to be most responsible for the "race problem" in American life. The well-publicized actions of Black civil rights activists in the 1950s and 1960s were hard to miss and were a major source of deepening anxieties and fears among many White Americans, who viewed direct action protest as a threat to their way of life. Some even understood them to be evidence of communist infiltration within US social and political organizations.[42] By rebuffing the suggestion that they seek help from the Urban League, a well-known African American civil rights organization, and denying their problems were tied to the burgeoning "race problem," LARASA's founding members distanced themselves from their counterparts in Denver's growing African American community and suggested that their organization's work to address Mexican American civil rights would not follow the same, radical path as that taken by the increasing number of Black activists challenging Jim Crow.[43]

Refusing to recognize that racial discrimination affected their community was one method of erasing the salience of race for Mexican Americans' lives. Another approach was simply to proclaim Mexican American whiteness, as if whiteness was the norm and did not exist as its own racial category. Daniel T. Valdes, a sociology professor, LULAC member, and frequent newspaper commentator, was emphatic in his claim to a White identity. While acknowledging the "uncertainty and ambiguity" that made racially categorizing Mexican Americans a process fraught with conflict, he used his expertise as a sociologist to provide scholarly legitimacy to his thinking on the matter. Claiming that 80 percent of the city's Spanish-surnamed population could trace their roots back to seventeenth- and eighteenth-century Spanish settlers, he pointed out the historical inaccuracy of comparing them to more recent Mexican arrivals. "What," he asked, "are the biological, cultural, political, and historical facts which must be known and used to properly label or name these people?" He began with the biological. He noted the differences in color and phenotype among "Spanish-origin citizens," but he invoked scientific authority when he said "the great bulk are anthropologically and biologically white Caucasians." Culturally, there were clear differences between Anglos and Hispanos, the term Valdes argued was the most appropriate. Their language, religion, and customs marked them as different but, he warned, this did not mean they were racially different from Whites. In fact, he even downplayed Indigenous cultural traditions within his community, remarking that their culture was "essentially European and Hispanic." Thus, even though there were some variations, Hispanos were racially *and* culturally White.⁴⁴ As members of the White race they did not have to worry about racism.

In his biography of well-known scholar and civil rights activist George I. Sánchez, historian Carlos Blanton notes this type of civil rights strategy among Mexican American activists in mid-century Texas. It was quite common. But while Blanton argues, at least in the case of Sánchez, that the racial terms used by activists and the strategies they employed to gain traction on their issues are not necessarily evidence of a strong belief in a White identity or an acceptance of anti-Black and anti-immigrant perspectives, it *is* telling that they continued to promote such ideologies.⁴⁵ It may have been strategic, but it had consequences nonetheless. By denying the importance of racism to their daily lives, they perpetuated the dangerous notion that it was a problem that only African Americans faced. The decade of the 1950s was a conservative period in American history, and Mexican Americans who fought for civil rights were limited in their ability to make radical demands. But when examined within the long history of claiming Spanish American identities and history, the civil rights strategies of the 1950s and early 1960s fit a well-established pattern that connects the late nineteenth century and the present. At any given moment there has always been a segment, varying in size, of the Mexican American community that believes itself to be racially and culturally distinct from other Mexican Americans and Mexicans. This has produced a range of ideologies and perspectives that privilege whiteness and US citizenship and that contribute to support for conservative, often racist, policy positions. In the post–civil rights era this has meant opposition to the radical politics of the Chicana/o movement, as well as anti-racist politics more generally. By the 1970s, the Chicana/o movement had shifted the racial politics of a large segment of the Mexican American community, yet it did not change all minds. Rather, it caused a great deal of division over race, identity, and civil rights.

MEXICAN AMERICAN CIVIL RIGHTS AND THE "OTHER WHITE" LEGAL STRATEGY

By the post–World War II period, the central mechanism for challenging discrimination in the courts was the Fourteenth Amendment's equal protection clause. Passed and ratified in the aftermath of the Civil War (1861–65), this principle of equal protection clearly was meant to apply to African Americans. But there were questions about whether it applied to other racialized groups. In the case of Mexican Americans, it took decades for the courts to finally rule that it did. Before that, as Mexican American civil rights activists and attorneys struggled to articulate the subordination they experienced in terms the courts would recognize, they developed a specific strategy, the "other White" argument, that held out two critical advantages. First, it enabled them to argue that state authorities (public school officials, for example) could not segregate Mexican American children from "other White" children. While this tactic did not challenge the constitutionality of segregation per se, it did allow them to attack the practice of separating Mexican Americans from Anglos. Second, the "other White" line of reasoning supported the long-standing contention that Mexican Americans were White, a legal argument that grew out of the 1848 Treaty of Guadalupe Hidalgo. This treaty, which ended the Mexican–American War and ceded northern Mexico to the United States, granted US citizenship to all Mexican citizens who resided in that area and chose not to leave. Because whiteness at that time was a prerequisite for US citizenship, they were therefore legally White.[46] In the words of legal historian Ariela Gross, Mexican Americans were "white by treaty."[47] By tracing the history of Mexican American legal claims to an "other White" racial identity, this section demonstrates the inability of the US legal system to reckon with the legacies of colonialism, particularly as they relate to the racial construction of Mexican Americans. Race, as the courts had determined it, was defined by the Black-White color line. By limiting civil rights attorneys' options for proving discrimination against Mexican Americans, the law simultaneously forced adherence to an ahistorical racial binary and reinforced the power of whiteness to dictate individual and group identity formation.

One of the prime methods of establishing a racial order that placed Whites on top was the development of segregation. This looked different in every community, but there were clear patterns. Anywhere there existed a significant population of Mexicans and/or Mexican Americans, housing and school segregation emerged as important racial projects.[48] By the 1930s many of these towns had created separate "Mexican" schools or developed other methods of maintaining as much separation as possible between White students and Mexican American students. Although there were no laws that mandated segregation for Mexican Americans, as there were for African

Americans in the South, segregation was propagated through formal policies and practices, often developed at the local level. One of the most common practices was to establish separate schools or separate classrooms within integrated schools for children who could not speak English. As Spanish speakers, the argument went, these students needed extra attention in learning English. Their presence in classrooms with Anglo students also brought down the quality of education for Anglos because teachers had to spend more time with non-English speakers. Thus, according to the rationales provided by school officials, Mexican Americans were segregated not because of their race but because of sound educational practice. They assumed that all Mexican Americans lacked sufficient English-language skills.[49] This was a common assumption in many Colorado schools as well.[50]

Of course, just because the central argument for segregation was seemingly race neutral did not mean the demand for segregated schools was not racially motivated. Many Anglos viewed Mexican Americans as a separate, inferior race and did not want their children in the same classrooms. A survey conducted by the *American-Statesman*, an Austin, Texas, newspaper, in the 1950s revealed that the majority of Anglos supported separate Mexican schools either because they feared racial mixing or because they believed Mexican Americans were culturally and/or intellectually inferior. "Most of those who approve of segregation make no attempt to cover up their prejudice against Latin-Americans," wrote the newspaper. "They say Latin-Americans are 'a different race,' 'socially inferior,' 'not clean,' 'we don't believe in mixing races.'"[51] Teachers often shared these perceptions. One student who attended a segregated Mexican American classroom in Monte Vista, Colorado, remembered the harsh treatment they received from educators:

> [Our teacher] would take us to the bathroom and wash our hands with a brush. She brushed us so hard that it almost made our knuckles bleed. While she was washing our hands she would say, "You dirty little Mexicans!" I remember some of us getting hit with a rubber hose. We were treated like animals. I still have nightmares about that school. I don't want to say that all Anglo teachers were like that. I did have some good Anglo teachers.[52]

In Greeley, Colorado, about fifty miles from Denver, Whites were hesitant about educating Mexican American children. Some felt it was pointless to educate them because they would end up working in the sugar beet fields anyway. Many actually feared that educating Mexican Americans too much would give them the tools to escape the sugar beet colonias. The district constructed a one-room schoolhouse specifically to educate Mexican Americans of all ages, those who had not already dropped out. Six-year-olds sat in the same classroom as thirteen-year-olds. Soon, enough people voiced concerns about the lack of age-appropriate curriculum that the district decided to construct a partition in the middle of the classroom. Elementary aged students were housed on one side and junior high aged students on the other. Rather than send these students to other schools in the district, school officials decided it was best to keep them segregated.[53] In most cases, a Spanish surname was enough to slot a student into a Mexican school. But as Carey McWilliams pointed out in 1947, the "common practice has been simply to assign all children with Spanish or Mexican names to a separate school. Occasionally, the school authorities inspect the children so that the offspring of a Mexican mother whose name may be O'Shaugnessy will not slip into the wrong school."[54] In their efforts to create and maintain segregated schools, local school officials saw no difference between Mexicans, Latin Americans, Hispanos, Spanish Americans, Spanish-speaking people, and Spanish-surnamed people. In South Texas, which had a relatively large population of Mexicans and Mexican Americans, about 90 percent of public schools were segregated, with separate schools for Anglos and Mexicans.[55]

Given its interest in promoting the full integration of Mexican Americans, LULAC emerged as a prominent challenger to public school officials' efforts to segregate Mexican American children. In 1930, just one year after it was founded, the organization filed the first legal challenge to the segregation of Mexican Americans. It challenged the Del Rio, Texas, school district's practice of placing Mexican American children in a separate elementary school. Central to its argument was the claim that you could not segregate White children from "other White" (Mexican American) children. Since Mexican Americans were no different from other White children, that is, the school district had no basis for segregating them. This argument then became the basis for Mexican American challenges to school segregation for the next three and a half decades and informed the civil rights strategies of Mexican Americans throughout the Southwest.[56]

In asserting their claims, Mexican American civil rights attorneys relied on case law that extended back to the nineteenth century, which declared that Mexican Americans were White.[57] While this was always the dominant legal strategy at mid-century, some of these lawyers pursued an alternative tactic that placed *racial* discrimination at the center of their argument. That is, they embraced the idea that Mexicans and Mexican Americans were non-

White and argued that Anglos discriminated against Mexican Americans because they were racially different. This was a starkly different argument from the "other White" claim made by lawyers in the aforementioned school segregation cases. Attorneys in several criminal cases, for example, went this route, only to be rebuffed because they could not overcome the presumption of Mexican American whiteness, a presumption not based in sociohistorical facts but on legal precedent. The courts recognized that Mexican Americans were different based on ethnicity, ancestry, or nationality, but they refused to accept that these kinds of distinctions were the same as race. Although these cases stemmed from criminal convictions and not school segregation, they are important for understanding the development of Mexican American civil rights strategies. In the case of Aniceto Sanchez, who tried to appeal his criminal conviction because the jury that convicted him did not include any Mexican Americans—he argued that he had not received a fair and impartial trial—the Texas Court of Criminal Appeals threw out the argument, noting that Mexican Americans "are not a separate race but are white people of Spanish descent, as has often been said by this court. We find no ground for discussing the question further."[58] Mexican Americans thus wore a "Caucasian cloak" that made it very easy for state authorities to discriminate against them without the fear of judicial intervention.[59] Segregation worked because Mexican American whiteness was denied in certain areas—the labor market, the political arena, the schools, and public accommodations, for example—and upheld in the courts. This is precisely how racial projects operate. Having failed to convince the courts that precedent was wrong—that Mexican Americans were not White—civil rights attorneys fully embraced the "other White" strategy.

This approach was validated by the US Supreme Court in 1954 when it heard a case dealing with the civil rights of Mexican Americans for the first time. In *Hernandez v. Texas* (1954), the justices heard the case of Pete Hernández, a criminal defendant challenging his murder conviction by an all-White jury in Jackson County, Texas. Hernández's legal team argued that because there were no Mexican Americans on the jury, he was denied the Fourteenth Amendment rights of equal protection and due process. They maintained that although Mexican Americans *were* White, the state of Texas treated them as a group separate from Anglos. In a landmark victory, the Supreme Court ruled unanimously that in Texas, Mexican Americans were treated as a "distinct class."[60] Its opinion, written by Chief Justice Earl Warren, pointed out the harsh discrimination Mexican Americans faced in Texas while simultaneously reinforcing their whiteness. This was exactly what Hernández's lawyers and those backing him had wanted. They had gained official recognition of their second-class status while also bolstering their claims to whiteness. As a result, Mexican American civil rights lawyers became firmly wedded to the "other White" argument.[61] This was about more than winning in the courtroom; it was also about finding legitimization as American citizens. In the post–World War II period, this "barrio Americanism" defined the activism of middle-class Mexican Americans like those pursuing school desegregation litigation.[62] This mindset, which promoted social uplift, assimilation, and patriotism, found its most salient feature in its appeal to whiteness and the subsequent development of the whiteness strategy. While some more privileged and light-skinned Mexican Americans did secure the benefits of full inclusion as American citizens over the course of the post–World War II period, most did not. Full belonging continued to elude Mexican Americans in the Southwest, regardless of the courts' affirmation of their legal whiteness.

To understand Mexican American racial formation in post–civil rights Denver, the interrelated histories of Spanish and American settler colonialism and the "other White" legal strategy must be considered together. Generations of Hispanos or Spanish Americans understood themselves to be the descendants of the Spanish colonizers, completely disconnected from Mexicans and Mexico. Within the region that encompassed northern New Mexico and southern Colorado, social relations were patterned after the social, economic, and political shifts that accompanied conquest, first by the Spanish, then by the Americans. It was in this context that *nuevomexicanos* constructed a shared identity that linked them to the settlers of centuries past, an identity and history many carried with them when they migrated north starting in the 1920s. In the postwar period, therefore, their understanding of civil rights issues was shaped by both the legacies of settler colonialism in the US West *and* the Black/White Jim Crow system that had come to dominate legal and common perceptions of race, education, and civil rights in the postwar United States. As the following chapters make clear, understandings of Hispano whiteness became a major part of Denver's school desegregation efforts and shaped how different groups of Mexican Americans perceived the issues and organized their support or opposition to the district court's order for district-wide desegregation.

TWO

Racial Migrations

THE MILE HIGH CITY IN TRANSITION, 1945–1969

BERNARD VALDEZ WAS BORN IN 1912 on a family farm near Cleveland, New Mexico, a small village northwest of Las Vegas. According to Valdez, his ancestors had settled in the area "sometime in the 1700s," and the land was passed down through generations until his grandfather died and the farm went to his uncle. In 1926, with few other options, his father gathered his wife and five children and joined the hundreds of other migrant farmworkers in the northeast Colorado sugar beet fields. If all the members of the family worked, his parents believed, they could earn enough to return to New Mexico at the end of the harvest season. Like so many others, they found out the hard way that making enough to return was nearly impossible. Their alternative plan was to stay the winter in Denver, the nearest major city. They never left northeast Colorado.[1]

Fourteen years old when his family came to the city, Valdez remembered entering the Denver Public Schools (DPS) and feeling isolated, unable to communicate with his teachers. As a poor, Spanish-speaking youth in an Anglo-dominated city, he experienced intense culture shock.[2] Returning to the fields in the spring, he helped supplement the family income. In 1933 he joined the Civilian Conservation Corps (CCC) in Colorado, which "delighted" his widowed mother because the family would now have a steady income of $25.00 a week. The camps gave him the opportunity to work with an educational adviser and learn from the other young men there, experiences that he credited with changing the direction of his life.[3] He then returned to high school in Fort Collins, Colorado, and, at the age of twenty-four, earned his diploma.[4]

After working his way through Colorado A&M College, which later became Colorado State University, Valdez ended up back in New Mexico, where he began working in the field of social welfare. After World War II opportunities in Denver lured him and his wife, Dora, back to Colorado. In 1948 he began working for the City Recreation Department, he later enjoyed a stint with the Denver Housing Authority, and finally, in 1963, he became the city's manager of welfare.[5] While continuing in this role, he became a member of the Denver Board of Education in 1972, a position he held for six years (see figure 4). As a school board member Valdez did not believe that desegregating the city's majority Mexican American schools would improve the quality of their education. In fact, he was a proponent of Mexican American community schools. Nonetheless, he often served as a tie breaker between anti-integrationists and integration proponents during the height of the school district's efforts to overturn a federal court order that required it to desegregate. He thus earned a reputation for being levelheaded and pragmatic on a board with several short-tempered and vocal members. But he never forgot what it was like to be that poor, Spanish-speaking student in the Denver schools, and he was a tireless advocate for bilingual and bicultural education.

Like Valdez, Rachel Noel became a prominent community member and educational advocate, but her work focused on improving the educational experiences of Black students. Also like Valdez, her life began somewhere else, in this case Hampton, Virginia. Born Rachel Bassette in 1918 to a prestigious Black family, Noel's early life was shaped by the educational aspirations of her parents and grandparents. Her grandfather was a bondsman, but after emancipation he became a lawyer and went on to found a school for Black children in 1895. Her father was also a lawyer, and her mother was a teacher, one of the few Black women to have earned a college degree at the time. Noel herself went on to earn a bachelor's degree in education from Hampton Institute and, in 1940, a master's degree in sociology from Fisk University. While at Fisk she met a young medical student named Edmond Noel, whom she married in 1942.[6]

Seven years later, in 1949, the Noels left the South behind and headed to Denver, where Edmond had accepted a position as a staff physician at Rose Medical Center.[7] At first they resided in the city's Five Points neighborhood, where the majority of Black residents lived and where Black newcomers, many of them from the South, found community. When their two children reached school age, Noel convinced her husband to move to the majority White, affluent neighborhood of Park Hill because, she said, the

FIGURE 4. Denver school board member Bernard Valdez speaking at the dedication of McGlone Elementary School in May 1978. An unknown woman and school board president Omar Blair sit behind him. Photo courtesy of The Denver Public Library, Western History Collection, WH1839.

FIGURE 5. Rachel Noel at DPS school board meeting, 1964. Photo courtesy of The Denver Public Library, Western History Collection, ARL117.

schools were much better. The Noels were one of only a couple of Black families in the area, and they experienced their share of discrimination. But Noel was determined to see her children, and other Black children, receive a quality education. She was active in the Park Hill Elementary School Parent Teacher Association (PTA), and she tried to stay apprised of her children's classroom experiences. In the early 1960s she noticed that the school district had started to change school boundaries in the area, pushing her son and daughter into nearly all-Black schools, where the level of academic work was far below that of their previous schools. She took her grievances to the next level and ran for the DPS Board of Education in 1965. When she won she became the first Black school board member in city history (see figure 5).[8]

For the first few years of her term Noel tried to work with school officials and the other board members to improve conditions for students in racially concentrated minority schools, usually to no avail. After Martin Luther King Jr. was assassinated in 1968, she decided it was time to push harder;

she introduced Resolution 1490, which ordered the DPS superintendent to develop a comprehensive integration plan by September 30, 1969.[9] When the board voted to implement the resolution it set into motion a decades-long struggle over the meaning of equal educational opportunity and race in a city that had always prided itself on its racial progressivism and spirt of equality but had yet to come to terms with the demographic changes of the postwar period.

The migration stories of Bernard Valdez and Rachel Noel tell a lot about the transformation of the Mile High City during and after World War II and about the educational aspirations of Mexican Americans and African Americans. As the city expanded, both in population and in physical space, it became a modern, multiracial metropolis. Between 1945 and 1970, the population of Denver and the surrounding suburbs more than doubled, growing from 612,128 to 1,229,798.[10] According to one government study, the population increase between 1950 and 1957 marked the city as the third fastest growing city in the country.[11] As was the case in other major western cities during this period, wartime jobs and the expansion of civil service sector work and defense industries after the war drove much of this growth. Lowry Air Force Base (see figure 6) and Fitzsimmons Army Hospital, the world's largest military hospital at the time, employed thousands. New job opportunities were created at bomber modification hangers at Denver's Stapleton Airfield, the Rocky Flats atomic energy plant, and the Rocky Mountain Arsenal, where nerve gas and other chemical weapons were made and stored.[12] Bomb-making facilities and missile plants, including the Glenn L. Martin Company (later Lockheed Martin), moved to the outskirts of Denver. Several other military contractors, including, among others, Rockwell International, Honeywell, Litton Industries, and Kaman Corporation, opened shop in the area. When the Air Force Finance Center relocated from St. Louis to Denver in 1951, the number of migrants increased further.[13] A growing city, moreover, created the need for an expanded professional class of doctors, lawyers, teachers, and others, as well as service workers.

Their stories also highlight one of the most important aspects of Denver's postwar history, the increasing numbers of African Americans and Mexican Americans who called the city home. Before World War II Denver's Black population never exceeded 7,000 people. The Mexican American population is harder to pinpoint with accuracy because the US Census did not count Mexican Americans or other Latinas/os separately and the population was so migratory. A 1940 study estimated the Mexican American population

FIGURE 6. Lowry Air Force Base in Denver, ca. early 1950s. A B-36B Peacemaker sits in front of Hangar No. 2. John D. Smilley took the photo while stationed at Lowry Air Force Base. Photo courtesy of History Colorado-Denver, Colorado, 93.152.14.

of the city to be 12,345, while the Denver Unity Council reported that in the mid-1940s the population was 14,631.[14] Several reports indicated that, starting in the 1920s, the population of Mexican Americans doubled or tripled during the winter, as migrant farmworkers made their way to the city.[15] During the two decades after the war, both African Americans and Mexican Americans experienced significant growth through migration and new births. By 1969 there were approximately 46,000 Blacks and 71,185 Mexican Americans in the city. With a total population of 493,000 that year, Denver was about 9.3 percent Black and 14.4 percent Mexican American.[16] Smaller but still significant communities of American Indians and Asian Americans also increased over the postwar period. When the Amache concentration camp, located in the southeastern corner of the state, closed in 1945, many of the 6,000 to 7,000 Japanese and Japanese Americans who had been incarcerated there remained in Colorado, making Denver their home.[17] And when the federal government began promoting urban relocation for American

Indians, Denver was one of the cities that participated in the program.[18] The end result, by 1969, was a thoroughly multiracial metropolis that had grown into one of the largest cities in the US West.

These migrations transformed the Mile High City forever. By 1969 the city and its public schools would be embroiled in a series of racial conflicts that stemmed from the demographic changes of the previous two and a half decades. While Denver was almost always segregated in one way or another, the growth of the Black and Mexican American populations forced new segregation patterns to emerge in both housing and the schools. Such patterns reveal the multiracial nature of racial formation. In order to understand the story of school segregation in Denver, multiple racial projects must be examined in relation to each other. Whereas African Americans were constructed by local Whites as a separate, non-White race, Mexican Americans were conceptualized as a problem group—the "Spanish American problem"—in need of assimilation, not White but not exactly not White, either. In practice this meant some Mexican Americans could integrate easily into the dominant society, but the majority remained too distinct for inclusion, their culture, color, and language too foreign for acceptance and their class too poor for acceptance. Based on these different experiences of racialization, African Americans and Mexican Americans developed very different notions of educational equality in the postwar city. For most African Americans, segregation was at the root of their educational problems, and only integration would bring about the changes for which they had long fought. Most Mexican Americans, conversely, understood the issue as one of cultural devaluation and eradication. Bilingual/bicultural education, they argued, would help restore some of their cultural losses. This belief prompted them to support stronger community schools, which were threatened by the integration plan promoted by African Americans. Yet even though these were the dominant arguments put forth by Black and Mexican American Denverites, neither group was monolithic in its thinking. Some African Americans strongly advocated for Black community schools, while Mexican Americans were even more divided on the issue. Whereas some fully supported integration, others rejected it outright, preferring to align themselves with White anti-integrationists who also opposed bilingual/bicultural education. These divergent viewpoints contributed to major political disagreements and uneasy alliances that gave shape to the legal battle that unfolded in the courts.

SPACE AND PLACE

A history of school desegregation necessarily must start with a history of segregation, one that is specific to the place under investigation. Denver's history of racial segregation is both typical and unique, given its particular racial makeup, migration patterns, city planning policies, spatial dynamics, and history. It was the discovery of gold in 1858 in the Platte and Cherry Creek Rivers that first brought large numbers of enterprising Euro-Americans to the area, although it had been a meeting ground for various Indigenous peoples, including the Arapaho, Cheyenne, and Utes, for centuries. The relentless search for and extraction of the area's natural resources is what put Denver on the map, along with transportation. The city's early spatial arrangements reflect these dynamics. Understanding that the future of their city depended on an influx of capital and permanent residents, early city boosters advocated for railroad development to connect their isolated city to other metropolises in the West, East, and South. Even though the Union Pacific railway bypassed Denver for Cheyenne, Wyoming, there still was a tremendous expansion of railways in the 1860s and 1870s. Along each line of this "spiderweb of steel," as Denver historians Stephen J. Leonard and Thomas J. Noel describe it, rail yards, factories, warehouses, and other heavy industries popped up, along with hotels, saloons, and brothels to service the increasing number of passengers coming through on their way to the West or back to the East.[19] Much of the city's built environment, then, sprang from the tracks.

During the 1920s, as the city experienced an increase in population and economic growth, many of the Euro-Americans who resided in the city's center began to purchase more expensive homes farther from the industrial core. By this point many people in Denver's relatively small Black community had moved into the central areas nestled between Auraria to the west and the Five Points neighborhood to the east, beginning a shift away from residential dispersal to concentration. As Euro-Americans left the Five Points area, in particular, Black tenants moved into their former dwellings, many of which were converted from single-family to multifamily homes. By 1929, the majority of Black residents had moved into Five Points in this manner. Racially restrictive housing covenants, later upheld by the Colorado Supreme Court, restricted their options, as did other forms of discrimination by real estate agents and landlords.[20] Black families continued to cluster in this neighborhood for the next two decades, although they lived in very small numbers in most city neighborhoods.[21] African Americans understood that while there was no law mandating segregation in the city, there were places they were not allowed. Denver clearly was a segregated city.[22]

During the 1920s and 1930s, Denver's Mexican American population fluctuated with the seasons, as migrant laborers came in and out of the city to the rhythm of the crops, particularly sugar beets. While there were Mexican Americans in other kinds of employment, like railroad work and coal mining, during this period most of them worked in the fields. The vast majority of these migrant farmworkers came from southern Colorado, Texas, and New Mexico, though a smaller number came from Mexico.[23] Writing in 1950, Samuel Liss of the President's Commission on Migratory Labor explained Colorado's centrality to the circuit of migrant farmworkers in the nation's sugar beet fields. "Colorado is a clearinghouse," he noted, "for workers for the sugar beet industry and canning processors."[24] Starting in the 1920s the northeast Colorado–based Great Western Sugar Company started recruiting Mexican and Mexican American workers in the US Southwest. One of the company's strategies for keeping labor costs down was to over-recruit workers in order to ensure a surplus. This allowed it to pay workers as little as possible, with the added advantage of lowering its costs for importing labor farther north. "It is cheaper to ship workers from Denver to Billings [Montana] than from San Antonio to Billings," the Denver Commission on Community Relations (CCR) reported in 1947.[25] Denver, then, became a sort of launching pad for the company's operations throughout the intermountain West. Whether they were recruited by the sugar companies or other labor contractors, or they came on their own initiative, thousands of Mexican American farmworkers passed through the state every year. Many of them stayed to work for a short period or often longer; some of them chose to stay the winter, as did Bernard Valdez's family.

Arriving in the city in the 1920s, these sojourners most often found their way to the Auraria neighborhood. Although it was once home to Denverites of all classes, the upwardly mobile escaped the grime, noise, and pollution of the industrial area as soon as they could. The introduction of horsecar lines in the 1870s and electric street cars in the 1880s sped up this process, so that by the early part of the twentieth century Auraria was a solidly working-class area.[26] With the arrival of increasing numbers of Mexican American migrants during the second decade of the century, the neighborhood became increasingly Mexican American.[27] As that happened the once economically vibrant community began to lose the economic base that supported it. Businesses closed, jobs were lost, and the built environment suffered. The pace of these changes was slow at first, but by the 1950s changes in transportation and manufacturing ensured Auraria's economic decline.[28] The neighborhood, by that point, was one of the poorest in the city.[29]

The housing patterns of Denverites shifted once again as the economic, demographic, and policy changes brought on by World War II and its aftermath caused overcrowding, sped up the deterioration of the city's core area physical infrastructure, and encouraged White migration farther from the central city.[30] Job discrimination was rampant, although some industries were more blatant about it than others. "Negroes and Spanish have a slight mental inferiority," explained one local employer in the 1940s.[31] By the 1950s, however, many non-Whites were employed in manufacturing, meatpacking, and railroad work. They made rock-hard mining equipment at Gardner Denver, underground gas tanks for service stations at Eaton Metal Products Company, radiator hoses for Gates Rubber, and boxes for Russell Stover Candies at Deline Box Company. Thousands toiled day after day in the stench of the city's many packinghouses. Armour, Swift, Cudahy, and Wilson were the biggest firms, but around a dozen more operated as well. Partly, these jobs became available because many of the Whites who had once worked them moved on to white-collar positions in the city's growing banking, investment, insurance, and telecommunications industries.[32] For Black and Mexican American families, these working-class jobs were highly coveted. They paid more and offered the opportunity to buy a home and participate in the growing consumer economy. Fewer non-Whites worked in jobs that required interaction with the White public. Department store clerks, servers, bank clerks, delivery truck drivers, telephone installers, and other such positions were open to Whites only, in large part because the companies maintained that their customers refused to be served by non-Whites.[33]

Although fewer African Americans and Mexican Americans were employed in white-collar positions, the availability of jobs with the federal government opened a crucial pathway to middle-class status that was unavailable to non-Whites in many other cities. Denver leaders liked to refer to their city as the "Little Capital of the USA" or "Little Washington" because of the high number of civilian jobs within nearly every federal department and agency. In 1958, according to the US Census Bureau, these departments and agencies provided work for 18,800 civil service employees, a number that only grew in the next decade.[34] Because these were federal positions, moreover, they largely were open to anyone who possessed the required skills and education. Black men and women filled many of these jobs, ensuring a sizable Black middle class in the city. Mexican Americans were also employed by the federal government but were less likely than Blacks to be hired because of lack of education and training. Some simply could not speak or read English well enough to fill out an application or sit through an interview. While the dearth of Mexican American federal employees was not the sole reason for the lack of a sizable Mexican American middle class, it certainly played an important role and helps explain why the city had a relatively large Black middle class and a very small Mexican American middle class.

Most Mexican Americans, in fact, found themselves within the working class or part of the growing poverty class. As a consequence, by 1955 Mexican American families were more likely than African American families to receive public assistance. Certainly other factors contributed to their socioeconomic status, but the inability of most Mexican Americans to secure decent-paying jobs was at the heart of this phenomenon. A full 50 percent of those receiving Aid to Families with Dependent Children (ADC) were Mexican American, while only 15 percent were Black. The remaining 35 percent were White.[35] At a time when Mexican Americans constituted about 11 percent of the population as a whole, their heavy dependence on the city welfare department is telling, and it contributed to the perception that they were a problem for the city. By 1967, average Mexican American household income was $4,636 annually, while that of Blacks was $5,031 and of Whites was $5,917.[36] Of 40,000 families living in poverty that same year, 48.5 percent were Mexican American, 22.6 percent were Black, and 28.9% were White.[37] The lower socioeconomic status of Mexican Americans in the city, relative to Black Denver residents, contributed to disagreements and tensions between the two groups throughout the ensuing two decades. This was particularly true once factories started shutting down or moving to the growing suburbs surrounding the city or to other states in the mid-1960s, a trend that continued throughout the 1970s.[38]

In 1949 the Denver Area Welfare Council conducted a study of the city's Mexican American community and noted that enumerating its population was difficult, but estimated that there were between 30,000 and 45,000 Mexican Americans living in the city. Almost half lived in a central area of the city that encompassed four census tracts, including Auraria. Approximately 81 percent lived in just ten census tracts, all of which were in the central city or west of the Platte River, the area broadly defined as the Westside.[39] As the Mexican American population expanded through natural growth and in-migration in the 1950s, it became even more visibly concentrated in these areas. Besides the Westside, there were also large pockets of residents in the core city area near Capitol Hill, where many Mexican American families settled among or near Black families, and Curtis Park, adjacent to Five Points.[40]

The postwar growth of the Black population also led to shifts in residential patterns. With new Black migrants arriving from the South and increased birth rates, Five Points and its adjacent neighborhoods were bursting at the seams. Overcrowding in older, dilapidated dwellings led to multiple problems, including malfunctioning heating and plumbing systems, hazardous living conditions, sickness, and increased crime. By the late 1940s middle-class Black families, like the Noels, chose to leave Five Points for less-crowded, more appealing areas. Usually this meant they moved eastward, into the outskirts of the Park Hill neighborhood, which was at that time a middle- to upper-class White neighborhood. Lionel Dean Lyles noted in his 1977 dissertation on Black neighborhood development in Denver that the population of Five Points actually decreased during the 1950s, a reversal of earlier trends. This decline, he argued, could be attributed to a significant increase in Black family income during this decade, a development that led to a large number of middle-class families migrating away from the older Black neighborhood.[41]

SEGREGATED NEIGHBORHOODS

These changes set the stage for conflict by the early 1960s, a decade that for many people revealed the racial inequities that structured housing and neighborhood identity. As in other cities, Denver's real estate markets and land use policies in the postwar period were guided by growth-minded city leaders, planners, developers, and real estate companies intent on ensuring racial segregation. For these entities, setting and enforcing policies that ensured segregation was rooted in the idea that property values were dependent upon neighborhood racial homogeneity. But for most people the connection between race and property values was simply the result of natural forces. Protecting one's property values then became a matter of ensuring one's neighborhood remained segregated.[42] While many people of all races argued that Denver did not have a segregation problem—there were people of all races in all areas of the city, after all—and tended to fall back on the point that the city was relatively progressive compared to those in the South, the Mile High City was not unlike other major urban areas in the nation. As Tom Romero notes, it was actually because so many people believed Denver was free of the racial past that haunted the South and North that metropolitan areas in the US West "became the greatest sites of land use innovation and the home to some of the most intense resistance to school integration."[43]

Racially restrictive housing covenants were introduced in Colorado starting in the 1920s and became more common in the next couple of decades as racially restrictive property rights were validated by state and local courts. In 1930, the Colorado Supreme Court heard the case of Mable and Edward Ziegler, who were suing their real estate developer for misrepresenting the racial exclusivity of a development in Jefferson County, adjacent to Denver. They claimed he owed them damages because they had purchased a lot in the development on the promise of such exclusivity, yet a Japanese family was able to move in next door. Although the neighborhood did not have a restrictive covenant, the court held that it was state policy "to recognize that 'a person who owns a tract of land . . . may prefer to have as neighbors persons of the [W]hite, or Caucasian race.'"[44] A decade later, the same court ruled against a Black plaintiff who tried to challenge the constitutionality of a restrictive covenant in Denver. With such legal backing, throughout the 1940s several city developments had active racially restrictive covenants that banned the sale of property not just to Black buyers, but to Mexican American, Japanese, and Jewish buyers as well.[45] By the 1950s, the CCR, a mayoral advisory committee, maintained that restrictive clauses were probably fair housing advocates' biggest obstacle to achieving integrated housing in the city. As in other metropolitan areas, Denver real estate agents, bankers, and other mortgage lenders formed agreements that prohibited them from selling to or financing properties in areas dominated by Whites to non-Whites.[46] Real estate agents even started listing properties in certain areas by including the caveat "no discrimination," instead of the common phrase "protected by covenants." In reality, this was merely a way of informing potential White buyers that this property was in a transitioning neighborhood and would soon be resegregated.[47]

More subtle practices also promoted a segregated cityscape. Convinced that African Americans would lower property values, real estate agents directed prospective Black buyers to traditionally Black neighborhoods.

Mortgage lenders made it especially difficult for non-White buyers who sought housing in a White neighborhood to secure financing, especially in areas where home values were higher. Even if they were approved, Black buyers often paid much higher interest rates for their loans, and/or the down payment was three to five times as much as it would have been for a White buyer.[48] When African Americans applied for housing in private developments, they often were allowed to file an application but faced constant delays. Agents did everything they could to discourage potential buyers, a practice that often led to the buyer walking away from the development.[49] So-called gentleman's agreements, moreover, had been a staple of Denver's housing market for years. According to Stirling Kahn, who trained as an apprentice for Denver real estate company Foster and Barnard in the 1950s, "There were certain understandings that you just didn't sell a home to any minority over a certain boundary line. There was nothing in writing.... You just became aware of it."[50]

Khan importantly revealed that housing discrimination was directed toward "any minority" and not just Black buyers. In 1947, representatives from twenty-three real estate companies or neighborhood improvement associations confirmed the existence of housing restrictions against Mexican Americans. The representatives, who were interviewed for a confidential study, noted that they did not have written policies, but it was well known by everyone in the business that you could not violate these restrictions. "People won't live near Mexicans and there is nothing that we, as salespeople, can do about this type of discrimination," a saleswoman explained matter-of-factly. "You cannot stay in business and do that."[51] Several of them justified such exclusions by describing Mexican Americans' unfitness for particular areas. They were "slow in paying rents, dirty, [had] no ambition, [and] ruined the houses in which they lived." Another agent summed up his objection by describing them as "an unscrupulous lot."[52]

Housing restrictions deeply affected Mexican Americans' sense of community belonging or lack thereof. Paul Sandoval, who served as a Colorado state senator in the 1970s, vividly recalled these agreements several decades later. "There was an unwritten rule that past York they would not sell you a house," he explained. "I can remember when I was young going out to Stapleton Airport to sell newspapers. York Street, you knew. That was the dividing line then. You just knew. Nothing but White past York." York Street was the customary dividing line between Whites and non-Whites in northeast Denver, though as that line shifted farther east in the 1950s with increasing numbers of non-White homeowners, particularly African Americans, the dividing line changed several times. Sandoval continued, "Later I can remember people saying, 'Christ, they passed York. But they're not gonna cross Colorado Boulevard.' Then they crossed Colorado and you heard, 'Oh, they're not gonna go to Dahlia. That's too beautiful an area.' I can remember those conversations, yeah." Using his own family as an example, he also described the feelings of shock and amazement he remembered feeling at the news that his uncle had purchased a large home on York Street. Later, his cousins purchased east of York and people said "'Jesus, you got a house *there*?'"[53]

As fair housing advocates pushed their agenda in the 1950s, public opinion among White Denverites revealed the ways that a local racial hierarchy, encompassing multiple racial groups, was taking shape in the city. As early as the late 1940s, members of the CCR recognized that Whites had differing reactions to the influx of these various groups into their city. "People in Denver are most in favor of discrimination against Negroes," a 1948 report read. It continued, "next against 'Spanish-Americans and Mexicans' and 'Orientals such as Chinese and Japanese;' least against Jews."[54] Perceptions were not unchanging, however. On the one hand, there was progress. Whereas once Jews had been systemically discriminated against, the Denver Coordinating Council for Education and Human Relations reported that restrictions against Jewish home buyers had nearly disappeared by the mid-1950s.[55] A 1954 study on housing integration, moreover, found a substantial increase in the number of Whites who were willing to sell to anyone, regardless of race, over the previous five years. While in 1949 only 15 percent of homeowners in White areas were willing to sell to anyone, by 1954 45 percent were willing to do so.[56]

On the other hand, Whites' willingness to live among people unlike them was contingent upon a number of factors, including class, color, and language. The same study revealed that Whites were more likely to sell to Mexican Americans or Japanese Americans than they were to African Americans. Of those surveyed, 57 percent said they would sell to a Japanese American or Mexican American buyer, while only 47 percent were willing to sell to a Black buyer.[57] Progress for some did not mean progress for everyone. One man who lived in the Capitol Hill area told an interviewer that he would not sell to a Black buyer or a "real Mexican."[58] Seemingly drawing a contrast between "real Mexicans" and Mexican Americans, his reluctance to live among Mexicans probably was based on color and class as much as nationality. Some real estate agents and housing association representatives, for example, tried to defend themselves against accusations that they had knowingly placed a Mexican family in a White neighborhood by arguing the family was Spanish. The president of the Montclair Improvement Association cited an example of a case in which a new family had moved into the area, and neighbors objected because they believed the family was Mexican. When he visited the family he discovered that the father was "a very high-type Spaniard not a Mexican." He described the man as well educated, with a college degree, and noted that he was active in community organizations. "I believe that he served on one of Denver's Mayor's Committees," he noted. When he explained all of this at the next association meeting the protesting parties dropped their complaints, but it was clear they remained concerned about the presence of the family.[59] A similar incident happened in the Barnum area, where a Mexican American family had recently moved. When neighbors threatened J. E. Squire of the Moon Realty Company, who had sold that family the house, he tried to soothe their fears by telling them the father was "a full-blooded Spaniard and had a right to live where he darn pleased. He was no Mexican." Although he distinguished between Spaniards and Mexicans in his defense of the sale—he did not state whether this appeased the neighbors—Squire also reverted to calling the father Mexican when he was in the intimacy of a confidential interview. "I would never sell to a Mexican in a White neighborhood again," he concluded.[60] Middle-class Mexican Americans were White enough to justify a sale but not White enough to risk such a scenario again.

These racial negotiations were also mediated by class considerations. The more affluent the neighborhood, the more important it was for real estate agents, mortgage lenders, and homeowners to maintain White exclusivity. Whereas Mexican Americans and Japanese Americans were found living in majority White developments with low or moderately priced homes, under $16,000, they were prohibited in areas with homes over $16,000.[61] Many Denver real estate agents supported racial housing restrictions, but they were most ardent in their defense of wealthy White neighborhoods. One agent explained, "I would not sell a house to a Mexican in any of the better sections regardless of his financial condition."[62] Such perspectives indicate that these agents did not work alone. Rather, they operated within an intentionally structured system of housing segregation that included real estate agents, mortgage lenders, and home insurers, as well as White home sellers and buyers. Whites were willing to accept some Mexican Americans, if they were of the proper socioeconomic status and had the right coloring (not too dark), but most people continued to see African Americans as too racially distinct for inclusion.

The 1959 Colorado Fair Housing Law, the first of its kind in the nation, did little to correct deeply imbedded discriminatory housing practices. The author of a 1963 report on housing attitudes in Five Points and the area east of it noted that in the course of his work he had listened to countless firsthand descriptions of discrimination when a Black buyer attempted to move into a White area. "I will not rent or sell to Negroes," one owner-realtor flatly stated. "The law that says I must is unconstitutional and I will not obey it."[63] Such opinions were widespread. The Metro Denver Fair Housing Center reported in its 1969 annual report that one of the biggest obstacles to providing affordable, fair housing in the city was the "great American institution" of racism. Noting the coded language that was frequently employed by those who wished to maintain race- and class-exclusive neighborhoods, the center's executive director condemned common phrases like "Save Our Neighborhood Schools," a nod to the then emerging conflict over school desegregation, and "Zoning Integrity."[64]

Even though Mexican Americans often did not face hurdles as difficult as those confronting African Americans, they still were overwhelmingly concentrated in dilapidated or deteriorating housing in older, overcrowded sections of the city. On the Westside, only 5 percent of the homes were considered standard housing, according to the Denver Planning Office. Some 70 percent were deteriorating, 25 percent had extensive structural issues, and 10 percent lacked even basic plumbing.[65] By 1964, about 27 percent of all Mexican American housing in the city was deteriorating.[66] Homeownership was very low among Mexican Americans; most tended to rent instead. They paid more and got less for their money than Whites who also lived in rentals.[67] High rents, housing discrimination, lack of housing, a deficient Denver Housing Authority, and urban renewal all contributed to the Denver housing crunch, especially for the poor and working classes.

The urban crisis that emerged at mid-century was compounded by an increasing population that included many African Americans and Mexican Americans. As in other cities that experienced similar demographic shifts in these years, rising racial and class tensions emerged as a defining feature of the era. These tensions looked different in different contexts, but the changing racial character of many American cities, in combination with overcrowding, more intense job competition, and the increasingly volatile debate over civil rights, was a prime factor. In Los Angeles racial tensions exploded in 1943 with the infamous zoot suit riots, wherein mostly White military personnel joined forced with White locals anxious about the increasing presence of Mexicans and Mexican Americans in the City of Angels to perpetrate violent attacks on Mexican American youth, as well as African American and Filipino youth.[68] Denver, which in the postwar period did not experience such open violence, remained steeped in a long-held belief in the region's racial tolerance and commitment to the ideals of racial democracy. Compared to many southern and northeastern cities embroiled in racial conflict, Denver appeared positively Eden-like, at least to its majority White population. Notions of rugged, western individualism undergirded such positive outlooks. In 1955 the *Rocky Mountain News* proclaimed the Mile High City a racial and humane frontier. Describing a recent study conducted on human relations, the article credited local residents for their progressive views on race-related matters. "This is heartening news but not unexpected," the article proclaimed, "because Denver, by tradition and for nearly a century, has the solid reputation of being a city reasonably free of narrow views on minorities."[69] Yet as many non-White city residents understood all too well, race was just as salient in Denver as it was in Birmingham, Selma, Boston, and Detroit. "For so long," wrote the *Denver Blade*, the city's major African American newspaper, "Denver has been known as the All American City, thought to be free of the strife and racial tensions of the less congential [sic] larger cities, but with the exodus of Blacks from the South and East came shatters of the myth of this city being the mountaintop promise land."[70] One need only look to northeast Denver for ominous signs of the conflict ahead. Middle-class Black residents of the Five Points neighborhood began inching eastward in the late 1940s due to overcrowding and a desire for better housing. As they moved farther east, they began to encroach on the highly desirable Park Hill area. By 1949, Park Hill homeowners were starting to voice their opposition. "I feel I have the right to choose my neighbors," one resident said, "and that's why I bought my property in a white neighborhood."[71] Others rejected outright racial language and insisted it was their property value that concerned them most. "Me, I don't mind Negroes; it wouldn't bother me or my family to be next door to them—but when they move in I can just kiss $5,000 goodby [sic] on the value of my home," argued a longtime Park Hill homeowner.[72] Whether through expressly racist language or the more subtle but no less effective rhetoric of property values, White Park Hill residents tried to keep Black families out. When a new two-block subdivision meant to alleviate some of the overcrowding in the Five Points and Whittier areas was proposed for the outskirts of the area, Park Hill citizens made their objections known: no Blacks allowed.[73] Plans for the subdivision were scrapped. But the eastward migration of African Americans continued over the next two decades.

By the mid-1950s, blockbusting began to rapidly change the outlying areas of the neighborhood from predominantly White to predominantly Black. Panic at the possibility of dwindling home values led to massive sell-offs, and real estate agents funneled in Black buyers only, essentially resegregating the area within a short time.[74] A 1958 survey of African American opinions on housing options revealed that most of those interviewed who were actively looking for homes outside the traditional Black area were looking toward Park Hill.[75] Out of this situation, some residents formed the Park Hill Action Committee (PHAC) in 1960 to prevent blockbusting and promote interracial harmony in the area.[76] Although Park Hill remained internally segregated, with Black families on the fringes of the community, Park Hill schools were effectively integrated several years before the *Keyes* drama began to unfold in the late 1960s. The PHAC would become one of the central grassroots organizations calling for city-wide school desegregation.

Over the course of the postwar period Denver became home to thousands of newcomers, who contributed to the diversification of the city's population and the transformation of the city's racial geography. These structural changes were informed by the development of a multiracial hierarchy that determined where groups were located in proximity to whiteness and blackness. Mexican Americans were simultaneously not White enough for full inclusion in the dominant society *and* just White enough to be allowed into certain neighborhoods, schools, and classrooms, depending on their color, class, and language. Some were welcomed as fellow Whites, others had their whiteness questioned and reluctantly accepted, while still others remained within an amorphous non-White group. The "Spanish American problem" became the shorthand way of referring to Mexican Americans as a whole, although, as chapter 1 demonstrated, many upwardly mobile, middle-class Mexican American men and women challenged such depictions by trumpeting their Spanish, settler origins. As the next chapter shows, these demographic and spatial shifts resulted in new public school policies and practices that manufactured segregated, unequal education.

THREE

Public Schools in Denver's Racialized Urban Geography

WITHIN THE RACIALIZED SPACES that made up the city of Denver were public schools that both reflected the segregated nature of neighborhoods and were themselves important in the construction of segregation. Over the course of the postwar period the racial composition of the Denver Public Schools (DPS) student body changed dramatically, altering the makeup of the schools. As these shifts occurred, DPS officials responded by implementing new practices and modifying old ones, all in the name of maintaining as much racial separation as possible. During the early twentieth century DPS administrators, city officials, and business leaders touted Denver's public schools as a beacon of democracy. The Colorado state constitution forbade racial segregation in the state's public schools, and the small number of private schools projected the appearance of an egalitarian system. The schools, therefore, were essential to city boosters' efforts to promote migration to the city. After a school building boom during the first few decades of the century, the Great Depression halted new construction between 1930 and 1946. This fact, paired with increased migration during and immediately after World War II and an increased birth rate, led to severe overcrowding in the schools by the 1950s.[1] The effects of this surplus of students were not felt equally throughout the district, and the problems that came with overpopulation were especially acute in the core city area and the northeast corner of the city, where most African Americans and many Mexican Americans were settling.

These new demographics and spatial dynamics produced new schooling experiences for the city's children. Updated administrative procedures, teaching practices, and curriculum revisions were implemented by administrators and teachers in an attempt to maintain segregation and mitigate racial conflict in newly diverse school environments. Mexican Americans and African Americans shared many educational experiences in the district, such as racist teachers and peers, poorer levels of academic achievement, high rates of absenteeism and dropouts, and a curriculum that ignored the historical and cultural contributions of their respective racial communities. But while these commonalities existed, these two groups of students also had very different schooling experiences based on how school officials racialized them. Black students, the majority of whom went to northeast Denver schools, were understood by many school authorities to be socially and intellectually inferior. Concentrating them in schools with few White students was the preferred method of maintaining educational separation. By redrawing school boundaries, implementing mobile units at Black schools that were over capacity, manipulating feeder schools, and creating optional zones, DPS administrators ensured the vast majority of Black students in the district would remain concentrated at particular schools. They also bused White students in over-capacity White schools to other White schools that were farther away than necessary, while refusing to do so with Black students. These practices, in combination with other methods, fabricated segregation. Multiple times between 1950 and the mid-1960s Black parents challenged the district on these procedures but were rebuffed by the school board and administrators, who insisted that race had never been a factor in their operations.[2]

Less visible, though no less damaging, was the suite of practices and policies that isolated Mexican American students within the Denver schools. To fully appreciate this system of racial discrimination requires an understanding of the ways teachers, principals, and other administrators racialized Mexican Americans, particularly in relation to White and Black students. As the Mexican American population grew in Denver, its members came to represent what White locals called the "Spanish American problem."[3] While there were several facets to this "problem," their performance and behavior in the schools were important parts of the crisis narrative developed by Denverites. As conceptualized in 1950 by the Denver Area Welfare Council, the problem was actually several problems. Poverty, substandard housing conditions, lack of access to health care, low levels of educational attainment, juvenile delinquency, a lack of cultural assimilation, and Anglo prejudices all contributed to the development of a major social problem for the city and its residents. In popular language, the "Spanish American problem" was a pathology, a set of inherent characteristics and a mode of behavior that defied societal norms. Writing in the postwar period, newspapers, social service agencies, mayoral committees, community organizations, and Denver school officials consistently referred to Mexican Americans with reference to this "problem," and it became the shorthand way of describing the social and cultural challenges that accompanied the transformation of the city as increasing numbers of racial "others" arrived in its neighborhoods.

For school officials in particular, the "Spanish American problem" required action. At schools with large and growing Mexican American populations, teachers and principals had to adapt to larger classes and find ways to serve more students with the same amount of resources. But they also had to mediate disputes between students of different racial, religious, and class backgrounds. In the late 1940s, conflict between Mexican American and Jewish students at Lake Junior High School, which resulted in several fights and other minor skirmishes on and off school grounds, epitomized the fear that many local Whites had come to feel about the growing presence of Mexican Americans. What began as adolescent rivalries quickly became gang warfare in the city's newspapers and other public discourse. Racialized notions of Mexican criminality and violence easily blended with neighborhood anxieties about the racial transformation of the area. Though the West Colfax corridor had been a Jewish neighborhood since the late nineteenth century, increasing numbers of Mexican Americans had been settling nearby in the Auraria neighborhood since the 1920s. In the 1940s they started to move into areas closer to the Jewish stronghold. Public schools that served this area, including Lake Junior High School, now had to contend with the shifting racial, class, and religious character of the student body.[4] In 1949, when these conflicts became headline news, Lake's student population was approximately 20 percent Mexican American and 20 percent Jewish. The remaining students were identified as Anglo.[5]

In the fall of that year fighting broke out between a number of these students as well as older adolescents from nearby high schools. The *Rocky Mountain News* proclaimed it a "gang battle" between thirty Spanish American and Jewish students, fought in front of an audience of three hundred.[6] Rumors and exaggerated accounts of the incident quickly spread.

According to some of the Jewish students, the Mexican kids carried "killing knives" and sometimes guns. Mexican Americans complained of the teachers who, they said, showed favoritism toward their Jewish classmates, many of whom called them "wetbacks" and "dirty Mexicans."[7] A former Lake PTA president remarked that there was prejudice on both sides.[8] In the end the simplified narrative that emerged from the incident was one of violent Mexican hoodlums bullying their Jewish peers, who were simply trying to get an education. The "Spanish American problem" was now firmly entrenched in the schools.

This problem, this way of conceptualizing and packaging ideas about Mexican American racial pathologies, is what Natalia Molina calls a "racial script."[9] As a project of racialization, the deployment of the problem narrative was incredibly effective at marking Mexican American bodies, homes, neighborhoods, and schools as deficient and dangerous. As utilized by some social workers and Mexican American community advocates, the problem script also challenged depictions of inherent filth, dysfunction, and violence by advancing an argument that placed class at the center. Rather than racial characteristics, the problems of the Mexican American community were instead attributed to intense poverty, often born of or intensified by racial prejudice. At the same time, these advocates blamed Mexican Americans' lack of assimilation into the dominant Anglo way of life, regardless of racial and/or class differences, as a cause of their indigent status. If they would only become more like Anglos, the problem would be solved.[10] Mexican American culture, traditions, and ways of life were thus marked as inferior. While certainly this narrative was less overtly racist and more attuned to the realities of life in poverty, its more subtle delineation of Mexican American inferiority was no less damaging.

Recognizing that the incidents at Lake Junior High were probably not the last racial conflict the schools would see and desiring a way to promote intercultural exchange and understanding, school officials adopted a philosophy of cultural pluralism that they implemented in the 1950s and early 1960s. Rooted in the experience of World War II and the need to defeat an enemy motivated by ethnic hatred, as well as a recognition that peace at home meant racial/ethnic tolerance and harmony, as an ideology cultural pluralism promoted intergroup exchange, celebration of the many cultures and communities that contributed to American life, and individualism. Racial prejudice, now deemed by cultural pluralists anathema to the American creed, was treated as a problem of individuals, one that could be solved by intercultural education, in particular.[11] As a central tenet of postwar racial liberalism, "racial individualism" displaced other frameworks for understanding the nation's "race problem," and in so doing it encouraged a host of interested parties, from social scientists to civic groups, foundation leaders to educators, to abandon more radical calls for New Deal–like social and economic policies in favor of tackling White prejudice and promoting a rights-based social and legal culture.[12] In practice this encouraged reform agendas rather than a complete dismantling of the structures that maintained White hegemony.

Cultural pluralism, in DPS's formulation, was a method of integrating the increasing number of Mexican American students into the schools without the kind of conflict that defined the Lake Junior High experience. It was not a true valuing of Mexican American history and culture but a superficial attempt at maintaining cordial race relations. "Although at the outset administrators believed that this philosophy would serve as a model for race relations in Denver's public schools," argues Tom Romero, "in time the method proved incapable of diffusing the multiple and divergent color lines taking shape in the city."[13] That is, DPS's cultural pluralist model of education failed to address the structural inequities that limited educational opportunity for the city's largest non-White group and facilitated the racialization of Mexican Americans as a problem race that needed extra help adapting to Denver's dominant (White) culture.

As a racial script, moreover, the "Spanish American problem" positioned Mexican Americans in the borderlands between Black and White. One factor that helped determine exactly where they fell in those borderlands—were they closer to blackness or whiteness?—was visibility. If Mexican Americans were present but their presence was not overwhelming, they were less of a problem. In the 1950s and early 1960s, as the percentage of Mexican American pupils in DPS grew, they were still a relatively small proportion of the student body. School officials recognized the potential for conflict but remained committed to a program of integration via assimilation. Cultural pluralism was the tool that would help them achieve this goal. At the same time the district made specific decisions that increased the racial concentration of Black students in certain northeast Denver schools. There was no effort to include them in the curriculum of the schools, as there was with Mexican Americans. The public schools, like other aspects of community life, operated within a larger social and cultural context in which race was critically important. As Neil Foley shows, Mexicans straddled the line between Black and White.[14] Mexican Americans' experiences in Denver public schools reveal similar dynamics.

As Denver schools maintained separate schools for most of the district's Black students, DPS found other methods to segregate Mexican American students. In many ways, separating Mexican Americans was an easier task than separating African Americans. School officials could argue that their policies were colorblind: the district was simply separating Mexican American children based on language and cultural differences. School officials made no effort to address the very real problems Mexican American students experienced; they simply placed them in second-tier classes and watched as their educational achievement fell behind that of White students, discipline problems mounted, truancy rates rose, and dropout rates skyrocketed. Because residential segregation was not as stark among Mexican Americans in the 1950s, they were not as clearly segregated as Denver's Black students. That did not mean that segregation did not occur. Rather than identifiable Mexican American schools—though these did exist by the mid-1960s, particularly at the elementary school level—there were identifiable Mexican American classrooms. Students were tested for comprehension levels in basic subjects and placed in certain tracks. Those placed in the college preparatory track were mostly White, while those placed in the vocational training track were majority Black and Mexican American. Moreover, a disproportionate number of Mexican American students were placed in special education classrooms, called remedial education, based on the district's assumption that they were slower learners and/or had no potential or desire to succeed.[15]

According to Mexican American parents and civic leaders, the primary reason for the lack of achievement and high dropout rate of Mexican American students was the school district's lack of cultural sensitivity and inability to reach those students who came from different cultural backgrounds. They argued that neither the majority of DPS teachers nor the administration understood the family and community backgrounds of non-Anglo students and also could not effectively communicate with students whose primary language was not English.[16] Teachers, they said, were on the front lines of the student educational experience. When Mexican American students looked up and saw an Anglo teacher in almost every classroom and at the helm of every school, they often disengaged, particularly when those teachers showed no interest in helping them succeed. The teachers appeared cold, as did the entire school system. The key to motivating students, argued many Mexican American parents and activists, was to get them to identify with the school system, to see their schools as an extension of their families and communities. Mexican American teachers were therefore crucial components of the learning environment for Mexican American students.[17] The students themselves recognized as much. "Our goal is to get an education," wrote Baker Junior High students Cindy and Cheri Trujillo in a letter to the editor published in 1969, "but there needs to be a better understanding between teachers and students."[18] Lena Garcia, a student at South High School, told the Denver Board of Education that most teachers were "insensitive" toward Mexican American students, and she pleaded with board members to hire more Mexican American and Black teachers.[19]

In 1965 there were only fifty-eight Mexican American teachers in the entire district, out of a total of 3,953, slightly over 1 percent. The majority of Mexican American students never even saw a Mexican American teacher.[20] By 1973, when *Keyes* was being considered by the Supreme Court, that number had risen to only 132, about 3 percent of the total number of teachers. This was at a moment when the district had thirty-eight schools that were over a third Mexican American. Twenty-one of those schools were over 50 percent Mexican American, and seven were over 75 percent Mexican American. The Latin American Research and Service Agency (LARASA) estimated that within a decade, as the population of Mexican Americans grew and Anglo families fled to the suburbs, the majority of DPS pupils would be Mexican American.[21] Believing these students were in crisis and that the situation was only going to get worse, the group urged the school board and the DPS administration to hire more Mexican American teachers, administrators and counselors. Radicalized Chicano youth demanded this change (see figure 7).

DPS perceived the problem differently. Its perspective was that Mexican Americans were the problem, not the district's curriculum, teaching methods, or learning environment. School officials accepted as a general premise that Mexican American culture was inferior and fostered students' lack of motivation and academic success. During the mid-1950s, as the "Spanish American problem" became more and more apparent to district officials and teachers, DPS implemented the Joint City-Schools Program, meant to encourage better communication between the schools, parents, and larger community.[22] One of the first steps this new organization took was an attempt to understand why achievement was so low among Mexican Americans. Its report indicted Mexican American culture and families and took almost no responsibility for the many problems these pupils encountered in Denver schools. The lack of parental involvement among Mexican Americans, for example, was the consequence of their lack of interest in their children's education rather than a result of their unfamiliarity with the school system, insecurities about being poorly educated themselves, or their inability to converse well in English.[23] One teacher at Baker Junior High

FIGURE 7. Mexican Americans protest in front of the DPS administration building, May 3, 1973. Photo by Ira Gay Sealy, *Denver Post*. Courtesy of The Denver Public Library, Western History Collection, X-28761.

School, located on the Westside, told the Denver Board of Education that "the reason [Mexican American] children do not want to read is because they are unhappy, frustrated, and unsocial, coming from family backgrounds that lack love for learning."[24] These assumptions only increased the likelihood that DPS would not institute changes that, by the late 1960s, Mexican American parents were demanding: bilingual and bicultural education programs and an increase in the number of Mexican American teachers, counselors, and principals.[25]

The Eurocentrisim of the school district thus fostered an environment that limited the success of many Mexican American students, pushed them out of the schools, devalued their cultural heritage, and erased the histories that led to Mexican American subordination in the United States. When these students and parents dared protest this treatment, they were ignored, silenced, or arrested, as was the case for several of the students who participated in the school walkouts in 1969. These experiences were the direct consequence of settler colonialism. As institutions, schools are meant to impart the ideological underpinnings that support settler societies, erase histories that reveal the violence and dispossession that created such societies, and police behavior that could rupture the illusion of exceptionalism. "This process of elision," notes gender studies scholar Rana Sharif, "speaks to the power of settler colonialism in erecting narratives that figuratively and literally remove unwanted bodies from history books."[26] This process, while denying Mexican American students a useful and emancipatory education, also aided in the construction of these students as a "problem." By denying the existence of a centuries-old history, DPS promoted the idea that Mexican Americans were newcomers who need only assimilate to the American way of life to succeed. Their inability to do so was evidence of their "problem" nature.

Visible educational inequities resulted from these dynamics. One of the most obvious identifiers of these inequities was the lower test scores of Mexican American students compared to White students and the high dropout rate of Mexican American students compared to both White and Black students. School officials did not maintain statistics based on race until 1962, and they did not release that information to the public until late 1967.[27] Nonetheless, teacher observations concluded that non-White students in majority non-White schools performed at lower levels than White students.[28] Two successive DPS superintendents recognized that students in the schools with majority Black and/or Mexican American students scored below expectancy. Dr. Kenneth E. Oberholtzer, superintendent from 1947 to 1967, and Dr. Robert D. Gilberts, superintendent from 1967 to 1970, both acknowledged the lower achievement of minority schools, though both maintained that race was not a factor in this outcome.[29]

Low achievement scores translated into other inequalities. The use of IQ tests and culturally biased standardized testing resulted in a disproportionate number of Mexican American students being placed in special education classes.[30] Once in these sections, students had little chance of returning to regular classrooms or of learning the skills and behaviors that were required for life success. Dr. Jose Cardenas, an educational expert who specialized in Mexican American student needs, maintained that the district's use of the Proficiency and Review (PAR) test, in particular, unfairly marked Mexican American students for failure due to both its biased nature and the district's overreliance on it as a predictor of academic achievement levels.[31] By the 1971–72 school year, when Mexican Americans comprised about 13.7 percent of total enrollment in the state of Colorado, they constituted 32 percent of students in special education classes and 30.2 percent of students held back to repeat a grade level. In Denver, with a higher percentage of Mexican American students, the situation was similar.[32]

Even the school buildings occupied by majority Black and Mexican American students were inferior, many lacking basic amenities and enough space to provide the kinds of educational programs that White students and parents took for granted. Dilapidated conditions were the norm, as was overcrowding. Elmwood, the school with the highest proportion of Mexican American students (92 percent), had no lunchroom. Meals were served from a table set up under a stairwell in the basement. And there were not enough tables for all four hundred students. Pupils were rushed through their meals so they could make room for those students still waiting for their food. The basement could not accommodate the long line of hungry students, so school officials propped open a door and they continued the line outside, even in the cold mountain West winters. There was no gymnasium or dedicated music room. DPS converted a small classroom into a gym in which students had limited space to play games. Another class doubled as a music room and a speech therapy room. Students were forced to share a single restroom, which also was located in the basement.[33] Referring to Elmwood, community activist Waldo Benavidez argued, "We do not want West Side elementary schools to be sardine cans where children do not know their teachers or principal and where they cannot get personal attention."[34]

With little incentive and even less encouragement, many Mexican American students moved through DPS with low expectations. They encountered hostile teachers and administrators, an educational system that did not value their culture or values, and in some cases a language they barely understood. Others could speak English effectively but had a difficult time reading and writing in English, a problem that school officials never recognized until it was pointed out to them in court proceedings. As a result, the dropout rate of Mexican American students was highest among any group in Denver.[35] LARASA estimated that by the early 1970s, one-third to one-half of all Mexican Americans in the Denver school system dropped out on an annual basis.[36] Moreover, its research concluded that Mexican American students who dropped out had already determined to do so by about the third grade. After that, it was merely a matter of how long they were willing to hold out before they formally exited the schools.[37]

Based on Mexican Americans' and African Americans' different experiences of racialization and schooling within DPS, parents, students, and activists within these two groups developed different ideas about educational equality and divergent strategies for improving their children's education. Among African Americans, a well-organized middle class took the lead in demanding school integration. For over a decade Black parents, with the help of local civil rights organizations like the National Association for the Advancement of Colored People (NAACP) and the Urban League, had been demanding school officials take seriously their pleas for integration. Their efforts yielded few concrete results. When Rachel Noel was elected to the school board she took up the cause; in the spring of 1968, after Martin Luther King Jr.'s assassination, she introduced the resolution that called on the DPS administration to develop an integration plan, thus initiating the process that would lead to litigation in 1969. (See figure 8.) Similar histories unfolded in cities nationwide. After the NAACP's victory in *Brown v. Board of Education*, Black activists around the country started to pursue their own litigation strategies or, at the very least, they began to seriously investigate the possibility of bringing lawsuits against local school districts. African Americans in the North and West were no different, even though *Brown* applied to state-sanctioned school segregation only. These parties were never fully convinced there was a real, meaningful difference between the segregation practiced in the South and that practiced in other parts of the country. In Denver members of the NAACP had been considering litigation as far back as 1956. By that time an informal study of the education students were receiving at majority Black schools and majority White schools had revealed stark disparities.[38] Many members of the Black community thus came to the conclusion that integration was the only way to guarantee equality. Black parent and state legislator George Brown reported, "I felt that if black youngsters were to get a full opportunity for an equal educational experience, that the only way they would get it would be that there would be white youngsters there who would be taken care of and as a result of them being taken care of the black youngsters would also have the same opportunity of being care of."[39] For parents like Brown, the question was not whether Black students needed White students next to them in class in order to succeed. Rather, it was a matter of ensuring school officials could not shortchange Black students. In order to properly serve White students, the district would have to pay attention to Black students and share resources equally. This perspective became the dominant Black view after 1956. Importantly, not all African Americans agreed that integration was the best path forward. Pockets of Black residents existed throughout the city that promoted strengthening Black community schools. The most widely embraced perspective, however, was that integration would provide Black children a more equal education.

FIGURE 8. African Americans supporting the Noel Resolution, May 16, 1968. Photo courtesy of The Denver Public Library, Western History Collection, X-28759.

While local concerns and the specific actions of Denver school authorities convinced Black Denverites that integration was the only way to achieve their schooling objectives, they were also influenced by the guidance of the national NAACP, which had already determined that integration was to be the primary educational strategy. In 1961, national NAACP leaders decided it was time to bring *Brown* north and west. Their victory against the New Rochelle, New York, school district laid the groundwork for a broader attack on so-called de facto segregation. "Schools segregated in fact are as harmful to our youth as are schools segregated by law," wrote June Shagaloff, author of a 1961 NAACP booklet, *The Jim Crow School—North and West: Facts for Action*. She continued, "We urge our branches to survey their systems and take some clear action to eliminate segregated schools wherever found."[40] Members of the local branch in Denver immediately began to investigate further DPS's policies and practices. Led by James Atkins, chairman of the branch's Education Committee, they began to follow the national organization's six-part plan that, ultimately, culminated in litigation. The road to *Keyes*, in fact, followed this plan precisely.[41]

Most Mexican Americans, whose children were not as starkly segregated in the schools as were Black children, maintained a different educational philosophy and pursued alternative strategies for winning better schools. Rather than integration, Mexican American parents and activists increasingly sought to develop and nurture stronger Mexican American community schools, where bicultural education could be emphasized and valued, bilingual education could be realized, and the neighborhood was seen as a resource instead of a hindrance to children as they learned and developed. These priorities, however, did not emerge until the late 1960s. Prior to that the only Mexican American organization working on education in the city was the Latin American Educational Foundation (LAEF) and, unlike African Americans, Mexican Americans did not have the benefit of a national organization active on this issue upon which to rely. The LAEF was established to address the very specific issue of funding college education for Mexican Americans. During the organization's first six years of existence (1949–55), it funded only eighty-seven students from the entire state.[42] Certainly this was a significant achievement. But it could not aid the vast majority of Mexican American students in the city. Other Mexican American organizations did recognize the importance of education and the need to address some of their concerns, but they seem to have worked on these issues piecemeal, without organization or cooperation from other groups.

The Colorado Federation of Latin American Groups, for example, argued that DPS needed to hire more Mexican American teachers.[43] Such groups also assisted area high schools and junior high schools in setting up Latin American student clubs, which aimed to provide spaces for socialization, learning about postgrad opportunities, and cultural awareness. They held dances, pageants, and monthly luncheons with "prominent" members of the community, all in the name of furthering a more positive image for Mexican Americans, one that challenged the depiction of their group as a "problem." In short, during the 1950s and early 1960s, much of the educational work of Mexican American community organizations was focused on social uplift, respectability, and the growth of the Mexican American middle class.[44]

The mid-1960s saw a turning point in the development of Mexican American educational goals and the organization of people and resources to achieve these goals. In 1964 a group of Mexican Americans, many of whom were also a part of the LAEF or other organizations, formed LARASA as an umbrella organization and research clearing house.[45] With funding from the United Way and, soon, other grant-awarding organizations, LARASA quickly became a household name. Over the next decade it became the most active and widely involved organization of Mexican Americans in Denver. When the group's Education Committee called a conference in the fall of 1965, they established for the first time a major educational agenda that went beyond providing college scholarships. The committee's primary objective was to improve Mexican American education within DPS. It was a "milestone" moment for the community.[46]

What proved to be a critical moment in local Mexican American educational organizing was also significant for the nation. In 1965 the National Education Association (NEA) published a landmark report on Mexican American education in the Southwest. It focused on five states—Arizona, California, Colorado, New Mexico, and Texas—as well as several bilingual education programs throughout the region.[47] The report was significant in the effort to achieve bilingual education in schools with a large number of Mexican American students.[48] It also highlighted the alienation that many Mexican Americans experienced in their schools, a result of few Mexican American teachers, forced assimilation, and disrespect for Mexican American cultural and linguistic traditions. Poverty, a reality for a large number of Mexican Americans in the Southwest, exacerbated these problems. To improve the education of Mexican Americans, the report said, school districts needed to promote bilingual education and the repeal of English-only laws.⁴⁹ Entitled *The Invisible Minority*, the report argued that one of the biggest obstacles to obtaining needed reforms was that school officials ignored Mexican American students, teachers, parents, and activists. Although they often were the largest non-White group in cities throughout the Southwest, Mexican Americans were invisible to policy makers and others tasked with implementing public policy. An article in the *Atlantic* a couple of years later similarly described Mexican Americans as "the minority nobody knows."⁵⁰ Such interpretations surely resonated with Mexican Americans in Denver, who struggled to get school officials to listen to and take seriously their educational demands, particularly when those same officials were busy defending themselves against African American claims that they segregated students.

However significant the mid-1960s were in the eyes of Mexican American educational advocates, in fact, most Denverites paid little attention. As Denver westsider Vincent Garza explained to educators at a statewide conference, "Too often this ethnic group [Mexican Americans] has been considered the invisible minority, in that society refuses to become aware of the multiple problems of the Mexican-American."⁵¹ By 1973, as the city awaited the Supreme Court's decision in *Keyes*, LARASA complained that even though they were putting in the work to study the problems Mexican Americans encountered in DPS and to develop recommendations for school officials, they were completely disregarded by the district. Sofie Zamora, the group's chairperson of the board, pointed out the double standards they encountered with DPS employees and school board members and decried the lack of attention to Mexican Americans. When a White housewife from south Denver complained to the board about a recent incident in which her five-year-old child had been dropped off by a district bus driver five blocks from their home, leaving the child alone and lost, board members were deeply apologetic and displayed great concern about what had transpired. Yet just minutes before this woman spoke at the school board meeting, the LARASA Education Committee chairman had described several concerns they had about the district's handling of the high Mexican American dropout rate. Since 1967, they emphasized, approximately five thousand Mexican American students had dropped out every year. Not only did LARASA's concerns not elicit the same kind of concern as the south Denver mother's, but they got no response at all. "There was neither a murmur from the Denver Board of Education, nor a moan from the Denver Public School Superintendent or members of his staff," Zamora charged. After pointing to several other instances in which the group's recommendations were ignored, she condemned DPS authorities for their refusal to do anything that might improve Mexican American educational outcomes. "Through consistent silence and inactivity," Zamora penned, DPS "has demonstrated that it does not possess the intellectual will to construct an original solution to the special problems of the Chicano and that it is not receptive to constructive suggestion from the community."[52]

As LARASA investigated the situation in the schools and developed strategies for improving the education of Mexican American youth, African American integrationists continued their assault on DPS for not taking any action to alleviate the growing concentration of Black youth. Meanwhile, Mexican American pupils were increasingly concentrated as well, particularly at the elementary school level. Activists had pushed the district to create a new study committee, the objective of which was to investigate and make recommendations about the problem of growing racial concentration in the schools. The Advisory Council on Equality of Educational Opportunity in the Denver Public Schools included representation from five civil rights organizations, including LARASA, the NAACP, the Congress on Racial Equality (CORE), the Park Hill Action Committee (PHAC), and the Anti-Defamation League (ADL), as well as parents, teachers, business leaders, and DPS administrators. It was chaired by a local attorney, William Berge, while Bernard Valdez served as its vice chair.[53]

From the beginning, the multitude of interests and identities on the council complicated the study process and highlighted the difficulties in trying to ensure equal educational opportunity in a multiracial city.[54] While the problem of unequal schools had multiracial components, DPS's approach to dealing with it was biracial. When the council considered its charge, it noted that the tasks it had been given were limited in scope. Council members were asked to consider the impact of the district's neighborhood school policy and to recommend policy changes or adaptations for the district's operations in Northeast Denver only; no other areas of the city were mentioned by the board. In its report, the council stated, "In view of the restricted charge, the Council felt inhibited in its considerations" of other problems, including the concentration of Mexican American students in particular schools.[55] In fact, in its official "Statement of the Problem," the council mentioned Black students only.[56] The council's biggest mistake was not recognizing the interconnectedness of the problems it was supposed to address: segregation in one area of the city influenced the educational outcomes in other areas, so any plan to address these concentrations would invariably influence the entire district. When the council pointed out the limitations of its study and suggested that other problems, including the segregation of Mexican American students, might be addressed at a later date, it put off the concerns of Mexican American parents and community members, making them secondary to the concerns of the Black community. It also highlighted the central paradox of Denver's desegregation dilemma. The district was not split along Black and White lines, yet from the beginning its approach to the problem had been guided by the assumption that segregation *was* a Black and White problem. Although many people pointed out the inequalities Mexican Americans faced in the schools, the problem was seen as separate from the desegregation question. The Advisory Council's attempt to compartmentalize the myriad problems confronting the district merely compounded an already deeply embedded system of racial inequality in the Denver school system. As a consequence, Mexican Americans were once again pushed to the margins.

Mexican Americans and African Americans had many of the same schooling experiences, but their specific encounters with DPS were guided by the different ways they were racialized. Whereas DPS was able to concentrate the majority of Black students racially into particular schools, the same could not be said for Mexican Americans, who were more residentially dispersed. Instead, school officials implemented a curriculum meant to assimilate Mexican American students and then tracked them into vocational courses or special education. Meanwhile, large numbers of both groups continued to drop out on an annual basis, and the school district ignored parent and community demands for increased attention and resources. By the mid-1960s many Mexican Americans had become more racially segregated as well, the result of increased population and residential concentration on the Westside, in Northwest Denver, and in the core city area. By the end of the decade, DPS had several schools that were majority Black, several that were majority Mexican American, and a few that were majority Black and Mexican American combined. When *Keyes* was filed in 1969, these racial dynamics forced the plaintiffs' attorneys to develop specific legal arguments that drew on *Brown* but significantly expanded that decision's meaning as well.

FOUR

Becoming Minority under the Law

IN THE WINTER OF 1970 George Bardwell testified in support of school integration proponents in *(Wilfred) Keyes, et al. v. School District No. One, et al.* (1973).[1] A mathematician at the University of Denver, Bardwell had been part of a team that spent eighteen months collecting information on student enrollment data, housing patterns, and school boundary decisions, as well as other evidence from the city's public school system. According to the plaintiffs, this evidence demonstrated that Denver Public Schools (DPS) had purposely segregated students by race. Although Black and White residents of Park Hill initiated the litigation, it involved all the district's students, including the largest non-White group in Denver, Mexican Americans. Using Bardwell's data, the plaintiffs argued that the district had intentionally created and maintained "majority Anglo" and "majority minority" schools. They combined Black and Mexican American students in the minority category.[2]

The listed plaintiffs were eight Black, Mexican American, and White families. Wilfred Keyes, lead plaintiff, was a Black chiropractor who filed on behalf of his daughter. Born and raised in Kansas City, Missouri, he attended segregated public schools and did not want his children to suffer the same inequities. When he and his wife moved to Denver in 1952 they began the process of purchasing a home in south Denver but quickly realized their new city was not what it seemed. Keyes decided to look into the neighborhood school first, which he found to be more than adequate. "It was a lovely school," he stated. "There was carpeting on the floor, good audiovisual equipment, new books, relevant instructional materials, and everything else needed for youngsters to achieve a quality education. One could easily see that this school was receiving its share of the taxpayers' money." But when he

FIGURE 9. Josephine Perez, 1971. Photo courtesy of Sheila Perez-Kindle.

revealed that his children would be attending that school, a district official told him that "this public school was for Whites." Instead of south Denver, then, the family chose a majority Black neighborhood in north Denver. There Keyes's two children enrolled at Mitchell elementary school, which, according to Keyes, was "not half as good as the one in the other neighborhood. [There was] no carpeting on the floor, no audiovisual equipment, no relevant instructional materials." He quickly determined that Mitchell was vastly inferior to the school he had viewed in south Denver. He explained, "These schools here are separate but certainly not equal. I decided to do something about this segregated school system."³

Josephine Perez, a Mexican American grassroots community activist, joined the *Keyes* lawsuit to represent Mexican Americans as a plaintiff on behalf of three of her children (see figure 9). She lived in the Lincoln Park neighborhood on the West Side, which located her right in the middle of a bustling community caught up in the momentum of the Chicana/o movement. When students walked out of West High School in 1969, she was one of many parents to attend community meetings in the aftermath. One of six parents elected to a group that operated as a liaison between students and DPS officials, she worked for years to promote Mexican American educational needs and demands.[4] During the summer of 1970 she worked as a teacher's aide for the Baker Junior High Extension Center, a program designed to assist at-risk students as they labored to achieve their life goals.[5] Working with and advocating for such students was a central part of her activist work. Born in Riverton, Wyoming, in 1923, Perez never attended school past the fourth grade. Instead, she joined her stepfather in the potato and sugar beet fields outside of town and assisted her mother at home. As she recalled years later, she could not speak English back then, and none of her teachers spoke Spanish. "I couldn't read," she remembered. "I felt so dumb." That memory must have remained with her throughout her life. At age sixteen she taught herself to read with *McCall's* and *True Story* magazines and the help of a family friend. As a parent she instilled the value of education in her children, even forcing them to handwrite passages from the family's prized encyclopedia collection during the summer when they were out of school. Later, when she was in her sixties, she decided to get her GED by enrolling in Denver's Emily Griffith Opportunity School. As it turned out, she did not need to take any classes; she passed the test on the first try.[6] Education, for Perez, formed the core of her self-identity and activist philosophy. Because she understood that getting a quality, equal education was essential to Mexican American students' futures, she committed her family to the integration cause.[7]

Both Keyes and Perez valued education and recognized its significance for their children, but their different racial and class backgrounds had produced different experiences with public schools and education more generally. Nonetheless, they came together in their efforts to achieve their goal: equal schooling for all children. The plaintiffs' decision to construct Blacks and Mexican Americans as "minorities," a collective in opposition to "Anglos," reflected the joint endeavor of Keyes and Perez by including all Denver pupils. Yet this strategy was also limited by its inability to speak to the divergent experiences of African Americans and Mexican Americans. For the school district's attorneys, it was an easy argument to challenge. There were no records that proved the district had ever utilized the category "minority" in its classification of students. Moreover, the district had never had any official policy of segregation. School officials were always, defense attorneys argued, race neutral.[8] But the choice to center their argument on an Anglo/minority binary made sense to the plaintiffs' attorneys, led by Gordon Greiner. With few legal precedents available to support a school desegregation case in a multiracial city where there had never been any law requiring segregation, attorneys were forced to develop a new approach. The traditional Black-White binary could not account for the kind of segregation that existed in Denver's public schools.

As in other cities without a history of legal segregation, school officials pursued a set of policies that created and maintained racially recognizable schools, even though they presented their actions as colorblind. These practices led to both segregated schools and segregated classrooms, all of which demonstrated a dynamic particular to Denver and other multiracial cities: multilayered segregation. There were schools that were majority Black, others that were majority Mexican American, and still others that were majority Black and Mexican American. In Houston, Texas, for example, school officials placed Black and Mexican American students in schools together and then argued Mexican Americans were White. This allowed them to claim they had desegregated city schools when, in fact, they had merely shifted non-White students in order to maintain majority White schools. Educational inequality thus operated on multiple levels and affected various groups of students in different ways. Lawyers pursuing school desegregation lawsuits in other parts of the US West also grappled with these complexities.[9]

Although historians and legal scholars have long recognized the significance of *Keyes*, the racial negotiations that grounded the litigation have not been fully explored. Both the plaintiffs and the defendants embraced a biracial understanding of discrimination litigation that ignored the multiracial realities of the city.[10] That is, their conception of race did not move beyond the Black-White binary to consider the unique racial positioning of Mexican Americans. Located somewhere between Black and White and viewed by local Whites as culturally and intellectually inferior, they presented attorneys in the case with a dilemma. By constructing Mexican Americans as minorities, the plaintiffs attempted to show they were more like Blacks than Whites. On the other hand, by challenging the Anglo/minority approach, lawyers for the district indicated that they believed Mexican Americans were more White than Black. As the litigation progressed the two sides regularly battled over the question of Mexican American racial identity. This kind of legal maneuvering is indicative of the ways the law operates to create and legitimize race. Its reliance on precedent ensures that any attempt to litigate questions relating to race, such as in school desegregation cases, is bound by predetermined rules that are themselves the product of past legal action or statutory design. In this way the law is as much a sociopolitical construction as a legal one. Thus, the law is never neutral or unencumbered by broader social, cultural, economic, or political influences. Yet even while the law is constructed in specific temporal and geographical locations, once a legal decision is made or a law passed, it goes on to act as universal doctrine, informing legal outcomes decades or even centuries later. According to critical legal scholar Ian Haney López, "One of the defining elements of law is its universal aspiration, its will to apply equally in all cases and across all situations." It is this feature of the law that perhaps most shapes the legal construction of racial categories and definitions, even though historical context does play a role. Because precedent establishes the rules of engagement, legal actors are limited in the arguments they can make, thus ensuring that radical or even moderate departures from these predetermined rules, regardless of their relevance for the legal questions at hand, are always suspect. This makes legal recognition of newer conceptions of race, as well as local understandings of racial hierarchies and identities, difficult for the courts to recognize.[11]

As Denver lawyers on both sides developed strategies for winning their cases, they depended on school desegregation case law, starting with the 1954 *Brown v. Board of Education* decision and its progeny, to define and give meaning to the racial classifications in question. When the plaintiffs' attorneys, led by Denver lawyer Gordon Greiner, determined to frame their argument around the Anglo/minority binary, they attempted to conform a local system of racial understanding to the imperatives of school desegregation law.

These debates over whether Mexican Americans were closer to blackness or whiteness illustrate another important component of racial formation.[12] In the constantly evolving struggle over who is and is not a full member of US society, relational racialization has played a central role. All racial projects, argues Natalia Molina, are connected across time and space. "Once attitudes, practices, customs, policies, and laws are directed at one group," she explains, "they are more readily available and hence easily applied to other groups." Even when these ideas, practices, and policies, which she calls "racial scripts," are questioned or condemned in reference to one group, they are always ready to be used against others. Racialized groups in the past, present, and future are always connected.[13] Molina's theory of racial scripts helps us understand how different racialized groups become excluded from full US citizenship. But what about efforts to win full inclusion for these same groups? Part of the purpose of this chapter is to demonstrate how a racial scripts approach can be useful for understanding post–civil rights legal battles. Relational racialization could both exclude *and* include. My analysis of the *Keyes* case reveals that, from the perspective of the plaintiffs, comparing Mexican Americans to Blacks was crucial to securing civil rights protections for both Mexican American and Black students. Proving they were minorities, in fact, was a key part of the plaintiffs' strategy for winning better schools for all students. Alternatively, comparing Mexican Americans to Whites, as the defendants did, raised questions about the plaintiffs' claims of educational discrimination. The decades-long battle over whether Mexican Americans were White or non-White informed the arguments of both sides.

By focusing on the early stages of the case, I show how and why the plaintiffs developed the minority construction and how it was contested. While Mexican Americans played a critical role in desegregating Denver schools, their participation in the case was more symbolic than real. It would take intervention by the Mexican American Legal Defense and Educational Fund (MALDEF), which did not occur until January 1974, to ensure that the courts considered the educational needs and demands of Mexican Americans. By that time the Anglo/minority binary was firmly entrenched in the debates over school desegregation in the city, limiting MALDEF's ability to secure equitable education for Mexican American students. Relational racialization in the name of inclusion, therefore, was no less exclusionary.

As the case moved up the court system, both the plaintiffs and the school district maintained their original arguments. At times they adjusted their rationales, providing insight into how they were thinking and strategizing as the case progressed, but their basic arguments remained the same. They developed their claims as they prepared their case for the district court trial. While the Supreme Court's decision has garnered attention from legal scholars and historians, earlier strategizing produced the ideas and arguments that shaped that decision. This chapter, therefore, focuses on the district court trial rather than the case before the Supreme Court. Such an approach allows me to detail the important ways that local context shapes how courts decide precedent-setting cases. Denver's school desegregation battle set a national precedent with profound nationwide implications. Understanding how and why the case was argued as it was establishes the significance of Mexican Americans to broader civil rights developments in the postwar United States.

Strategically, multiracial student populations presented civil rights attorneys with a challenge. In order to prove school segregation had taken place in the post–*Brown v. Board of Education* period, plaintiffs had to show not only that each group experienced discrimination, but also that each group was indeed a recognized racial/ethnic minority.[14] The racial uncertainties that defined the Mexican American experience made this a difficult task. On the one hand, they were legally White. This had been true since 1848, and it was confirmed in several important court decisions between 1897 (*In re Rodriguez*) and 1954 (*Hernandez v. Texas*), as well as by the US Census Bureau, which continued to categorize Mexican Americans as racially White. Many Mexican Americans, moreover, argued for White racial classification. This occurred in Denver and throughout the Southwest. In 1966 Mexican Americans organized a collective challenge to the Denver Police Department's practice of classifying them as "Mex," "Mexican," or "U.S. Mexican" on police reports. Responding to the pressure, the chief of police announced that they would be marked as "white" or "Caucasian" in the future.[15] On the other hand, Mexican Americans increasingly made claims on the state by pointing to a legacy of racism. By 1969 their highly visible challenges to a system that had kept them locked in poverty and socially, culturally, and politically marginalized had an impact on the ways that Mexican Americans were racially constructed. Almost anyone could open a newspaper and see stories about the rising consciousness and protest activity of the Chicana/o movement, whether those stories featured farmworker strikes, struggles over land, school walkouts, or a national gathering of Chicana/o youth in Denver. And government officials were finally starting to take notice. In 1967 President Lyndon Johnson created the Inter-Agency Committee on Mexican American Affairs in response to increasing pressure from Mexican American organizations and the rising visibility of their dissatisfaction. Occurring alongside the civil rights movement, the Chicana/o movement helped crystallize, in the eyes of many Americans, Mexican Americans as an aggrieved non-White group.

Although contradictory, these two constructions of Mexican American racial identity reinforced each other precisely because they were opposing formations. The fact that these two different racial projects existed simultaneously points to the significance of racial ambiguity in the construction and maintenance of a regional racial hierarchy. Historians have demonstrated how Mexican Americans' not-quite-White racial status worked to keep them locked into subordinate positions and unable to challenge discrimination in the courts.[16] In the post–civil rights period this porousness continued to work against Mexican Americans as they tried to access the benefits of recent civil rights legislation and court victories. Becoming minority under the law was an incredibly important hurdle that had to be cleared before the courts would overrule the long-standing legal precedent that they were White.

When the *Keyes* plaintiffs filed their lawsuit, Mexican American legal minds were only beginning to see the benefits of abandoning the "other White" argument. For the first time, lawyers representing Mexican Americans looked to *Brown* to lay the foundation for their civil rights claims.[17] The reasons for this shift in strategy are complex, but two important changes, one in the realm of policy and one in the realm of ideology, help explain it. First, the passage of the 1964 Civil Rights Act provided vast new legal rights that applied not just to education but to jobs, housing, and public accommodations as well. Being able to claim racial discrimination now proved incredibly useful in Mexican Americans' fight to achieve full inclusion. Asserting whiteness was no longer the most obvious path to victory in the post–Civil Rights Act period. As Nancy MacLean argues, "It enabled Mexican Americans to embrace non-white identity without assuming the risk involved when discrimination was legal."[18] Second, the rise of the Chicana/o movement by the late 1960s helped solidify, for many Mexican Americans, a new way of thinking about their racial identity. Rejecting whiteness and assimilationist politics as not only impractical but also culturally damaging and ineffective, these individuals forged an identity that was both racially distinct and politically radical. To claim one's self as *Chicana/o* was to assert this new politicized understanding of racial identity.[19] Combined, the end of Jim Crow and the rise of the Chicana/o movement dramatically altered the political landscape for Mexican Americans fighting for equal schools.[20]

After assuming they were White for so long, however, the courts proved reluctant to accept otherwise. When the recently established MALDEF tried to intervene in a school desegregation case in Houston, Texas, arguing Mexican Americans deserved representation because they constituted a separate, identifiable minority group, the judge in the case refused to accept this new argument. "Content to be 'White' for these many years now," he wrote in his denial of MALDEF's petition, "when the shoe begins to pinch, the would-be Intervenors wish to be treated not as Whites but as an 'identifiable minority group.'"[21] Before Mexican American civil rights attorneys could lead a successful challenge to school segregation, they had to prove that Mexican Americans were, in fact, a separate minority group.[22]

In Denver, the plaintiffs' legal team arrived at the same conclusion. They constructed a racial binary between Anglo and minority students, and they embraced a definition of segregation that strongly linked it with racial imbalance. Convincing the courts to discard the "other White" argument meant they had to move to the other extreme; they had to prove Mexican Americans were more like Blacks than Whites. Legal precedent had already established that Mexican Americans were White and that school segregation involved the unlawful separation of Black students from White students.[23] To win their case the plaintiffs needed to develop an argument that conformed to these parameters but that also could account for the locally specific racial understandings and hierarchies that informed the racial geography of the schools.

Although they were well-intentioned, contends legal scholar Michael Olivas, their focus on the Black-White color line was doomed from the start. They failed to see that their work to desegregate the nation's schools, concentrated in the South up to that point, had to be reworked for the US West, where Mexican Americans were too large a group to be ignored. That is, their focus on racial balance failed to address Mexican American educational needs and demands, which centered on the implementation of bilingual programs and culturally relevant curriculum. Olivas writes, "This myopic, singular focus ... ended up setting desegregation against bilingual education instruction, a conundrum that need not have occurred."[24]

Olivas's criticism is fair, but he has the benefit of hindsight and two decades of scholarship that challenges the Black-White paradigm.[25] According to Juan Perea, this paradigm, the dominant paradigm of race in the United States, is "the conception that race in America consists, either exclusively or primarily, of only two constituent racial groups, the Black and the White."[26] In fact, the plaintiffs' decision to construct Mexican Americans as "minorities" along with Blacks reaffirmed the Black-White paradigm because it erased the distinct racialization of Mexican Americans that informed their educational experiences in Denver. Rather than highlight the ways school officials discriminated against Mexican Americans, they chose to focus on Black experiences. In effect, they collapsed racial difference into one "minority" category and then tried to demonstrate the educational inequalities between Anglos and minorities.[27]

Earlier in the century officials at the US Bureau of Naturalization similarly collapsed all non-White, non-Black groups into one "nonwhite" category for the purpose of excluding them from naturalizing as US citizens. Citing the US Supreme Court decisions in *Ozawa v. United States* (1922) and *United States v. Bhagat Singh Thind* (1923), these officials denied Japanese persons and Asian Indians the right to naturalize because they were not White. Even though these cases did not deal with the racial identity of Mexicans, many naturalization officials argued that they applied to Mexicans, who were also racially located somewhere between Black and White, and rejected their applications. In so doing they reinvented Mexicans as "nonwhite," a malleable racial category that was not "Black" or "White." Marking them non-White was only possible because they were racialized in relation to other groups. Because Asians were already seen as perpetually foreign and non-White, grouping Mexicans into the same ambiguous category made it possible to exclude them as similarly foreign and non-White.[28]

The same racial process played out in 1969, this time with an entirely different goal. By that time Blacks were already understood to be a historically oppressed group. The civil rights upheavals of the 1960s had proven as much. By grouping Mexican Americans with Blacks, the plaintiffs tried to show that they, too, were oppressed minorities deserving of the same civil rights protections as Blacks.[29] Moreover, both groups suffered educational inequities and were clearly seen as distinct from Whites. While the effort to lump Mexicans into a "nonwhite" category with Asians in the 1920s stemmed from efforts to prohibit them from gaining inclusion as US citizens, the push to group Mexican Americans with Blacks in a "minority" category in 1969 originated from a desire to extend the benefits of full US citizenship to them.

For the purpose of inclusion, however, comparing Mexican Americans to Blacks and grouping them together had limited utility in school desegregation cases because the Black-White paradigm still shaped understandings of race. The defendants challenged the notion that the two groups of students were the same because relational racialization had taught them Mexican Americans were not Black, and only Blacks could claim a history of state-imposed segregation. As Mexican Americans had no such history, at least not one that was recognized by the courts, their racial identity had to have been different and their claims of discrimination immaterial. The plaintiffs, on the other hand, understood that Mexican Americans were not Black, but they positioned them closer to blackness than whiteness. Only when they were racialized in comparison to Blacks and Whites, that is, could Mexican Americans become "minority." Yet categorizing both groups into one minority category and demonstrating the concentration of Mexican American and Black students in the Denver schools did not translate into an effective argument for *why* segregation looked different for these two groups of students or *how* an unequal educational system had disparately affected Mexican American pupils. Any effort to comprehend the racial processes at work in *Keyes* must account for the influence of long-standing debates over Mexican American whiteness, the changed policy arena of the post–civil rights period, and the exclusionary power of relational racialization.

THE LEGAL STRATEGY: CONSTRUCTING AN ANGLO/MINORITY BINARY

In theory the Anglo/minority binary had several benefits. Most importantly, it allowed the plaintiffs to link the *racial* discrimination experienced by Black students, already recognized by the courts in school desegregation cases, to the discrimination experienced by Mexican Americans, previously understood in terms of *ethnicity*.[30] Whatever its benefits, in practice the plaintiffs' approach proved problematic. During pretrial conferences and the district court trial, lawyers for the school district challenged both the classification of Mexican Americans as "minority" and the practice of grouping Mexican American and Black students in order to prove segregation. Both the courts and the federal government had long categorized Mexican Americans as White, which the defendants used against the plaintiffs. Further complicating the case was the fact that it was brought at the same time the federal government was beginning to recognize the discrimination experienced by Mexican Americans and other Latinas/os in the United States. For example, the Equal Employment Opportunity Commission designated "Spanish Americans" as minorities on its EEO-1 form starting between 1965 and 1966, and the US Commission on Civil Rights incorporated Mexican Americans into its published reports with its two-volume study on school segregation, published in 1967.[31]

The Anglo/minority binary, however, was only part of the plaintiffs' overall approach to winning the case. The second major argument they presented, related to the first, was that racial imbalance in Denver schools was evidence of segregation. Up to that point in the history of litigation challenging racial segregation in public schools, the courts had determined that state-mandated segregation was unconstitutional. The remedy was to remove racial qualifications for school attendance. No court had determined that racial imbalance alone, without a law requiring separate schools for different races, was a violation. To determine which schools were racially imbalanced, the plaintiffs used a mathematical construct that calculated the probability that a school's racial makeup would have arisen by chance. Lead plaintiffs' attorney Gordon Griener argued that northeast Denver schools were segregated in the traditional sense, meaning these schools were at least 90 percent one race. Other city schools were not segregated in the same sense but they were still purposely racially imbalanced, the result of the same district practices that created segregated northeast Denver schools. Schools with at least 70 percent combined Black and Mexican American students were included under this definition. Both of these instances, therefore, represented violations of *Brown*.[32]

Once they established these violations Greiner's team sought to prove that the district had established policies knowing they would create further racial imbalance. Without a record of state-mandated segregation, the plaintiffs tried to demonstrate that school officials ignored community concerns about the creation of racially recognizable schools. Even though they knew particular policies would perpetuate segregation, Greiner argued, they implemented them anyway. The plaintiffs also tried to show how segregation limited educational opportunity for Black and Mexican American students. They brought in statistics that demonstrated various educational inequities for both sets of students, including test scores, years of teacher experience, and rates of school suspensions and dropouts. During the trial, the plaintiffs submitted several pieces of evidence that compared the educational experiences of Anglo and minority students. To prove their arguments Griener presented several charts and graphs depicting the racial categories that informed their strategy: "Anglo," "Black," "Hispano," and "minority," indicating both Black and Hispano (see figure 10).[33] During questioning the plaintiffs' attorneys and their witnesses used the terms *Anglo* and *minority* often, clearly trying to reinforce the Anglo/minority binary that grounded their case.

The defense focused its strategy on three intertwined points. First and foremost, the district's attorneys argued, DPS never formally utilized race in its operations, and Colorado's state constitution had always forbidden racial segregation in the schools. Without a clear intent to segregate there was no constitutional violation. Moreover, school districts had never been held accountable for residential patterns, nor had they ever been held to the standard that racial imbalance equaled segregation. The defendants insisted

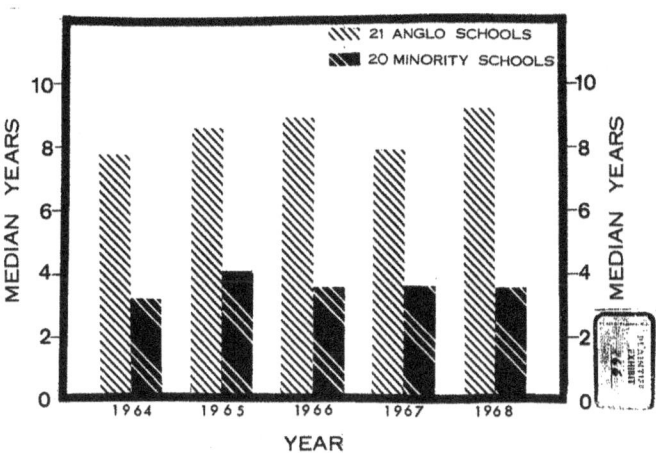

FIGURE 10. Median years of DPS experience, elementary school teachers, 1964–1968." Source: Plaintiffs exhibit 266, *Keyes v. School District No. 1*, 1969, *Appendix, Supreme Court of the United States*, vol. 2, October 1971, No. 71–507, p. 2066a.

that the plaintiffs' definition of segregation, racial imbalance, was a "remarkable definition" with no legal precedent.[34] Thomas Creighton, lead counsel for DPS, noted that several of the schools the plaintiffs claimed were segregated were substantially White, so that he believed they were moving toward "a novel definition of segregation."[35] That is, he implied that an all-White school was the natural and expected outcome of unbiased school policy. The existence of such unremarkable schools could never be evidence of racial segregation.

Related to these arguments, the defendants also challenged the plaintiffs' racial categories. During cross-examination they pressed the plaintiffs' witnesses to define their terms and demonstrate the racial thinking of school officials. If the plaintiffs could not show the specific ways they had racially categorized students and that "minority" was a conscious grouping, utilized by the district to maintain "Anglo" schools and "minority" schools, then the plaintiffs' argument was irrelevant. From the perspective of the defense, grouping Blacks and Mexican Americans was a clear manipulation of racial understanding, which dictated that the categories "Black" and "Hispano" were not the same thing. Combining these two groups defied the logics of race. Armed with this reasoning, the defendants pushed back against the Anglo/minority binary the plaintiffs had built.

If the court allowed this argument to proceed the defendants would be burdened in two ways. First, the category "minority" included many more students, which created a wider range of implications for Judge William Doyle to consider. Not only would the district have to defend against the argument that it operated a dual system in northeast Denver; it also would have to show that race was never a factor in its citywide operations. If Judge Doyle ruled against the school district the constitutional remedy required of it potentially could be more comprehensive, requiring more sustained attention and resources from the board of education, school administrators, and teachers.

Complicating the plaintiffs' efforts to construct Mexican Americans as minorities was the fact that they were focused on Black students from the beginning. Black parents, activists, and a number of community organizations had tried to get the district to integrate northeast Denver schools for over a decade. The 1968 Noel resolution and the subsequent integration resolutions all dealt with schools in and around Park Hill. Robert Connery, one of the plaintiffs' lawyers, recalled that Park Hill was the "crucible" of the entire case.[36] Very few Mexican Americans, however, lived in that area.[37] The plaintiffs included Black, White, and Mexican American parents and DPS students. Although their strategy for proving segregation revolved around a very carefully constructed Anglo/minority binary, a strategy that relied on Mexican Americans, much of the plaintiffs' evidence displayed a traditional, biracial understanding of race in the United States. It centered the experiences of Blacks and Whites.

All evidence, in fact, suggests that Park Hill was the primary focus of the litigants. It is not surprising, given the pattern of settlement, the reality of housing discrimination, and the actions of school officials in response to the rapid shift in the racial character of the neighborhood. This history mirrors the processes occurring in countless other cities in the postwar period. But Denver, like many other western cities, was different. It was not a city defined by the color line but was instead defined by multiple color lines, boundaries that explained not just housing patterns and job segregation but the educational experiences of a multiracial student body.[38] The plaintiffs seemed to recognize this, given their decision to include Mexican Americans, but their understanding of Mexican American experiences was limited. Mexican Americans thus were a part of the plaintiff class, but the plaintiffs' lawyers did not fully represent their specific needs, which revolved around bicultural and bilingual education programs.[39]

Many Mexican Americans, moreover, had already voiced their opposition to integration plans that merely shuffled students around in the name of racial balance. In the fall of 1968, as the school district debated integration plans, Chicana/o movement leader Rodolfo "Corky" Gonzales and other activists from the Crusade for Justice interrupted a school board meeting to protest the direction of integration deliberations. Gonzales insisted that the solutions being offered, "busing" in particular, would not solve the inequalities that existed in DPS.[40] He argued that integration was "a misleading proposition in regards to solving the problems imposed upon the children of the Mexican American segment of this society."[41] Activists like Gonzales resented the implication that Mexican American students would do better in school if they sat next to a couple of White students. Because they believed the school system was rooted in a history of colonialism and Eurocentrism, only major philosophical, pedagogical, and curricular changes would begin to address the educational inequities that Mexican Americans faced. Recent public meetings and school board hearings, moreover, had demonstrated that Mexican Americans were not unified in their viewpoints. At several such gatherings in 1969 they were split on the question of integration and "busing," with some supporting the integration plan and wanting it to go further and others rejecting any kind of transportation program for the purpose of racial balancing.[42] Clearly, the belief that racial balance would provide better schools for all students was not universal among members of the plaintiff class.

As both parties prepared for trial the Anglo/minority binary became contentious. During a pretrial conference the defense focused on breaking it down by challenging the inclusion of Mexican Americans in the plaintiff class. Although Josephine Perez and three of her children were listed as plaintiffs, the defendants suggested that Mexican Americans should not be included. The argument could be made, they said, that Mexican Americans did not want to be included. Defendants' co-counsel Kenneth Wormwood explained to Judge Doyle, "I don't think they really know what's going on here.... [S]ome of these Hispano members I think are quite happy to be where they are."[43] Wormwood's comments reveal two important points. First, the defense believed it had something to gain from excluding Mexican Americans, which indicates that the school district feared their inclusion in the plaintiff class. Indeed, without Mexican Americans, the plaintiffs' two-part strategy for tackling school segregation would not have made sense. Removing them from the class would have meant a major hurdle had been overcome. Second, Wormwood's reasoning behind his opposition to the inclusion of Mexican Americans implies that the defense believed Mexican Americans not only opposed the lawsuit but were actually content with the schools. On the one hand there was some evidence he was correct. Within the previous year various Mexican American groups had questioned the goal of racial balance, which is precisely what the plaintiffs were trying to win. The Crusade for Justice's well-publicized protest was just one instance of opposition. On the other hand the defendants' claim that Mexican Americans were "quite happy" with their present schools was a hollow attempt to spin Mexican American dissatisfaction with the schools into an argument for why they opposed desegregation. The insistence that racial balance would not provide equal schools for Mexican Americans was grounded in a critique of the schools that challenged the educational philosophy of the district. It was not simply a rejection of racial balance. Just months before *Keyes* was filed, in the midst of citywide debates over the merits of integration, hundreds of Mexican American students protested the schools by walking out of their classrooms and into the streets. Student activists presented to school administrators a list of demands that emphasized curriculum, pedagogy, and representation. It did not include a call for racial balance.[44] Indicating that he at least recognized Mexican American dissatisfaction with the schools, Judge Doyle dismissed the defendants' argument and allowed the plaintiffs to include Mexican Americans in their suit.

The trial on merits, in which the plaintiffs asked Judge Doyle to rule DPS a dual school system, began on February 2, 1970. If he ruled that segregation did exist, then he had to decide whether it was intentional or a product of forces outside the control of the school district. Was DPS's neighborhood school policy merely a clever way of maintaining segregation? Finally, did racially imbalanced schools create and/or increase inequalities in the educational opportunities available to Denver public school children?

As the plaintiffs presented their case they relied on the Anglo/minority binary, which again drew the attention of the defense. Greiner's first witness was Paul Klite, a physician who had temporarily left the University of Colorado Medical School to work full time collecting, analyzing, and organizing the data to be presented in court.[45] He explained a number of exhibits that showed the ways school officials had intentionally created and maintained majority Anglo and majority minority schools. Through the selection of new school building sites, gerrymandering school boundaries, the creation of optional attendance zones, the use of mobile classroom buildings, busing, and the use of a limited open enrollment plan, DPS had followed a program of systemic segregation that negatively affected both Black and Mexican American students. In his questioning, for example, Greiner asked Klite about the 1950–53 controversy surrounding the new Manual High School, located in the predominantly Black neighborhood of Five Points. The district had chosen a site that promised it would be a majority Black school and then set the boundaries to ensure it would be almost exclusively Black, even establishing an optional zone at the edges of the Black community, a transitioning area, so that White families living there could send their children to majority White East High School. When parents and community activists challenged school officials on their plan and proposed alternative sites that would ensure an integrated school, they were ignored.[46]

During its cross-examination the defense focused substantial attention on the racial categories Klite used in his testimony. Referring to a table that showed how many Anglo and minority students had participated in the district's voluntary open enrollment plan in 1966, defense co-counsel Michael Jackson asked him to explain why he had created a table comparing "Anglo schools" and "minority schools." Klite explained that a table with three categories, White, Black, and Hispano, would have had too many columns to be meaningful. With this admission the witness revealed an important truth behind the Anglo/minority binary: only by combining Black and Mexican American students into one "minority" category could segregation in Denver schools be made recognizable in the nation's court system. In order to prove DPS had violated the civil rights of Black *and* Mexican American students, the plaintiffs had to manipulate racial categories, a strategy that reveals further the ways that the law operates to construct race. While precedent establishes the parameters within which lawyers must make their case, they always are able to maneuver, in various ways, through and around these doctrinal boundaries.[47]

Revealing this racial fraudulence, as the defendants saw it, might help persuade Judge Doyle to reject the plaintiffs' arguments. Responding to Klite, Jackson pressed his question further. He seemingly was at a loss to understand the witness; no distinction between "Black" and "Hispano" students had been made in the creation of these tables? Rather than challenge the validity of the argument Greiner was making with Klite's testimony—in this case, that the district used the Limited Open Enrollment program as a cover for a segregated school system—the defense went after the plaintiffs' racial reasoning.

A similar interaction occurred later during George Bardwell's testimony, when he described the 1962 school boundary changes that affected Morey, Byers, and Cole Junior High Schools. The plaintiffs tried to make the point that in drawing the boundaries the way it did, the district intended to keep minority and Anglo students in separate schools as much as possible while still maintaining the posture of colorblindness. Greiner wanted to demonstrate how the movement of Black families into these areas prompted the district to gerrymander boundaries to maintain the concentration of Black students at Cole, even though parents and community members had pointed out to DPS other, seemingly more pragmatic, boundary options that would break down these concentrations. The plaintiffs continued to use the terms *minority* and *Anglo* to describe the students involved in this boundary change, but because "minority" and "Hispano" were not Census Bureau categories, it was impossible to present data on the numbers of Mexican Americans living in each enumeration district.[48] The exhibit, therefore, depicted the percentage of "nonwhite" individuals in the areas north and south of Morey who were involved in the 1962 boundary change.

As in earlier civil rights litigation, Mexican Americans' racial uncertainty created a great deal of skepticism about the equal protection claims of the plaintiffs. Recognizing the discrepancy between the plaintiffs' racial categorization of Mexican Americans and the Census Bureau's, the defense raised important questions about their data. When Ris asked Bardwell to explain whether Mexican Americans were included in the non-White category in the census enumeration district data, Bardwell struggled to answer the question. "So," Ris interrupted, "you have no figures then as to what these minorities consisted of or the non-whites consisted of?" "Oh, yes, what they consisted of—Negro and Oriental. Non-white does not include Hispano." Yet the plaintiffs had very carefully built their argument around the "minority" category and the Anglo/minority binary. How could Mexican Americans be minority if the Census Bureau did not include them in the "nonwhite" classification? Realizing it had an opening to challenge their minority grouping—and thus create a significant doubt as to the validity of their case—the defense pressed Bardwell to admit the flimsy basis of the grouping. "Well, in many of your figures here today you have used Hispano as being equivalent to non-white, have you not?" Bardwell's response was to point out that "minority" and "nonwhite" were not the same thing. This was the first time the plaintiffs had even uttered the word *non-White*, and it was solely because that was the only information available from the census.[49]

Ris picked up on the implications of Bardwell's revelation and moved to strike the evidence as unsubstantiated. "Just so we have our terms correct, Dr. Bardwell, in some of your figures this morning, when you were talking about Anglo and minority, did minority in those instances include Hispano?" "Minority includes Hispano, that's correct," Bardwell emphasized. "So," Ris asked, "for some purposes Hispanos are minorities and other purposes they are Anglo?" Here was the critical question. Were Mexican Americans White or non-White? The plaintiffs were trying to argue a school segregation case based on a clear-cut racial division: Anglo versus minority. At the same time, there was no legal definition for *minority*. Did minority mean the same thing as non-White? The defense apparently had been operating under that assumption.⁵⁰

This possibility is supported by the next exchange. Greiner objected to Ris's line of questioning, arguing that the defense was "mischaracterizing what the witness's testimony has been." Judge Doyle allowed Ris to continue his questioning, and Bardwell answered that the Census Bureau included Hispanos in the "White" category. Not satisfied, Ris asked him to relate his *personal* understanding of where Mexican Americans were racially located. "I am talking about your testimony generally from when you started testifying this morning," he emphasized.

Bardwell responded that Hispanos were included in the "minority" category but not the "nonwhite" category. He seemed to tangle himself up as he tried to articulate the plaintiffs' strategy. This was partly because they were trying to cook the available evidence, but it was also because they were trying to conform a complex multiracial reality to the binary rules of law. Because school desegregation litigation since *Brown* relied on a binary understanding of race, lawyers had to make a solid case that racial discrimination was at the center of pupil experiences to prove that school districts deliberately segregated students. If Mexican Americans were White, then those Denver schools with high percentages of Black and Mexican American students—minority schools, in the plaintiffs' argument—were not segregated because there was no racial difference between Mexican Americans and Anglos. Both were White.⁵¹

In fact, school officials in Texas had been using the argument that Mexican Americans were White for several years, effectively deploying the "other White" argument to delay desegregation in their schools. The 1964 Civil Rights Act included provisions that withheld federal funds from states that continued to racially discriminate and directed the US Department of Health, Education, and Welfare (HEW) to issue guidelines for school desegregation. Although the Civil Rights Act included "national origin" minorities in its language, HEW took a more limited approach in its interpretation of "racial discrimination," investigating and publishing statistics within the "Black" and "White" categories only. When Texas schools began placing Black and Mexican American students in schools together, arguing that Mexican Americans were White in order to delay desegregation, HEW did not protest. It was not until the late 1960s that HEW officials began collecting statistics on "Spanish Surnamed Americans," and not until 1970, when it began publishing its series of "Mexican American Studies," that it began to actively investigate allegations of school discrimination against Mexican Americans.[52] *Keyes*, therefore, was brought before the district court at the very moment when federal officials were transitioning into a new period of racial categorization. What this transition meant for legal and commonsense understandings of race, however, was not clear.

It certainly was not clear in Judge Doyle's court. Upon Bardwell's admission that Mexican Americans were "minority" but not "nonwhite," Ris further questioned the racial division the plaintiffs had created. If "minority" did not mean "nonwhite," then what did "white" mean?

"But, now," Ris asked, "is there any distinction between Anglo and white?"

"Yes," Bardwell replied. "The white category in the Bureau of the Census does include Hispano and—of course, if that information were available separately, it would have been broken down. . . . In the case of the school district data, that information is much more detailed and it is possible then to go ahead and talk about Anglo students as not including Hispano."[53]

Feeling he had laid a basis for rejecting the testimony, Ris objected to the exhibit on the ground that it lacked specificity. Once again the plaintiffs could not define their racial categories. Perhaps recognizing the complexities involved in the case, or through sheer curiosity and a desire to get to the bottom of the district's practices, Judge Doyle allowed Bardwell to continue. This was the pattern of legal maneuvering that framed the plaintiffs' argument to the court. Although the case inherently dealt with race—it was, after all, a school desegregation case—no one guessed that racial understandings would become such a prominent feature of the litigation. Race was supposed to be commonsense.

When the plaintiffs rested their case they had tried to prove two things: that the school board deliberately segregated northeast Denver schools and that other city schools were racially imbalanced. Both constituted intentional segregation and thus violated *Brown*. The quality of education at Anglo schools was better, the result of more experienced teachers, more updated and modern facilities, more advanced curriculum, and a focus on college preparation. At minority schools the academic performance of students lagged behind. Not only were students segregated, but the plaintiffs showed that DPS had a sustained practice of placing Black and Mexican American teachers in minority schools and White teachers in Anglo schools. Finally, Greiner brought in educational experts and psychologists to explain to the court how segregation was harmful to children's educational, social, and psychological development. The defendants, possibly believing Judge Doyle would never rule in favor of the plaintiffs with no evidence of an actual state policy of segregation, limited their defense to the argument that all actions taken by school officials had been race neutral.

On March 21, 1970, Judge Doyle issued his opinion, declaring DPS guilty of segregating students. The plaintiffs' evidence proved that the district had taken state action to segregate northeast Denver schools. Regarding the second half of the plaintiffs' two-part strategy, however, Judge Doyle remained unconvinced. Without a demonstration of state action to prove the district was segregating the so-called minority schools, the court could not find a Fourteenth Amendment violation. Remarkably, although the court did not find purposeful segregation, it did find that the quality of education at some of the minority schools was so inferior that it violated the "separate but equal" doctrine established by *Plessy v. Ferguson*. DPS therefore had a constitutional responsibility to correct these inequalities.[54]

Yet the district did not have an obligation to remedy the situation at all the minority schools. Skeptical that grouping Mexican Americans and Blacks into a single minority category was a justified practice for the purpose of declaring a school segregated, Judge Doyle refused to recognize those schools that were not identifiably Black *or* Mexican American. Schools with high concentrations of Blacks *and* Mexican Americans, that is, were not racially isolated.[55] Morey Junior High School, for example, had a student population that was over 70 percent minority (52.4 percent Black, 18.6 percent Mexican American, and 26.8 percent White), making it a racially imbalanced school according to the plaintiffs. Revealing his acceptance of the defendants' earlier objections, Judge Doyle questioned the permissibility of this grouping. He indicated that to do so challenged accepted legal definitions of racialized groups.

Even so, Judge Doyle had difficulty making sense of Mexican Americans' racial positioning. Noting that the plaintiffs used the term *Anglo* to describe Whites—perhaps in order to differentiate between Whites and Mexican Americans—he took notice of the "other White" argument and dismissed it. Mexican Americans, he argued, were different from Whites.[56] Next, he commented on the argument that they were minority, the opposite of Anglo. In making this determination, the opposite of Anglo equated to blackness, and the question became: Could blackness be associated with Mexican Americans? Judge Doyle opined: "One of the things the Hispano has in common with the Negro is economic and cultural deprivation and discrimination. However, whether it is permissible to add the numbers of the two groups together and lump them into a single minority category for purposes of classification as a segregated school remains a problem and a question."[57]

Mexican Americans were not White, but they were not Black, either. The court's challenge, then, was to determine how the color line applied to Denver. For the time being, Judge Doyle left the question unanswered, but he suggested that because both Mexican Americans and Blacks had comparable experiences of poverty, prejudice, and discrimination, their racial identities were more similar than different. What this meant for Denver's school system had yet to be decided. If they were definitively non-White, then DPS was legally obligated to bring schools like Morey up to par with majority Anglo schools. If they were White, the district was under no such obligation.

Within days of Judge Doyle's ruling the school district filed an appeal. Eight days later the plaintiffs cross-appealed, citing Judge Doyle's rejection of their Anglo/minority strategy, as well as his refusal to find neighborhood schools unconstitutional when they produced segregation as the basis for their appeal.[58] In June 1971 the US Court of Appeals for the Tenth Circuit confirmed the district court's ruling on northeast Denver schools; the school district intentionally segregated these schools and was constitutionally obligated to desegregate them. While the court agreed with Judge Doyle that DPS was not guilty of segregating the core city minority schools, it rejected his order that school officials improve the quality of education at those schools. Judge Doyle's order in this matter, according to the court, was judicial overreach.[59] Once again, neither party was satisfied. Within months the plaintiffs petitioned the US Supreme Court for a writ of certiorari to review the decision of the Tenth Circuit, a petition that was granted on January 17, 1972.

As the first northern school desegregation case to reach the Supreme Court, *Keyes* immediately garnered national attention. If the court ruled in favor of the plaintiffs, it would set a national precedent that even school districts with no history of state-sanctioned segregation policy could be found in violation of the Constitution. For districts everywhere outside the South, the outcome of this litigation could not be more important. "The big questions before the court," reported the *Wall Street Journal*, "are whether school segregation, regardless of its cause, is unconstitutional because of its harmful effects, and, if so, what must be done to uproot it?"[60] The *Washington Post* was even more succinct. Its headline read, "Legality of Neighborhood Schools at Issue in Denver."[61] With such high stakes, Gordon Greiner was joined by James M. Nabrit III of the National Association for the Advancement of Colored People (NAACP) Legal Defense Fund when the case was argued before the court in October 1972.

At issue for the plaintiffs were two major aspects of the lower courts' rulings. They argued that the lower courts had required too great a burden of proof for determining that the district's core city minority schools were segregated. Both courts had decided that they had to prove segregatory intent for each school, a nearly impossible requirement. Their second argument dealt with the method of defining a segregated school. Judge Doyle had classified any school with 70 percent or more Black students or 70 percent or more Mexican American students as segregated. Fifteen of the core city schools fell under this definition, leaving out twelve schools with large populations of combined Black and Mexican American pupils. The plaintiffs reiterated the argument they had made before the district court, that a school was segregated if it had a combined population of Blacks and Mexican Americans in excess of 50 percent. These minority schools were vastly inferior to the city's Anglo schools. Thus, the racial identity of Mexican Americans was once again a primary issue, this time before the nation's highest court. In short, the justices had to decide whether they were White or non-White.

However the court resolved this issue, it would have major implications for school districts around the nation. Multiple northern and western cities were in the midst of their own school equality battles, and the racial uncertainty of Mexican Americans and other Latinas/os proved to be a central theme. Puerto Ricans in New York City and Boston were attempting to assert their interests, a herculean task given the focus on Black-White racial dynamics. Like many Mexican Americans in Denver, they sought bilingual education programs that would foster not only bilingualism but also pride in Puerto Rican culture and heritage.[62] Meanwhile, in San Francisco, clashes over the merits of integration versus bilingual education and community schools were just as controversial as in Denver. A large and organized Chinese community voiced strenuous opposition to integration schemes that would break apart their community schools. When *Keyes* made its way to the Supreme Court, lawyers representing these San Francisco interests well understood the case's significance for their own clients' educational concerns, and they submitted a brief to the court. This intervenor class consisting of "Spanish speaking/Spanish surname," "Negro/Black," "Other White," and "Asian" students in the San Francisco public schools argued against the Denver plaintiffs by making a case for the legal uncertainty of racial categories and the constitutional soundness of neighborhood school policies. As parties to the San Francisco school desegregation case, *(David) Johnson, et al. v. San Francisco Unified School District, et al.*, this multiracial group opposed desegregation efforts on the basis that "neighborhood schools" were best able to nurture and educate students of diverse backgrounds, many of whom needed special language programs. *Johnson* followed relatively the same trajectory as *Keyes*. In 1969 Black plaintiffs filed a lawsuit against the San Francisco school district, alleging violations of *Brown*. Two years later, in July 1971, the US District Court for the Northern District of California ruled in favor of the plaintiffs and ordered the schools to desegregate. Finally, the defendant school district appealed to the Ninth Circuit Court of Appeals, which in March 1972 set the case aside until after the Supreme Court ruled in *Keyes*.[63]

While lawyers representing the San Francisco group made several arguments, one of their core claims addressed the Denver plaintiffs' construction of Mexican Americans as minority, synonymous with African Americans. Racial classifications, they asserted, are always suspect and always arbitrary. When utilized in a "multi-racial and multi-ethnic community," they would lead either to a denial of equal protection or a denial of due process, or both.[64] In San Francisco, school assignment plans other than those based on neighborhood burdened students of "Chinese, Latin, and Filipino ancestry" the most.[65] Hoping to capitalize on Mexican Americans' historic racial uncertainty, they targeted the Denver plaintiffs' understanding of Mexican American homogeneity. "'Hispano,'" they wrote, "is not defined universally as plaintiffs suggest." Instead, Hispanos were the descendants of Spaniards who had settled in the US Southwest centuries prior and were not equivalent to other Latinas/os. To demonstrate they were critiquing more than terminology, they also challenged the notion that all Hispanos were non-White, calling such an argument "fallacious, malicious sometimes, and always unjustified." Here, lawyers cited Denver professor and community advocate Daniel T. Valdes, discussed in chapter 1.[66] By picking up on the different racial subjectivities of Mexican Americans in Denver and the legacy of Spanish colonialism more generally, these attorneys highlighted a central point: speaking on behalf of all Mexican Americans was politically impossible. The group was too heterogeneous in terms of race, color, and political ideology to assume Mexican Americans all felt the same way about what was best for their children's education. To argue they were all non-White, moreover, was historically unjustified. These arguments directly challenged the Denver plaintiffs' grouping of Mexican Americans and African Americans into a single "minority" category.

Recognizing that the outcome in *Keyes* would set a precedent for multiracial cities around the nation, the San Francisco attorneys concluded this line of argumentation by pointing to the absurdity of such relational racialization. "For the same reasons which motivate plaintiffs in the case at bar," they wrote, "there is a compulsion to widen the 'Negro' group to include Mexican Americans in Corpus Christi, Hispanos in Denver, Chinese in San Francisco, Puerto Ricans in New York and American Indians in Arizona."[67] As in Denver, civil rights lawyers in all of these places were in the midst of their own challenges to school segregation in multiracial districts and they, too, had found it useful to compare different racialized groups to African Americans. If this kind of thinking was allowed to go forward, the San Francisco intervenors maintained, then the courts would be required to recognize all sorts of other groupings and inequalities. Boys, for example, scored lower on achievement tests than girls. "If plaintiffs' theory were correct," they opined, "one should conclude that boys are suffering from a lack of equal educational opportunity in predominantly male classrooms. Should we then be required by the Constitution to balance boys with girls more closely? Or should we be required to reclassify boys for special treatment as 'Negroes?'" Taking their rhetorical questioning to ridiculous lengths, they asked, "Or should we be required to develop equations on the order of the Lorenz transformation by which we may weight Negroes, Blacks, Chinese, Japanese, Mexicans, Filipinos, Samoans, boys, girls, Hispanos, Indians, Armenians, Italians, Germans, Russians and so on?"[68] Such an absurd conclusion was the point. They hoped to draw the court's attention to the logical fallacy of the Denver plaintiffs' construction of Mexican Americans as minorities comparable to African Americans.

On June 21, 1973, the Supreme Court issued its decision. In a 7–1 ruling, the justices agreed with the lower courts that Park Hill schools were segregated and that the segregation was de jure.[69] This was a major blow to school districts outside the South; school officials could no longer rely on the argument that they were not constitutionally required to eradicate segregation not caused by explicit state law. The court then remanded the case back to Judge Doyle to determine whether northeast Denver was a unique situation or whether the district, as a whole, was a dual system. If the plaintiffs could prove that segregation occurred in one area of the district, then it reasonably could be assumed that it occurred in other areas of the district. The burden of proof thus fell on DPS to show that racial discrimination did not motivate its district-wide policies. If the school district could not prove that northeast Denver was a unique case, then it had "the affirmative duty to desegregate the entire system 'root and branch.'"[70] This was a tremendous victory for the plaintiffs because now school officials would have to prove the racial neutrality of their decisions over the previous two decades. If they could not convince Judge Doyle, then a system-wide remedy represented the only constitutionally sound relief.

Having ruled on the first complaint, the court then turned to the question of whether Mexican American and Black students could be grouped into one "minority" category for the purpose of defining a segregated school. It had to make legal sense of Mexican Americans' uncertain racial positioning. Judge Doyle had ruled they could not be grouped together, implying that he was uncomfortable with the ambiguity of Mexican American racial identity. He knew Mexican Americans were different from Anglos, but he was also certain they were different from African Americans. The Supreme Court disagreed that these two groups of students could not be grouped together, officially designating Mexican Americans as legally minority.[71] For the first time in the post–civil rights period the court ruled on Mexican Americans' racial identity, situating them in relation to African Americans. Beyond confirming their minority status, however, the justices did not elaborate.

A close reading of the court's opinion indicates that Mexican Americans' precarious racial position was no more solidified than it had been before *Keyes* went to trial. Instead of using the evidence to highlight how Denverites uniquely racialized Mexican Americans, Justice William Brennan, who wrote the opinion, continued to depend on relational racialization to make clear the ways that Anglo society discriminated against them. In Denver, Brennan said, there was ample proof that "Hispanos and Negroes have a great many things in common."[72] The District Court in Colorado itself had recognized that both groups suffered the same "economic and cultural deprivation and discrimination."[73] Thus, the lower courts had erred in not allowing the combination of the two groups into one minority category.

Without a legal precedent for Mexican American *racial* difference, the court continued to view the difference as ethnic. According to Justice Brennan, there was ample precedent for this kind of reading. In *Cisneros v. Corpus Christi Independent School District* (1970), the US District Court for the Southern District of Texas ruled that Mexican Americans were a protected class and had a right to seek equal protection under the Fourteenth Amendment. Citing *Hernandez v. Texas* in its decision, the Texas court determined that Anglos treated Mexican Americans in Corpus Christi as non-White and segregated them into different schools and classrooms based on their perceived racial difference.[74] The only Supreme Court ruling on which they could rely was *Hernandez*, an important Mexican American civil rights case but one that was won by evoking the "other White" argument. Here, the specific word choice of the court is significant. The court wrote, "Denver is a tri-ethnic, as distinguished from a bi-racial, community."[75] If Mexican Americans were non-White, then why didn't the court describe Denver as a triracial community? The justices had clearly heard enough evidence to convince them that Whites in the city thought of Mexican Americans as non-White and that they had historically been subject to social, economic, and political exclusion throughout the Southwest. "Though of different origins," the court wrote, "Negroes and Hispanos in Denver suffer identical discrimination in treatment when compared with the treatment afforded Anglo students."[76] But Whites in the city did not treat African Americans and Mexican Americans the same way. They were racialized in distinct ways, a fact the court failed to recognize. Of course, one of the primary reasons it did not acknowledge the separate histories of racialization for African Americans and Mexican Americans was that the plaintiffs had not made a distinction. In the presentation of its case, the plaintiffs' attorneys had constructed both groups of students as minorities. The court agreed. Its opinion reflected both an affirmation of discrimination against Mexican Americans in Denver and a rejection of multiracial formations.

By conflating racial and ethnic identity, the court ignored the historical construction of difference and engaged in a process of relational racialization in order to make sense of Mexican Americans' social status vis-à-vis African Americans. Because these two groups experienced "identical discrimination," they occupied similar positions within the local social hierarchy and belonged in the same "minority" category. The court did not attempt to differentiate between the educational histories of African Americans and Mexican Americans. The category "minority" provided no distinctions between groups; they were the same in the eyes of the court. Thus, there were no distinctions required in formulating a remedy for a constitutional wrong. What worked for one group would work for another, and since African Americans were historically marked as "the other" in the US racial system, *minority* became synonymous with blackness. This would have serious consequences for Mexican American students once the district court tried to fashion a suitable desegregation remedy. For the time being, however, the Supreme Court's ruling on Mexican American racial identity meant that a much higher number of Denver schools were segregated because the majority of students enrolled were either African American or Mexican American. Under Judge Doyle's interpretation, such a school would not have been considered segregated because Mexican Americans were minority but still, for all intents and purposes, White.

The court's failure to acknowledge the history of Mexican American racialization also made it easy for local residents to continue to debate the racial categorization of Mexican Americans and the meaning of racial difference in a multiracial city. As the next chapters detail, the decision of the nation's highest court did not end the school desegregation controversy in Denver, nor did it settle the question of Mexican American racial identity. As the Denver community struggled to come to terms with the court's ruling and implement a workable desegregation remedy, racial categories remained in flux, and Mexican American educational demands remained unfulfilled.

FIVE

"Not White, Yet Not, in the Old-Style Parlance, 'Colored'"

"NOW ALTHOUGH IT IS TRUE that Hispano children often suffer the same educational inequities as blacks," opined the editors of the *Denver Post* three days after the Supreme Court handed down its ruling in *Keyes*, "it is also true that most Hispanos in Denver—the articulate ones at least—apparently do not want their children to have the same degree of school integration sought by most blacks."[1] As these comments indicate, the court's decision to include Mexican Americans in the same "minority" category as African Americans and its remand of the case back to the District Court in Denver for further proceedings dramatically altered the ramifications of the case. It was not just northeast Denver they were talking about but the entire district. The Supreme Court had just opened the door to a massive desegregation plan that would include all the city's public school children, and Mexican Americans were central to that outcome. From the editors' vantage point in June 1973, however, Mexican Americans did not seem to favor integration.

What led them to this conclusion? What were the editors conveying when they used the phrase "most Hispanos"? Who were the "articulate ones"? Were there other, apparently "nonarticulate" ones calling for integration, or something else? What, in this context, did "articulate" mean? These are some of the questions this chapter addresses. Although the nation's highest court had determined Mexican Americans were racially positioned on the non-White side of the color line, local negotiations and conflicts over racial identity and politics continued to define the relationship of the Mexican American community to desegregation. As *Keyes* moved up the court circuit, it became highly politicized, polarizing the city even further along racial lines and intensifying cultural and political divisions among Mexican Americans.

On the one hand, there was some evidence that Mexican Americans opposed integration. Since 1968, when the school board first started to seriously debate integration and develop a desegregation plan, the Mexican American community had housed vocal opponents of desegregation. But for many of these individuals, opposition was not as simple as the *Denver Post* made it sound. Many of them were not necessarily opposed to the idea of integration, but they were unconvinced that racial balance would bring about the kind of educational opportunities they wanted for their children and their communities. Of primary concern to many was developing bilingual-bicultural education programs that, they argued, would boost Mexican American's educational achievement and stem the tide of students dropping out of school. Philosophically, moreover, the argument that integrating with White students would, on its own, promote better learning and achievement among Mexican American students was anathema to a growing number of parents, students, and activists who were drawn to the politics of the Chicana/o movement. For them, the problem with the schools was not that they did not have an opportunity to learn with and from White students; rather, it was that teachers and administrators did not value the cultural background of Mexican American students and did not believe they would ever amount to anything but low-wage workers or criminals. In short, integration with White students meant nothing if the schools did not also make major structural and pedagogical changes. Some African Americans also made these arguments, in some cities more than others. In New York City, for example, Black community control advocates organized for more Black and Puerto Rican parental participation in the running of I.S. 201, a Harlem school composed of Black and Puerto Rican students. They called for a "radical redistribution of power" in school-community relations that they contended would finally address the many flaws in their children's education.[2]

Other Mexican Americans resented the argument, made by the plaintiffs in *Keyes*, that they were minority and needed judicial intervention in order to obtain quality schools. For these individuals, school desegregation litigation was yet another example of the harms being done by the civil rights movement, the Chicana/o movement, and other rights movements of the late 1960s and 1970s. Many were committed to a politics of accommodation and moderation, and they rejected the notion that they were an oppressed minority. Some, in fact, had achieved significant upward mobility. Following the rules, not rejecting them, was key to making it in US society.

School desegregation litigation, as it unfolded in Denver, threatened their precarious positions within the dominant (White) society.

On the other hand, there also were many Mexican Americans who supported integration efforts in Denver. Many of these individuals worked in the schools or with community organizations that sought to improve the quality of education for Mexican American students. Although they had not participated extensively in the litigation, they had been pushing school officials to adopt their reforms for several years. Particularly after Mexican American students protested their experiences in Denver Public Schools (DPS) by walking out in 1969 and again in 1970, various community entities, some of which worked directly with the schools, did research, wrote reports, spoke at school board meetings, and met with administrators to achieve their goals. Much of this work was for naught, as DPS almost never seriously considered their input. Although Mexican Americans had been plaintiffs in the case from the beginning, their specific critiques of the schools and recommendations for improvement were largely ignored. Nonetheless, many of these advocates believed in the merits of integration and supported the plaintiffs in *Keyes*.

While the *Denver Post* editorial ignored these various opinions within the Mexican American community, it did highlight both the centrality of Mexican Americans to the case and the lack of consensus over the question of racial balance, even after the Supreme Court ruled. At the height of the Chicana/o movement, when activists tried to foster community unity to bring about major societal changes, significant divisions emerged over key aspects of Chicana/o identity. The existence of so many different viewpoints among Mexican Americans had long been a feature of Mexican American community formation and civil rights politics. As social movement scholars tell us, social movements require both radical or militant wings and moderate or conservative wings. For change to happen, the larger society must be convinced change is necessary, and that often occurs through the intracommunity politicking that goes on between the radicals and the more established, moderate community advocates. These diverse perspectives balance each other and make the more moderate calls for change seem more plausible and appropriate, compared to the demands of the radicals.[3] The burgeoning Chicana/o movement and its radical roots forced Mexican Americans to confront these long-standing community divides. In Denver, groups like the Crusade for Justice significantly shifted the terrain on which these battles were waged. As radical Chicanas/os gained momentum, adherents, and press coverage, more and more Mexican Americans had to grapple with how they understood their own identity and culture. They had to face old questions in a new social and political environment. By the late 1960s and early 1970s the culture wars of the previous decade and the passage of major civil rights reform had done much to alter the ways ordinary Americans viewed issues like race and civil rights. School desegregation in Denver surfaced as a critical issue for Mexican Americans at precisely this moment, as some were in the midst of a radical transformation and others were doubling down in their defense of older identity formations that privileged Spanish settler history and political moderation. These differing perspectives emerged prominently in encounters over school desegregation. *Keyes* burst open fissures that had long existed among Mexican Americans and accelerated the retreat of Mexican American moderates and conservatives away from the Chicana/o movement and other civil rights movements of the period. Rather than fully transforming Mexican American racial identity, this period helped strengthen older ideas about racial and ethnic identity that privileged cultural difference over racial otherness and sharpened the divide between Mexican Americans and African Americans.

THE DENVER CHICANA/O MOVEMENT

By the mid-1960s many Mexican Americans in the city, particularly the youth, came to view themselves in stark opposition to Whites. As in other cities throughout the Southwest and the nation, these individuals were adopting new racial identities and a new political consciousness that was much more radical than those who continued to self-identify as Hispano or Spanish American. For these Chicanas/os, racial and class differences explained their second-class status in society, not their individual moral, social, or economic failings. Assimilation, they argued, was a *gabacho* method for submitting to White, middle- and upper-class domination. It would never lead to the type of liberation they envisioned for their communities. Only by toppling the system of White supremacist capitalism would they achieve their goals. Partly, this social awakening was a response to the failure of the moderate, assimilationist civil rights groups, like the League of United Latin American Citizens (LULAC) and the American G.I. Forum (AGIF), to make any substantial positive change in the lives of ordinary Mexican Americans. But it also emerged from the powerful labor organizing of the United

Farm Workers and the successes of the Black freedom struggle, which had won substantive victories by the mid-1960s and influenced multiple civil rights mobilizations.[4] In Denver the institutional home of this awakening was the Crusade for Justice. Founded by Rodolfo "Corky" Gonzales in Denver in 1966, the organization was centrally concerned with the ongoing problem of police brutality within Mexican American neighborhoods. (See figure 11.) For years Gonzales and his allies had been documenting these cases and urging the creation of a citizen's review board to investigate claims of police discrimination and misconduct, a demand that went unheeded. Police violence thus played a critical role in politicizing Crusade members and many in the wider Mexican American community. Similar dynamics played out in multiple cities across the Southwest, including Los Angeles, where Mexican Americans and the Los Angeles Police Department had a long-standing contentious relationship based on the well-documented anti-Mexican violence perpetrated against the city's Mexicans and Mexican Americans.[5]

The shift to a Chicana/o identity and politics reflected these distinct experiences of protest, police repression, and violence. As young Chicanas/os watched the civil rights struggles unfolding around them, they developed an idea of race and protest that explained the often violent response of Whites to the demands of people of color. When African Americans marched in Selma, for example, they were met with extreme violence. When young Chicanas/os walked out of high schools to protest the low quality of education they received, police in riot gear greeted them. As the same narrative played out over and over throughout the late 1960s and early 1970s, they began to see themselves as people of color, in stark contrast to Whites intent on beating them down through police repression and violence.[6] Media bias, in combination with police brutality, also contributed to an emerging sense of Chicana/o subjectivity. As Crusade members printed in every issue of their newspaper, "*El Gallo* was born out of frustration and determination for the truth. The truth about our people is never printed in the major newspapers." The message concluded that it would be the "VOICE of the people."[7] By connecting police misconduct and violence, as well as media bias, with the everyday discrimination that many Mexican Americans experienced, *El Gallo* pinpointed the structural mechanisms giving shape to Chicana/o political mobilization and racial identity transformation in the late 1960s.

Adopting a Chicana/o identity meant rejecting the mythology of the "Spanish fantasy past" and any identification with European-ness. "As to his feeling of his racial heritage, he is more apt to be proud of his Indian side

FIGURE 11. Rodolfo "Corky" Gonzales, 1968. Photo courtesy of The Denver Public Library, Western History Collection, WH1971.

than his Spanish," wrote one author in an article that was reprinted in the Crusade's newspaper. For Chicanas/os there was no pride to be felt in identifying with the Spanish "*entremetido* (intruder) who came and destroyed a people."[8] It meant identifying with "*la raza*," the people on the street, living and working within the barrios, or the campesinos, toiling in the fields that fed America. Claiming one's self as Chicana/o was a political statement as much as a racial one, a fact that even the youngest adherents picked up on. In seventh-grade student Rosalie Montoya's poem "Chicano Power," she wrote that in order to possess Chicano power one must first *be* Chicano. Yet being Chicano was not a matter of skin color. She wrote:

> To Have Chicano Power
>   You have to mean it.
>   You have to prove it, and
>   You have to be Chicano
> If not in the shade of your skin
> Then in your HEART.[9]

Being Chicana/o in one's heart meant, above all else, casting off the colonialist logic of White supremacy. Whiteness, then, was to be critiqued and not valued. But whiteness was not just a skin color; it was also a mentality. It was an ideology that poisoned the minds of its adopters and harmed the movement for liberation that was developing at the grassroots level (see figure 12).

Deep divides over race and political philosophy thus emerged among the city's Mexican Americans. More established leaders continued to practice the politics of moderation, assimilation, and working within the system for incremental change. While many of them celebrated their cultural ancestry, they eschewed the radical racial politics of the Chicana/o movement. On the other side stood leaders like Corky Gonzales, who boldly and defiantly preached about Chicana/o cultural nationalism and the need for liberation among a people who were used to accommodation. Racial and political subjectivity worked in tandem for all facets of the community. That is, people's politics informed their racial identity, just as their racial identity influenced their politics.

As the Crusade for Justice and Gonzales regularly made newspaper headlines, divisions in the Mexican American community deepened: some sided with the movement and its militant ethos, while others distanced themselves from it as much as possible. Gonzales had once helped organize the city's Mexican American residents behind Democratic Party candidates for local, state, and national elections. He even headed up the Colorado ¡Viva Kennedy! campaign, but by the mid-1960s he had abandoned mainstream Democratic politics and put all his energy into more radical efforts. "I'm an agitator and a trouble-maker," he stated, "That's my reputation, and that's what I'm going to be."[10] While this kind of antiestablishment language

FIGURE 12. Chicanos protest in front of the DPS administration building, February 11, 1970. One protester holds a sign that reads, "Chicano means power," highlighting the radical roots of Chicano identity formation and political mobilization. Photo courtesy of The Denver Public Library, Western History Collection, X-21598.

was popular with Crusade members and sympathizers, others in the city, including many other Mexican American leaders, viewed Gonzales and his organization with distaste. In one of several editorials discussing Gonzales in the city's two major newspapers, Alex Johnson criticized the Crusade's popular leader and the hundreds of followers who showed up at demonstrations. In language that was becoming increasingly popular, Johnson lamented President Lyndon Johnson's Great Society and urged his fellow "Spanish-Americans" to work hard and take responsibility for their own lives. He expressed clear disdain for the emerging Chicana/o movement and its leadership in Denver, noting that he and others like him did not need a spokesman, especially one like Gonzales, to speak for him. As a responsible, hardworking American, he did not need public assistance and resented that some big shot thought it was up to him to save "Spanish-Americans" when he had already saved himself.[11] John Rosales, a member of the Pueblo, Colorado, city council who was profiled by the *Rocky Mountain News* in 1966, similarly voiced his distrust of movement leaders. "I don't like the idea of someone else being a spokesman for me," he said after he explained his aversion to public demonstrations as a tactic of political mobilization.[12] Both he and Johnson revealed their aversion toward the increasing publicity that the Chicana/o movement was achieving. Their sense of individual autonomy and success was offended by movement politics.

The Crusade was also viewed unfavorably by longtime Mexican American community advocates because of its militancy and association with blackness. Taking their cues from the civil rights and Black power movements, members rejected customary political tactics and preferred more overt actions like marches, walkouts, and other public displays of dissatisfaction, anger, and pride. One of their frequent tactics was to interrupt the meetings of various public bodies (city council, mayoral meetings, and school district meetings, for example), take over the proceedings, and make their demands. From the perspective of more assimilationist Mexican Americans who strove to be taken seriously by their elected representatives, such displays in otherwise orderly public forums revealed both a dismissal of authority and a tendency toward chaos. State Representative Frank Anaya, elected from a majority Mexican American city district, believed that Gonzales's militancy needed to be kept in check. Members of the Mile High chapter of the AGIF, he noted, were used to having to release public statements repudiating Crusade actions. "In the interests of responsible leadership," Anaya reported, the AGIF also had prepared signs to use in counterpicketing at Crusade demonstrations. Respectability politics played an important role in their civil rights work, which meant that they needed to make sure "the public gets the right impression."[13] Anaya and his fellow AGIF members viewed the Crusade's radicalism with suspicion and embarrassment.

For the Crusade for Justice, social movement organizing began by being in the community. It meant getting in the trenches and learning about what was really plaguing people. When Gonzales was accused of merely trying to gain public attention for himself, an argument made frequently by his detractors, Crusade members jumped to his defense and insisted that his interest was in achieving meaningful change for the vast numbers of ordinary Mexican Americans. Crusader John Haro argued that Gonzales was recognized as a leader in the Mexican American community because he actually spoke to regular people about their problems. The traditional Mexican American leadership, in his view, had failed to do so, and now they resented that the Crusade was gaining members and attention. Responding to a letter critical of Gonzales and his organization, Haro wrote, "Perhaps [the author] should leave her ivory towers—talk to some of the people in the 'barrios' (ghettos), and ask them about the Crusade for Justice and its leader—rather than speaking to those who jump from cause to cause, never seeing one cause out to fruition and attempting to defeat what they have left by petty innuendos and personalities."[14] When researchers at the University of Denver conducted a study of Mexican American leaders in the city, they found that Gonzales was the most recognized, particularly among poor people.[15]

THE CONGRESS OF HISPANIC EDUCATORS

When the Supreme Court declared that Mexican Americans were non-White for the purpose of school desegregation, it set into motion a series of debates that centered on the role of Mexican Americans in the desegregation plan. Now that the high court had issued its decision and it was clear DPS was going to be desegregated, several parties, hoping to influence the final plan, intervened in the case. One of these groups was the Congress of Hispanic Educators (CHE). Established in 1968, the group represented Mexican American teachers in Colorado but also counselors, parents, and other interested community members. In early 1974, the Denver chapter of the CHE obtained legal counsel with the Mexican American Legal Defense and Educational Fund (MALDEF) and filed a motion to intervene in the case on the side of the plaintiffs.[16] While they supported the goal of integration, MALDEF attorneys also insisted that Mexican American students required bilingual education programs, curriculum that fostered knowledge of and appreciation for their history and culture, and more Mexican American teachers and counselors. As it had done in several other school desegregation cases, MALDEF intervened to protect the interests of Mexican Americans who did not want to be used as "pawns, puppets, and scapegoats" in efforts to achieve racial balance between White and Black students.[17]

Whereas MALDEF was a national organization focused on the Southwest, the CHE was local, and its members were not only deeply concerned about the quality of education Mexican Americans received in Denver schools but also enmeshed in the school system themselves. As DPS employees they had a special obligation to the students in their classrooms and schools. In a report summarizing the participant-initiated 1968 Workshop to Develop Human Resources among Mexican American Teachers, at which the CHE was established, Fernie Baca Moore noted that this was an important moment for their community. Many of the participants had long felt isolated in DPS, but now they could organize together. As one participant wrote, "The workshop has given us unity, closed the communication gap among us, and made us aware of others and provided direction."[18] Other participants remarked that the workshop helped them develop a sense of pride in their cultural heritage, which they then could take back to the schools. "I changed many of my beliefs," one reported, "and I have become *very* proud of what I am."[19] Based on the report and participants' reflections, it is clear that the workshop served as both an education and an awakening. It was a moment of community building but also consciousness raising.

In the following years the group's members were incredibly active, both at the state level and within DPS. They did research, wrote reports that they then submitted to Denver school officials, accompanied administrators on teacher recruitment trips, spoke at school board meetings, and stayed up to date on the developing school desegregation issue. Several matters were recurring themes in their efforts to improve education for Mexican Americans, including curriculum development, use of Title I funds for low-income areas, parental involvement, the need for DPS to hire and promote more Mexican Americans, and integration. During the winter of 1969, as school officials worked to develop an integration plan after passage of the Noel resolution the previous spring, the CHE submitted two separate reports to the school district that outlined the educational needs of Mexican American students and the solutions the organization believed would address the many problems that currently plagued them. The first item discussed in both reports was integration, indicating its significance in the formation of the group's educational philosophy. "Integration," one report stated, "is a vital and fundamental step towards attaining quality education for the Hispano child, as well as for all children."[20] While the CHE recognized that integration alone would not solve all of Mexican American students' problems, it "strongly recommend[ed]" that current efforts to desegregate Denver schools be expanded to include Mexican Americans.[21] At that time the district's proposal was focused specifically on northeast Denver, where few Mexican Americans lived. The CHE's insistence that Mexican Americans be included in the plan, even before *Keyes* was filed, demonstrates that Mexican American educational advocates were interested in achieving desegregation along with other reforms.

The CHE's journey from its origins to its intervention in *Keyes* reveals how members' shifting racial subjectivities informed their tactics and, eventually, their decision to get involved in the litigation. Hints that this transformation was already underway at the CHE's founding meeting appear in the words of some of the speakers. LARASA executive director Charles Tafoya spoke to the conference participants about the rural folk culture of northern New Mexico and southern Colorado, where many Denver Mexican American families had originated. He discussed the isolated nature of their communities and their "Spanish" origins. But he concluded by noting that more and more Hispanos were abandoning the "Spanish or fantasy heritage" for identification with the "Mexican-Indian."[22] His use of the phrase "Spanish or fantasy heritage" indicates not only that he was familiar with the work of noted lawyer and journalist Carey McWilliams, who first used "Spanish fantasy heritage" to describe the historical fiction that underlay identify formation among many elite Mexicans and Mexican Americans, but also that he accepted McWilliams's argument. Claims to a Spanish colonial past were, for most Mexican Americans, illusions that were now being reconsidered.[23] According to the report summarizing the Workshop to Develop Human Resources among Mexican American Teachers, moreover, participants developed "a willingness to identify with a minority group."[24] The inclusion of this statement in the document suggests that this had been an important aspect of their discussions. Just as the courts in *Keyes* grappled with whether or not Mexican Americans were minority, so too did Mexican American teachers as they worked together to develop solutions to the educational problems their community faced. It is significant that one of the first things they did was collectively agree they were, in fact, part of a minority group.

Acknowledging the Spanish fantasy past and agreeing that Mexican Americans were minority did not settle the identity question. Over the course of the next several years the group's recruitment materials and reports illustrate that it continued to wrestle with the question, suggesting that the multiple currents of thinking that emerged from the larger Mexican American community influenced the CHE. An informational pamphlet produced in 1968 or 1969 displays revealing indicators of how the group situated itself (see figure 13). The bottom of the cover depicts three colonial-era ships that represent the Spanish colonial past, suggesting that members continued to associate with the Spanish heritage that was central to Hispano identity. But the pamphlet also includes signs that its members were proud of their indigenous past. Each letter in "CHE" contains simple, geometric designs

FIGURE 13. Congress of Hispanic Educators pamphlet, ca. 1968–1969. Photo courtesy of The Denver Public Library, Western History Collection, WH2334.

reminiscent of those found in Aztec artwork. Combined, the ships and the designs conveyed to anyone who picked up the pamphlet that the CHE was an organization committed to *mestizaje*. The inclusion of the word "Viva" at the top, so as to read "Viva Congress of Hispanic Educators," reveals that group members very much thought of their organization as a part of the growing Chicana/o movement and helps demonstrate how the organization conceptualized Mexican American racial subjectivity.[25] At protests and community events, "¡Viva la raza!" could be read on signs and heard from chanting attendees, and the newspaper of the Crusade for Justice frequently used "viva" to evoke a particular combination of emotions (pride, righteous indignation, and urgency) in its readers. Overall, the CHE's choice of imagery and its inclusion of a common Chicana/o rallying cry indicates that its sense of identity was in the midst of an evolution.

By July 1973 the evolution was complete. The cover of a counseling institute program celebrates Aztlán, the mythical homeland of the Aztecs and a foundational element of Chicana/o nationalism. Written at the 1969 Chicano Youth Liberation Conference in Denver, a national youth gathering that galvanized the movement, *El Plan Espiritual de Aztlán* (The spiritual plan of Aztlán) articulated both a distinct bronze racial identity and a plan for achieving Chicana/o liberation. Its opening statement declared that Chicanas/os were "a bronze people with a bronze culture.[26] For the CHE to embrace Aztlán, its members would have had to accept the racial politics of the Chicana/o movement; they would have had to understand their racial identity as brown, not White. When they joined forces with MALDEF and intervened in *Keyes*, this understanding of their history and identity took center stage in their justification for intervention.

In its motion to intervene, MALDEF noted the Supreme Court's determination that both African Americans and Mexican Americans had similar experiences of prejudice and discrimination in the Southwest. But it moved from that point to highlight the findings of the US District Court in Texas that found Mexican Americans were an identifiable class for the purposes of the Fourteenth Amendment.[27] As such, MALDEF attorneys argued, Mexican American students had a right to their own representation because they had unique educational needs that were not being addressed by the Denver plaintiffs. In fact, their interests *could not* be represented "because the existing plaintiffs who are primarily Blacks, and their counsel lack exposure to the diverse problems that confront the Chicano community."[28] The difficult task of devising a plan for equal educational opportunity in the

Denver schools was further complicated by the fact that the interests of Black students and Mexican American students might be in competition. "The existing plaintiffs cannot adequately and forcefully represent [both groups] in such a competitive situation," MALDEF insisted.[29]

According to MALDEF attorneys, the CHE had a right to intervene in the case because of Mexican Americans' unique (non-White/non-Black) racial positioning. Proving this argument, of course, meant overcoming the racial uncertainties that had always worked against Mexican American civil rights efforts. Three points supported the attorneys' contention. First, Mexican Americans had a significant stake in the outcome of the court's decision regarding a desegregation remedy. The courts had already recognized that Mexican American students experienced discrimination within the Denver schools, and they would have to abide by whatever plan the court devised. Acknowledging that transportation probably was going to be a major part of the plan, MALDEF attorneys insisted that Mexican Americans be treated equitably, which meant that they would not bear the brunt of "busing" and would not simply be shuffled into middle-class schools "where they will be made to feel inferior and will be discriminated against by students, teachers, administrators, and staff because of their poverty and inalienable racial characteristics."[30] Hoping to capitalize on the newly emerging argument that Mexican Americans were racially distinct, MALDEF put great effort into situating Mexican American students in contrast to both Black and White students. As persons with "inalienable racial characteristics," Mexican Americans were a separate, identifiable racial group not currently being represented by the plaintiffs.

Second, MALDEF had to show that it was not intervening to sabotage the desegregation plan, a result of the long-standing legal argument that Mexican Americans were White. In other school desegregation cases, White parent groups had tried, mostly unsuccessfully, to intervene while the courts were developing remedies as a way of interjecting their anti-integration viewpoints into the planning process. When Mexican Americans tried to intervene in a Houston, Texas, school desegregation suit, claiming they had both a clear interest in the case and a constitutional right to seek relief as minority persons, the court rejected them on the ground that they had always been treated as Whites in Texas courts.[31] That opinion was overturned on appeal when the Fifth Circuit rejected the decision regarding the intervention of Mexican Americans and, as MALDEF pointed out, the question of Mexican American whiteness was later litigated by the Supreme Court in *Keyes*. By law, Mexican Americans were now non-White.[32] To drive the point home, MALDEF's memo cited the Fifth Circuit's ruling in the Houston case, *Ross v. Eckels*, several times, indicating that the attorneys may have been concerned their motion to intervene would be denied on the basis of their clients' perceived whiteness and thus their perceived interest in undermining the plaintiffs' efforts. In addition to situating Mexican Americans as non-White, MALDEF also noted its interest in working with the plaintiffs to ensure equal education for both Black and Mexican American students. In numerous school desegregation cases, MALDEF argued, "*White* parents or other parents attempted intervention to oppose integration, while the Chicano parents here seek not to oppose integration, but to ensure that the court's remedy: (1) treats all children equitably, and (2) considers the exigencies of Chicano education." Later, MALDEF emphatically stated, "Chicanos cannot be counted as whites for any purpose in the *Keyes* desegregation suit."[33]

Finally, MALDEF pointed out that although the plaintiff class had included Mexican Americans from the beginning, the case had been "clearly Black dominated."[34] Most of the evidence the plaintiffs presented in court dealt with establishing discrimination against Black students. This was apparent in their choice to focus on Park Hill schools. While Mexican Americans constituted about 25 percent of the city's population as a whole, the Park Hill area was only about 10 percent Mexican American. As such, MALDEF maintained, "It only requires a syllogistic conclusion for the Court to find that the emphasis of *Keyes* has not been on Chicanos."[35] If it had been, the plaintiffs might have taken note of the May 25, 1970, US Department of Health, Education, and Welfare (HEW) Memorandum to School Districts with More Than Five Percent National Origin-Minority Group Children, which MALDEF now presented to the court for consideration. HEW recognized "the particular discrimination directed at Chicanos," a point the plaintiffs had not made a part of their strategy.[36] MALDEF thus sought intervention by arguing, "This case is for us, and about us—but without us."[37] This statement accurately captured the political and legal precarity that Mexican Americans faced in the post–civil rights context. *Keyes* was a legal challenge to unequal schooling for both African Americans and Mexican Americans. Its outcome had significant consequences for the educational opportunities and outcomes for all students. It was, thus, *for* Mexican Americans. The case also was about the proper application of racial knowledge. Were Mexican Americans White or non-White? Could the plaintiffs group African

Americans and Mexican Americans into one "minority category"? Determining Mexican American racial identity was a critical part of the district court trial and as the case moved up the circuit to the Supreme Court. *Keyes* was, therefore, *about* Mexican Americans and their position in the US racial hierarchy. MALDEF astutely phrased both points in its motion to intervene but also emphasized that up until that point in early 1974 the plaintiffs did not fully represent Mexican American interests. Now that Mexican Americans were official minorities under the law, it was essential that the courts take the time to acknowledge their divergent experiences. Without such recognition they would be forced to accept minority status without the corresponding ability to challenge the specific discriminatory practices that harmed Mexican American youth.

MALDEF's argument pivoted on the power of racial distinction. In fact, the lawyers used the term *Chicano* as opposed to *Hispano* to make their case that Mexican Americans were racially different from both Whites and Blacks. *Hispano* identified ethnicity, a term that had come to mean "other White" and celebrated cultural difference while rejecting racial otherness. It denoted a Spanish colonial identity that increasing numbers of Mexican Americans in Denver were rejecting. *Chicano*, by 1974, had come to indicate racial pride and awareness that *la raza* represented a group quite different from both Blacks and Whites. Vilma Martinez, general counsel for the CHE and MALDEF president, pointed out a couple of months later, "The anomalous position of the Chicano—not white, yet not, in the old-style parlance, 'colored'—has been one of the roots of Chicano tragedy in this country and has produced a history of legal struggle for equal educational opportunity that has been as difficult as, and at the same time, significantly different from, that waged by black Americans."[38] While the plaintiffs centered their case on the construction of Mexican Americans as analogous to Blacks, an argument accepted by the Supreme Court, MALDEF maintained that Mexican Americans' uncertain racial positioning was what made their situation both distinct from African Americans and particularly difficult to litigate. Prior to the late 1960s Mexican American civil rights lawyers had developed a legal strategy for combating discrimination and segregation in the schools that compared them to Whites. They were "other White," a designation that was not quite White but certainly was not Black. In *Keyes* the plaintiffs' Anglo/minority binary relied on comparing Mexican Americans not to Whites but to Blacks. In both instances relational racialization made it easier to convince the courts that Mexican Americans had legal standing under the Fourteenth Amendment, but such efforts had not led to real equality in the schools. Martinez's insights in this regard demonstrate why positioning them as Chicanas/os, not Black and not White, was so crucial to MALDEF's efforts.

CONFRONTING SCHOOL DESEGREGATION

The Mexican American interveners and members of the Crusade for Justice highlighted their nonwhiteness, but not all Mexican Americans agreed they were racially distinct from Whites, and not all accepted the political and ideological changes taking place within their community. For most of the postwar period, the city's Mexican American leaders had worked to craft an image of themselves as hard-working citizens who deserved full inclusion in Denver's civic affairs, as Americans first. Local attorney and Colorado state senator Roger Cisneros explained, "We are American citizens first and Spanish-Americans second." While he acknowledged that Corky Gonzales and the Crusade for Justice were doing good work, he could not agree with their tactics. Many people in the community, he explained, had already assimilated and did not agree with Gonzales. He lived in a predominantly Anglo area, attended a Protestant church, and raised his children to recognize that "being Spanish doesn't mean as much as it used to."[39] Mexican Americans did experience discrimination, he conceded, but he argued that it was *their* job to change, "to show discrimination should not exist."[40] DPS teacher Uvaldo "Sam" Chavez, who identified as Hispano and said Mexican Americans in Denver descended from the Spanish pioneers of New Mexico, maintained that "to trace one's ancestry to these people is to boast of one's real Americanism. The heritage of the Southwest really has nothing to do with the Mexican Revolution."[41] Being "American" thus equated to linkages to the European colonial past, not revolutionary Mexico, an argument that challenged depictions of Chicana/o pride that celebrated the peasant leader Emiliano Zapata and other symbols of the revolution.

The professional successes and middle-class lifestyles of Mexican Americans like Cisneros and Chavez propelled them to leadership roles, and they adopted the perspective that assimilation was the key to making it in an Anglo-dominated urban environment. "We want to contribute to the predominantly North European culture of our city," reported Daniel T. Valdes, "and to be integrated into it."[42] Cisneros proudly explained that his children did not know Spanish. They "have learned the value of education ... and have placed less value on ancestry."[43] For such individuals, moving out of poverty required that they play by the rules of the dominant society, a perspective that put them at odds with the radical philosophy emerging from the Chicana/o movement. "If you're 35, have a family, a decent job and a chance to make your place in the world, you aren't too impressed with what the militants have to say," reported one Mexican American West Sider, a parent of four children with an income of $6,000 a year.[44] Overturning a system that had actually worked for them did not make sense, nor did the racial politics coming out of the movement. Rejecting Chicano identity and politics went hand in hand. "I am a born Spanish-American, born in Denver. I am proud of being Spanish, not Mexican, Chicano, etc.," one person wrote in a letter to the *Rocky Mountain News* in 1970. They questioned why so many Mexican Americans were buying into the revolutionary movements of the times, particularly the "illiterate Chicanos" who did not seem to understand what would help them the most. Here, "illiterate Chicanos" most likely referred to poor people, many of whom had dropped out of school before graduation. This individual clearly linked race and class in their interpretation of the Chicana/o movement and in their situating of themselves outside the movement, as both "Spanish" and literate (not poor).[45]

These politics remained a force within Mexican American communities, even as Chicana/o movement radicals worked to transform the ways Mexican Americans engaged with their histories, understood their identities, and fought for justice. The publicity generated by the Chicana/o movement, most of which focused on the Crusade for Justice and its actions on a variety of issues, reinforced these older ideas by forcing people to explain and defend why they opposed the newer ideas and approaches generated by young Mexican Americans. Compelled to make a case for why they spurned the movement, more people went public with their racial politics than ever before. These debates were a central characteristic of Mexican American community relations in the late 1960s and 1970s, a point demonstrated by the several meetings held in an effort to unite various factions for the betterment of their schools and neighborhoods.[46] Members of the Crusade for Justice engaged in these conversations as well by arguing that Mexican Americans opposed to their vision were traitors and sellouts. Sometimes referring to them as "Spanglos," Crusaders criticized their "establishment" behavior and lack of support for the movement. But the term also conveyed a critique of "Spanish American" identities. Claiming to be Spanish and refusing more radical politics, for movement adherents, transformed one into an Anglo, or at least positioned them as Anglo adjacent.[47]

Denver's school desegregation drama offers a useful lens through which to view Mexican Americans' diverse racial and political subjectivities. Whereas problems like police brutality and access to low-income housing affected only segments of the wider Mexican American community, the public schools touched almost everyone. Many Mexican Americans were content to stay out of the debates brewing over police violence and gentrification because, quite simply, these conversations did not apply to them personally. But everyone with public school children was affected by the court's order to break up segregated schools. Their children's futures were on the line. For the CHE, desegregation offered an opportunity to rebuild their community through cultural and historical education. Lacking the influence they needed to force the school district to embrace their cultural differences as an educational benefit and feeling neglected by a system of government that continually ignored their demands, they began to view desegregation litigation as a new method for achieving their vision of educational equity. After noting the ambivalence many Mexican Americans felt about desegregation, educator Everett Chavez explained that many in the community felt they had lost their cultural ties through generations of industrialization and urbanization. The *Keyes* case presented an opportunity "to reconstitute through academic endeavors some of [their] cultural losses."[48] When he was asked whether this related to the growing movement for Chicano nationalism, Chavez answered affirmatively but very carefully qualified his response by describing the different viewpoints that existed within the community. Not only did people not agree on what to call themselves—Hispanos, Spanish Americans, Mexican Americans, Mexicans, or Chicanos—they also embraced very different cultural and political positions. Not everyone agreed that it would be a good thing to emphasize their cultural distinctiveness. This included very real differences of opinion when it came to speaking and teaching the Spanish language. "Some don't want to have anything to do with Chicano culture," he articulated, "but there are those who do."[49]

Like members of the CHE, other Mexican Americans filtered their perceptions of school desegregation through the lens of race. Transformations in identity and racial politics were taking place within the community in the late 1960s, but many of the old ideas remained. Guadalupe San Miguel Jr. argues that as Mexican Americans in Houston mobilized around school desegregation litigation, they united around a shared brown racial identity in order to protect their interests.⁵⁰ In Denver, conversely, the *Keyes* case sharpened divisions over racial identity and ideology and raised important questions about Mexican Americans' minority status. If they, as a collective, could not even agree whether they wanted to be desegregated, how could the courts force the school district to include them in the plan? As city residents came to terms with the certainty of desegregation, the uncertainty of Mexican American racial identity came more into focus.

As one of the primary centers of the Chicana/o movement in Denver, the Crusade for Justice was an important vehicle for mobilization around important issues like education. Along with police brutality, education was a constant concern of group members. In the spring of 1968 school board member Rachel Noel introduced a resolution that called for a district desegregation plan. While the board put off the vote on the resolution to the next meeting, Denver citizens jumped into action. Community meetings were held throughout the city as people of differing opinions gathered support for their viewpoints. In northeast Denver, where the problem of racially concentrated Black schools was most apparent, support for Noel's motion was widespread. Two Crusade members, Andres De Pinedo and Eloy Espinoza, attended a meeting that had been called to plan a picket line protest in support of Noel. The two supported the desegregation motion so strongly that they attempted to persuade meeting participants to take more radical action. Rather than a simple picket line, they argued, they should plan a student walkout that was similar to the East Los Angeles walkouts that had just occurred.⁵¹ It was the students, after all, who were "the real victims of bigoted, inadequate education."⁵² The Los Angeles action had been planned and led by Mexican American students who were fed up with the everyday racism of their teachers, the Eurocentric focus of their history courses, and the large number of Mexican Americans who dropped out every year. But the students who walked out in support of their Mexican American peers were diverse. Many Black students joined them. For De Pinedo and Espinoza, solidarity between Black and Mexican American students was critical for success. The Crusade newspaper staff, moreover, seemed to view the Noel resolution favorably and linked the need for desegregation with the plight of Mexican Americans in the nation's schools. The news item about the community meeting and the participation of De Pinedo and Espinoza appeared on the same *El Gallo* page as a piece about a Mexican American student protest in Albuquerque, New Mexico, and two pieces about the growth of the Brown Berets and Black Berets in the Southwest, which emphasized their role in supporting Mexican American student movements.[53] In the spring of 1968, before the school district had taken any action on Noel's proposed resolution, the city's largest and most vocal Mexican American civil rights organization took a strong, if not unequivocal, pro-desegregation stance.

By the following fall the organization reversed course by publicly expressing its critiques of desegregation. In October 1968, as DPS debated Superintendent Robert Gilbert's desegregation plan, Corky Gonzales and several Crusade members interrupted the school board's meeting to protest the proposed plan's failure to address the educational needs of the Mexican American community. On live television being broadcast on Denver's public station, Gonzales insisted that the solutions being offered, "busing" in particular, would not solve the inequalities that existed in DPS.[54] Several black beret–wearing Crusade members joined him on stage, while others filled the room singing "We Shall Overcome" in Spanish. Although Gonzales had been scheduled to speak later in the meeting, his refusal to follow board procedures angered several board members, who demanded that the microphones and cameras be turned off. Undeterred, Gonzales pulled out a bullhorn and proclaimed, "We can no longer remain silent in the face of this devastating monster that perpetuates the myth that European whites or Anglos are the only symbols of success and power in this society."[55] He listed a series of demands that included free education for all Mexican Americans from preschool through college, bilingual education from preschool through college, DPS recognition and protection of the cultural rights embodied in the Treaty of Guadalupe Hidalgo, and a requirement that all teachers reside in the neighborhoods in which they teach. Gonzales also addressed Superintendent Gilberts's desegregation plan specifically, demanding that each neighborhood school complex, a central component of the plan, have its own school board composed of people from the community, with no at-large members.[56] As a whole, these demands revolved around three central aspects of radical Chicana/o philosophy: recognition of the poverty affecting a large segment of the Chicana/o community, bilingual and bicultural education, and community control. In a reversal of the educational goals of earlier Mexican American civil rights advocates, these activists rejected assimilation and integration as a means of educating and preparing Mexican American students. Such a viewpoint did not easily coexist alongside efforts to integrate the Denver schools.

Gonzales's statement also demonstrates the significance of race and class for understanding the anti-integration viewpoint taken by the Crusade, even though members supported the goal of equal education for Black students as well as Mexican Americans. When he discussed the limitations of integration as a plan for achieving equal education, one of his central points was that none of the school board members represented Mexican American interests. "There is not one of you who lives in our Barrios," he exclaimed, "there is not one of you who looks like us."[57] The specific educational needs of poor Mexican Americans were quite different from those of middle-class Blacks, who were the major force behind integration efforts. Even though Rachel Noel, herself a middle-class Black woman, understood and often supported Mexican American educational reform efforts, her focus on integration as a strategy for obtaining educational equality left little room for exploring alternative methods.[58] Part of the problem, as Crusade members saw it, was that integration talk proceeded in a biracial Black-White manner and eclipsed opportunities to interrogate the divergent racial and class backgrounds of Denver students. Their conceptualization of themselves as a colonized people, a major tenet of Chicana/o liberation philosophy, was always centrally about their racial and class identities compared to the dominant White society.[59] Integration would do little to address the historical inequities birthed by colonization.

Like the Crusade for Justice, the Colorado La Raza Unida Party (LRUP) opposed school desegregation as an effective method for achieving high-quality education. The LRUP was established in 1970 in Crystal City, Texas, and a Colorado party quickly followed. "La Raza Unida is a political party of and for La Raza," Manuel Lopez wrote in the *Denver Post*. It was a direct challenge to the two-party system and, in particular, the Democrats, who courted Mexican American votes but served the interests of White, corporate America. "The aim of La Raza Unida is to educate our people about the economic and political system that is oppressing them," Lopez concluded.[60] In 1970 the party's first official platform did not state a position on integration, desegregation, or "busing," but it did emphasize community control in the administration of public schools. Rather than a central school board, each neighborhood school should have a board made up of people who lived in neighborhood.[61] In 1971 the party ran three candidates for the Denver school board, all of whom articulated an anti-desegregation stance that mirrored the perspective of the Crusade. At a press conference to announce their candidacies they explained that "busing" would not solve the problem of segregation. Candidate Soledad Martinez argued that "busing" was an "artificial approach" since the same buses that carried children outside their segregated neighborhoods returned them to those same communities at the end of the school day. "Busing," moreover, merely produced more tensions within the schools, insisted candidate David Sandoval. The third candidate, Eloy Espinoza, was the same young Crusader who had spoken so forcefully in favor of desegregation prior to the passage of the Noel resolution. Just a couple of years later his viewpoint seemingly had been transformed. By 1971 he was running opposed to "forced busing."[62]

This reversal of opinion on the issue of desegregation was not an anomaly. The historical record demonstrates that some Mexican Americans expressed multiple perspectives over the course of the city's desegregation battle, illustrating the shifting nature of racial and political commitments in a period of intense political polarization and racial conflict. Even within the CHE, there was not consistency. DPS teacher James Esquibel, for example, started off opposed to desegregation because he was a firm supporter of Chicana/o community schools. As a third-grade teacher he was happy to be placed at Fairmont Elementary School in west Denver, a majority Mexican American school in a majority Mexican American neighborhood. Judge Doyle's 1974 court order, however, transferred many Fairmont students to other schools, and he was reassigned to Moore Elementary School. At first he did not support these changes, convinced they would result in decreased educational quality for Mexican Americans. After one year at Moore, he changed his mind and began to recognize the value of a desegregated educational environment. Not only did he report improved attendance by Chicana/o students; he also described improved student interactions. Working bus duty after school he got to watch students as they waited in line and boarded the buses. Based on these observations, he stated, "It's only an eight-minute ride, true, but I really think they have a good feeling for Moore school."[63] Other Mexican Americans' viewpoints also changed. West Sider Germaine Aragon wrote two letters to the editor of the *West Side Recorder*, one after the school board elections in the spring of 1969 and the other two years later, in the spring of 1971. In her first letter she lamented the results of the election, which went to James Perrill and Frank Southworth, and regretted that these "foes" of integration would now be joining two other "foes" to ensure the end of integration efforts in Denver schools. "We residents of the West Side are unhappy about the results of the school board elections," she wrote. "For the sake of the children and every community in Denver we hope and pray that something constructive is set up for this next semester."[64] Notably, that newspaper clearly was in favor of integration. The front page of the issue printed after the election proclaimed, "Our sympathy: Following the school board election—to all Denver school children who will not be going to school with children from different social, ethnic and economic backgrounds. Now we must work even harder for improved education."[65]

Like Crusade member Espinoza, Aragon's understanding of the issues presented by desegregation changed dramatically within a couple of years. "Now we are asking you, the Denver Board of Education, 'Don't you ever hear us, or choose to hear us?'" she demanded in April 1971. "In the last school board election, every precinct in the Hispano community voted to maintain the neighborhood school concept. Does it mean nothing to you? To us it does. We do not want to be bussed anywhere."[66] These differing perspectives on desegregation are perplexing. How are we to read their "antibusing" stances in 1971, given their staunch support for the Noel resolution in 1968 and 1969? On the surface, Espinoza's and Aragon's "antibusing" stance seems at odds with their public expression of support for the Noel resolution, in the case of Espinoza, and their dissatisfaction with the victory of anti-integrationists Perrill and Southworth, in the case of Aragon. One strong possibility is that they supported the efforts of Black parents and activists to achieve integration in northeast Denver, the focus of desegregation efforts in 1968 and 1969, but they opposed efforts to use schools with high proportions of Mexican Americans to achieve racial balance. Moreover, their strident rejection of "busing" can be best understood as an expression of their belief that Mexican American community schools were most equipped to provide quality education for Mexican American students. Closing those schools, as several of the proposed plans recommended, and transporting West Side students to other areas of the city where they might lose the benefit of bilingual education, breakfast programs, and curriculum in Mexican American history and culture seemed to be counterintuitive to many Mexican American students, parents, and activists.[67] Aragon, like Espinoza, was deeply enmeshed in Chicana/o educational activism. During the 1969 West High School walkouts, her son Larry was arrested along with several other protesting students, and she began working with Crusade for Justice members who were organizing on the West Side.[68] Their "antibusing" sentiment provides support for Tom Romero's contention that many Mexican Americans in the city who opposed the breakup of West Side community schools "appropriated the 'neighborhood school' philosophy held by many 'Whites' who opposed busing" as a way of making their viewpoints heard.[69] Without a receptive audience for their specific grievances regarding their children's experiences in DPS, they adopted "antibusing" rhetoric and arguments to advance their own causes, a strategy that ultimately failed to secure their demands.

One way to gauge the diversity of Mexican American perspectives on desegregation is to examine the 1971 school board election. That a quarter of the twenty candidates were Mexican American demonstrates that they were concerned with the direction of the schools, particularly when the issue of desegregation was occupying so much of DPS's time. All five, including three LRUP candidates, opposed the *Keyes* plaintiffs' efforts to win desegregation because they preferred to focus on improving neighborhood schools.[70] Although they agreed about the undesirability of "busing," they very much disagreed about the purpose of public schools, the reasons for low Mexican American achievement, and the racial politics that underlay debates over equal educational opportunity. As the first school board election since the highly contentious 1969 race, which resulted in the election of two anti-integrationist candidates and the rescission of the integration resolutions, a lot was riding on it. Judge Doyle's desegregation plan had been in effect since the fall, and the case had not yet been heard before the Appeals Court. It is likely that many people believed the decision would be overturned. It was, after all, the first time a federal court had ruled a school district with no history of state-sanctioned segregation was in violation of *Brown*. On the chance that it was not overturned, pro-desegregation and anti-desegregation forces wanted to be sure the school board would vote their interests. For Mexican Americans, it had been two years since the student walkouts at West High School, the first big push for attention to their educational demands. Since that time two other walkouts involving large numbers of Mexican American youth had rocked West and North High Schools, as well as several junior high schools. Although DPS officials implemented small changes, like the creation of the Hispano Lay Advisory Committee, the district still had not made much progress. Getting a Mexican American elected, many argued, was an important step toward initiating positive action. In one sense, they were victorious. Three of the five Mexican American contenders finished in the top ten, demonstrating the popularity of their message. And one of them, lawyer and former Colorado state representative Bert Gallegos, won a seat by receiving the highest number of votes of any of the candidates.[71] He became the first Mexican American to serve on the DPS Board of Education (see figure 14). In another sense, however, the mixed election results illustrate the divisions over racial and political ideologies that existed within the Mexican American community. The three

FIGURE 14. New DPS school board members being sworn in, May 25, 1971. Left to right: Theodore Hackworth, Robert Crider, Bert Gallegos, and Colorado Supreme Court justice Paul Hodges. Photo by Duane Howell, *Denver Post*. Courtesy of the *Denver Post* via Getty Images.

LRUP candidates were highly critical of DPS. They viewed education as essential but believed the Anglo-oriented nature of school governance and curriculum was damaging to non-White children. Education, party members believed, was the basis for Chicana/o futures. Their lives would be guided by the kind of education they received as youths. It was essential, therefore, that the schools meet the "unique social and cultural assets of Chicano communities."[72] Whereas many DPS teachers and administrators saw these unique traits and experiences as the reason for Mexican American students' lower achievement levels and high dropout rates, those who adopted a "Chicana/o" identity rejected such assessments. To be Chicana/o was to be proud of one's racial identity and cultural heritage and adamant about the importance of Chicana/o history, traditions, and practices. The LRUP's dismissal of desegregation as a strategy for improving the schools was based on members' firm belief in the need for the schools to embrace Chicanas/os' unique cultural and historical contributions and their focus on Chicana/o community control. From their perspective, "busing" for racial balance would provide neither.

Bert Gallegos, by contrast, resisted the politics of the Chicana/o movement. As a former state representative and active community member, he accepted as a basic premise that government was essentially sound. When he was appointed by DPS in 1969 to the new Hispano Lay Advisory Committee, he undertook the role of mediator between the Mexican American community and the school district.[73] He was not there to challenge the school board, nor was he there to demand major changes to the operation of the schools. Shortly after the student walkouts at North High School in 1970 he appeared before the school board to emphasize the committee's willingness to work with the board, and he very clearly juxtaposed the work it was doing to the more radical tactics of Chicana/o students and their allies. Telling board members that the committee was dedicated to cooperating with them, he noted that he did not speak for all Mexican Americans in the city, only those of "good will."[74] Reiterating this point several times, clearly he hoped to demonstrate to school officials that his committee would work through the proper channels to enact change.

After the district court ruled in *Keyes*, Gallegos's support for Mexican American education took on a fervent "antibusing" tone. Speaking to the school board in March 1971 about the district's plans for desegregation, he noted that there were more than 100,000 Mexican Americans in the city, and they would not be pushed around by "judicial fiat," an increasingly popular argument with White anti-integrationists. He argued that Mexican American precincts had voted convincingly for "antibusing" candidates in the 1969 school board election and that it was unconstitutional for a single judge to overrule the will of the majority. He pointed out that he always had had progressive views on civil rights, but he also believed in the separation of powers. When the majority of people vote for a particular viewpoint, he insisted, their will must be followed.[75] From the sidelines, Gallegos's appeal must have sounded a lot like those coming from anti-integrationists nationwide. During an exchange with anti-integrationist school board member James Perrill, Gallegos was asked to elaborate on Mexican Americans' position regarding their concentration in certain schools. He argued that Mexican Americans could live wherever they wanted; there was no discrimination. The reason they were concentrated in certain neighborhoods and thus certain schools was the lower economic standing of those families.[76] They had not experienced housing discrimination. The argument flew in the face of the experiences of countless Mexican American families who had faced hostile landlords, realtors, and banks and who were now being pushed out of their homes in the name of urban renewal. His analysis also failed to recognize the centrality of race to class standing in the city. Job discrimination and a lack of education meant that many Mexican Americans were only qualified for working-class jobs. Gallegos's relatively privileged class position hindered his ability to understand the role that race played in creating high levels of Mexican American poverty and contributed to his belief that Mexican Americans were in the majority, not the minority. A month later Gallegos's views were front and center when he announced his bid for a seat on the school board. Running on an "antibusing" campaign, he claimed to represent the views of the majority of Mexican Americans in the city. "[Hispanos] are incensed because Judge Doyle's order singles them out from the mainstream of American society," he said, an order that "apparently is based on certain findings that Denver schools attended by Hispanos are achieving below the national norm."[77] Here Gallegos revealed his disapproval of arguments that separated him, and Mexican Americans generally, from "the mainstream of American society." Yet he appeared completely out of touch with the realities of Mexican American educational experiences in the city. He resented the fact that Judge Doyle's plan marked him as different.

Gallegos represented the exception, not the rule, when it came to Mexican American upward mobility. Born in Santa Fe, New Mexico, and schooled in Pueblo, Colorado, he firmly identified as Hispano and proudly embraced a Spanish settler history. "My family traces back to old California and New Mexico pioneers," he explained. As an adult he was firmly middle class, having earned his bachelor's and law degrees in Colorado and worked for years as a successful lawyer and legislator.[78] By the early 1970s, he had served on several different community organizations, had volunteered his time on various civic councils, and was living in affluent Park Hill. Gallegos began his political career by serving multiple terms in the Colorado legislature, first as a Democrat and then as a Republican. Switching parties in 1962, he claimed he was not going to be a rubber stamp for the Democratic Party, which he accused of taking Mexican American votes for granted. "You can save this state by voting Republican," he explained to Mexican American luncheon attendees, "otherwise you'll be third and fourth class citizens all your life."[79] All of this informed his racial politics. He believed in working hard to move up the economic ladder and in assimilation to achieve social and political legitimacy, and he was rewarded for these beliefs. In short, he was a practitioner of what one historian has called "barrio Americanism." He epitomized the moderate, middle-class professional whose identity as an American defined his approach to reform for his community.[80] The Chicana/o movement, the *Keyes* case, and the racial implications of both challenged the life he had built within the American mainstream.

For Bernard Valdez, also a member of the Mexican American middle class, the issues presented by school desegregation litigation were more complicated than Gallegos perceived them. First as an active member of the community who participated in several organizations dedicated to Mexican American advancement, and second as a member of the Denver Board of Education, Valdez tried to forge a middle ground between integration proponents and opponents.[81] In political terms this meant that he did not stake a strong position on the question of desegregation. Sometimes he voted with the board's three anti-integrationists, while at other times he voted with the three pro-integrationists. Always, he tried to "keep both sides working for the betterment of education for the children of Denver."[82] In racial terms Valdez's middle ground approach raised complicated questions for integration advocates. Like many others of his class, he described Mexican American difference in cultural terms. Race was a matter of color, and Mexican Americans, in his estimation, were the same color as Whites. They did not face the same "color barriers" as African Americans, and as a result their understanding of themselves was not grounded in color. Again, he struggled to explain how they were different, but he used the term *value system* to convey the ways in which difference was conceptualized by many in the Mexican American community. Based on his explanation, it is clear that value system equated to ideas about racial mixing and cultural retention. "We are quite different in how we achieve education," Valdez noted. "Our hangups [*sic*] on education are long-range culturally rooted and not color rooted and, frankly, my feeling is that a good educational program, even though our children were 100 percent isolated, would do the job for us."[83] Critically, he expanded by arguing against the practice of grouping Mexican Americans with African Americans as racial minorities. One of the reasons it was so difficult to articulate how Mexican Americans conceptualized their identity was that racial difference had been understood in Black and White terms for so long. "It is difficult to express because usually the majority community puts us both in the same hat or in the same bucket, and in how we feel about ourselves we are quite different."[84]

These reflections about race, culture, color, and identity demonstrate the multiple ways that people create meaning out of their differences, but these meanings do not exist in a bubble. They are developed, refined, and deployed within particular social, economic, and political contexts. "If we understand race and culture as political categories, where lines of inclusion and exclusion are constantly shifting," argues historian Sonia Song-Ha Lee, "then we must recognize that people of color constructed their racial and cultural identities through a political process."[85] While Mexican American conceptions of identity were forged over centuries and in relation to other sociocultural groups, these ideas were always political and often had contemporary implications across a broad spectrum of social and political life. In the politically contentious battles over civil rights enforcement in the post–civil rights era, making decisions about personal and group identity and evoking particular histories of colonial relations and legacies were shaped by dominant ideas about race, poverty, and culture. So prevalent by the late 1960s were notions of antiblackness, cultural poverty, and White innocence that many Mexican Americans could not help but be influenced by them. When they were threatened with the breakup of their schools, a threat made very real with the order to desegregate, these dominant tropes entered into their arguments. But as Song-Ha Lee points out in her study of Puerto Rican civil rights mobilizations in New York City, some Puerto Ricans in the 1960s took a different path as they sought to create better schools for their children. Rather than reject coalitions with African Americans and identify bilingual education as inherently incompatible with school desegregation efforts, these activists constructed a shared identity as "minorities," one that allowed them to work together to create the kind of schools both Puerto Ricans and African Americans sought for their children.[86] In Denver, different choices were made, choices that reflected the multitude of identities and political ideologies that existed within the Mexican American community. Mexican American parents and activists who adopted the mantle of "antibusing" in the name of protecting bilingual education made a clear statement about where their sympathies lay, and it was not with African Americans seeking desegregation. While Whites in Denver treated both Mexican Americans and African Americans as second-class others, many Mexican Americans conceptualized their own identities in opposition to blackness.

By 1973, when the Supreme Court issued its decision in *Keyes*, questions about the meaning of equal educational opportunity gripped the Denver community. Different factions debated the merits of various proposals, but the primary conversation revolved around "busing" for racial balance. Certainly, there was no agreement among African Americans that it was the solution to unequal schools. From the very beginning there were Black parents, students, and activists who argued for stronger community schools, but the dominant message was that they wanted integration. No such dominant message existed for Mexican Americans. Instead, people embraced various perspectives and changed their minds over the course of a number of years. How Mexican Americans responded to the push for school integration was informed by the broader social, cultural, and political context, in which civil rights were a central factor. The emergence of a robust Chicana/o movement in the late 1960s shifted, for many Mexican Americans, the terms of the debate over equal schooling and provided a framework for challenging DPS practices and prejudices. Yet this shift was not accepted by everyone. Instead, many Mexican Americans shunned the racial politics and ideology of the movement and actively worked to undermine them.

Understanding Mexican Americans' different viewpoints on school desegregation illuminates these community divisions. Some supported the goals of integration proponents. Others were sympathetic to the educational demands of African Americans, but they held firm to the notion that stronger community schools would best serve Mexican American students. Finally, a third group arose as strong opponents of desegregation. In all cases, people's comprehension of the issues and their advocacy choices were the result of how they conceptualized Mexican American racial identity and engaged in civil rights politics. By the time the CHE intervened in the case and Judge Doyle tried to implement district-wide desegregation, many more Mexican Americans had entered the public debate. How they framed their positions reveals their relationship to the changes taking place in American society during the critical period after major civil rights reform in the mid-1960s and demonstrates how ordinary Mexican Americans, when their children's education was on the line, helped reshape racial ideology in the post–Jim Crow nation.

SIX

"American," Not "Minority"

MEXICAN AMERICANS AND COLORBLINDNESS

"WHAT DO YOU DO when you cannot document his ancestry?" It was a seemingly simple inquiry, but one with a complicated past and far-reaching ramifications. Naomi Bradford, a woman who identified as part Hispano and part Navajo, posed the question to the Denver Board of Education in November 1974, seven months after the US District Court in Denver had ordered system-wide desegregation of the city's public schools. The ultimate goal of the desegregation plan was racial balance among the district's five racial groups. This meant, of course, that before individual students could be placed in the plan, they had to be racially classified by school officials. Bradford's question about documenting ancestry was only the beginning. She asked further, "Can an individual demand to be classified as minority because of dark skin? Can a person of mixed ancestry switch from one racial classification to another? Does a married Anglo woman who bears a Spanish surname qualify to be Hispano?"[1] Her questions, and their implications, concerned school board members. They also revealed a troubling reality. Court-ordered school desegregation plans were vulnerable not only because they were politically contentious but also because the very basis of these plans, racial classification, was a historically fraught process. Denver parents opposed to "forced busing" discovered that this gave them a way to challenge the legitimacy of the court's order. Because race was so difficult to pin down, they implied, any plan that relied on racial categorization was invalid. Such logic was extended to support their larger claim, that court-ordered desegregation plans were unconstitutional and un-American.

Naomi Bradford was not the only parent to raise these issues with the school board. After Judge Doyle issued his district-wide desegregation plan, detailed in this chapter, several parents and other Denverites made the existence of mixed-race families a major feature of their anti-integrationism. While they used the term *mixed race* broadly—presumably, any mixture of races was included—it was Mexican American or White parents of mixed Mexican American–White children that spearheaded the campaign. Mexican Americans' complicated racial history and the multiple racial formations that existed within the Denver Mexican American community provided important context for Bradford's questioning. How these debates were resolved had consequences for the city's children, families, and communities. Yet my study of the rocky road to resolution unmasks not just the fluidity of racial identity but also the political utility of racial uncertainty in civil rights legal battles. At stake was high-quality education, but also whiteness itself. To protect the benefits accrued by whiteness, people like Naomi Bradford put their racial ambiguity to work. By pointing out the arbitrariness and flexibility of racial identity, they acted to preserve not only their own whiteness but the entire system of White domination that civil rights activists were challenging in places like Denver and in cases like *Keyes*.

By the 1970s racial identity trials were a phenomenon of the past. With no racial restrictions on immigration, naturalization, marriage, or other rights of citizenship, there was no need to litigate race in order to enforce exclusion.[2] In the post–civil rights period, however, determining race for the purpose of inclusion became an important political battleground. Recent civil rights legislation, Great Society programs, and the courts provided new avenues for subordinated groups to claim the benefits of full American citizenship, but these claims did not go uncontested, particularly if the claimants were racially ambiguous. Who could claim "minority" status? How would "race" be determined, and who would determine it? With so much at stake in *Keyes*, race became one of the primary weapons of desegregation foes, who used the uncertainty inherent to racial classification to challenge not only the extent of court-ordered desegregation plans but their very legitimacy as well.

This chapter also focuses on the 1970s as a significant moment in the development of colorblind racial ideology. The two decades following the 1964 Civil Rights Act represent a temporal borderland that lay between two different legal racial regimes. Under the pre-1964 regime the nation's legal institutions were tasked with determining race in order to uphold racial distinctions in the law.[3] A prohibition against marriage between a Black man and a White woman could not be enforced unless some legal actor, a county clerk or marriage bureau office worker, in this case, concluded that the man was indeed Black and the woman was indeed White. Yet these legal institutions were remarkably inconsistent in how they determined race, particularly when it came to deciding the racial positioning of people marked as not clearly Black or clearly White. Jurists, policy makers, and state bureaucrats could utilize evidence from science, social science, common sense, and the law, in addition to appearance and performance of racial identity, to legitimize their decisions. This was true even when the courts contradicted themselves, as they did in *Ozawa* and *Thind*.[4] The malleability and contingency of race are what made it so powerful a tool of exclusion. This was evident particularly in the US West, where racial diversity had always shaped understandings of race, as well as the laws and policies that policed the boundaries of inclusion.[5] Racial categorization, therefore, was a crucial technology in the maintenance of White supremacy.

In the post-1964 regime, colorblind racial ideology came to define the possibilities and limitations of antidiscrimination law by providing the intellectual framework for a new judicial interpretation of the US Constitution. It also provided a useful discourse for ordinary Americans opposed to civil rights but who desired a more neutral, less overtly racist language for expressing their hostility. By the mid-1980s colorblind racial ideology had become the dominant mode of expressing this opposition.[6] Between roughly the mid-1960s and the mid-1980s, the temporal borderland, political and legal struggles over the reach of the Fourteenth Amendment, and debates over the methods of civil rights enforcement created the perfect breeding ground for new forms of massive resistance to take shape. Of course, race-neutral or colorblind arguments against integration had been used for decades. Even in the South, as middle- and upper-class Whites fled the cities for the suburbs, their arguments in favor of racial exclusivity shifted from supporting racial segregation to advocating individual rights for property owners.[7] But in the post–civil rights period, as the federal government took on a larger role in enforcing desegregation, race-neutral logic took on new meaning, ultimately transforming how many people and the courts interpreted the Fourteenth Amendment. Today, legal scholars maintain that colorblind constitutionalism—simply, the belief that the US Constitution prohibits the government from classifying people on the basis of race—is rooted in its adherents' reading of the *Brown* decision.[8] While *Brown* laid the legal precedent by invalidating racial segregation, it was subsequent civil rights battles that laid the political groundwork for this interpretation to gain dominance among jurists and laypeople alike.[9]

A close interrogation of this period reveals the on-the-ground processes that made the transition between legal discrimination and colorblind constitutionalism so effective. "In borderland spaces," argue Mary Dudziak and Leti Volpp, "we can see what the law *does* in American history and American culture."[10] We can unpack the ways that legal norms and practices contribute to both formal and informal structures of racial subordination. In the post-1964 temporal borderland, before the law could develop fully the rules and parameters of a new legal racial regime, the rules and parameters of the old regime were reimagined for a new sociolegal context. The porousness of race, once a requirement for the continued legitimacy of legal racial exclusions, now played an important part in the race work unfolding in the post-1964 period. Racial classification was not a newly ambiguous or contingent process. It was just that its *purpose* had changed. Now its malleability was no longer an open secret, used under the guise of popular, scientific, or legal legitimacy. Its flexibility was the very characteristic of race utilized by many anti-integrationists in the name of fairness, transparency, and individualism. Before the courts could articulate fully a colorblind reading of the US Constitution, a diverse group of officials, pundits, and ordinary people helped pave the way by invoking the old logics of race for a new, nefarious purpose: obstructing civil rights.[11]

Like the pre-1964 period, the existence of people marked as not clearly White and not clearly Black made racial classification all the more useful. In Denver, the multiracial character of the case presented several avenues of opposition to the court's desegregation order. As chapter 5 revealed, Mexican Americans not only joined those who supported integration efforts, many challenged the plan. Although their objectives for doing so often differed from those of Whites, they frequently adopted the same rhetoric and tactics. Some, like Naomi Bradford, challenged the school district's racialization of their mixed-race children in order to point out the absurdity, as they saw it, of an integration plan that required racial balance. Others tried to put the courts to work for them in their efforts to remove their children from the desegregation order and maintain their presence in schools serving White interests. In the wake of national efforts to roll back the gains of the civil rights movement, efforts promoted by both major political parties, corporations, think tanks, and conservative legal scholars, some Hispano (White)-identified Mexican Americans used the emerging tropes of colorblindness as a way of holding onto the few gains they had made from their privileging of whiteness and White political interests. This examination of Mexican

American racial and political subjectivities contributes to a fuller understanding of the evolution of colorblind racial ideology.

COLORBLINDNESS IN MODERN AMERICA

Colorblind racial ideology is the dominant system of racial understanding in the United States today and has been incredibly powerful in shaping the course of US racial politics since the 1970s. As a set of ideas, colorblindness revolves around the notion that race no longer matters, that it is a meaningless social category. Its adherents maintain that while race used to play an important role in American life, the civil rights victories of the mid-1960s ended racial restrictions in the law, thus setting the nation on course for a colorblind future. With racism outlawed in public life, the argument goes, it is no longer important. By ignoring race and denying its relevance for modern society, proponents contend they are advancing the vision of 1950s–1960s civil rights activists like Martin Luther King Jr. Crucially, the belief that race is irrelevant extends to the argument that any use of race is not only unfair, immoral, and undemocratic, it is also unconstitutional. As an ideology, colorblindness derives its power from its adherents' ability to ignore structural racism; indeed, it requires that they ignore much of American history. In so doing, they help replicate the historical status quo: a US society very much stratified and ordered by race. "Rather than a recipe for a just society," argues George Lipsitz, "colorblindness constitutes a core component of a long-standing historical whiteness protection program."[12]

Starting in the 1940s and greatly accelerating in the 1970s, anti-integrationists deployed colorblindness in their efforts to fight integration, particularly in housing, schooling, and the workplace. The origins of colorblind racial ideology can be found in these battles. Constructed as a more moderate and civil strategy for opposing civil rights, colorblindness was increasingly adopted by people who found overt racism and racial violence, one of the most common methods of racial intimidation and resistance to integration, distasteful. Massive resistance to school desegregation after the 1954 *Brown* decision, many of these covert racists believed, was politically and economically damaging. By deploying arguments in favor of "freedom of choice" and "freedom of association," proponents of colorblindness led the way in opposing the advances of civil rights activists in school, neighborhood, and workplace integration. Devoid of race on the surface, these racially coded appeals celebrated the right of individuals to choose who they lived near or where they sent their children to school. After all, who could disagree that freedom was a right of US citizenship? By the 1970s, court orders for school integration that included transportation—what opponents derisively called "busing"—expanded opposition to school integration, particularly in cities outside of the South. As the "antibusing" movement grew, so too did the popularity and embrace of colorblind arguments. The language of "busing" was, in fact, colorblind racial ideology at work. By developing their opposition around the method of integration, rather than integration itself, anti-integrationists in the North and West could maintain that they were not racist and that their hostility toward court-ordered desegregation had nothing to do with race.[13]

In the 1970s, proponents of colorblindness developed two new strategies in their quest to roll back the civil rights gains of the previous decade. The first was their embrace of "reverse racism" as an argument against race-conscious civil rights remedies. Arguing that these remedies, such as affirmative action or racial balance in the schools, were unfair to Whites, champions of this perspective claimed they were victims of racism in reverse. Many went so far as to say such remedies were actually "reverse discrimination" and were just as unconstitutional as were racial requirements for school attendance or employment. This shift in strategy, according to Michael Omi and Howard Winant, was a critical step toward the full development of colorblind racial ideology because it "reframed racism as a zero-sum game" and enabled civil rights opponents to claim they were anti-racist.[14] By reframing racism in this way, anti-integrationists disconnected it from the sociohistorical context from which it emerged, thus erasing the relationship between subordination and domination that dictated the operation of race and racism. In 1974, for example, White policemen in Detroit filed a federal lawsuit against the city's African American mayor for implementing an affirmative action hiring and promotion plan. By painting themselves as members of an oppressed group within the new legal culture of group rights, they charged that the plan unfairly punished them for being White men, an injustice they called "reverse discrimination."[15] White opponents of school integration adopted similar arguments in their battles against "busing." In 1972, New York representative Norman Lent, cosponsor of an "antibusing" bill being considered by Congress, maintained that "if it was wrong in 1954 to assign a black child to a particular school on the basis of race, it is just as wrong to do the same thing to other children in 1972. This is 'Jim Crowism' in reverse."[16]

The second strategy anti-integrationists developed in their quest to overturn race-conscious civil rights policies emerged from the same colorblind logic Representative Lent employed in his articulation of "Jim Crowism in reverse." Not only did anti-integrationists claim that race-conscious policies were unfair to Whites, now they denounced any effort to racially categorize people as discriminatory, even if the goal of racial categorization was to remedy civil rights infringements. According to this reasoning, any use of racial categories, regardless of its purpose, was antithetical to the civil rights mission and a clear violation of the US Constitution. In order for contemporary colorblind racial ideology to take root, its adherents needed to move beyond racially coded arguments and claims of reverse discrimination and repudiate race itself. Because race was no longer relevant in the post–civil rights period, they argued, there was no need to racially classify people or store racial data. A White parent in Denver explained at a US Commission on Civil Rights hearing that he had been in favor of using "busing" for integration in the late 1960s and early 1970s. But once he discovered the court was requiring students be categorized "by their appearance or family names," he turned against the court-ordered plan. "This concept in its totality defeats the entire purpose of desegregation," he claimed.[17] Racial classification, according to this reasoning, was harmful regardless of whether its purpose was the enforcement of racial requirements for school attendance or the assignment of students for desegregation purposes. This thinking was so dominant among conservative intellectuals and legal scholars, and so effective at convincing people that race consciousness was unfair, immoral, and illegal, that it developed into the foundation of the Supreme Court's interpretation of race and antidiscrimination law. Colorblind constitutionalism became so entrenched in civil rights law that by the first decade of the twenty-first century, a plurality of the court agreed with its basic tenets.[18]

Colorblind constitutionalism was not developed by the Supreme Court alone. Legal scholars, intellectuals, think tanks, corporate interests, and ordinary people constructed its basic contours through their contestation of integration. In the post–civil rights period, it was the popular embrace of colorblindness that perhaps most propelled its continued development.[19] Examining this process with Latinas/os in mind sheds new light on how the transition from Jim Crow to colorblindness occurred. In the temporal borderland between the passage of the 1964 Civil Rights Act, which ended legal segregation, and the full emergence of colorblind racial ideology, questions over Mexican American racial identity helped grassroots opponents of race-conscious policies like court-ordered racial balance plans chart out new forms of resistance.[20]

THE FINAL ORDER AND DECREE, 1974

The District Court in Denver issued its final order and decree on April 17, 1974. It included several different provisions for ensuring racial balance, including redrawing school boundaries, a part-time pairing plan, and transporting students. Under the Finger Plan, so named because it was developed by Dr. John A. Finger, the court-appointed expert, a school was considered desegregated when it reached 40 to 70 percent Anglo in the case of elementary schools, and 50 to 60 percent Anglo in the case of secondary schools. In some instances, Judge Doyle said, deviations could be expected and might even be desirable. Importantly, the Finger Plan exempted four predominantly Mexican American schools—Garden Place, Del Pueblo (formerly Elmwood), Cheltenham, and Swansea elementary schools—from the order, saying that some racial concentration in these schools was justifiable because of the desire to maintain or implement bilingual/bicultural programs. These schools were 77 to 88 percent Mexican American.[21] Boulevard Elementary School later was exempted, bringing the list to five majority Mexican American schools. Judge Doyle implied that schools needed to provide equal opportunity for all students; otherwise the dismantling of segregated schools would lose some of its value. Though he did not frame his decision in these terms, his careful attention to the Mexican American Legal Defense and Educational Fund's (MALDEF) arguments indicates that he believed school desegregation needed to transcend the Black-White binary. "It seems particularly important at the present time," he insisted, "that the Denver educational system be responsive to the educational needs of minority black *and* Chicano students as well as those of the majority Anglos."[22] Additionally, the court ordered Denver Public Schools (DPS) to implement the Cardenas Plan, a proposal written by Dr. Jose A. Cardenas and submitted to the court by the Congress of Hispanic Educators (CHE).[23]

In many ways the Cardenas Plan represented the spirit of what Mexican American parents, students, and activists had been demanding for the last several years. When Crusade for Justice members interrupted school board meetings and voiced their opposition to "busing" as a means of creating better schools for Mexican Americans, they articulated an alternative vision of school integration based on Mexican Americans' particular experiences of racialization. So did those students who walked out of West High School almost four years earlier to protest a school system that devalued their culture, limited their opportunities, and eventually pushed them out. For these students, integration with White students would not necessarily create an environment that was conducive to their educational success.

At the heart of the Cardenas Plan was a fundamental shift in the way education was understood, as well as the way public schools were conceptualized. Dr. Cardenas called for major changes in curriculum and personnel, but also in the philosophical underpinning of the entire district. Most school systems were organized around and for the "Anglo Saxon white middle class English speaking population," he argued in court.[24] In order to correct this deficit school officials needed to alter their thinking and approach to education. The schools must be reoriented for minority students, he said, taking into consideration both the race and class of the students at each school. Teachers and administrators had to prepare themselves to go out into the community to communicate more effectively with students and their parents, rather than requiring parents to come to the schools. The schools, moreover, had to make it the responsibility of teachers and other school officials to instill a sense of pride and self-worth in each student, and they must provide the basic resources and mechanisms for every student to learn, develop, and thrive in a multicultural, modern world.[25]

CHALLENGES TO RACIAL CLASSIFICATION IN THE SCHOOL BOARD ROOM

Even though the Supreme Court had determined Mexican Americans were an identifiable class under the Fourteenth Amendment, and MALDEF was pursuing their interests as a distinct racial group, the racial wrangling that had been a feature of the litigation since the beginning intensified. The Denver public had been debating the issue of desegregation and racial balance for several years. Starting in 1974, some parents and other residents began to challenge court-ordered racial balance by disputing the validity of racial categorization. As a form of resistance to Judge Doyle's district-wide plan, challenges to racial categorization took several forms, and Mexican Americans were often at the center. First, desegregation opponents protested the very notion that each student's race had to be documented by the school district and used to determine their school assignment. How could this be legal, they asked, when the Colorado Constitution forbade this very act? Title IV of the 1964 Civil Rights Act, moreover, explicitly rejected racial balance remedies. Nolan Winsett, president of the Denver anti-integration group Citizens Association for Neighborhood Schools (CANS), consistently made this argument.[26]

Second, anti-integrationists criticized the process of racialization. Before school officials could begin to develop a plan, they had to make sure each student's race was officially recorded. DPS practice had long depended on teacher observation of students to determine their race, and this continued during the desegregation era. Sometimes they utilized surname and/or language. Often, marking children's race encompassed several of these practices, particularly when there was some question about their race. DPS parent Marguerite Cordova complained to school board members that teacher observation was fraught with "many inaccuracies brought about by color of skin, hair, and eyes and the sound of the name."[27] Lila Lewis, demonstrating Cordova's point, presented board members with pictures of each of her four children and asked them if they could identify the race to which they belonged. Her point was that her children's race easily could be mistaken. Because they had varying skin shades and facial features, they were inconsistently racialized by the school district. When she asked for documentation from DPS, school officials sent her a letter that named two of her children as "Hispano" and two of them as "Other," even though all four children had the same parents and the same last name. She told the board there were thousands of students just like her children who were being incorrectly classified.[28] Because race was so uncertain, these parents implied, it was not a solid basis upon which to base a desegregation plan that would shift thousands of students to other schools.

This objection to the process of racialization led to the third manner in which anti-integrationists utilized anti-classification arguments. Racial identities were, in fact, so difficult to pin down that only parents could identify their child's "true" race. If racial balance was going to go forward, they argued, parents had *a right* to name their child's race. "No one could state with any degree of accuracy," insisted Robert Weaver, "the ethnicity or race of a child except the mother or father."[29] Several parents, concerned about how their mixed-race children were being classified by the district, demanded that parents be sent a survey that would allow them to designate officially their child's race. If they found that school officials had misclassified them, moreover, they should be allowed to change it. Taking this argument a step further, some parents argued for the inclusion of a "mixed-race" category, which would represent more accurately the thousands of "half and half" students in the district. As Lila Lewis explained after she showed her children's photos to school board members, "neither Judge Doyle nor the [School] Board had the right to designate which ethnic background her own children must belong to."[30] Recognizing the ambiguity of racial categories gave parents the ability to claim a particular status in order to manipulate their child's placement in the district's scheme to create racial balance. Treating race solely as identity enabled parents like Lewis to discount the structural mechanisms of race that produced segregated schools in the first place.

These racial negotiations and the racial politics that informed them, as historians of race in Latin America and the Caribbean remind us, hid structural racism under the veneer of mixed-race racial enlightenment. By drawing DPS's attention to the fact that school officials had failed to account for all their children's racial parts, the various components of their distinct racial admixture, these parents engaged in a politics of *mestizaje* as one tactic of many in their attempt to overturn court-ordered desegregation. *Mestizaje*, the dominant racial ideology of Mexican and other Latin American and Caribbean societies, promotes and celebrates racial hybridity as a source of unity, strength, and democracy in the modern nation. Yet like all racial triumph narratives, *mestizaje* has not led to more fair and equitable societies but instead has given rise to the notion that race does not matter and has hidden deep racial inequities. Those who benefit from the existence of racial hierarchies often defend such advantages with reference to this racial democracy that *mestizaje* supposedly birthed.[31] In a similar pattern, Denver parents attempted to use their children's racial mixedness as a more socially acceptable way of challenging their inclusion in the desegregation plan. On the surface, it looked like these parents simply wanted to ensure mixed-race children were accurately enumerated and placed in the plan. But underneath such benign requests lingered a deep sense of injustice and desire to destabilize the entire desegregation effort.

Once the court approved a plan to allow children to stay in their neighborhood schools if their presence contributed to racial balance at that school, the district was inundated with demands from parents that they be able to choose their child's race.[32] As a result the district had to ask Judge Doyle to define minority categories. If some pupils are going to be exempt from "busing," DPS explained to the court, "it is necessary that certain standards be established for determining whether a child is a minority child for these purposes."[33] At a court conference in June, Judge Doyle addressed the defendants' request, stating that he would not require the district to "measure and add up the percentage of parentage." If a parent claimed their child was minority, he maintained, "that's the end of it as far as I am concerned.[34] He seemed hesitant to issue more concrete definitions, assuming it was not necessary for the district to successfully implement his desegregation plan. From the perspective of school officials, who had to deal with the day-to-day execution of the plan, the court needed to issue specific guidelines for determining who qualified as a minority child and to which racial classification they belonged. By June, the district had already heard from many parents on the question of racial definitions and expected more to follow. Already antagonistic toward the court's plan, school officials now had to navigate the complicated terrain of the racial borderlands that existed in the ideological space between Black and White.

The plaintiffs, too, were concerned about the ways that racial ambiguity was being used to pick apart the desegregation plan. Gordon Greiner was particularly troubled about two possible scenarios. First, he wondered about students with "a Chicano parent and an Anglo parent." How would they be classified? The fact that several parents with Mexican American children kept insisting on a mixed-race category had to have influenced his preoccupation with this issue. As outspoken opponents of the court's order, what did these parents stand to gain from the creation of such a category? And how would mixed race fit into the plaintiffs' Anglo/minority argument that had won over the Supreme Court? Greiner had to have considered the possibility that a mixed-race category could jeopardize any plan for racial balance and could give the district a way of appealing Judge Doyle's ruling that DPS was a dual system. He worried also that White parents might try to claim minority status for their children in order to remain in their neighborhood school.[35]

That so much time was spent on these issues reveals the precarious nature of court-ordered school desegregation, and of legal remedies for civil rights violations more generally. Such remedies relied on racial categorization, yet the process of racially identifying students was much more complicated than many in the legal community were willing to address. In part, this resulted from the courts' refusal to recognize the deep, structural connections between school and housing segregation. While some Supreme Court justices understood that segregated schools in the North and West (and, increasingly, in the South) stemmed from segregated neighborhoods, most reasoned that segregated housing was the consequence of economics, demographics, and individual housing choices. School districts were not culpable for such phenomena. Justice Lewis F. Powell, in a separate opinion in *Keyes* (concurring in part and dissenting in part) elevated this perspective when he opined that an offending school district could remedy unconstitutional segregation simply by adopting a neighborhood school policy without regard to race/ethnicity.[36] If the court had not avoided the interconnectedness of schools and housing, it could have established doctrine like that urged by Justice William O. Douglas in *Keyes*. For Douglas, state action was the key, regardless of which arm of the state created, through discriminatory policy, segregated neighborhoods and thus segregated schools. "When a state forces, aids or abets, or helps create a racial 'neighborhood,'" Douglas wrote, "it is a travesty of justice to treat that neighborhood as sacrosanct in the sense that its creation is free from the taint of state action."[37] Such a decision would have more firmly rooted findings of school district segregatory action in longer histories of state action to manifest and perpetuate segregated housing and may have forestalled the kind of racial wrangling that Denver experienced in the aftermath of Judge Doyle's order for system-wide desegregation.

Greiner's strategy in court, moreover, reinforced a strict racial divide between Anglos and minorities that was impossible to police. The long history of racial mixing wrought by the colonization of North America, first by Europeans and then by Americans, made identifying "Indians" and "Hispanos" particularly problematic.[38] Were Hispanos Indians? Could Indians with an Anglo parent or grandparent also be Hispano? Racial hybridity defied the legal categories established by the state to maintain social and economic exclusion. At times racial mixed-ness enabled people to transgress rigid social and legal boundaries, while at others it proved to be the very characteristic that signified inferiority. Euro-Americans viewed Mexicans, in particular, as a degraded, hybrid race, composed of the worst elements of Spanish, African, and Indian characteristics and demeanors. "As would naturally be the case," wrote US attorney W. W. H. Davis, who served in New Mexico in the 1850s, "a people so various in their origin as the Mexicans, and in whose veins flows the blood of three distinct races, would present a corresponding diversity of character. They possess the cunning and deceit of the Indian, the politeness and spirit of revenge of the Spaniard, and the imaginative temperament and fiery impulses of the Moor."[39] Indeed, it was the racial uncertainty of Mexicans, the messy, racial fusion and confusion they generated, that prompted many congressmen to vote against New Mexico and Arizona statehood. At the same time, however, Mexicans' hybridity allowed some to escape the worst forms of racial discrimination. This is what induced many Mexicans and Mexican Americans to reject indigeneity and embrace efforts to secure the rewards of (White) settler colonialism.

Racially categorizing mixed-race bodies was a fluid process that changed based on time- and place-specific context. In the post–civil rights period various state entities placed people into one of several racial categories in order to enforce civil rights legislation or judicial decisions like *Keyes*. In this context, the purpose of racialization had changed, as had some of its mechanizations. But the reasons motivating many parents' use of racial knowledge remained the same. They adopted the language of racial uncertainty to preserve the privileges of whiteness. To address the race questions raised by parents, Judge Doyle finally issued an order that dictated four minority categories for the district to use: "American Indian," "Oriental," "Black," and "Hispano." He also laid out the process whereby school officials would assign racial classifications. DPS was to continue its normal practice, teacher observation, unless a parent claimed their child's race was incorrectly documented. In that case the parent could fill out an affidavit with the correct race, which the district would then recognize. As per a request made by Greiner, probably in order to monitor the number of parents changing their child's race in an attempt to exempt them from the desegregation plan, Judge Doyle also ordered that the school administration keep track of these affidavits and file periodic reports to the court on the usage of this process.[40] Greiner's concerns about the demands for a mixed-race category and the use of these new racial affidavits indicate that he was suspicious of the emerging anti-classification arguments being used by anti-integration advocates.

His suspicions soon proved justified. Within a matter of months parents of DPS students had filed two hundred affidavits requesting that their child's race be changed. Although this was less than 1 percent of the entire district, two hundred students was not an insignificant number when one considers the delicate racial balancing the court was trying to achieve with its plan.[41] By October a controversy over racial classification erupted in southwest Denver, where several of the most vocal opponents of the desegregation plan lived. Using the official racial classification affidavit, fifty-seven parents of children at Johnson Elementary School changed their child's race, claiming they had been identified mistakenly as Anglo when they were American Indian. Angered at "being used" in the city's "busing" controversy, local

American Indians protested the false Indian claims in a meeting with school officials. "When more than 50 people file affidavits that they are Indian in 1974," noted Manson Garreaux, director of the Denver Indian Center, "it looks like people are playing at being Indian again."[42] Playing Indian, of course, had a long and contentious history in the United States. Dressing and playing as Indians, appropriating Indian culture, and imagining an "authentic" Indian past were common traditions in American culture, traditions that helped those who participated in such play to construct more "authentic" American selves. Lost in the chaotic modernity of post–World War II American life, as Philip Deloria demonstrates, Whites who appropriated Indianness in this period sought meaning and personal identity in a society they perceived as lacking in authenticity. The Indian—proud, free, rebellious, committed to nature and community—provided the essential backdrop onto which Americans could latch for comfort and purpose, while simultaneously confirming Americanness as civilized and modern in comparison to the "savagery" of Indianness. Closely connected to the postwar crisis of meaning and identity was increasing racial anxiety, as understandings of race and culture were transformed, and the civil rights movements of the era grew in adherents and prominence.[43] School desegregation efforts around the country reinforced many people's sense that something had gone terribly wrong in American culture and society. When Denver parents suddenly became Indian in 1974, they joined a long line of Americans, stretching from the Revolution to the present, who adopted Indian dress, culture, and even identity.

Regardless of how many people now claimed their children were Indian, reports showed that there had been no American Indian children at Johnson in the previous three years.[44] Executive Director of Pupil Services James O'Hara at DPS noted that at the time the disputed Johnson claims were brought to the district's attention, officials had already approved 148 Indian affidavits and were processing 20 more. Without any specific directions for approving parents' assertions of Indianness, O'Hara said they were accepting all of them "at face value."[45] Already aware of the ways the desegregation plan's challengers were implementing anti-classification arguments, district administrators' lack of attention to the manipulation of the affidavit system reveals the expediency of such tactics. On a practical level, with legal options running out for school officials, legitimizing parents' concerns about the ambiguity of race proved a useful way to disrupt implementation of Judge Doyle's plan. Parents and DPS administrators thus were partners in the larger movement to undo the civil rights advances of the previous two decades. By playing along, accepting falsified Indian claims "at face value," school officials continued their long-standing commitment to preserving the property value in whiteness.

One parent, more than any other, led the way. Naomi Bradford was the mother of three DPS children, a resident of southwest Denver, president of the Johnson School Parent Teacher Association (PTA), a member of CANS, and a future Denver school board member. Her questioning about racial classification procedures, which opened this chapter, is only one example of her constant work to dismantle court-ordered school desegregation. She and her spouse, Ronald Bradford, spoke at nearly every school board meeting and public hearing to denounce racial balance as unconstitutional and unworkable. Her leadership in the crusade against "forced busing" was so well regarded that in 1975 she was elected by Denver residents to the DPS Board of Education, where she spent several years doing everything in her power to stall implementation of Judge Doyle's plan and limit its effectiveness.[46]

In many ways, Bradford fit the mold of Americans who viewed themselves as "caught in the middle," part of a group that President Richard Nixon famously named the "Silent Majority."[47] "The great silent majority of Americans," he strategically pronounced, were not selfish for opposing higher taxes and were not racist for opposing school desegregation schemes that took their child out of the neighborhood school. As a political ploy, such arguments appealed to the cross-class alliance of White Americans whose primary interest was to protect their economic and racial privileges. "Echoing from the grassroots to the White House," notes Matthew Lassiter, "these narratives of white victimization and suburban heroism transformed the landscape of Southern and national politics and repudiated the history of metropolitan inequality" that had become ever more apparent by the late 1960s.[48] Bradford's activism as a parent and then as a school board member (see figure 15) reverberated with populist sentiment. "I was a peace-loving PTA president whose biggest delight in life was setting up PTA functions," she reported. "I was no activist. But I had to set it all aside to roll up my sleeves and fight for neighborhood schools."[49] Like many middle-class White women, her central political focus was on fighting "forced busing," a movement that reflected the segregationist, consumerist, and anti-tax ideologies of the postwar era. Evoking their motherhood to protect their prerogatives as consumer citizens, these women challenged "busing" as a

FIGURE 15. School board member Naomi Bradford speaking at a school board meeting, 1976. Photo courtesy of The Denver Public Library, Western History Collection, WH2129.

violation of constitutional, property, and parental rights. Yet race remained central to their movement.[50]

Bradford and others like her, Mexican Americans who found radical civil rights activism distasteful and un-American, introduced new dynamics to the conservative consensus over civil rights in the 1970s.[51] Her conservatism, particularly her antagonism toward court-ordered desegregation, must be analyzed within the context of the larger debate over civil rights in the post–civil rights period. Her work to dismantle integration was deeply racialized, not only because she sometimes utilized overtly racist language in her tirades against fellow school board members and supported the project of systemic educational inequity, but also because she took advantage of the confusion the racial borderlands presented.[52] Moreover, the fact that she was Mexican American gave her a useful way of deflecting accusations that she was an anti-integrationist and complaints that she did nothing for the Mexican American community.[53] A focus on the legal borderlands of court-ordered desegregation reveals the significant role that Mexican Americans played in the transformation of American politics in the 1970s. Their new legal minority status gave them credibility when it came to talking about civil rights issues, but many of them resented being grouped into the minority category. Some, like Naomi Bradford, joined the growing conservative movement, while others, Mexican Americans frustrated at their inability to win the reforms *they* wanted, ended up adopting many of the same arguments and rhetoric as their White, conservative counterparts. Embracing the politics of whiteness, in turn, continued the long tradition of Mexican Americans who put their tenuous whiteness to work toward the goal of securing a more privileged position in the hierarchical structure of US society.

Whether Bradford came up with the idea to claim her children were American Indian is not certain. What is clear is that she was PTA president of the school at the center of the controversy, and she frequently served as a spokesperson for their efforts. Once the high number of claims coming from parents in southwest Denver was investigated and Bradford was questioned about her claim to an Indian identity, she explained that although she was not a member of the tribe, she was Navajo. According to an interview she later gave a local newspaper, her mother was "Navajo and Hispano," and her father was "part Indian." While her politics persuaded others to lump her in with White anti-integrationists, she told the reporter, "Anyone who looks at me can tell I'm either Hispanic or Indian."[54] The irony of this comment, considering her many statements pointing to the inability of school officials to visually racialize students correctly, clearly did not concern her and further demonstrates the political opportunism of the language of racial uncertainty. At other times she spoke of being "one-fourth Navajo," indicating that she viewed race as a matter of "blood." On the one hand, Bradford's understanding of her racial identity embodied the spirit of *mestizaje* that was so central to the racial politics of the Chicana/o movement. She recognized that her ancestors were both indigenous and European, and she saw no contradiction in identifying as Mexican, Hispano, and American Indian at different points in her life. By claiming her Navajo ancestry, in fact,

FIGURE 16. Naomi and Ronald Bradford and their three children, 1978. Left to right: Rhonda, Joan, and Ralph. Photo courtesy of The Denver Public Library, Western History Collection, WH2129.

she did precisely what movement activists encouraged: she reclaimed her indigenous roots. On the other hand, she was motivated to claim particular identities in order to disrupt Judge Doyle's plan for racial balance and affirm her commitment to the politics of whiteness. In claiming to be American Indian in the fall of 1974, she was not only trying to exempt her own children from being "bused" to another school. She was trying to maintain systems of racial advantage from which she and her family had benefited (see figure 16).

The reason so many parents had not identified their children as American Indian before, Bradford argued, was that there was no need to racially classify them before court-ordered desegregation.[55] That is, there was no advantage parents like her could gain from being minority prior to the court order. Now that minority status secured Johnson students a way out of "busing," many parents rushed to make use of it. The Supreme Court's decision in *Keyes* that Mexican Americans were non-White, followed by the District Court's order for district-wide desegregation, dramatically altered the racial identity claims of hundreds of individual Denver residents. The law, in this space of ambiguity, produced new racial guidelines for people to follow in their pursuit of material benefits. That so many parents tried to manipulate the system forced Judge Doyle to take further action to define racial categories. While he previously had ordered that parents' claims of racial identity would stand, in the case of American Indians he now said that parents must be able to prove they had a "substantial" amount of "Indian blood"—perhaps 50 percent, he suggested. American Indians present at a meeting with DPS immediately protested such a recommendation, as they had a right to name their own community members. As Indian educator Bill Roberts explained to school officials, this was an important right of sovereignty.[56] Nonetheless, Judge Doyle ordered that any parent who had filed an affidavit claiming their child was American Indian now had to refile with proof they qualified to be Indian.[57]

Many of the parents who had submitted American Indian affidavits chose not to resubmit, and their children were reclassified as whatever category they had been the previous year. Several others, however, remained defiant by refusing to file another affidavit. Thirty families, including the Bradfords, wrote a joint letter to DPS that demanded more concrete definitions of all racial groups, not just American Indians. They argued that demanding proof of Indian-ness, while not requiring it for those claiming other racial identities, was unfair and tantamount to discrimination.[58] A couple of days later these parents appeared before a school board public hearing to air their grievances. Based on the personal details they reported, many of the families were mixed race, with one parent being Mexican American. None of the parents who spoke claimed their children were part Black, a fact that suggests both the undesirability of blackness and the continuation of American preoccupations with the one-drop rule. In US racial understandings, whiteness and blackness appeared easily distinguishable. Both popular and legal thinking held that an individual was Black if they possessed one drop of Black "blood." This rule of hypodescent was not firm because "Black" people frequently "passed" in and out of whiteness.[59] Nonetheless, the *idea* that blackness was easy to discern remained a constant aspect of US racial ideology. Maintaining White hegemony, in fact, depended on this fiction. Such thinking was evident in the lack of Denver parents purporting to have part-Black children. Claiming blackness, unlike Indianness, easily could be disproven because the markers of blackness were thought to be so much more visible; it was "common sense."

Mexican Americans, moreover, already were at least partially Indian according to US conceptions of racial hybridity. Parents Betty McClain and

Donna Thorberg, both of whom had filed Indian affidavits, protested the DPS practice of teacher observation and use of surname to determine race. McClain, like Lila Lewis before her, presented photographs of her children as evidence of the district's inability to correctly classify each child. She noted their dark skin and hair and told board members they were "half Spanish." Despite this, teachers had documented them "as Anglo because their father was Anglo."[60] Thorberg's family dynamics were even more complicated. She explained that her two eldest children, whose last name was McBride, had been classified as "Other" by school officials, while her youngest child, whose last name was Romero, had been classified as "Hispano." Consequently, her "Hispano" child was exempted from "busing," while her two "Other" children were "bused" to another school. She claimed this had created a negative environment in her home because her children recognized that their different school assignments were based on "skin color." In an attempt to unify her home and prevent "permanent psychological division" in her family, she said that she filed Indian affidavits for the two older children, "rightfully claiming their Indian blood."[61] The DPS boardroom may not have been a court of law, but Thorberg's proclamation that her children possessed "Indian blood" and her insistence that they be classified as American Indian sounded a lot like the testimony heard in racial determination trials of the pre-1964 period. On a pragmatic level, sending one's children to two different schools based on perceptions of their race must have seemed ridiculous to parents like her, and perhaps even caused real hardships. On an ideological level, pointing this out was a potent political strategy in the battle against civil rights. (See figure 17.)

Parent after parent whose American Indian affidavits had been denied spoke on these hardships. In nearly all of their comments, they protested their loss of authority to identify their own race in a way that preserved the racial status quo and expressed frustration with school administrators and Judge Doyle for questioning their motivations in filing their affidavits. In a perfect example of the trope of reverse discrimination taking shape during this period, one parent demanded to know, "Does [my] skin have to be black, brown, yellow, etc. before the public officials feel [I] could be discriminated against?" Another resented that her claim had been rejected by the district, and she accused Judge Doyle of calling her and her parents liars. Both of her grandparents, she said, had been "born on a Cherokee Indian Reservation in Kentucky."[62] This history of school desegregation unveils a fundamental reorientation of the meaning and application

FIGURE 17. "Dr. Doyle's Bureau of Indian Authenticity," cartoon by John P. Trevor, 1974. The cartoon is a comment on racial classification for "busing" purposes. Trevor criticizes both the notion that parents of Johnson schoolchildren could claim their children were American Indian—he notes that the school PTA (under Naomi Bradford) was leading the charge—*and* the idea that the courts could somehow confirm a person's ethnicity. Courtesy of The Denver Public Library, Western History Collection, 2015.024 ART.

of race in the lives of ordinary Americans, who used the changes of the post–civil rights period to their advantage. People who had never had to consider whether or not they were not White—they simply lived as Whites, accruing its privileges and benefits—were now arguing to the contrary. Determined to challenge the integration order through whatever means they could, these parents wielded racial uncertainty as a weapon. The deception and pure audacity of White parents who made these claims demonstrates the persistence of anti-integrationists in their quest to undo the civil rights victories of the previous decade. By so forcefully pursuing the American Indian strategy, they highlighted a centuries-long problem—the fluidity of race—in a modern, civil rights context, and revealed vulnerabilities in remedial law. Mexican Americans were particularly suited to participate in these unfolding dynamics, given the history of Mexican American racial classification, the fact that they already were a hybrid race (according to US racial ideology), and the higher number of interracial Mexican American–White marriages and relationships that resulted in mixed-race children.[63]

That this emerged as a tactic of anti-integration activists reveals colorblind ideology in formation. "People don't know about the ethnic business," Lila Lewis explained to the *Denver Post*, "so we told them."[64] Her cynical description of racial classification as the "ethnic business" demonstrates that she and fellow CANS activists had already latched onto the anti-classification rhetoric that now dominates colorblind approaches to attacking race-conscious civil rights remedies. Their focus on mixed-race children, moreover, indicates that anti-integration activists in the 1970s had already learned an important lesson of the post–civil rights period. As Peggy Pascoe compellingly argues, *Loving v. Virginia* (1967) played a central role in the conservative reworking of colorblindness by removing, once and for all, racial qualifications for marriage. Interracial marriages and, in particular, the increasing births of mixed-race children, were proof that the United States had finally moved beyond race.[65] Opponents of court-ordered desegregation in Denver used the presence of mixed-race children to point out irregularities in the school district's process of racial classification, thus raising critical questions about the practicality and legality of racial balance schemes.

By 1974 Denver residents still had not resigned themselves to the reality of court-ordered desegregation. Neither had the school district. The DPS Board of Education voted to appeal Judge Doyle's final order and decree, and the Cardenas Plan was one of their central points of contention. School officials had great difficulty accepting the order for bilingual education; courses in Mexican American history and culture; and, in particular, the idea that public schools were responsible for the intellectual, social, *and* cultural well-being of their students. Ordering racial balance was one thing, district attorneys argued, but dictating educational philosophy was something entirely different that went well beyond the requirements of the US Constitution. Recognizing Mexican Americans' specific histories of racialization proved to be too onerous for school officials.

Meanwhile, Mexican Americans chose different paths in their quest for better schools. Some exited the district completely, opting for the alternative Chicana/o school set up by the Crusade for Justice in 1970. Others tried to work within the parameters of Judge Doyle's plan, hoping that the courts finally could force DPS to adopt the kinds of programs and policy changes for which they had been advocating for a decade. Finally, some Mexican Americans continued to oppose desegregation, and they turned to the courts as well. The challenges to racial classification raised by parents like Naomi Bradford, Lila Lewis, Betty McClain, and Donna Thorberg proved to be just one tactic. Mexican American racial uncertainty, always available to enforce their exclusion from American life, now provided multiple avenues of opposition to civil rights enforcement. In the next phase of resistance Mexican Americans refused to be identified as minorities, thus challenging the entire framework of racial classification in the post–civil rights period.

CHALLENGES TO RACIAL CLASSIFICATION IN THE COURTS

Two years later, in February 1976, Loisa (Sanchez) Van Schoick complained to school board members that her son, a first grader at Swansea Elementary School, had been sent out into the hallway to read a book while other students received instruction in Spanish. Swansea was one of several schools to implement a bilingual-bicultural program, limited as it was, and Van Schoick had opted to exclude her son. Feeling he was being neglected by the school, she charged that the program took away valuable classroom time that could have been devoted to more rigorous academic training. Bilingual education, she believed, was not an appropriate teaching method, and students should only be instructed in English. Even though the school granted her request to exclude her child, she still expressed outrage and alleged DPS was depriving students like him. Such an audacious argument made sense only within a social environment predicated on the politics of whiteness. White racial innocence ensured parents like Van Schoick (Mexican Americans who subscribed to whiteness) would understand themselves as victims of a civil rights crusade gone too far. Although Van Schoick was Mexican American, she was adamantly opposed to bilingual-bicultural education, not only for her own children, but for all Denver schoolchildren. She also maintained that the order for school desegregation was a cancer on the people of the city. In protesting the Swansea bilingual-bicultural program, she concluded that such curriculum was not necessary "in a community with a lot of Hispano last names but not a lot of Hispano people."[66] Devoid of context, such a statement could have multiple meanings. But by February 1976, several factors were converging to make families in the Swansea school area more concerned about the future of their children's education and more apt to challenge the court's order.

Six months earlier the Appeals Court for the Tenth Circuit had returned its decision on the appeal and cross-appeal of Judge Doyle's final order and decree. Its decision largely affirmed the District Court's plan, although it did reverse four aspects of it. First, the court determined that the order for part-time pairing did not go far enough to ensure equality of educational opportunity; only a full-time pairing program was sufficient to meet constitutional requirements. Second, the circuit judges overturned Judge Doyle's order for the creation of the East-Manual Complex in Northeast Denver. Third, the court decided that the maintenance of five predominantly Mexican American elementary schools, exempted from the pairing plan by Judge Doyle in order to ensure the successful implementation and operation of bilingual-bicultural education programs, was not allowable. Bilingual-bicultural programs were not a legal excuse for maintaining segregation, the court wrote in its opinion, and it remanded the issue back to Judge Doyle to decide whether there was some other justifiable reason for excluding the five schools. If not, then they must be desegregated along with the other schools. Finally, the court ruled that Judge Doyle's order for the implementation of the Cardenas Plan went too far, and it was overturned.[67] For school officials, the court's decision ensured that the district would have to move forward with a full-time desegregation plan. Although both DPS and the plaintiffs appealed to the US Supreme Court, their appeals were denied in December 1975. Judge Doyle ordered both parties to develop a full-time desegregation plan that included the five previously exempted Mexican American elementary schools, which included Swansea.[68] Just two days later, Van Schoick made her objections to school board members, who now were tasked with deciding if her children's school would become a part of the desegregation plan and whether or not a bilingual-bicultural program would be maintained there.

These consequences, as parents like Van Schoick saw them, were the result of a faulty racial classification process that separated Mexican Americans from majority society. Many people in the neighborhood, she indicated, had Spanish surnames but did not identify as Hispano. Certainly they did not consider themselves to be a part of a separate minority race. While many Swansea students may have appeared Hispano on paper, she insinuated, they did not need the kinds of educational reforms that many Mexican American advocates said they needed. Such an assertion went against the very logic of including bilingual-bicultural education in the desegregation plan and further discredited the notion that particular educational programs were required for different racial/ethnic groups. It also revealed, once again, the ways that Mexican American racial ambiguity made implementing civil rights remedies a challenging process. Some Mexican Americans thought of themselves as racially distinct from Whites, a distinction that merited alternative educational methods like bilingual-bicultural education. Judge Doyle accepted this rationale in his approach to desegregation in the city. Others rejected a non-White subjectivity and the educational programs that groups like the CHE and MALDEF viewed as essential to the academic success of non-White children.

With the appeals process exhausted, Denverites opposed to Judge Doyle's desegregation plan found themselves running out of options yet still were determined to fight it. Some Mexican American opponents, refusing to concede defeat, advanced a set of arguments that raised questions about their minority status and the school district's ability to correctly classify them. While parents had been making similar claims since at least 1974, it was not until the spring of 1976 that they took these arguments to the next level by completely rejecting minority classification and reinvigorating the old argument that they were "American." Long a civil rights strategy of Mexican Americans who fought for full inclusion in US society, this simple yet rhetorically powerful argument reemerged in the mid-1970s under a much-changed social, cultural, and legal environment. Here, their embrace of "American" identities served not only to distinguish themselves as deserving (White) citizens but also to help establish a new way of thinking about race and rights in the post–civil rights period, a new way of thinking that reworked not just the nature of racial classification, but its very meaning as well.

Loisa Van Schoick joined a group of Mexican American parents in her neighborhood to contest the inclusion of Swansea in DPS's desegregation plan. A month after Van Schoick chastised the school board for running a bilingual-bicultural program, fellow Swansea area parent John Garcia presented to board members a petition with five hundred signatures, reportedly gathered in just one day, of Swansea parents who objected to the inclusion of their school in the desegregation order. Their petition listed several benefits of the school and its teachers and specifically named its bilingual-bicultural program as a factor in wanting to keep their children at that school. "At Swansea," the petition read, "we have a very good teaching staff. Most of them really care if the children learn or not."[69] Clearly, not all of the parents who signed the petition worried that desegregation would undermine bilingual-bicultural education. Van Schoick's commitment to ending Swansea's bilingual-bicultural program reveals that she had other motivations. Neither she nor any of the others who spoke in support of the petition, moreover, showed any concern for Black students. Schools in majority Black areas of the city, they implied, were plenty good enough for Black students.

Although Mexican American teachers at Swansea were unanimous in their support for the school's inclusion in the desegregation plan, many Swansea parents insisted that the neighborhood and the school were already integrated and they did not want their children to be "bused" anywhere.[70] Parent Blas Canales told the board that he saw no benefit to "busing" and argued that forcing his children to go to another school ensured that the United States "was no longer a free country." Manuel Gonzales, another Swansea parent, spoke in support of the petition and asked that the district's legal counsel do what they could to change the laws so that children did not have to be "bused" away from their neighborhoods. In response Naomi Bradford proclaimed that the law could be changed; they just needed to work with the national movement against "forced busing." Their ultimate goal, she explained, was a constitutional amendment banning "busing" for racial balance.[71] Whether or not the majority of Swansea parents supported Bradford's "antibusing" stance is irrelevant. Their protest against the inclusion of *their* children in the desegregation plan was enough to prop up the burgeoning national "antibusing" movement in Denver.

"Anti-busing" discourse, like that put forward by these parents, was not uncommon among Mexican Americans opposed to school desegregation. As previous chapters have shown, their interests were often quite different from those of the majority of White parents who disagreed with the court's integration orders. Regardless of their motivations, however, their acceptance and utilization of popular "antibusing" arguments allied them with the growing White opposition to school desegregation nationwide. By 1976 stories on the nightly television news and other media coverage had conveyed the message that cities across the nation were experiencing a "busing crisis." Images of White mothers marching from Pontiac, Michigan, to Washington, D.C., to protest "busing"; public statements condemning court orders for "busing" by Presidents Richard Nixon and Gerald Ford; and local news stories about the *Keyes* case kept the issue front and center.[72] The violence of "anti-busing" activists in Denver and nationally heightened the sense, for many Americans, that "busing" was a national tragedy. Shortly after Judge Doyle first ordered transportation to effect desegregation, multiple bombs ripped through the DPS school bus yard, destroying or damaging

FIGURE 18. Burned DPS school buses after several bombs exploded inside them, February 5, 1970. Firefighters work and a helicopter with spotlight hovers above. Photo courtesy of the *Denver Post* via Getty Images.

forty-six buses and other vehicles (see figure 18).[73] Bombs also were planted at the homes of Judge Doyle, school board member James Perrill, named plaintiff Wilfred Keyes, and others involved in the lawsuit. Luckily, no one was seriously injured.[74] Still others received threats of bombs and/or other violence. Rachel Noel, who had first initiated desegregation as a school board member, recalled "the many nights that concerned friends would follow her home from board meetings to ensure that no harm would come to her."[75] Similar anti-integrationist violence wreaked havoc around the nation.

While the media focused on several cities undergoing court-ordered desegregation in the early 1970s, television coverage of events in Boston was particularly influential. Network news stories framed the issue as one sided by completely ignoring the histories of school segregation that had led to litigation in the first place and narrowed in on the violent confrontations between "antibusing" protestors and law enforcement officers that sometimes ensued. News producers thus constructed Boston as the symbol of the "busing crisis" in the United States. Beamed into their homes nightly, these news stories riveted viewers and helped sell the idea that "busing" was indeed an American crisis.[76] Mexican Americans consumed these news stories, too, and some were likely persuaded by them. For a community that had struggled to get anyone to pay attention to their schooling needs, the pull of "antibusing" arguments, which clearly were forcing people to take notice, must have been powerful. By linking their specific grievances with "busing," these Mexican American parents signed what Neil Foley has called a "Faustian pact with whiteness."[77]

The Swansea petition made little difference to the deeply divided school board. The day after parents submitted it, members voted 4–3 to pass Resolution 1897, which directed DPS administrators to work with the plaintiffs and intervenor CHE's attorneys to stipulate to a plan that desegregated the entire district. Five days later, their stipulation was filed with the district court.[78] Under the plan the five predominantly Mexican American schools were desegregated. Swansea, a school in north Denver, was paired with Holm Elementary School in the southeastern corner of the city. Children were to attend one school for grades 1 through 3 and the other school for grades 4 through 6. Kindergarteners were to remain at their neighborhood school, and students would be transported to their paired facility. Starting in the 1976–1977 school year, Swansea families, along with families across the district, would become subject to the court's order for city-wide, full-time desegregation.

The Swansea parents' petition was only the first step these parents took to air their opposition to the new desegregation plan. Feeling they had been unheard and unwilling to passively abide by Judge Doyle's latest court order, they, too, turned to the courts for help. On March 16, 1976, they filed a formal complaint with the US District Court for the District of Colorado, challenging the legality of that same court's order in the *Keyes* case. *(Susan Anita) Garcia, et al. v. The Board of Education, School District No. 1, et al.* alleged that the school district was using a system of "discriminatory classification" to achieve balance based on "race, color, and ethnic background." The listed plaintiffs consisted of eight Mexican American families, including that of Loisa Van Schoick, and the plaintiff class was defined as "all children of Hispano ancestry in the community served by Swansea Elementary School now being classified by defendants as 'minority' students." The petition argued that these children's Fourteenth Amendment rights were being violated by the district's practice of racial classification and "busing." Like Swansea parents' earlier petition to DPS, the complaint listed their desire to maintain bilingual-bicultural education in addition to several other benefits of the school, but their general argument was shaped by their rejection of racial classification, a central component of colorblind racial ideology. In particular, they objected to the way they had been racialized by the courts and, subsequently, by the school district. "Plaintiffs are of Hispano ancestry and are being labeled and classified by defendants as 'minority' students," their complaint stated. Several times, in fact, they rejected the term *minority*, and insisted they were "American." Since they had long before learned that to be fully American meant being White, their rhetorical choice here was clear. They were White. Articulating their identities in ethnic terms, they opposed being racially classified with Black students as minorities and explicitly distanced themselves from Black integration proponents. The parents also objected to the argument that their interests had been represented in *Keyes* by the CHE. "The 'Congress of Hispanic Educators,'" they argued, "did not represent the Hispano community and most certainly did not speak for plaintiffs or plaintiffs' community."[79] In short, they challenged their racialization as non-White and argued that because they had been categorized as minority, they were being discriminated against by the district. Here was colorblind logic in action. Arguing they were being unfairly racially categorized by school officials, who had been ordered to officially racialize them as minority in the first place, these Mexican American parents refused the social, cultural, and legal changes brought on by civil rights reform in the postwar period. Content to identify and be identified as Hispano, they felt wronged by the legal effort to erase their Spanish history and settler (i.e., American) status.

Understanding these parents' motivations and the legal logic their attorneys employed in building their case requires attention to multiple, converging factors. The long history of Mexican American other-whiteness dramatically informed the actions of these parents in their pursuit of quality education for their children. An important aspect of this history was a legacy of antiblackness in Mexican American racial formation that influenced the structure of their argument to the court. Finally, while it was the Swansea parents who decided to challenge the desegregation plan, it was their lawyers who wrote the complaint and developed their argument. And they did so according to the standards and practices of US law. Thus, analyzing the complaints and briefs submitted by the *Garcia* plaintiffs requires a recognition that these documents do not so much reveal the candid thoughts and reasoning of the Mexican American plaintiffs as they are evidence of the ways the law operates to limit the potential arguments and evidence that might be used in any given case. Forced to develop an argument that conforms to past precedent, lawyers are always working within a conservative legal system that has little room for new approaches or claims. Bound by legal rules yet focused on getting Mexican American children in Swansea out of the desegregation plan, the *Garcia* plaintiffs' lawyers determined to present their clients as victims of an antidiscrimination lawsuit gone too far. Mexican Americans, according to this legal logic, were victims of the civil rights movement.

DPS attorneys asked for a dismissal of the case. While many in the district supported the spirit of *Garcia*—certainly they objected to "busing" for racial balance, as did the Swansea parents—they also were aware of their obligations under Judge Doyle's order in *Keyes*. Naomi Bradford and fellow anti-integrationist school board member Ted Hackworth took a particular interest in the *Garcia* lawsuit and were angry that their attorneys requested the case be dismissed. No deliberate segregation had ever taken place in the Swansea area, Bradford insisted, therefore these parents had a right to be heard by a court of law. Hackworth and Bradford even asked DPS attorneys if they could file briefs in support of the *Garcia* plaintiffs, as individual members of the DPS Board of Education.[80] The lawsuit, in fact, supported Bradford's longtime argument that most Mexican Americans were opposed to "busing" and did not want to be a part of any desegregation plan.[81] In *Garcia* she saw an opportunity to further delegitimize racial classification for racial balance purposes.

District Court judge Richard Matsch dismissed *Garcia* on the grounds that the issues raised had already been litigated in *Keyes*.[82] He acknowledged the difficult task of designing and implementing a desegregation plan and highlighted the ambiguities that arise in such complex processes. Questions around racial classification were particularly fraught. "It may be conceded," Judge Matsch wrote, "that there is an artificiality in identifying segregated schools through quotas and that there is some incongruity in requiring government agencies to use race and ethnic origin as criteria for measuring the need for affirmative action to redress the deprivation of opportunity because of past policies involving the use of such invidious classifications." Yet if he allowed the lawsuit to move forward, the result would be "a flood of new suits" requiring the nation's courts to relitigate school desegregation cases time and time again.[83] Judge Matsch's point was to illustrate the practical, legal consequences of hearing the lawsuit, but he also exposed the inability of the law to fully address structural racism. If such a flimsy category as racial identity could dismantle two decades of school desegregation litigation, the law held only limited potential for redressing centuries of institutionalized whiteness.

The fact that a group of Mexican Americans opposed their inclusion in a plaintiff class seeking school desegregation and framed their opposition in colorblind terms demonstrates how some Mexican Americans used their flexible racial identities to challenge the direction of civil rights in the 1970s. The district court's dismissal of their case only further emboldened them, and they appealed to the Tenth Circuit Court of Appeals. Like their initial complaint, their brief to the appeals court emphasized their right to an education free from racial/ethnic labeling and their status as American citizens. "Long ago," their attorneys argued, "residents of this part of the city abandoned ethnic and racial labeling, and proudly consider themselves as Americans and neighbors."[84] By opening their argument with this statement, the *Garcia* plaintiffs set the stage for the claims that would follow. Their entire challenge to Swansea's inclusion in Judge Doyle's desegregation plan was built on these two separate but related assertions. While the court defined their children as minority, they refused to succumb to any insinuation that they did not belong. As "Americans and neighbors" they were entitled to call themselves what they wanted, live where they wanted, and go to school where they wanted, all entitlements of whiteness denied to Black students and their families. In fact, they stated, DPS had never discriminated against them prior to March 12, 1976, when the school board included Swansea in the desegregation plan. Instead of being dissatisfied with their children's school, they were pleased with the "superior" education they received there. One of their major arguments was that the courts had never found any discrimination to exist specifically at Swansea. The new 1976 desegregation plan targeted them for inclusion based solely on their racial classification as minorities.[85] This assertion made little sense, given the courts' rulings in *Keyes*. The Supreme Court had determined that the existence of de jure segregation in one part of the city created the presumption that it existed in other parts of the district as well. If DPS could not show that northeast Denver was a separate and unique part of the city, then the District Court must rule the entire district was a dual system. Thus, the plaintiffs did not need to prove segregation in each and every school.[86] On remand, the District Court then found DPS to be an illegal, dual system. The only constitutional remedy was district-wide desegregation, which included Swansea.[87]

Swansea parents employed two strategies to demonstrate their children were not minority. First, they insisted that if they must be categorized then the appropriate term was *Hispano*. Unlike the CHE and its MALDEF attorneys, who used the term *Chicano*, these Mexican Americans did not believe they were a part of a separate race. "If labeling is necessary, and plaintiffs resent such demeaning characterizations," their brief stated, "plaintiffs are of 'Hispano' ancestry."[88] For them, classification as minority was debasing and did not accurately convey their membership in the dominant White majority. Later, attorneys again commented that the plaintiffs "take issue with being classified a 'minority.'" But they took that argument even further by clearly linking Hispanos with whiteness. "What is now called 'Hispano,'" they maintained, "has traditionally been Caucasian."[89] Such arguments were not new within the Mexican American community, but here the *Garica* plaintiffs connected claims of Hispano whiteness to their adoption of colorblind racial ideology. Like the parents who argued before the Denver school board for a mixed-race category for their part–Mexican American children, these parents also maintained racial mixture was a central part of their identities. Many Hispanos in the Swansea community, they asserted, "are far from being full or even half blood 'Hispano.'" Although they did not provide a definition of "Hispano," they connected Hispano-ness to a mixed-race past, informing the court that "the 'Hispano' ancestral line" originated with the blending of two separate races—blackness did not calculate into their understanding of *mestizaje*, a common ideological maneuver in Latin American countries. By the 1970s, they implied, centuries of racial mixture had nearly erased any semblance of nonwhiteness.[90] It was this mixture, this uncertain amalgam that made their racial categorization as minority offensive and, perhaps even more critical, unreliable. They informed the court that if allowed to present their argument, they would demonstrate that "such classification *in their case* is meaningless."[91] If, in the case of Mexican Americans, racial categories were meaningless, how was the court supposed to order a racial balance plan that depended on such categories?

Once again, the ideology of *mestizaje* played an important part in Mexican Americans' conceptualization of themselves in relation to other groups, particularly African Americans. Situating these actions within the long history of Latin American racial theorizing around racial mixture helps elucidate their political meaning. In his seminal treatise *Nuestra América (Our America)*, Cuban nationalist José Martí argued for the development of a pan–Latin American identity and political consciousness that would overthrow European colonialism and US global dominance. Like José Vasconselos in Mexico, he urged the adoption of *mestizaje* as a means of unifying the Latin American people. "A Cuban is more than white, black or mulatto," he wrote, "there can be no racial animosity because there are no races."[92]

As historian Michelle McKinley points out, Martí's logic extended to the ability of the modern nation to enforce racial exclusion. If there were no races because everyone was mixed race, the nation could not implement or police things like segregation. Conceptualized as beneficial and necessary for the establishment of a more just and equitable society, such arguments were widely embraced in the early twentieth century.[93] Rather than result in fairness and equality, as scholars of modern Latin America have demonstrated, such discourse merely hid from plain view the racial workings of societies very much stratified by race.[94] These dynamics are similar to what unfolded in the post–civil rights United States. Mexican Americans, unable to favorably position themselves in relation to the long-standing Black/White paradigm, turned to arguments cemented in Latin American understandings of race as a way of making sense of their own positionality and the efforts of the US racial state to redress the harms of racial segregation. By grounding their claim of discrimination in Mexican American racial uncertainty, racial hybridity, and a discourse of whitening over time (also prominent in Latin America), the *Garcia* plaintiffs, and others like them around the nation, contributed new modes of thinking about race and civil rights that demonstrate the on-the-ground process of racial formation in post–Jim Crow society. These new modes of thinking helped transform colorblind racial ideology, already embraced and advanced by conservative intellectuals, think thanks, and jurists, from a general belief in race neutrality to further race-specific objectives like segregation to a belief in racial anti-classificationism as the ultimate method of safeguarding whiteness.

The second strategy *Garcia* parents used to prove they were not minority was to point to the malleability of racial categories and racial quotas, particularly when it came to Mexican Americans. Racial balance, they maintained, was a policy that demanded "arbitrary, numerical classifications and forced transportation based on such classification."[95] While the focus of their lawsuit was on proving the school district had discriminated against Hispanos by basing school assignments on racial/ethnic identity, they also maintained a firm "antibusing" stance and used colorblind arguments to tie "forced transportation" to the use of illegal, inaccurate racial categories. Calling racial classification a "mechanical fiction-upon-fiction approach," they challenged both the school district's practice of racially sorting students and the court's ability to legally mandate such a process when it was clear racial categorization was neither dependable nor impartial.[96] The pairing plan that required some Swansea students to "bus" to Holm, lawyers wrote, was based on a plan that mandated participation only by schools "which do not meet certain artificially established ethnic guidelines."[97] Thus, not only was racial categorization a flawed practice, but so was the method for determining which schools had to participate. Under Judge Doyle's plan DPS was to set school assignments using a court-designated ratio of Anglo students. Elementary schools needed to fall within 40 and 70 percent Anglo. Anything outside that range was segregated.[98] According to the *Garcia* plaintiffs, this range was both random and harmful. Swansea, they pointed out, was a mere forty-three Anglo students away from falling within the court-ordered ratio. If not for the absence of three Anglo students per class, the school would have been considered integrated and left out of the pairing plan.[99] Moreover, the very foundation of the plan was suspect because the court's adoption of the plaintiffs' racial categories was based on misguided, perhaps even deliberately falsified information.[100] The claim that Hispanos were actually Caucasian reinforced this approach because it meant that if only a few Hispanos were racialized as White, the court would consider Swansea desegregated, ensuring it would not participate in "busing." From their perspective, the court had too easily accepted the argument that all Mexican Americans were a distinct non-White race. If there were such glaring inaccuracies in the usage of the Hispano category, then common sense dictated that there probably were problems with the other two court-designated classifications, Black and Anglo, as well. The uncertainty of Mexican American racial identity made it possible to question the entire system of racial classification in the post–civil rights period.

Another strategy for relaying their rejection of minority classification was to pit themselves against African Americans, whom the *Garcia* parents understood to be the instigators behind the push for school desegregation in the city. This was achieved in several ways. Not only was their challenge to being labeled minority about their desire for whiteness, it was also about their fear of being associated with blackness. By combining African Americans and Mexican Americans into a single category and defining that category as antithetical to whiteness, the *Keyes* plaintiffs and then the federal courts had similarly positioned each group. In order to prove they were the unwitting victims of this chain of events, this group of Mexican Americans took every opportunity to situate themselves in opposition to Black parents, students, and civil rights activists. Partly this was achieved by ignoring the record in *Keyes*. Over and over again, in various ways, the lawyers for the *Garcia* plaintiffs maintained that it was only African Americans who wanted integration. Thus, they were to blame for the current state of affairs. "Plaintiffs' community was not and never has been part of the *Keyes* case," they insisted. Any defense that argues otherwise was "totally without merit."[101] Mexican Americans had never wanted to be a part of any desegregation action, according to this approach. They did not mention Josephine Perez or her three children, who were listed as plaintiffs on the original complaint in *Keyes*, nor did they mention the intervention of the CHE on the side of the plaintiffs. The only reference to the CHE, in fact, appears near the end of the brief when the *Garcia* plaintiffs explain that this organization of Mexican American teachers did not represent them.[102] "Appellants have no relationship whatever with the plaintiffs in *Keyes* and plaintiffs in *Keyes* are not dependent in any way upon Swansea's inclusion in the 'plan.'"[103] By maintaining that they were uninvolved in desegregation matters from the beginning and relating their separation from African American integration proponents, they rewrote the history of the case to suit their own purposes.

Swansea parents also revealed their antiblackness by employing a spatial approach in their analysis. Throughout their brief they displayed a keen awareness of the city's racial geography and its corresponding class dynamics. By describing Swansea as an established, integrated community with a good school that had never disappointed its residents, and by juxtaposing it with the northeast Denver neighborhoods that were at the center of desegregation efforts, they depicted their community as spatially and conceptually separate from and indeed superior to those in the northeast corner of the city, where the majority of African Americans resided. With a recent history of racial unrest, northeast Denver had undergone many changes in the postwar period. The rapid growth of the Black population, the existence of a relatively large Black middle class, and the migration eastward of Black families from Five Points into Park Hill had resulted in many tensions, including but not limited to challenges to school segregation. By 1976 parts of Park Hill had become majority African American. As more Black families moved in, more White families moved out, and fears grew of a completely transitioned neighborhood and plummeting home values. Many Denverites, therefore, understood northeast Denver to be a community in racial distress, with all its corresponding problems. Swansea, conversely, was described by the *Garcia* plaintiffs as a long-standing community with families that had lived there "by choice for many generations." Rather than a neighborhood in distress, it was thriving. Rather than being segregated, it was composed of a "wholesome mixture of various ethnic backgrounds."[104] From their perspective, Swansea was the antithesis of Park Hill, and it existed outside the physical space wherein racial conflict was most apparent. It was, in other words, a colorblind community, one that had survived the torrent of racial conflict that defined the postwar period relatively unscathed and now existed as a post-racial utopia.

This careful comparison between Swansea and Park Hill also aided the *Garcia* plaintiffs as they made one of their central arguments: *Keyes* arose in another part of the city and they, parents of Swansea schoolchildren, were never consulted about their desire for desegregation. The original lawsuit, they asserted, involved only "a certain segment of the black community in a certain part of the city." As the case moved forward, "at the black community's urging," the federal courts expanded the groups and neighborhoods involved so that the litigation eventually resulted in "a quasi-punitive 'remedy' wholly disproportionate to the alleged wrong and parties involved."[105] Not only did this once again rewrite the history of *Keyes* to suit their own interests, it also positioned their non-Black neighborhood in opposition to Black northeast Denver. How could Swansea have a segregation problem, they implied, when "that controversy had arisen in another part of the city?"[106] To them, there could be no segregation problem in Swansea because there were no races in Swansea. People "in this part of the city [had] abandoned ethnic and racial labeling" long before.[107] Within the physical space of their neighborhood, where blackness was invisible, Mexican Americans easily had blended into the community and lived in harmony with its other residents.

While lawyers for the *Garcia* plaintiffs used spatial analysis to distinguish Swansea from northeast Denver, they also employed a Black/non-Black construction of minority identity that reinforced their distinction from African Americans and reflected antiblackness within the Mexican American community. This enabled them to once again depict themselves as victims in the battle to achieve school desegregation, but it was a tricky strategy. In the post–civil rights period, it was no longer acceptable to overtly oppose civil rights. The new, colorblind language of opposition was rooted in its adherents' agreement that legal discrimination must be eliminated. Thus, any strategy for challenging a court's finding of segregation and its order for desegregation had to be carefully constructed in this new language. Challengers had to come across as sympathetic to victims of discrimination and even as allies in the struggle to destroy race-based practices. But, they believed, there were limits. Civil rights remedies could only go so far before they infringed on other people's rights. Opponents constructed "busing," for example, as a solution gone too far. "Antibusers" argued that forcing children to ride buses to schools outside their neighborhoods solely to create racial balance was judicial overreach, a remedy disproportionate to the magnitude of the offense that punished people who were not responsible for creating segregation in the first place. This argument also contained another element of colorblind racial framing: White racial innocence. In the post–civil rights nation, with no legal barriers to equality, it became difficult for many people to see the mechanisms keeping racial hierarchies in place. That is, racism's structural nature was largely invisible, and the people who benefited from it were able to deny its existence. When racial inequities did come to light, as happened in school desegregation cases, this denial helped justify anti-integrationists' refusal to accept court-ordered desegregation plans. After all, *they* were not racist. *They* had not caused segregation. They should not, therefore, be penalized for it. The *Garcia* plaintiffs strategically utilized similar claims several times. Early on, for example, they stated that the desegregation plan adopted by DPS in March 1976 "prejudicially goes too far and raises serious constitutional questions."[108] Given their minority positioning in *Keyes*, however, their challenge to the plan contained novel dimensions that demonstrate how some Mexican Americans adopted and adapted emerging colorblind arguments to advance their interests. While they generally recoiled at the suggestion that they were minority, they also reluctantly accepted the designation in some parts of their brief in order to demonstrate their nonblackness, a critical maneuver that went to the heart of their argument. The *Keyes* plaintiffs, according to this logic, had gone so far beyond their original intent, the eradication of segregated schools in northeast Denver, that they even presumed to represent groups who had nothing to do with the calls for integration in that part of the city. In fact, the *Garcia* plaintiffs maintained, the adopted plan harmed the "non-black minorities involved" by robbing them of "the superior educational opportunities [they had] worked long and hard to attain."[109]

By situating themselves as non-Black minorities the *Garcia* plaintiffs erected a wall between Mexican Americans and African Americans that assisted them in remaking Black integration demands into unreasonable, unconstitutional punishments for Mexican Americans. Such a strategy also enabled them to deny the key finding in *Keyes*: DPS's entire school structure, including attendance zones, building sites, teacher assignments, suspension rates, and resource allocations, was discriminatory. Denver's public schools *were* segregated. Later, they argued that while the courts and the Denver school district had an obligation to undo past discrimination—a concession that placed them firmly within a post–civil rights, colorblind framework—such state bodies had "no 'discretion' to discriminate against a particular minority group at the instance of another."[110] Put another way, these Mexican Americans claimed that the courts had no recourse for remedying school segregation in a multiracial city because what was best for one minority group might be detrimental for another. This was a much more useful framing of the issues than the anti-integration arguments being put forth by White parents, whose interests were suspect to the courts. Mexican Americans, conversely, could be counted on to represent a nonbiased perspective because they, like African Americans, were minorities.

In deploying a Black/non-Black understanding of minority identity the *Garcia* plaintiffs built upon already deeply entrenched ideas about Black poverty, underachievement, and cultural pathology, ideas that merely reproduced colorblindness. Using culture and class as proxies for race, they embraced and perpetuated an argument in race-neutral terms that was very much about race, blackness in particular. A common practice in the post–World War II period, this colorblind sleight of hand built on social science of the era, especially Daniel P. Moynihan's *The Negro Family: A Case for National Action* (1965). Moynihan argued that the high rate of African American poverty was caused not by structural patterns of racial discrimination in employment and housing but by African Americans' cultural propensity for destructive behavior, which led to an increased rate of Black single mother–headed households. His ideas, in combination with those from similar studies, became central pillars of postwar racial discourse.[111] As Kimberlé Crenshaw has pointed out, this race-neutral discourse has been put to effective political use by bolstering the myth of a post–civil rights colorblind society based on meritocracy and equal opportunity.[112]

The *Garcia* plaintiffs' version of the case pitted deserving Mexican Americans against undeserving African Americans. In the initial brief to the court, their attorneys claimed that the *Keyes* plaintiffs' inclusion of Mexican Americans in the plaintiff class, "at substantial taxpayer expense, and without voluntary participation or representation of non-black minorities involved, threatens to deprive at least this non-represented group of the superior educational opportunities it has worked long and hard to attain."[113] Explicit in this statement was an admission of inequality and comparative privilege. Implicit was the assumption that African Americans had not worked long and hard to achieve better education. Rather, they expected the federal government, through legislative and judicial interventions, and the American taxpaying public to provide them with what they wanted without hard work and without respect for what other, non-Black minorities had already accomplished on their own. In this way the *Garcia* plaintiffs cast themselves as a sort of model minority, a group of ethnically different people whose presence in the city had at one time created many tensions and conflicts but who now had attained assimilation and upward social mobility. Model minority scholarship is now focused on Asian Americans, whom many in the United States construct as *the* model racial other in modern American society, yet several of the same processes that lent themselves to the development of the Asian American model minority construct played out for some Mexican Americans as well. According to historian Ellen Wu, the trope of the Asian American model minority is based on the notion that they are "a racial group distinct from the white majority, but lauded as well assimilated, upwardly mobile, politically nonthreatening, and *definitively not-black*."[114] She demonstrates how Asian Americans transformed from permanently unassimilable aliens ineligible for citizenship into the model minority over the course of the postwar period. In the 1940s and 1950s, the immediate post-exclusion era, Whites began to view Chinese and Japanese as entitled to citizenship but still non-White. It was during the 1960s, as Black freedom struggles began to pick up steam, that Asian American nonblackness became more central to their racialization than their nonwhiteness. As a minority group that was "definitively not-black," Asian Americans performed important cultural and political work in the construction of a new national racial order that emerged in the post–civil rights period.[115] In some places and in similar ways, Mexican Americans also contributed to these efforts. The Asian American model minority construct was formed in specific social, economic, and geopolitical contexts, but it is undeniable that the postwar race work that situated non-Black minorities in opposition to Black minorities also involved some Mexican Americans and other Latinas/os. The *Garcia* plaintiffs understood themselves to be fully integrated into their community, a working-class area with a long history of neighborhood pride and self-reliance, and they demonstrated over and over again their politically nonthreatening nature. They simply wanted to be left alone to send their children to the "neighborhood school." While they rejected being defined as minorities and cast themselves as Caucasian, they also recognized the importance of distinguishing themselves as non-Black minorities. If they were going to be minority, as the Supreme Court determined, they preferred to be a non-Black minority. When compared to Blacks, according to this thinking, Swansea parents were deserving citizens who, through no fault of their own, were now being forced by the courts and DPS to participate in a desegregation plan based on nothing but their racial classification. These seemingly contradictory claims, that Mexican Americans were both not minority *and* a non-Black minority, highlight how whiteness does its dirty work. Even when it leads its adherents to make oppositional arguments, it maintains its dominance.

Further adopting colorblind rhetoric for their own purposes, Swansea parents claimed that the adoption of a desegregation plan that included their community was reverse discrimination. No court, they explained, had ever found segregation to exist specifically at Swansea Elementary School. Thus, any desegregation plan that included their children and assigned them based on illegal racial categories was a denial of due process.[116] Once again, their argument was built on an erroneous foundation. The *Keyes* plaintiffs did not need to prove segregation existed in every school for them to win system-wide desegregation. This kind of logical fallacy is common in all reverse discrimination arguments. For their constructed sense of victimhood to make sense, proponents of the reverse discrimination trope must always ignore or downplay the structural nature of racism, as well as the legal doctrine grounding courts' findings of discrimination in the first place. By presuming to speak for all Mexican Americans, Swansea parents argued, the *Keyes* plaintiffs instigated a legal process that "brought about prejudicial discrimination against the Swansea School community," discrimination that forced them to endure "arbitrary numerical classifications and forced transportation."[117]

At issue here was not the legality of "neighborhood school" policies or the debate over whether northern and western school districts were guilty of de jure or de facto segregation. These were common issues raised by White parents who claimed reverse discrimination in their challenges to court-ordered desegregation. Rather, the *Garcia* plaintiffs set out to prove that one minority group, in their pursuit of constitutional rights, could not deprive another minority group of *their* constitutional rights. "Refusal to permit the Swansea community to speak for itself is even worse discrimination that that sought to be corrected by the initial complaint in *Keyes*," they wrote. "Discrimination regardless of the motivation is still discrimination. Damage resulting from classification based on race or ethnic background is of no less effect simply because discrimination is at the instance of another minority group."[118] Three important points emerge from these Mexican Americans' deployment of the reverse discrimination argument. First, by embracing this strategy they once again allied themselves with White desegregation opponents in their challenge to "busing." Rather than urging the court to ensure more educational resources were transferred to Swansea and all of north/northeast Denver, they propagated a familiar anti-integrationist approach to court-ordered desegregation. Like all "antibusing" arguments, putative flaws in the remedy were not corrected but were used as a justification for no remedy at all. Second, positioning themselves in agreement with White anti-integrationists provided further substantiation for their claim to whiteness. By adopting and putting to use the language of White innocence and colorblindness, they hoped to demonstrate to the court the ways that the *Keyes* plaintiffs had unfairly victimized them. Finally, even though they linked themselves to whiteness, their legal minority status helped legitimize the reverse discrimination claim by rhetorically removing the potential harm of whiteness. Whereas Whites might be suspected of racism for advancing a reverse discrimination argument, fellow minorities could be counted on to maintain a commitment to equality. In the case of some White-identified Mexican Americans, this commitment rang hollow as they continued to seek the advantages such whiteness conferred.

In the end, the *Garcia* plaintiffs were unsuccessful in their effort to challenge Swansea's inclusion in system-wide desegregation. In April 1978 the appeals court affirmed the lower court's decision, agreeing that the issues the case presented had already been litigated in *Keyes* and that Swansea parents had indeed been represented in that case, by either the CHE or CANS. The court did, however, take note of the unique nature of their lawsuit. "This appeal is apparently one of first impression and is premised on an unique factual situation," the court wrote in its published opinion. "It involves a suit by members of a minority group seeking to stop the desegregation of their neighborhood school."[119] Although Mexican Americans had been making their critiques of racial balance plans known for several years, the three-judge panel in Denver still found it strange to encounter a group of Mexican Americans opposed to desegregation. By the late 1970s, case law, with help from *Keyes*, had firmly established that Mexican Americans were not White but were a minority group akin to African Americans. That new normal, however, was not so long in the making. Only a decade earlier Mexican American "other whiteness" had been an established legal fact, and not everyone was as quick as the courts in accepting this change. Swansea parents' challenge to the way their children were racialized by the courts and DPS demonstrates that whiteness still held great appeal and even greater rewards. Their arguments, moreover, fit a growing movement in the 1970s toward colorblind racial ideology. By refusing to be classified as minority, the *Garcia* plaintiffs not only revealed their fear of being grouped with African Americans, they also embraced a crucial tenet of colorblindness: anti-classification politics. Because Mexican Americans were so racially uncertain, there was no way they could be properly categorized. Centuries of racial mixture had produced a hybrid people that legal racial classifications could not contain. Finally, in their efforts to get their children off the bus, these Mexican American parents proved they were willing to utilize the same type of anti-Black claims that animated White resistance to school desegregation. In the process they revealed themselves as inheritors of a historical legacy that went back centuries and helped explain their own adoption of Hispano identities, even in the wake of a movement to reject these longstanding and divisive ideologies. Denver may have been one of the centers of the Chicana/o movement, but it was also a site of continued struggles over Mexican American racial identity and civil rights politics.

Conclusion

On a cold winter morning in February 1976, parents, students, school officials, community activists, members of the media, and others gathered at the Federal Building in downtown Denver. It was the first day of a three-day hearing before the US Commission on Civil Rights, in town to hear testimony about the city's school desegregation progress. Outside, a group of about fifty anti-integrationists protested the hearings because the commission refused to hear from more "anti-busers." This, according to the protestors, proved the commissioners were engaging in an unfair process of investigation that privileged the perspective of "pro-busers."[1] Besides Denver, the commission also held hearings in Boston, Tampa, and Louisville. Combined with open meetings in four other cities, an extensive study of twenty-nine school districts, and a national survey, these hearings formed the basis of the commission's August 1976 report, *Fulfilling the Letter and Spirit of the Law: Desegregation of the Nation's Public Schools*. It provided a comprehensive examination of how the Supreme Court's *Brown* decision was being implemented across the nation, with particular focus on the origins of litigation, public response to desegregation orders, the different types and effectiveness of desegregation planning, the length of time each district had been dealing with desegregation, and the general ways desegregation was implemented. When commissioners presented the report to the president and Congress, they summarized its major arguments. "For every Boston and Louisville," the letter of transmittal stated, "there are dozen[s] of other communities, which have received no headlines and attracted no television coverage, where desegregation is proceeding without major incident." Compared to the violence of desegregation in Boston and Louisville, Denver's experience had been relatively smooth and peaceful. In fact, this was one of the things the commissioners were most interested in understanding during the hearings. The commission's second point was that although much progress had been made, there was still a lot of work to be done to ensure full equality of educational opportunity in the nation's public schools. In Denver, the commission found an intransigent school board and administration, the members of which had been dragging their feet on the issue for years, including when it came to the problems that most concerned Mexican Americans.[2]

Specifically, the commission's investigation of the Denver situation found that school officials were unwilling to develop and implement robust bilingual-bicultural programs, and they resisted any kind of affirmative action hiring program for Mexican Americans. Both were required under Judge Doyle's court order, but according to several people who testified at the hearing, Denver Public Schools (DPS) had so far failed to comply. One person called school officials' efforts in this area "ineffective, fumbling, weak, and inadequate."[3] School board minutes from the previous two years and the reports of the Community Education Council, a court-appointed citizen's council that monitored the district's implementation of the court order, confirm this interpretation.[4] Not only did some school board members and DPS administrators move slowly, they also actively undermined their own efforts by, for example, refusing to apply for federal grant money that would help pay for bilingual-bicultural programs. From the perspective of commission members, this was something that needed immediate attention. The nation's most prominent civil rights monitoring body recognized Mexican Americans' complaints and made them an important part of its analysis of school desegregation in Denver. This was a remarkable transformation from just a decade earlier, when Mexican Americans were touted as "the invisible minority" and could not get federal officials to pay attention to their needs and demands. In this sense, school desegregation efforts had provided an important avenue of change for Mexican Americans interested in improving their children's education. Commissioners not only recognized that Mexican American educational concerns were inseparable from the school desegregation issue, it also advocated on their behalf. Yet the report, as comprehensive as it was, merely glossed over the deep divisions that characterized Mexican American perceptions of school desegregation, race, and civil rights. Bilingual-bicultural education *was* an important educational goal for many Mexican Americans, but there were others who vehemently opposed it, not only for its pedagogical value, but also because of what such programs implied about Mexican Americans. For such individuals, bilingual-bicultural education separated Mexican Americans from the American mainstream. It marked them as different in a society they had worked hard to assimilate into.

By eliding Mexican Americans' multiple perspectives on school desegregation, perspectives that were divulged during the three-day hearing, the commission's report did not accurately represent the complexity of the opposition to the Denver school district's implementation of Judge Doyle's order for city-wide desegregation. As the nation's premier civil rights body, established to investigate the "Negro problem" in American life, perhaps the commissioners were just as unprepared to acknowledge the workings of race and racism as applied to Mexican Americans as US Department of Health, Education, and Welfare (HEW)'s Office for Civil Rights had been just a few years earlier. Now that Mexican Americans were widely considered to be one of several "minority" groups, it is also possible that the commissioners simply did not identify or view as significant those Mexican Americans whose racial identities and racial politics did not conform to movement ideologies or legal decisions like *Keyes*. The Appeals Court for the Tenth Circuit did remark in *Garcia*, after all, that the case presented "an unique factual situation."[5] By that the court meant that it was peculiar to encounter a lawsuit by a group of minorities challenging school desegregation. Such a thing must have seemed utterly contrary to the judges and others who had kept up with the racial shifts of the previous decade.

What these jurists missed was the subtle reworking of race and racial ideology that had been underway in the post–civil rights period. While the courts may have confirmed Mexican Americans' minority status in US culture and society, the power of whiteness was still too great to abandon wholesale. Memories of Hispanos' White settler past continued to shape how many Mexican Americans in Denver conceived of their individual and group identities. Claiming whiteness was no longer a civil rights strategy, as it had been in Mexican Americans' challenges to school segregation and other forms of discrimination earlier in the century. Now it was a strategy for defeating civil rights. Even the slightest hint of Mexican American whiteness, moreover, provoked questions about whether Mexican Americans were legitimate beneficiaries of civil rights legal protections and race-based social policy, questions that raised doubt about the direction of civil rights in the 1970s. In this way, Mexican Americans' historic racial uncertainty became a useful tool in efforts to dismantle the nation's civil rights apparatus.

The US District Court for the District of Colorado monitored DPS's implementation of its court orders on school desegregation over the next several decades, until 1995, when the court granted the district unitary status and released it from the court's oversight. Between the mid-1970s and the mid-1990s, as the city's public school population got smaller and less White, meeting the court's mandate for racial balance became increasingly more difficult. School board members and administrators used this fact in their attempts to get the court to recognize they had done all they could to overcome Judge Doyle's ruling that DPS was a dual school system. Numerous times throughout the 1980s the district tried to prove it had met its obligations under the law, all to no avail. As long as there were racially concentrated schools; unmet hiring goals for Black and Mexican American teachers, counselors, and administrators; and educational disparities between White and minority students, the court said that school officials had failed to meet its mandates. Not only that, but there was mounting evidence that the district had purposely avoided taking action that would alleviate some of the worst inequities. In short, *Keyes* did not bring about the kind of educational equality that integration advocates had hoped it would. At the same time, proponents of stronger Black and Mexican American community schools gained momentum and converts. By the early 1990s, there were signs that majorities in both groups desired an end to desegregation efforts. By that time, the memory of Mexican Americans who supported and fought for integration had faded, and the only thing most people remembered was that "Hispanics didn't want busing in the first place."[6]

The notion that Mexican Americans had always been opposed to "busing" and had nothing to do with integration efforts in the city reinforced an oversimplified narrative that Mexican Americans were monolithic in their schooling concerns and racial politics. As the city's battle over desegregation demonstrates, Mexican Americans had at least three different perspectives on the question of integration and racial balance. One group, led by Mexican American teachers and parents like Josephine Perez, pushed for desegregation as a means of providing educational enrichment and equality for all students. They did not blindly accept that racial balance would provide everything they wanted, but they were convinced that in order for DPS to implement meaningful reforms like bilingual-bicultural education, a foundation of equality needed to be laid first. The second and largest group, consisting of other teachers, parents, and community activists like members of the Crusade for Justice, also recognized that the school district had a long history of neglect when it came to Mexican Americans. Like integration advocates, they pushed school officials to adopt bilingual programs and implement curriculum in Mexican American history and culture. Rather than wasting money and other resources on creating racial balance, they insisted on putting those resources toward creating better schools as they already were constituted. Many in this group believed strongly that Mexican American community schools were best suited to provide quality, emancipatory education for students and neighborhood residents alike. Thus, they agreed with the argument that DPS operated an unequal school system, but they rejected integration as a flawed solution that was unable to correct the core problems they identified in the district's operation. Finally, the third group was made up of those Mexican Americans who opposed desegregation on the same grounds that many Whites did. These individuals disagreed that DPS was a dual school system. They insisted that their children had never received unequal education and, moreover, they resented civil rights politics and found such politics to be un-American. Many in this cohort were happily assimilated into middle-class American culture, and they refused not just desegregation but bilingual-bicultural education as well. Recognizing these divergent viewpoints is critical for fully understanding the racial politics of the post–civil rights period. While Mexican Americans did not agree on the question of desegregation in the Denver schools, each of their perspectives was informed by the key racial transformations of the period.

By the early twenty-first century colorblind constitutionalism was deeply rooted in civil rights jurisprudence, as well as public perceptions of race and equality. It is a truism, in fact, that today most Americans celebrate colorblindness as the height of racial equality. After the election of Barack Obama in 2008, the nation basked in the glory of finally achieving a "post-racial" society. The conservative co-opting of colorblindness in the aftermath of *Brown* and the subsequent struggle over its meaning and substance in US society and culture produced a powerful weapon. In the struggle for racial justice, civil rights opponents wield colorblind ideology with remarkable success. Mexican Americans did not invent colorblindness, but some did participate in its expansion and many continue to propagate its tenets today. If we want to challenge colorblindness in US society, it helps to understand how it has infiltrated Mexican American communities. This history is only one part of that larger story. Unpacking the rest of it will be a difficult but necessary process that may go a long way toward breaking down the colonial mindset of Mexican American whiteness.

NOTES

INTRODUCTION

1. Dick Davis, "West High School Student Demonstration," 1969, Denver file folder, Western History Collection, Denver Public Library.
2. "Summer in March: Denver Student [sic.] Become Restless in March," *Denver Blade* 9, no. 24 (25 March 1969): 1. See also Westside Action Ministry, "Supplement to the West Side Recorder, March 1969," *West Side Recorder* 5, no. 9 (March 1969): insert.
3. Wilfred Keyes et al. v. School District No. 1, Denver, Colorado, et al., Civil Action C-1499, U.S. District Court for the District of Colorado, June 19, 1969.
4. Guadalupe San Miguel Jr., *"Let All of Them Take Heed": Mexican Americans and the Campaign for Educational Equality in Texas, 1910–1981* (Austin: University of Texas Press, 1987); Glen Linden, *Desegregating Schools in Dallas: Four Decades in the Federal Courts* (Dallas: Three Forks Press, 1995); Kristi L. Bowman, "The New Face of School Desegregation," *Duke Law Journal* 50, no. 6 (April 2001): 1751–1808; Stephen H. Wilson, "*Brown* over 'Other White': Mexican Americans' Legal Arguments and Litigation Strategy in School Desegregation Lawsuits," *Law and History Review* 21 (Spring 2003): 145–194; Guadalupe San Miguel Jr., *Brown, Not White: School Integration and the Chicano Movement in Houston* (College Station: Texas A&M University Press, 2005); Mark Brilliant, *The Color of America Has Changed: How Racial Diversity Shaped Civil Rights Reform in California, 1941–1978* (Oxford: Oxford University Press, 2010), 58–88, 227–256; Daniel Martinez HoSang, *Racial Propositions: Ballot Initiatives and the Making of Postwar California* (Berkeley: University of California Press, 2010), 91–129; Brian Behnken, *Fighting Their Own Battles: Mexican Americans, African Americans, and the Struggle for Civil Rights in Texas* (Chapel Hill: University of North Carolina Press, 2010), 195–223; Neil Foley, *Quest for Equality: The Failed Promise of Black-Brown Solidarity* (Cambridge, MA: Harvard University Press, 2010), 94–139; Sonia Song-Ha Lee, *Building a Latino Civil Rights Movement: Puerto Ricans, African Americans, and the Pursuit of Racial Justice in New York City* (Chapel Hill: University of North Carolina Press, 2014),

165–210; Tatiana M. F. Cruz, "'We Took 'Em On': The Latino Movement for Educational Justice in Boston, 1965–1980," *Journal of Urban History* 43, no. 2 (2017): 235–255; David G. García, *Strategies of Segregation: Race, Residence, and the Struggle for Educational Equality* (Berkeley: University of California Press, 2018); and Rand Quinn, *Class Action: Desegregation and Diversity in San Francisco Schools* (Minneapolis: University of Minnesota Press, 2020).

5. Martinez HoSang, *Racial Propositions*; Brilliant, *Color of America Has Changed*; Behnken, *Fighting Their Own Battles*; Song-Ha Lee, *Building a Latino Civil Rights Movement*; and Cruz, "'We Took 'Em On.'"

6. Ronald Reagan, press conference transcript, February 17, 1970, box GO 155, file Research File—Education—Busing, Ronald Reagan Governor's Papers, Ronald Reagan Library, Simi Valley, California, as cited in Brilliant, *Color of America Has Changed*, 237.

7. "Press Release #441," as cited in Brilliant, *Color of America Has Changed*, 237.

8. Michael Omi and Howard Winant, *Racial Formation in the United States*, 3rd ed. (New York: Routledge, 2015), 124–127, quote on 125.

9. On the "common sense" of race, see Ian F. Haney López, *Racism on Trial: The Chicano Fight for Justice* (Cambridge, MA: Belknap Press of Harvard University Press, 2004), esp. part 2; Ariela J. Gross, *What Blood Won't Tell: A History of Race on Trial in America* (Cambridge, MA: Harvard University Press, 2008), 16–47; and Omi and Winant, *Racial Formation in the United States*, 126.

10. Laura E. Gómez, *Manifest Destinies: The Making of the Mexican American Race* (New York: New York University Press, 2008), 49–84.

11. Adrian Bustamante, "Los Hispanos: Ethnicity and Social Change in New Mexico," (PhD diss., University of New Mexico, 1982); John R Chávez, *The Lost Land: The Chicano Image of the Southwest* (Albuquerque: University of New Mexico Press, 1984); Sarah Deutsch, *No Separate Refuge: Culture, Class, and Gender on an Anglo-Hispanic Frontier in the American Southwest, 1880–1940* (New York: Oxford University Press, 1987); Charles Montgomery, *The Spanish Redemption: Heritage, Power, and Loss on New Mexico's Upper Rio Grande* (Berkeley: University of California Press, 2002); John M. Nieto-Phillips, *The Language of Blood: The Making of Spanish-American Identity in New Mexico, 1880s–1930s* (Albuquerque: University of New Mexico Press, 2004); Pablo Mitchell, *Coyote Nation: Sexuality, Race, and Conquest in Modernizing New Mexico, 1880–1920* (Chicago: University of Chicago Press, 2005); Gómez, *Manifest Destinies*; and Linda C. Noel, "'I Am an American': Anglos, Mexicans, *Nativos*, and the National Debate over Arizona and New Mexico Statehood," *Pacific Historical Review* 80, no. 3 (August 2011): 430–467.

12. Richard Nostrand, "The Hispano Homeland in 1900," *Annals of the Association of American Geographers* 70, no. 3 (1980): 382–396.

13. James A. Atkins, *Human Relations in Colorado: A Historical Record* (Denver, CO: Colorado Department of Education, Division of Elementary and Secondary Education, Office of Instructional Services, 1968), 203.

14. Daniel T. Valdes, "Spanish-Origin Citizens: People without a Name," *Denver Post*, 5 September 1965, 19.

15. The scholarship on Mexican American whiteness in the twentieth century is deep. See, in particular, David G. Gutiérrez, *Walls and Mirrors: Mexican Americans, Mexican Immigrants, and the Politics of Ethnicity* (Berkeley: University of California Press, 1995); Neil Foley, *The White Scourge: Mexicans, Blacks, and Poor Whites in Texas Cotton Culture* (Berkeley: University of California Press, 1997); Stephanie M. Wildman, "Reflections on Whiteness and Latina/o Critical Theory," *Harvard Latino Law Review* 2 (1997): 307–316; Neil Foley, "Becoming Hispanic: Mexican Americans and the Faustian Pact with Whiteness," in *Reflexiones 1997: New Directions in Mexican Americans Studies*, ed. Neil Foley (Austin: Center for Mexican American Studies, University of Texas, 1998), 53–70; Claire Sheridan, "'Another White Race': Mexican Americans and the Paradox of Whiteness in Jury Selection," *Law and History Review* 21, no. 1 (Spring 2003): 109–144; Wilson, *"Brown* over 'Other White'"; Neil Foley, "Partly Colored or Other White: Mexican Americans and Their Problem with the Color Line," in *Beyond Black and White: Race, Ethnicity, and Gender in the U.S. South and Southwest*, ed. Stephanie Cole and Alison M. Parker (College Station: Texas A&M University Press, 2004), 123–144; Thomas A. Guglielmo, "Fighting for Caucasian Rights: Mexicans, Mexican Americans, and the Transnational Struggle for Civil Rights in World War II Texas," *Journal of American History* 92 (March 2006): 1212–1237; Ariela J. Gross, "'The Caucasian Cloak': Mexican Americans and the Politics of Whiteness in the Twentieth Century Southwest," *Georgetown Law Journal* 95, no. 2 (January 2007): 337–392; Adrian Burgos Jr., *Playing America's Game: Baseball, Latinos, and the Color Line* (Berkeley: University of California Press, 2007); Gómez, *Manifest Destinies*; Gross, *What Blood Won't Tell*, 253–293; Benjamin H. Johnson, "The Cosmic Race in Texas: Racial Fusion, White Supremacy, and Civil Rights Politics in Texas," *Journal of American History* 98, no. 2 (September 2011): 404–419; Carlos Kevin Blanton, *George I. Sánchez: The Long Fight for Mexican American Integration* (New Haven, CT: Yale University Press, 2014); and Tyina L. Steptoe, *Houston Bound: Culture and Color in a Jim Crow City* (Berkeley: University of California Press, 2015). See also Clara E. Rodríguez, *Changing Race: Latinos, the Census and the History of Ethnicity* (New York: New York University Press, 2000); and Julie A. Dowling, *Mexican Americans and the Question of Race* (Austin: University of Texas Press, 2014).

16. San Miguel, *"Let All of Them Take Heed"*; Bowman, "New Face of School Desegregation"; Wilson, *"Brown* over 'Other White'"; San Miguel, *Brown, Not White*; Neil Foley, "Over the Rainbow: Hernandez v. Texas, Brown v. Board of Education, and Black v. Brown," in *"Colored Men" and "Hombres Aquí"*: Hernandez v. Texas *and the Emergence of Mexican-American Lawyering*, ed. Michael A. Olivas (Houston: Arte Público Press, University of Houston Press, 2006), 111–122; Richard Valencia, *Chicano Students and the Courts: The Mexican American Legal Struggle for Educational Equality* (New York New York University Press, 2010); Foley, *Quest for Equality*; and Philippa Strum, *Mendez v. Westminster: School Desegregation and Mexican-American Rights* (Lawrence: University Press of Kansas, 2010).

17. Hernandez v. Texas, 347 U.S. 475 (1954). See Sheridan, "'Another White Race'"; Ariela J. Gross, "Texas Mexicans and the Politics of Whiteness," *Law and*

History Review 21, no. 1 (Spring 2003): 200–201; Wilson, "*Brown* over 'Other White,'"161–164; Ignacio M. García, *White but Not Equal: Mexican Americans, Jury Discrimination, and the Supreme Court* (Tucson: University of Arizona Press, 2008); and Gross, *What Blood Won't Tell*, 253–293. See also the edited volume on *Hernandez* by Olivas, *"Colored Men" and "Hombres Aquí"*.

18. Cheryl I. Harris, "Whiteness as Property," *Harvard Law Review* 106, no. 8 (June 1993): 1707–1791, esp. 1729–1731.

19. Foley, *White Scourge*, 13. The most influential historian of this interpretation is Neil Foley. See Foley, "Becoming Hispanic"; Foley, "Partly Colored or Other White"; Foley, "Straddling the Color Line: The Legal Construction of Hispanic Identity in Texas," in *Not Just Black and White: Historical and Contemporary Perspectives on Immigration, Race, and Ethnicity in the United States*, ed. Nancy Foner and George M. Frederickson (New York: Russell Sage Foundation, 2004), 341–357; Foley, "Over the Rainbow"; and Foley, *Quest for Equality*. See also Gutiérrez, *Walls and Mirrors*; Sheridan, "'Another White Race'"; Ian Haney López, "White Latinos," *Harvard Latino Law Review* 6 (2003): 1–4; Guglielmo, "Fighting for Caucasian Rights," 1231–1235; Michael Phillips, *White Metropolis: Race, Ethnicity, and Religion in Dallas, 1841–2001* (Austin: University of Texas Press, 2006), 121–148; Behnken, *Fighting Their Own Battles*; and Brilliant, *Color of America Has Changed*.

20. Carlos K. Blanton, "George I. Sánchez, Ideology, and Whiteness in the Making of the Mexican American Civil Rights Movement, 1930–1960," *Journal of Southern History* 72, no. 3 (August 2006): 569–604; Emilio Zamora, *Claiming Rights and Righting Wrongs in Texas: Mexican Workers and Job Politics during World War II* (College Station: Texas A&M University Press, 2008), 9–10, 121; María Josefina Saldaña-Portillo, "'How Many Mexicans [Is] a Horse Worth?': The League of United Latin American Citizens, Desegregation Cases, and Chicano Historiography," *South Atlantic Quarterly* 107, no. 4 (Fall 2008): 809–831; Gross, *What Blood Won't Tell*, 253–293; Cynthia E. Orozco, *No Mexicans, Women, or Dogs Allowed: The Rise of the Mexican American Civil Rights Movement* (Austin: University of Texas Press, 2009); Johnson, "Cosmic Race"; and Blanton, *George I. Sánchez*, 125–204. See also Julie M. Weise, *Corazón de Dixie: Mexicanos in the U.S. South since 1910* (Chapel Hill: University of North Carolina Press, 2015).

21. Martinez HoSang, *Racial Propositions*, 20–21.

22. I follow historian Matthew F. Delmont, who puts "busing" in quotation marks to demonstrate its constructed nature. I keep both "busing" and "antibusing" in quotes throughout the book. The "busing" frame obscured the fact that school desegregation was about remedying a constitutional violation. It hid the histories of deliberate government policies that had created housing and school segregation in the first place. Opposition to "busing" was merely a (seemingly) race-neutral way to oppose integration. *Why Busing Failed: Race, Media, and the National Resistance to School Desegregation* (Berkeley: University of California Press, 2016), 3–4.

23. US Commission on Civil Rights, *1961 Commission on Civil Rights Report: Housing* (Washington, DC: Government Printing Office, 1961), 1. On postwar suburban development, segregated housing, and metropolitan inequality, see

Kenneth T. Jackson, *Crabgrass Frontier: The Suburbanization of the United States* (New York: Oxford University Press, 1987); Thomas J. Sugrue, *The Origins of the Urban Crisis: Race and Inequality in Postwar Detroit* (Princeton, NJ: Princeton University Press, 1996); Arnold R. Hirsch, *Making the Second Ghetto: Race and Housing in Chicago, 1940–1960* (Chicago: University of Chicago Press, 1998); Becky M. Nicolaides, *My Blue Heaven: Life and Politics in the Working-Class Suburbs of Los Angeles, 1920–1965* (Chicago: University of Chicago Press, 2002); Robert O. Self, *American Babylon: Race and the Struggle for Postwar Oakland* (Princeton, NJ: Princeton University Press, 2003); Kevin M. Kruse, *White Flight: Atlanta and the Making of Modern Conservatism* (Princeton, NJ: Princeton University Press, 2005); David Freund, *Property: State Policy and White Racial Politics in Suburban America* (Chicago: University of Chicago Press, 2007); Richard Rothstein, *The Color of Law: A Forgotten History of How Our Government Segregated America* (New York: Liveright, 2017); and Keeanga-Yamahtta Taylor, *Race for Profit: How Banks and the Real Estate Industry Undermined Black Homeownership* (Chapel Hill: University of North Carolina Press, 2019).

24. The Supreme Court also placed limitations on the use of "busing." Swann v. Charlotte-Mecklenburg Bd. of Educ., 402 U.S. 1, 30 (1971). See also Gary Orfield, *Must We Bus? Segregated Schools and National Policy* (Washington, DC: Brookings Institution, 1978); J. Harvie Wilkinson III, *From Brown to Bakke: The Supreme Court and School Integration, 1954–1978* (New York: Oxford University Press, 1979), 134–150; Bernard Schwartz, *Swann's Way: The School Busing Case and the Supreme Court* (New York: Oxford University Press, 1986); Frye Gaillard, *The Dream Long Deferred* (Chapel Hill: University of North Carolina Press, 1988); James T. Patterson, Brown v. Board of Education: *A Civil Rights Milestone and Its Troubled Legacy* (New York: Oxford University Press, 2001), 155–159; Richard Kluger, *Simple Justice: The History of* Brown v. Board of Education *and Black America's Struggle for Equality*, rev. ed. (New York: Vintage Books, 2004), 762–768; and Delmont, *Why Busing Failed*, 129–133.

25. Milliken v. Bradley, 418 U.S. 717 (1974). See also Orfield, *Must We Bus?*; Wilkinson, *From Brown to Bakke*, 216–249; Kluger, *Simple Justice*, 765–767; Paul R. Dimond, *Beyond Busing: Reflections on Urban Segregation, the Courts, and Equal Opportunity* (Ann Arbor: University of Michigan Press, 2005), 97–120; Patterson, Brown v. Board of Education, 178–183; and Delmont, *Why Busing Failed*, 114–141.

26. Colo. Const. art. XIV, § 3; Colo. Const. art. XX, § 1; and Chungmei Lee, *Denver Public Schools: Resegregation, Latino Style*, The Civil Rights Project, Harvard University, January 2006, 3. See also Franklin J. James and Christopher B. Gerboth, "A Camp Divided: Annexation Battles, the Poundstone Amendment, and Their Impact on Metropolitan Denver, 1941–1988," *Colorado History*, no. 5 (2001): 129–174; Tom I. Romero II, "Our Selma Is Here: The Political and Legal Struggle for Educational Equality in Denver, Colorado, and Multiracial Conundrums in American Jurisprudence," *Seattle Journal for Social Justice* 3, no. 1 (Fall/Winter 2004): 119–120; and Rachel Guberman, "The Real Silent Majority: Denver and

the Realignment of American Politics after the Sixties" (PhD diss., University of Pennsylvania, 2015), 34–49.

27. See Harris, "Whiteness as Property"; George Lipsitz, *The Possessive Investment in Whiteness: How White People Profit from Identity Politics*, rev. and expand. ed. (Philadelphia: Temple University Press, 2006); and Ira Katznelson, *When Affirmative Action Was White: An Untold History of Racial Inequality in Twentieth-Century America* (New York: W. W. Norton, 2005).

28. Matthew D. Lassiter, *The Silent Majority: Suburban Politics in the Sunbelt South* (Princeton, NJ: Princeton University Press, 2006). See also Lizabeth Cohen, *A Consumer's Republic: The Politics of Mass Consumption in Postwar America* (New York: Vintage, 2003); Self, *American Babylon*; Kruse, *White Flight*; and Martinez HoSang, *Racial Propositions*.

29. Gary Orfield and Susan E. Eaton, *Dismantling Desegregation: The Quiet Reversal of* Brown v. Board of Education (New York: New Press, 1996); Gary Orfield and Erica Frankenberg, with Jongyeon Ee and John Kuscera, *Brown at 60: Great Progress, a Long Retreat and an Uncertain Future*, The Civil Rights Project/Proyecto Derechos Civiles, 15 May 2014.

30. The distinction between de jure and de facto segregation, as several scholars have shown, is no longer useful. As Matthew Lassiter argues, "The label of de facto segregation is so historically loaded—so wrapped up in artificial binaries between South and North, between the educational and residential areas, between deliberate state action and private market forces, between White culpability and White innocence—that historians should discard it as an analytical and descriptive category and evaluate it instead as a cultural and political construct." Matthew D. Lassiter, "De Jure/De Facto Segregation: The Long Shadow of a National Myth," in *The Myth of Southern Exceptionalism*, ed. Matthew D. Lassiter and Joseph Crespino (Oxford: Oxford University Press, 2009), 28. See also Brett Gadsden, *Between North and South: Delaware, Desegregation, and the Myth of American Sectionalism* (Philadelphia: University of Pennsylvania Press, 2012); Delmont, *Why Busing Failed*; Ansley T. Erickson, *Making the Unequal Metropolis: School Desegregation and Its Limits* (Chicago: University of Chicago Press, 2016); and García, *Strategies of Segregation*.

31. Hernandez v. State, 251 S.W. 2d 531, 535 (1952), citing Sanchez v. State, 243 S.W.2d 700, 701 (1951).

32. Chief Justice Earl Warren, who wrote the opinion, stated "Whether such a group exists within a community is a question of fact." Hernandez v. Texas, 347 U.S. 475, 478 (1954). See also Jorge C. Rangel and Carlos M. Alcala, "Project Report: De Jure Segregation of Chicanos in Texas Schools," *Harvard Civil Rights-Civil Liberties Law Review* 7, no. 2 (March 1972), 342–344.

33. Brown v. Board of Education of Topeka (Brown II), 349 U.S. 294, 301 (1955).

34. Michael J. Klarman, *From Jim Crow to Civil Rights: The Supreme Court and the Struggle for Racial Equality* (New York: Oxford University Press, 2004), 314, citing Brown v. Board of Education of Topeka (Brown II), 349 U.S. 294 (1955).

35. Kwame Ture and Charles V. Hamilton, *Black Power: The Politics of Liberation* (New York: Random House, 1967).

36. Neil Gotanda, "A Critique of 'Our Constitution Is Color-Blind,'" *Stanford Law Review* 44, no. 1 (November 1991): 1–68; Robert C. Smith, *Racism in the Post-Civil Rights Era: Now You See It, Now You Don't* (Albany: State University of New York Press, 1995); Howard Winant, "Racism Today: Continuity and Change in the Post-Civil Rights Era," *Ethnic and Racial Studies* 21, no. 4 (1998): 755–766; Ian F. Haney López, "Race and Colorblindness after *Hernandez* and *Brown*," in *"Colored Men" and "Hombres Aquí"*, ed. Michael A. Olivas (Houston: Arte Público Press, 2006), 41–52; Christopher W. Schmidt, "*Brown* and the Colorblind Constitution," *Cornell Law Review* 94, no. 1 (2008): 203–238; Clarence Taylor, "Hurricane Katrina and the Myth of the Post-Civil Rights Era," *Journal of Urban History* 35, no 5 (2009): 640–655; Eduardo Bonilla-Silva, *Racism without Racists: Color-Blind Racism and the Persistence of Racial Inequality in America*, 3rd ed. (New York: Rowman & Littlefield, 2009); Ian Haney López, *Dog Whistle Politics: How Coded Racial Appeals Have Reinvented Racism and Wrecked the Middle Class* (Oxford: Oxford University Press, 2014); and Omi and Winant, *Racial Formation in the United States*, 217–221.

37. Omi and Winant, *Racial Formation in the United States*, 105–136. On the social construction of race, also see Ian F. Haney López, "The Social Construction of Race: Some Observations on Illusion, Fabrication, and Choice," *Harvard Civil Rights-Civil Liberties Law Review* 29 (1994): 1–62.

38. Ian Haney López, *White by Law: The Legal Construction of Race*, 10th anniversary ed. (New York: New York University Press, 2006), 93.

39. Most histories of racial formation focus on one or the other (top-down or bottom-up), though some include both perspectives. For top-down studies, see Haney López, *White by Law*; Nyan Shah, *Contagious Divides: Epidemics and Race in San Francisco's Chinatown* (Berkeley: University of California Press, 2001); Mae M. Ngai, *Impossible Subjects: Illegal Aliens and the Making of Modern America* (Princeton, NJ: Princeton University Press, 2004); Gross, *What Blood Won't Tell*; Gómez, *Manifest Destinies*; Peggy Pascoe, *What Comes Naturally: Miscegenation Law and the Making of Race in America* (Oxford: Oxford University Press, 2009); and Natalia Molina, *How Race Is Made in America: Immigration, Citizenship, and the Historical Power of Racial Scripts* (Berkeley: University of California Press, 2014). For bottom-up studies, see David R. Roediger, *Wages of Whiteness: Race and the Making of the American Working Class* (New York: Verso Books, 1991); Neil Foley, *White Scourge*; Matthew Frye Jacobson, *Whiteness of a Different Color: Immigrants and the Alchemy of Race* (Cambridge, MA: Harvard University Press, 1999); Claire Jean Kim, *Bitter Fruit: The Politics of Black-Korean Conflict in New York City* (New Haven, CT: Yale University Press, 2000); Thomas A. Guglielmo, *White on Arrival: Italians, Race, Color, and Power in Chicago, 1890–1945* (New York: Oxford University Press, 2004); Laura Pulido, *Black, Brown, Yellow and Left: Radical Activism in Los Angeles* (Berkeley: University of California Press, 2006); Burgos, *Playing America's Game*; Scott Kurashige, *The Shifting Grounds of Race: Black and Japanese Americans in the Making of Multiracial Los Angeles* (Princeton, NJ: Princeton University Press, 2008); Martinez HoSang, *Racial Propositions*; Lilia Fernández, *Brown in the Windy City: Mexicans and Puerto Ricans in Postwar Chicago* (Chicago:

University of Chicago Press, 2012); Song-Ha Lee, *Building a Latino Civil Rights Movement*; and Steptoe, *Houston Bound*.

40. Omi and Winant, *Racial Formation in the United States*.

41. For a wider discussion of the policy debates and decisions that shaped federal recognition of different "minority" groups, see John D. Skrentny, *The Minority Rights Revolution* (Cambridge, MA: Harvard University Press, 2004). An important critique of Skrentny is Kevin R. Johnson, review of *The Minority Rights Revolution*, by John D. Skrentny, *American Journal of Legal History* 47, no. 3 (July 2005): 315–317.

42. Martinez HoSang, *Racial Propositions*, 12. See also Song-Ha Lee, *Building a Latino Civil Rights Movement*, 6; and Omi and Winant, *Racial Formation in the United States*.

43. My understanding of racial formation as relational is informed by Tómas Almaguer, *Racial Fault Lines: The Historical Origins of White Supremacy in California* (Berkeley: University of California Press, 1994); Foley, *White Scourge*; Kim, *Bitter Fruit*; Pulido, *Black, Brown, Yellow, and Left*; Natalia Molina, *Fit to Be Citizens? Public Health and Race in Los Angeles, 1879–1939* (Berkeley: University of California Press, 2006); Kurashige, *Shifting Grounds of Race*; Fernández, *Brown in the Windy City*; Ellen D. Wu, *The Color of Success: Asian Americans and the Origins of the Model Minority* (Princeton, NJ: Princeton University Press, 2014); Molina, *How Race Is Made in America*; Song-Ha Lee, *Building a Latino Civil Rights Movement*; and Steptoe, *Houston Bound*.

44. Eleanor G. Crow, *A Time for Change and Challenge: Civil Rights in Colorado, 1966–1968*, Colorado Civil Rights Commission Activities Report, 1969.

45. Wildman, "Reflections on Whiteness," 311.

CHAPTER 1. (UN)MAKING MEXICAN AMERICAN
RACIAL IDENTITY, 1848–1964

1. "Education for Latins Goal of New Group," *Denver Post*, 15 September 1949, 35.

2. LAEF pamphlet, "Strength for America," n.d., box 1, Bernard Valdez Papers, unprocessed, WH1839, Western History Collection, Denver Public Library, Denver, CO (hereafter WHC-DPL).

3. Newspaper clipping, photograph and caption, "Latin American Foundation in Spotlight," *Rocky Mountain News*, n.d., box 1, Bernard Valdez Papers.

4. Well-known sociologist Julian Samora, who taught at the University of Notre Dame from 1959 to 1985, was born in southern Colorado; attended Adams State Teacher's College in Alamosa, Colorado; and worked with other Mexican Americans in Denver and around the state on a wide range of issues, including education. He was a frequent conference participant and speaker for various Mexican American organizations in Denver in the 1950s and 1960s. Julian Samora for Community Service Clubs, Inc., "An Application to the Boettcher Foundation for Funds in Support of an Adult Education Program among Colorado's Hispanic Citizens,"

n.d., ca. 1953, box 1, Bernard Valdez Papers. For more on Samora and his legacy, see Alberto López Pulido, Barbara Driscoll de Alvarado, and Carmen Samora, eds., *Moving beyond Borders: Julian Samora and the Establishment of Latino Studies* (Urbana: University of Illinois Press, 2009).

5. Stephen J. Pitti, *The Devil in Silicon Valley: Northern California, Race, and Mexican Americans* (Princeton, NJ: Princeton University Press, 2003), 99. See also Carey McWilliams, *North from Mexico: The Spanish-Speaking People of the United States* (Philadelphia: J. B. Lippincott, 1949).

6. Bert Gallegos and Elwood Murray to [local community organizations], n.d., ca. 1950, box 1, Bernard Valdez Papers.

7. Executive Order, Proclamation: Coronado Week, 13–20 August 1950, box 1, Bernard Valdez Papers.

8. George J. Sánchez, *Becoming Mexican American: Ethnicity, Culture, and Identity in Chicano Los Angeles, 1900–1945* (New York: Oxford University Press, 1993); David G. Gutiérrez, *Walls and Mirrors: Mexican Americans, Mexican Immigrants, and the Politics of Ethnicity* (Berkeley: University of California Press, 1995); Pitti, *Devil in Silicon Valley*; Molina, *Fit to Be Citizens?*; Gabriela Arredondo, *Mexican Chicago: Race, Identity, and Nation, 1919–1936* (Urbana: University of Illinois Press, 2008); Lilia Fernández, *Brown in the Windy City: Mexicans and Puerto Ricans in Postwar Chicago* (Chicago: University of Chicago Press, 2012); and Tyina L. Steptoe, *Houston Bound: Culture and Color in a Jim Crow City* (Berkeley: University of California Press, 2015).

9. Richard Tucker, "'Handle for Understanding' Provided: Valdez," *Rocky Mountain News*, 7 May 1966, 42.

10. Denver Area Welfare Council, Inc., "The Spanish-American Population of Denver: An Exploratory Survey," July 1950, 3, folder 10, box 8, Denver Commission on Community Relations Papers, WH903, WHC-DPL (hereafter CCR Papers).

11. Denver Area Welfare Council, "Spanish-American Population of Denver," 6, folder 10, box 8, CCR Papers.

12. Steptoe, *Houston Bound*.

13. "The Spanish American in Denver," Commission on Community Relations internal report, n.d., ca. 1964, 24, folder 1, box 6, CCR Papers. For more on the contested historical memory of Juan de Oñate, see Sarah Horton, "New Mexico's Cuarto Centenario and Spanish-American Nationalism: Collapsing Past Conquests and Present Dispossession," *Journal of the Southwest* 44, no. 1 (2002): 49–60; Phillip B. Gonzales, "History Hits the Heart: Albuquerque's Great Cuartocentenario Controversy, 1997–2005," in *Expressing New Mexico: Nuevomexicano Creativity, Ritual, and Memory*, ed. Phillip B. Gonzales (Tucson: University of Arizona Press, 2007), 207–232; Michael L. Trujillo, *Land of Disenchantment: Latina/o Identities and Transformations in Northern New Mexico* (Albuquerque: University of New Mexico Press, 2009), 27–56; Vanessa Fonseca-Chávez, "Contested Querencia in *The Last Conquistador* (2008) by John J. Valdez and Cristina Ibarra," in *Querencia: Reflections on the New Mexico Homeland*, Vanessa Fonseca-Chávez, Levi Romero, and Spencer R. Herrera (Albuquerque: University of New Mexico Press, 2020), 79–97.

14. Alejandro Lipschütz, *El Indoamericanismo y el Problema Racial en las Americas* (Santiago: Editorial Nascimento, 1944). For an explanation of how pigmentocracy operated in the context of the US Southwest, see Ramón A. Gutiérrez, *When Jesus Came, the Corn Mothers Went Away: Marriage, Sexuality, and Power in New Mexico, 1500–1846* (Stanford, CA: Stanford University Press, 1991). Ian Haney López argues that the logic of racial thinking, particularly as it is codified in the law, has played a prominent role in the physical appearance of our society. He states, "While admittedly laws cannot alter the biology governing human morphology, rule makers can and have altered the human behavior that produces variations in physical appearance. In other words, laws have directly shaped reproductive choices." *White by Law: The Legal Construction of Race*, 10th anniversary ed. (New York: New York University Press, 2006), 11. See also Peggy Pascoe, *What Comes Naturally: Miscegenation Law and the Making of Race in America* (Oxford: Oxford University Press, 2009); and Pablo Mitchell, *Coyote Nation: Sexuality, Race, and Conquest in Modernizing New Mexico, 1880–1920* (Chicago: University of Chicago Press, 2005).

15. Gutiérrez, *When Jesus Came*; Douglas Monroy, *Thrown among Strangers: The Making of Mexican Culture in Frontier California* (Berkeley: University of California Press, 1990); Tomás Almaguer, *Racial Fault Lines: The Historical Origins of White Supremacy in California* (Berkeley: University of California Press, 1994); and Miroslava Chávez-García, *Negotiating Conquest: Gender and Power in California, 1770s to 1880s* (Tucson: University of Arizona Press, 2004).

16. Linda Gordon, *The Great Arizona Orphan Abduction* (Cambridge, MA: Harvard University Press, 1999).

17. Chávez-García, *Negotiating Conquest*, 67. David Montejano similarly observed within Texas that "money whitens." *Anglos and Mexicans in the Making of Texas, 1836–1986* (Austin: University of Texas Press, 1987), 85.

18. McWilliams, *North from Mexico*.

19. Richard Nostrand, "The Hispano Homeland in 1900," *Annals of the Association of American Geographers* 70, no. 3 (1980): 382–396, quotes on 382. See also Richard L. Nostrand, "The Hispanic-American Borderland: Delimitation of an American Culture Region," *Annals of the Association of American Geographers* 60, no. 4 (1970): 638–661; and Richard L. Nostrand, "Mexican Americans circa 1850," *Annals of the Association of American Geographers* 65, no. 3 (1975): 378–390.

20. Nostrand's thesis was intensely debated within the pages of the *Annals of the Association of American Geographers* between 1981 and 1984. Those who disagreed with him questioned his use of terminology without justification, his conflicting evidence, and his methodology. See Niles Hansen, "Commentary: The Hispano Homeland in 1900," *Annals of the Association of American Geographers* 71, no. 2 (1981): 280–282; and J. M. Blaut and Antonio Ríos-Bustamante, "Commentary on Nostrand's 'Hispanos and Their Homeland,'" *Annals of the Association of American Geographers* 74, no. 1 (1984): 157–163.

21. Laura E. Gómez, *Manifest Destinies: The Making of the Mexican American Race* (New York: New York University Press, 2008), 25. Historians have thoroughly

debunked these assertions. See, for example, Deena J. González, *Refusing the Favor: The Spanish-Mexican Women of Santa Fe, 1820–1880* (New York: Oxford University Press, 1999); María E. Montoya, *Translating Property: The Maxwell Land Grant and the Conflict Over Land in the American West, 1840–1900* (Berkeley: University of California Press, 2002); and Anthony Mora, *Border Dilemmas: Racial and National Uncertainties in New Mexico, 1848–1912* (Durham, NC: Duke University Press, 2011).

22. Thomas Hall, "Comment on the Nostrand, Hansen, Nostrand, Blaut and Ríos-Bustamante, Nostrand Debate" (paper presented at the annual meeting of the Western Social Science Association, Fort Worth, Texas, 1985), cited in Sylvia Rodríguez, "The Hispano Homeland Debate Revisited," *Perspectives in Mexican American Studies* 3 (1992): 98.

23. Adrian Bustamante, "Los Hispanos: Ethnicity and Social Change in New Mexico" (PhD diss., University of New Mexico, 1982); John R. Chávez, *The Lost Land: The Chicano Image of the Southwest* (Albuquerque: University of New Mexico Press, 1984); Charles Montgomery, *The Spanish Redemption: Heritage, Power, and Loss on New Mexico's Upper Rio Grande* (Berkeley: University of California Press, 2002); and John M. Nieto-Phillips, *The Language of Blood: The Making of Spanish-American Identity in New Mexico, 1880s–1930s* (Albuquerque: University of New Mexico Press, 2004).

24. Sarah Deutsch, *No Separate Refuge: Culture, Class, and Gender on an Anglo-Hispanic Frontier in the American Southwest, 1880–1940* (New York: Oxford University Press, 1987).

25. Gómez, *Manifest Destinies*, 136–191; and Noel, "'I Am an American': Anglos, Mexicans, *Nativos*, and the National Debate over Arizona and New Mexico Statehood." *Pacific Historical Review* 80, no. 3 (August 2011): 430–467.

26. Phillip B. Gonzales, "'La Junta de Indignación': Hispano Repertoire of Collective Protest in New Mexico, 1884–1933," *Western Historical Quarterly* 31, no. 2 (Summer 2000): 161–186, quotes on 161–162. Also see Nieto-Phillips, *Language of Blood*, 13–14.

27. *El Independiente*, 7 November 1901, translation by John Nieto-Phillips, cited in Nieto-Phillips, *Language of Blood*, 14.

28. See Sharrona Pearl, *About Faces: Physiognomy in Nineteenth-Century Britain* (Cambridge, MA: Harvard University Press, 2010).

29. Chávez, *Lost Land*, 85–106; Nieto-Phillips, *Language of Blood*, 145–205; and Montgomery, *Spanish Redemption*. See also McWilliams, *North from Mexico*.

30. McGregor, "Our Spanish-American Fellow Citizens," *Harper's Weekly*, 20 June 1914, 7. My thanks to John R. Chávez, *Lost Land*, 92 for the source.

31. Enrique Hank Lopez, "Back to Bachimba: A Hyphenated American Discovers That He Can't Go Home Again," *Horizon* 9, no. 1 (Winter 1967): 80.

32. Lopez, "Back to Bachimba," 80. *Manito* is short for *hermanito*, meaning little brother, and was also a term used by many *nuevomexicanos* from northern New Mexico to refer to each other. See Levi Romero, "Following the Manito Trail: A Tale of Two Querencias," in *Querencia: Reflections on the New Mexico Homeland*,

ed. Vanessa Fonseca-Chávez, Levi Romero, and Spencer R. Herrera (Albuquerque: University of New Mexico Press, 2020), 308–324.

33. "The Spanish-Americans in Denver Area Speak," *Rocky Mountain News*, 19 February 1954, newspaper clipping, folder 26, box 11, Rodolfo "Corky" Gonzales Papers, WH1971, WHC-DPL (hereafter Corky Gonzales Papers).

34. Gutiérrez, *Walls and Mirrors*.

35. Mario T. García, "Americans All: The Mexican-American Generation and the Politics of Wartime Los Angeles, 1941–1949," *Social Science Quarterly* 65 (June 1984): 278–289; Mario T. García, *Mexican Americans: Leadership, Ideology, and Identity, 1930–1960* (New Haven, CT: Yale University Press, 1989); Benjamin Márquez, *LULAC: The Evolution of a Mexican American Political Organization* (Austin: University of Texas Press, 1993); Craig A. Kaplowitz, *LULAC, Mexican Americans, and National Policy* (College Station: Texas A&M University Press, 2005); Neil Foley, "Over the Rainbow: *Hernandez v. Texas, Brown v. Board of Education*, and Black v. Brown," in *"Colored Men" and "Hombres Aquí": Hernandez v. Texas and the Emergence of Mexican-American Lawyering*, ed. Michael A. Olivas (Houston: Arte Público Press, University of Houston Press, 2006), 111-122; and Carlos Kevin Blanton, *George I. Sánchez: The Long Fight for Mexican American Integration* (New Haven, CT: Yale University Press, 2014), 145–162.

36. Minutes, Spanish American Advisory Committee Meeting to the Denver Commission on Community Relations, 23 October 1963, 1, folder 33, box 1, CCR Papers; and Metropolitan Council for Community Service, Inc., "Report on the Latin American Research and Service Agency," May 1964, 5, folder 20, box 48, Latin American Research and Service Agency Records, WH1842, WHC-DPL (hereafter LARASA Records).

37. Ariela J. Gross, *What Blood Won't Tell: A History of Race on Trial in America* (Cambridge, MA: Harvard University Press, 2008).

38. See Michael Omi and Howard Winant, "Ethnicity," in *Racial Formation in the United States*, 3rd ed. (New York: Routledge, 2015), 21–51.

39. Gutiérrez, *Walls and Mirrors*.

40. Julie A. Dowling, *Mexican Americans and the Question of Race* (Austin: University of Texas Press, 2014).

41. María Elena Martínez, *Genealogical Fictions: Limpieza De Sangre, Religion, and Gender in Colonial Mexico* (Stanford, CA: Stanford University Press, 2008); and Ben Vinson III, *Before Mestizaje: The Frontiers of Race and Caste in Colonial Mexico* (New York: Cambridge University Press, 2018). For an examination of the operation of antiblackness in contemporary Mexico, see Christina A. Sue's ethnographic study of Veracruz, *Land of the Cosmic Race: Race Mixture, Racism, and Blackness in Mexico* (New York: Oxford University Press, 2013).

42. Ellen Schrecker, *Many Are the Crimes: McCarthyism in America* (New York: Little Brown, 1998); Mary L. Dudziak, *Cold War Civil Rights: Race and the Image of American Democracy* (Princeton, NJ: Princeton University Press, 2000); and Thomas J. Sugrue, *Sweet Land of Liberty: The Forgotten Struggle for Civil Rights in the North* (New York: Random House, 2009).

43. Although Rachel Noel, a Black woman, was one of LARASA's founding members, it is likely that she left the construction of the group's philosophical framework and identity to Mexican Americans. A program from a 1987 recognition of LARASA founders lists Noel as one of the founders. "Founder's Recognition," 13 September 1987, 4, folder 111, box 20, LARASA Records.

44. Daniel T. Valdes, "Spanish-Origin Citizens: People without a Name," *Denver Post*, 5 September 1965, 19.

45. Blanton, *George I. Sánchez*. See also Benjamin H. Johnson, "The Cosmic Race in Texas: Racial Fusion, White Supremacy, and Civil Rights Politics in Texas," *Journal of American History* 98, no. 2 (September 2011): 414–418; and Gabriela González, *Redeeming La Raza: Transborder Modernity, Race, Respectability, and Rights* (New York: Oxford University Press, 2018), 167–189. For an alternative reading of George I. Sánchez's racial politics, see Neil Foley, *Quest for Equality: The Failed Promise of Black-Brown Solidarity* (Cambridge, MA: Harvard University Press, 2010).

46. The Naturalization Act of 1790 established that only "free white persons" could become naturalized citizens. With the passage of the Fourteenth Amendment in 1868, Blacks were also eligible for naturalization. Legally, then, after 1868 one needed to be either White or Black to qualify. Naturalization Act of 1790, 1 Stat. 103 (1790); and Haney López, *White by Law*.

47. Gross, *What Blood Won't Tell*, 254.

48. Omi and Winant define a racial project as "simultaneously an interpretation, representation, or explanation of racial identities and meanings, and an effort to organize and distribute resources (economic, political, cultural) along particular racial lines." *Racial Formation in the United States*, 125.

49. Guadalupe San Miguel Jr., *"Let All of Them Take Heed": Mexican Americans and the Campaign for Educational Equality in Texas, 1910–1981* (Austin: University of Texas Press, 1987); Gilbert G. Gonzalez, *Chicano Education in the Era of Segregation* (Philadelphia: Balch Institute Press, 1990); and Steven H. Wilson, "*Brown* over 'Other White': Mexican Americans' Legal Arguments and Litigation Strategy in School Desegregation Lawsuits," *Law and History Review* 21, no. 1 (Spring 2003): 145–194.

50. Rubén Donato, *Mexicans and Hispanos in Colorado Schools and Communities, 1920–1960* (Albany: State University of New York Press, 2007).

51. Joe Belden, "Minority of Texans Favors Separation for Latin Students," *Austin American-Statesman*, 9 June 1950, Texas State Library and Archives Commission, Austin, Archives and Information Services Division, Records, TGNC box 1989/59-18, cited in Gross, *What Blood Won't Tell*, 269.

52. Anonymous interview conducted by Rubén Donato, October 1998, quoted in Donato, *Mexicans and Hispanos*, 94.

53. Donato, *Mexicans and Hispanos*, 71.

54. Carey McWilliams, "Is Your Name Gonzales?," *Nation*, 15 March 1947, 302.

55. Wilson, "*Brown* over 'Other White,'" 155.

56. Independent School District v. Salvatierra, 33 S.W. 2d 790 (Tex. Civ. App., 1930). A similar case was filed in San Diego in 1930. See *Roberto Alvarez vs. the*

Board of Trustees of the Lemon Grove School District* (1931) (commonly known as the Lemon Grove Incident). For more, see Robert R. Alvarez Jr., "The Lemon Grove Incident: The Nation's First Successful Desegregation Court Case," *Journal of San Diego History* 32, no. 2 (Spring 1986), https://sandiegohistory.org/journal/1986/april/lemongrove/. Also see Wilson, "*Brown* over 'Other White'"; Kristi L. Bowman, "The New Face of School Desegregation," *Duke Law Journal* 50, no. 6 (April 2001): 1751–1808; and Margaret E. Montoya, "A Brief History of Chicana/o School Segregation: One Rational for Affirmative Action," *Berkeley La Raza Law Journal* 12, no. 2 (Fall 2001): 159–172. A milestone case was *Mendez v. Westminster*, litigation filed on behalf of Mexican and Mexican American children in Orange County, California. See Mendez v. Westminster School District, 64 F. Supp. 544 (S.D. Cal. 1946), and Westminster School District of Orange County v. Mendez, 161 F.2d 774 (9th Cir., 1947). See also Gonzalez, *Chicano Education in the Era of Segregation*; Vicki L. Ruiz, "South by Southwest: Mexican Americans and Segregated Schooling, 1900–1950," *OAH Magazine of History* 15, no. 2 (Winter 2001): 23–27; Richard Kluger, *Simple Justice: The History of* Brown v. Board of Education *and Black America's Struggle for Equality*, rev. ed. (New York: Vintage Books, 2004), 399–400; Jeanne M. Powers and Lirio Patton, "Between *Mendez* and *Brown*: *Gonzales v. Sheely* (1951) and the Legal Campaign against Segregation," *Law and Social Inquiry* 33, no. 1 (Winter 2008): 127–171; Philippa Strum, *Mendez v. Westminster: School Desegregation and Mexican-American Rights* (Lawrence: University Press of Kansas, 2010); and Mark Brilliant, *The Color of America Has Changed: How Racial Diversity Shaped Civil Rights Reform in California, 1941–1978* (Oxford: Oxford University Press, 2010), 58–88.

57. See In re Rodriguez, 81 F. 337 (W.D. Tex., 1897), which legal historian Steven Wilson calls "the beginning of the Mexican American civil rights canon." Wilson, "*Brown* over 'Other White,'" 152. See also Haney López, *White by Law*; and Martha Menchaca, *Naturalizing Mexican Immigrants: A Texas History* (Austin: University of Texas Press, 2011), 109–159.

58. Sanchez v. State, 243 S.W.2d. 700, 701 (Tex. Crim. App. 1951). See also Salazar v. State, 193 S.W.2d 211 (Tex. Crim. App. 1946). For more on these two cases, as well as others, see Claire Sheridan, "'Another White Race': Mexican Americans and the Paradox of Whiteness in Jury Selection," *Law and History Review* 21, no. 1 (Spring 2003): 109–144; Gross, *What Blood Won't Tell*, 280–281; and Ignacio M. García, *White but Not Equal: Mexican Americans, Jury Discrimination, and the Supreme Court* (Tucson: University of Arizona Press, 2008), 84–95.

59. Ariela J. Gross, "'The Caucasian Cloak': Mexicans Americans and the Politics of Whiteness in the Twentieth Century Southwest," *Georgetown Law Journal* 95, no. 2 (January 2007): 337–392; and Gross, *What Blood Won't Tell*, 253–293.

60. Hernandez v. Texas, 347 U.S. 475 (1954). See also Sheridan, "'Another White Race'"; Ariela J. Gross, "Texas Mexicans and the Politics of Whiteness," *Law and History Review* 21, no. 1 (Spring 2003): 195–205; Wilson, "*Brown* over 'Other White,'"161–164; García, *White but Not Equal*; and Gross, *What Blood Won't Tell*, 253–293. See also the edited volume on *Hernandez* by Michael A. Olivas, ed.

"Colored Men" and "Hombres Aquí": Hernandez v. Texas *and the Emergence of Mexican-American Lawyering* (Houston: Arte Público Press, University of Houston Press, 2006).

61. Wilson, "*Brown* over 'Other White,'" 164; and Gross, *What Blood Won't Tell*, 288.

62. García, *White but Not Equal*. Also see Thomas A. Guglielmo, "Fighting for Caucasian Rights: Mexicans, Mexican Americans, and the Transnational Struggle for Civil Rights in World War II Texas," *Journal of American History* 92, no. 4 (March 2006): 1212–1237; and Lorena Oropeza, *¡Raza Sí! ¡Guerra No! Chicano Protest and Patriotism during the Viet Nam Era* (Berkeley: University of California Press, 2005), 11–46.

CHAPTER 2. RACIAL MIGRATIONS

1. Art Branscombe, "Valdez Puts Hispano Goals on Scales," *Denver Post*, 4 April 1976, 20.

2. Branscombe, "Valdez Puts Hispano Goals on Scales," 20.

3. Mile High Chapter 7, "Bernard Valdez," *Colorado Civilian Conservation Core* (blog), accessed 15 September 2017, https://coloradoccc.org/people/bernard-valdez/.

4. Biographical Note, Bernard Valdez Papers, 1949–2007, WH1839, WHC-DPL.

5. Branscombe, "Valdez Puts Hispano Goals on Scales," 20.

6. "Rachel Noel (1918–2007)," Denver Public Library, accessed 15 September 2017, https://history.denverlibrary.org/rachel-noel-1918-2008.

7. He was the first Black doctor employed by a Denver hospital. "Rachel Noel (1918–2007)."

8. Noel was also the first Black woman in the state of Colorado to be elected to public office. "Rachel Noel (1918–2007)."

9. "Rachel Noel (1918–2007)"; and Resolution 1490, Denver Board of Education, 25 April 1968, folder 6, box 1, Rachel Noel Papers, ARL117, Blair-Caldwell African American Research Library, Denver Public Library (hereafter BCAARL).

10. Phil Goodstein, *Denver in Our Time*, vol. 1, *Big Money in the Big City: A People's History of the Modern Mile High City* (Denver: New Social Publications, 1999), 32; Population Figures, US Census, received from the Denver Regional Council of Governments (DRCOG), n.d., folder 35, box 51, William McNichols Papers, WH1015, WHC-DPL.

11. Robert L. Perkin, *The First Hundred Years: An Informal History of Denver and the Rocky Mountain News* (Garden City, NY: Doubleday, 1959), 575. Perkin cited a report published by the City of Houston Planning Office in 1957. Denver's population grew 37.5 percent; Houston, at 41 percent, ranked second; and San Diego, at 55 percent, ranked first.

12. Perkin, *First Hundred Years*, 571–573.

13. Frederick D. Watson, "Removing the Barricades from the Northern Schoolhouse Door: School Desegregation in Denver" (PhD diss., University of Colorado, 1993), 9.

14. James Patrick Walsh, "Young and Latino in a Cold War Barrio: Survival, the Search for Identity, and the Formation of Street Gangs in Denver, 1945–1955" (MA thesis, University of Colorado at Denver, 1996), 26.

15. Walsh, "Young and Latino in a Cold War Barrio," 26. See also Sarah Deutsch, *No Separate Refuge: Culture, Class, and Gender on an Anglo-Hispanic Frontier in the American Southwest, 1880–1940* (New York: Oxford University Press, 1987), 132.

16. Watson, "Removing the Barricades," 7; and "Colorado Population Statistics, Estimated Population by Counties and Minority Group Classifications, 1969 Estimates," table I, in Eleanor G. Crow, *A Time for Change and Challenge: Civil Rights in Colorado, 1966–1969* (Colorado Civil Rights Commission, December 1969). The metropolitan area had a total population of 1,229,798, of which 4.1 percent was Black and 11.3 percent was Mexican American. The total minority population of Metro Denver was 16.8 percent. Population Figures, US Census, folder 35, box 51, William McNichols Papers.

17. According to Robert Harvey, many of the former internees settled near the Larimer area of Denver. Although the Japanese and Japanese American population was only about 323 in 1940, in 1946 it was over 3,000. *Amache: The Story of Japanese Internment in Colorado during World War II* (Dallas, TX: Taylor Trade Publishing, 2004), 191.

18. Between 1952 and 1971, 6,144 relocation applicants were processed by the Field Relocation Office in Denver. Another 2,490 job training applicants applied for the Adult Vocational Training program in the city. Azusa Ono, "The Relocation and Employment Assistance Programs, 1948–1970: Federal Indian Policy and the Early Development of the Denver Indian Community," *Indigenous Nations Studies Journal* 5, no. 1 (Spring 2004): 27–50.

19. Stephen J. Leonard and Thomas J. Noel, *Denver: Mining Camp to Metropolis* (Boulder: University Press of Colorado, 1990).

20. Gregory J. Hobbs Jr. "Personal Memoir: Judge William E. Doyle and Governor Ralph L. Carr: Peers for Equal Justice," *Denver University Law Review* 90, no. 5 (2013): 1133.

21. Lionel Dean Lyles, "An Historical-Urban Geographical Analysis of Black Neighborhood Development in Denver, 1860–1970," (PhD diss., University of Colorado at Boulder, 1977), 92–93. Lyles's work shows that in general, the farther the neighborhood was from the city core, the fewer Black residences there were. These areas had between one and twelve separate Black households. See figure 18, "Black Households in Denver, 1941," p. 96.

22. Lyle Dorsett, *The Queen City: A History of Denver*, 2nd ed. (Boulder, CO: Pruett Publishing, 1985), 103–107; James Harvey, "Negroes in Colorado" (MA thesis, University of Denver, 1941), 41–67; Lyles, "Historical-Urban Geographical Analysis," 75–77; and George H. Wayne, "Negro Migration and Colonization in Colorado, 1870–1930," *Journal of the West* 15, no. 1 (January 1976): 102–120.

23. Fred O. Ford, "History of Migrant Labor in Colorado," 60th Annual Conference of Social Welfare Panel on Migrant Labor, 11 October 1950, 3, folder 20, box 5, CCR Papers; and Paul S. Taylor, *Mexican Labor in the United States, Valley of the South Platte, Colorado*, University of California Publications in Economics vol. 6, no. 2 (Berkeley: University of California Press, 1929), 110–111.

24. Samuel Liss to Allan Hurst, Chairman, Governor's Committee on Migrant Labor, 16 August 1950, 1, box 5, folder 20, CCR Papers.

25. "General Statement and Historical Background of the Spanish-Speaking People in Denver," 1947, 3, folder 15, box 8, CCR Papers.

26. Brian Page and Eric Ross, "Envisioning the Urban Past: GIS Reconstruction of a Lost Denver District," *Frontiers in Digital Humanities* 2 (August 2015): 3, https://doi.org/10.3389/fdigh.2015.00003.

27. Magdalena Gallegos, "The Forgotten Community: Hispanic Auraria in the Twentieth Century," *Colorado Heritage* 2 (1985): 5–20.

28. Page and Ross, "Envisioning the Urban Past," 4.

29. Gallegos, "The Forgotten Community."

30. On migrations to major cities during and after the war and the housing crises these migrations helped create, see Thomas J. Sugrue, *The Origins of the Urban Crisis: Race and Inequality in Postwar Detroit* (Princeton, NJ: Princeton University Press, 1996); Arnold R. Hirsch, *Making the Second Ghetto: Race and Housing in Chicago, 1940–1960* (Chicago: University of Chicago Press, 1998); Robert O. Self, *American Babylon: Race and the Struggle for Postwar Oakland* (Princeton, NJ: Princeton University Press, 2003); Todd M. Michney, "Constrained Communities: Black Cleveland's Experience with World War II Public Housing," *Journal of Social History* 40, no. 4 (Summer 2007): 933–956; Donna Jean Murch, *Living for the City: Migration, Education, and the Rise of the Black Panther Party in Oakland, California* (Chapel Hill: University of North Carolina Press, 2010); Lilia Fernández, *Brown in the Windy City: Mexicans and Puerto Ricans in Postwar Chicago* (Chicago: University of Chicago Press, 2012); and Tyina L. Steptoe, *Houston Bound: Culture and Color in a Jim Crow City* (Berkeley: University of California Press, 2015).

31. Quoted in Leonard and Noel, *Denver*, 391–392.

32. Richard Gould, *The Life and Times of Richard Castro: Bridging the Cultural Divide* (Denver: The Colorado Historical Society, 2007), 72–76, 82.

33. "Consumers for Fair Employment Launched," *All Told*, official newsletter of the Denver Coordinating Council for Education and Research in Human Relations, 26 November 1957, 1, folder 3, box 1, CCR Papers.

34. Perkin, *First Hundred Years*, 572; and Goodstein, *Denver in Our Time*, 1:16.

35. Denver Department of Public Welfare, "The 'Spanish-American Problem,'" 28 February 1956, 1, folder 22, box 5, CCR Papers.

36. Crow, *Time for Change and Challenge*, 23.

37. At that time, poverty was defined as a family of four living on $3,000 or less a year. Crow, *Time for Change and Challenge*, 23.

38. Gould, *Life and Times of Richard Castro*, 82-83.

39. Denver Area Welfare Council, Inc., "The Spanish-Speaking Population of Denver: An Exploratory Study," July 1950, 10–11, 15, folder 10, box 8, CCR Papers.

40. Memo, Commission on Community Relations, n.d., 2, folder 18, box 1, CCR Papers; and Phil Goodstein, *Denver in Our Time*, vol. 2, *DIA and Other Scams* (Denver: New Social Publications, 2000), 178.

41. Lyles, "Historical-Urban Geographical Analysis," 127.

42. Kenneth T. Jackson, *Crabgrass Frontier: The Suburbanization of the United States* (New York: Oxford University Press, 1985); Sugrue, *Origins of the Urban Crisis*; Hirsch, *Making the Second Ghetto*; Kevin M. Kruse, *White Flight: Atlanta and the Making of Modern Conservatism* (Princeton, NJ: Princeton University Press, 2005), chs. 2 and 3; Carl Nightingale, *Segregation: A Global History of Divided Cities* (Chicago: University of Chicago Press, 2012), 7; and Ansley T. Erickson, *Making the Unequal Metropolis: School Desegregation and Its Limits* (Chicago: University of Chicago Press, 2016).

43. Tom I. Romero II, "*Kelo, Parents* and the Spatialization of Color (Blindness) in the *Berman-Brown* Metropolitan Heterotopia," *Utah Law Review* 3 (2008): 953.

44. *Chandler v. Zielger*, 81 Colo. 1, 5 (1930), as cited in Tom I. Romero Jr., "Of Race and Rights: Legal Culture, Social Change, and the Making of a Multiracial Metropolis, Denver 1940–975" (PhD diss., University of Michigan, 2004), 52.

45. Romero, "Of Race and Rights," 52–53.

46. "Realtors Profit from 'Ghetto': Denver Inquirer Feature; 'People Are Talking . . . ,'" *Denver Inquirer*, 23 February 1953, folder 4, box 2, Keyes (Wilfred) v. Denver School District Records, 1969–1986, Accession 1, COU: 931, University of Colorado Boulder Libraries, Special Collection, Archives and Preservation Department, Boulder, Colorado (hereafter Keyes Records).

47. Mrs. Kenneth Whiting, "The Picture of Housing in Denver, 1955–1962," speech given at the Coordinating Council luncheon, 16 October 1962, folder 5, box 2, CCR Papers.

48. "Realtors Profit from 'Ghetto,'" *Denver Inquirer*, 23 February 1953, folder 4, box 2, Keyes Records.

49. Edward Miller to Edward Rothstein, 30 November 1955, 1–2, folder 4, box 2, Keyes Records.

50. Stirling Kahn, interview by Stan Oliner, videotape, 23 March 1994, Colorado Historical Society [now History Colorado], as cited in Gould, *Life and Times of Richard Castro*, 84.

51. "General Statement and Historical Background of the Spanish-Speaking People in Denver," 1947, 37–38, folder 15, box 8, CCR Papers.

52. "General Statement and Historical Background," 34, folder 15, box 8, CCR Papers.

53. Paul Sandoval, interview with Richard Gould, tape recording, Denver, Colorado, 25 May 1994, in Gould, *Life and Times of Richard Castro*, 86 (emphasis in original).

54. "A Report of Minorities in Denver with Recommendations," ca. 1948, 16–17, folder 1, box 1, CCR Papers.

55. Whiting, "Picture of Housing in Denver," folder 5, box 2, CCR Papers. Historians have shown that by World War II, Jews had transformed from "in-between peoples" to Whites. By mid-century they were fully assimilated into American life and able to take advantage of the benefits of whiteness, including homeownership in racially restricted areas. James R. Barrett and David Roediger, "Inbetween Peoples: Race, Nationality, and the 'New Immigrant' Working Class," *Journal of American Ethnic History* 16, no. 3 (Spring 1997): 3–44. See also Matthew Frye Jacobson, *Whiteness of a Different Color: Immigrants and the Alchemy of Race* (Cambridge, MA: Harvard University Press, 1999); Karen Brodkin, *How Jews Became White Folks and What That Says about Race in America* (New Brunswick, NJ: Rutgers University Press, 1998); and David Roediger, *Working toward Whiteness: How America's Immigrants Became White; The Strange Journey from Ellis Island to the Suburbs* (New York: Basic Books, 2005). For insights into Jewish experiences of discrimination and violence in early-twentieth century Denver, see Michael Lee, "Dirty Jew-Dirty Mexican: Denver's 1949 Lake Junior High School Gang Battle and Jewish Racial Identity in Colorado," *Ethnic Studies Review* 35 (2012): 135–155.

56. "Racial Bias Wanes: More People Willing to Sell Homes to Anyone," *Denver Post*, 2 September 1954, folder 4, box 2, Keyes Records. The study consisted of telephone interviews with 101 individual homeowners in White neighborhoods with home values ranging from $6,000 to $40,000.

57. "Racial Bias Wanes," *Denver Post*, 2 September 1954, folder 4, box 2, Keyes Records.

58. "Racial Bias Wanes," *Denver Post*, 2 September 1954, folder 4, box 2, Keyes Records.

59. "General Statement and Historical Background," 31, folder 15, box 8, CCR Papers.

60. "General Statement and Historical Background," 37, folder 15, box 8, CCR Papers

61. Edward Rothstein to Edward Miller, 30 November 1955, 1, folder 4, box 2, Keyes Records.

62. "General Statement and Historical Background," 32, folder 15, box 8, CCR Papers.

63. James F. Reynolds, "A Neighborhood Survey in a Residential Section of Denver, Colorado," report for the Mayor's Commission on Community Relations, 1963, 2, folder 1, box 1, Rachel Noel Papers.

64. Metro Denver Fair Housing Center, Inc., "Report of the Executive Director," 31 December 1969, 5, folder 13, box 51, William McNichols Papers.

65. Gould, *Life and Times of Richard Castro*, 39.

66. "The Spanish American in Denver," folder 1, box 6, CCR Papers.

67. "Spanish American in Denver," folder 1, box 6, CCR Papers.

68. Edward J. Escobar, *Race, Police, and the Making of Political Identity: Mexican Americans and the Los Angeles Police Department, 1900–1945* (Berkeley: University of California Press, 1999); and Elizabeth Escobedo, *From Coveralls to Zoot Suits:*

The Lives of Mexican American Women on the World War II Homefront (Chapel Hill: University of North Carolina Press, 2013).

69. "Toward the Full American Dream," *Rocky Mountain News*, 12 May 1955, 44.

70. "Denver Next Black Mecca," *Denver Blade*, 18 February 1969. See also the first installment of this story, "Denver Next Black Mecca," *Denver Blade*, 14 February 1969.

71. "Smashing against the Invisible Wall," Editorial, *Denver Post*, 17 April 1949, folder 5, box 2, Keyes Records.

72. "Smashing against the Invisible Wall," *Denver Post*, 17 April 1949, folder 5, box 2, Keyes Records.

73. "Smashing against the Invisible Wall," *Denver Post*, 17 April 1949, folder 5, box 2, Keyes Records.

74. Whiting, "Picture of Housing in Denver," folder 5, box 2, CCR Papers.

75. Charles Gray, "Initial Report: Survey of Negro Opinion on Housing Problems and Negro Housing Demand," in cooperation with the Denver Coordinating Council for Education and Research in Human Relations, 16 August 1958, 3, folder 1, box 2, CCR Papers.

76. Meeting Minutes, Commission on Community Relations, 27 February 1961, 2, folder 26, box 1, CCR Papers; Whiting, "Picture of Housing in Denver," folder 5, box 2, CCR Papers; and Goodstein, *Denver in Our Time*, 2:62.

CHAPTER 3. PUBLIC SCHOOLS IN DENVER'S
RACIALIZED URBAN GEOGRAPHY

1. Phil Goodstein, *Denver in Our Time*, vol. 2, *DIA and Other Scams* (Denver: New Social Publications, 2000), 49–50.

2. Jessica Pearson and Jeffrey Pearson, "Keyes v. School District No. 1," in *Limits of Justice: The Courts' Role in School Desegregation*, ed. Howard I. Kalodner and James F. Fishman (Cambridge, MA: Ballinger Publishing, 1978), 167–222; Frederick D. Watson, "Removing the Barricades from the Northern Schoolhouse Door: School Desegregation in Denver" (PhD diss., University of Colorado at Boulder, 1993); Sharon Ruth Brown-Bailey, "Journey Full Circle: A Historical Analysis of *Keyes v. School District No. 1*" (PhD diss., University of Colorado at Denver, 1998); and Goodstein, *Denver in Our Time*, vol. 2.

3. Historians have identified a similar construction, the "Mexican Problem," in several other places, but the process whereby Anglos developed or adopted this racial script looks slightly different in each locale. Carey McWilliams, *North from Mexico: The Spanish-Speaking People of the United States* (Philadelphia: J. B. Lippincott, 1949), 206–226; David Montejano, *Anglos and Mexicans in the Making of Texas, 1836–1986* (Austin: University of Texas Press, 1987), 179–196; George J. Sanchez, *Becoming Mexican American: Ethnicity, Culture, and Identity in Chicano Los Angeles, 1900–1945* (New York: Oxford University Press, 1993); Gilbert G. Gonzalez, "The 'Mexican Problem': Empire, Public Policy, and the Education of Mexican

Immigrants, 1880–1930," *Aztlán* 26, no. 2 (Fall 2001): 199–207; Robert L. Treviño, "Facing Jim Crow: Catholic Sisters and the 'Mexican Problem' in Texas," *Western Historical Quarterly* 34 (Summer 2003): 139–164; Gabriela Arredondo, *Mexican Chicago: Race, Identity, and Nation, 1919–1936* (Urbana: University of Illinois Press, 2008), 80–107; Cynthia Orozco, *No Mexicans, Women, or Dogs Allowed: The Rise of the Mexican American Civil Rights Movement* (Austin: University of Texas Press, 2009), 59; and Joseph L. Locke, "The Heathen at Our Door: Missionaries, Moral Reformers, and the Making of the 'Mexican Problem,'" *Western Historical Quarterly* 49 (Summer 2018): 127–153.

4. Michael Lee, "Dirty Jew-Dirty Mexican: Denver's 1949 Lake Junior High School Gang Battle and Jewish Racial Identity in Colorado," *Ethnic Studies Review* 35 (2012): 137–139.

5. Meeting Minutes, Meeting Held Concerning "Lake Junior High Incident" Reported in the *Rocky Mountain News*, 3 October 1949, 4, folder 27, box 8, CCR Papers.

6. "Garden Hose Cools Fighting Spirit: Gang Battle at School Broken Up by Woman," *Rocky Mountain News*, 1 October 1949, 22.

7. Meeting Minutes, Mayor's Committee on Human Relations, 11 October 1949, 1, folder 3, box 1, CCR Papers; Louis L. Sidman to Nathan Perlmutter, 4 October 1949, folder 3, box 6, CCR Papers; and J. Peter Brunswick to CCR Staff, confidential re: Lake Junior High School Incident, 4 October 1949, folder 3, box 6, CCR Papers.

8. Lee, "Dirty Jew-Dirty Mexican," 142.

9. Natalia Molina, *How Race Is Made in America: Immigration, Citizenship, and the Historical Power of Racial Scripts* (Oakland: University of California Press, 2014), 7.

10. Denver Area Welfare Council, Inc., "The Spanish-American Population of Denver: An Exploratory Survey," July 1950, 105–106, folder 10, box 8, CCR Papers.

11. Daryl Michael Scott, "Postwar Pluralism, *Brown v. Board of Education*, and the Origins of Multicultural Education," *Journal of American History* (June 2004): 71; and Leah N. Gordon, *From Power to Prejudice: The Rise of Racial Individualism in Midcentury America* (Chicago: University of Chicago Press, 2015).

12. Gordon, *From Power to Prejudice*.

13. Tom I. Romero, II, "Our Selma Is Here: The Political and Legal Struggle for Educational Equality in Denver, Colorado, and Multiracial Conundrums in American Jurisprudence," *Seattle Journal for Social Justice* 3, no. 1 (Fall/Winter 2004): 75. Romero covers DPS's adoption of cultural pluralism, which some advocates called the "Denver Experiment," on 77–80.

14. Neil Foley, *The White Scourge: Mexicans, Blacks, and Poor Whites in Texas Cotton Culture* (Berkeley: University of California Press, 1997).

15. Similar practices existed in other parts of Colorado. See Ruben Donato, *Mexicans and Hispanos in Colorado Schools and Communities, 1920–1960* (Albany: State University of New York Press, 2007), 70–81.

16. LARASA, "Recommendations of the Latin American Research and Service Agency to the Denver Board of Education and the Denver Public School System:

The Goals and Objectives of the Chicano Community and Their Impact on the Denver Public Schools," ca. 1974, folder "LARASA," box 21, unprocessed, Polly Baca Papers, WH1793, DPL-WHG; Mexican American Legal Defense and Educational Fund, "Intervenor's Memorandum with Respect to Minority Teacher Employment and Bilingual-Multicultural Education," *Keyes v. School Dist. No. 1*, Civil Action No. C-1499, US District Court for the District of Colorado, 4 April 1974, 4, no. 14, book 3, box 25, Keyes Records.

17. Manuel Gomez (Chairman, LARASA Education Committee) to Don Hefley (President, Denver Classroom Teachers Association), 4 May 1973, 2, folder "LARASA," box 21, unprocessed, Polly Baca Papers.

18. Cindy [Trujillo] and Cheri Trujillo, letter to the editor, *West Side Recorder* 6, no. 1 (May 1969), 2.

19. "South Pupils Ask Removal of Principal," *Rocky Mountain News*, 30 October 1970, 7, newspaper clipping in scrapbook (September–November 1970), folder 19, box 12, Corky Gonzales Papers.

20. Table, "Elementary Faculty, Racial Composition, 1963–68, Number," Plaintiffs' Exhibit 244, 2055a–2056a; Table, "Junior High Faculty, Racial Composition, 1963–68, Number," Plaintiffs' Exhibit 304, 2082a; Table, "Senior High Faculty, Racial Composition, 1963–68, Number," Plaintiffs' Exhibit 275, 2075a, all in *Keyes v. School Dist. No. 1*, Appendix, Supreme Court of the United States, October Term 1971, No. 71-507, Vol. 5. Note: the tables for junior high and senior high faculty are mislabeled. The table with the title for junior high faculty is actually for senior high faculty, and the table for senior high faculty is actually for junior high faculty.

21. LARASA, "Proposal to the Denver Board of Education to Activate the Hispano Advisory Committee," 1973, 1, folder "LARASA," box 21, unprocessed, Polly Baca Papers.

22. The Joint City-Schools Program was also affiliated with the Commission on Community Relations and included DPS staff members and representatives from various community organizations. James A. Atkins, *Human Relations in Colorado: A Historical Record* (Denver: Colorado Department of Education, Division of Elementary and Secondary Education, Office of Instructional Services, 1968), 163.

23. Joint City-School Project, "Some Problems Related to the Membership of Spanish Children and Youth in the Denver Public Schools," 24 February 1956, folder 22, box 5, CCR Papers. Another, more comprehensive report on minorities in Denver maintained a similar stance in regard to the educational problems of Mexican American students. Denver Commission on Human Relations, *Inventory of Human Relations, 1954–1955: Summaries and Recommendations*, in Cooperation with the Anti-Defamation League of B'Nai B'Rith, the Denver Urban League, Japanese American Citizens League, Adult Education Council, Anti-Discrimination Division of the State Industrial Commission, Western District of the National Conference of Christians and Jews, State Employment Service, League of United Latin American Citizens, and the United Packinghouse Workers of America (1955), 164–216.

24. Denver Board of Education, Minutes of Meeting, 23 April 1970, 19–20.

25. During this period bilingual/bicultural education was promoted by Latina/o education advocates around the nation, who understood it to be a curriculum that integrated and valued the Spanish language as well as Latina/o perspectives, histories, and culture. A 1975 special issue of *Inequality in Education* that focused on bilingual/bicultural education stated that it was "a process of total self-development by which a person learns and reinforces his or her own language and culture while at the same time acquiring the ability to function in another language and behave on occasion according to the patterns of the second culture." Alex Rodriguez, "Introduction," *Inequality in Education,* no. 19 (February 1975): 4.

26. Rana Sharif, "The Right to Education: From La Frontera to Gaza: A Brief Communication," *American Quarterly* 62, no. 4 (December 2010): 857.

27. Martin Moran, "Race Was Never a Factor, Ex-Superintendent Says," *Rocky Mountain News*, 18 February 1970, folder 6, box 2, Keyes Records.

28. Denver Commission on Human Relations, *Inventory of Human Relations*, 168.

29. Oberholtzer maintained that native ability, home environment, the educational level of the parents, the motivation of students, and income level were all contributors, just not race. Moran, "Race Was Never Factor, Ex-Superintendent Says," folder 6, box 2, Keyes Records. Gilberts argued socioeconomic background was the major factor contributing to the lower scores of students in minority schools. Robert D. Gilberts Testimony, Hearing on Preliminary Injunction, *Keyes v. School Dist. No. 1*, 17 July 1969, 289.

30. These classes were called Educable Mentally Retarded (EMR). Brief of Appellee-Plaintiff-Intervenor Congress of Hispanic Educators, *Keyes v. School Dist. No. 1*, US Court of Appeals for the Tenth Circuit, Nos. 74-1349, 74-1350 and 74-1351, 15 October 1974, 21-22, book 3, box 26, Keyes Records. See also Mary Ellen Leary, "Children Who Are Tested in an Alien Language: Mentally Retarded?," *New Republic*, 30 May 1970, 17–18.

31. Congress of Hispanic Educators, in consultation with Dr. Jose. A. Cardenas, "Addendum to the Intervenor's Education Plan for the Denver Public Schools," 5 February 1974, 23–24, no. 55, book 2, box 25, Keyes Records.

32. Brief of Appellee-Plaintiff-Intervenor Congress of Hispanic Educators, *Keyes v. School Dist. No. 1*, US Court of Appeals for the Tenth Circuit, Nos. 74-1349, 74-1350, 74-1351, 15 October 1974, 17, book 3, box 26, Keyes Records.

33. "Elmwood: A West Side Tragedy," *West Side Recorder* 6, no. 9 (January 1970), 3.

34. "Elmwood," 3.

35. Appendix III: Pupil Dropout Rates, *Keyes v. School Dist. No. 1*, 313 F. Supp. 61, 89 (D. Colo. 1970); Tentative Draft, "A Proposal for Community Involvement in a Desegregated School System, Denver, Colorado," prepared by the Commission on Community Relations for the Emergency School Assistance Program, 1 December 1970, 12, folder 2, box 2, Keyes Records; "Table 4: Estimated Student Dropouts for Anglo and Chicano Student Populations in the Denver Public Schools," attached to letter, Manuel Gomez (Chairman, LARASA Education Committee) to Don

Hefley (President, Denver Classroom Teachers Association), 16 April 1973, folder "LARASA," box 21, unprocessed, Polly Baca Papers.

36. LARASA, "Recommendations of the Latin American Research and Service," folder "LARASA," box 21, unprocessed, Polly Baca Papers.

37. Manuel Gomez (Chairman, LARASA Education Committee) to Don Hefley (President, Denver Classroom Teachers Association), 4 May 1973, folder "LARASA," box 21, unprocessed, Polly Baca Papers.

38. Watson, "Removing the Barricades," 18–19.

39. Court Testimony, Trial on Merits, *Wilfred Keyes, et al. v. School District No. 1, Denver, Colorado, et al.*, US District Court for the District of Colorado, 2–20 February 1970, 871a, in *Appendix, Supreme Court of the United States*, vol. 2, October 1971, No. 71-507.

40. June Shagaloff, *The Jim Crow School—North and West: Facts for Action*, July 1961, 1, as quoted in Watson, "Removing the Barricades," 40.

41. The plan urged "1. Fact-finding, 2. Recommendations, 3. Mobilizing community support, 4. Conferences with the School Board, 5. Protests (sit-ins, pickets, and marches), and 6. Litigation." Shagaloff, *Jim Crow School*, 4, cited in Watson, "Removing the Barricades," 41.

42. LAEF Press Release, n.d., ca. 1955, 1, folder "LAEF," box 1, Bernard Valdez Papers.

43. "Denver Schools Lag Behind in Employment of Latins," newsletter, Colorado Federation of Latin American Groups, 10, no. 1 (February 1962), 8, folder "Latin American Conference of Colorado," box 1, Bernard Valdez Papers.

44. Newsletter, Colorado Federation of Latin American Groups, 10, no. 1 (February 1962), folder "Latin American Conference of Colorado," box 1, Bernard Valdez Papers; Newsletter, Colorado Federation of Latin American Groups, 10, no. 2 (August 1962), folder "Latin American Conference of Colorado," box 1, Bernard Valdez Papers; and Bob Jain, "A Denver Post Special Report: The Spanish-American in Denver," *Denver Post*, 19 July 1965, 31.

45. Spanish American Advisory Committee Meeting to the Denver Commission on Community Relations, Minutes, 23 October 1963, 1, folder 33, box 1, CCR Papers; Metropolitan Council for Community Service, Inc., "Report on the Latin American Research and Service Agency," May 1964, 5, folder 20, box 48, LARASA Papers.

46. LARASA, Meeting Minutes, folder "LARASA," box 24, unprocessed, Polly Baca Papers; Richard Tucker, "'Handle for Understanding' Provided: Valdez," *Rocky Mountain News*, 7 May 1966, 42, folder 9, box 12, Corky Gonzales Papers.

47. National Education Association, *The Invisible Minority: Report of the NEA-Tucson Survey on the Teaching of Spanish to the Spanish-Speaking* (Washington, DC: Department of Rural Education, National Education Association, 1966).

48. Guadalupe San Miguel Jr., *Contested Policy: The Rise and Fall of Federal Bilingual Education in the United States, 1960–2001* (Denton, TX: Al Filo: Mexican American Studies Series, University of North Texas Press, 2004), 12; and William Robbins, "Language and Cultural Diversity: Monroe Sweetland, Adalberto

Guerrero and the Bilingual Education Act of 1968" (paper presented at the Western History Association, Tucson, AZ, October 12, 2013).

49. National Education Association, , *Invisible Minority*.

50. Helen Rowan, "A Minority Nobody Knows," *Atlantic* (1967): 47–52, box 48, LARASA Collection, WHG-DPL.

51. "'Education Has Failed the Mexican-American'... Garza," ca. 1968, newspaper clipping, scrapbook, January 1968–December 1968, folder 10, box 12, Corky Gonzales Papers.

52. Sofie Zamora, "Wounded Knee Is Denver, Colorado," n.d., ca. April 1973, 2, 8, folder "LARASA," box 21, unprocessed, Polly Baca Papers. See also Sofie Zamora, "Chicano Community's Concerns in Choice of School Administrator," editorial, *Denver Post*, ca. 1973.

53. Advisory Council on Equality of Educational Opportunity in the Denver Public Schools, *Final Report and Recommendations to the Board of Education School District Number One, Denver, Colorado* (Denver: Denver Public Schools, 1967), 17–18.

54. Romero, "Our Selma Is Here," 87.

55. Advisory Council, *Final Report and Recommendations*, 16.

56. Advisory Council, *Final Report and Recommendations*, 27–29.

CHAPTER 4. BECOMING MINORITY UNDER THE LAW

1. *Keyes* was filed in US District Court for the District of Colorado on 19 June 1969. Complaint for Permanent Injunction and Declaratory Judgement, *Keyes v. School Dist. No. 1*, Civil Action No. C-1499 (D. Colo. 19 June 1969).

2. Court Transcript, Civil Action C-1499, 2–20 February 1970, in *Appendix*, vol. 2, *Supreme Court of the United States*, October term 1971, No. 71-507, *Wilfred Keyes, et al.* (hereafter cited as Court Transcript, 2–20 February 1970); and US Commission on Civil Rights, *Hearing Before the United States Commission on Civil Rights: Hearing Held in Denver, Colorado*, 17–19 February 1976 (Washington, DC: Commission on Civil Rights, 1977), 21–22.

In 1969 the student population of Denver Public Schools was 15.8 percent Mexican American, 12.7 percent Black, and 70.7 percent White. Keyes v. School District No. 1, 445 F.2d 990 n. 1 (10th Cir. 1971).

3. Janet Bingham, "Lawsuit Tough but Vital for Keyes Family's Dream," *Denver Post*, 18 August 1994, A-24; and Jim Kirksey, "Keyes, Whose Suit Brought Busing to Denver, Dies," *Denver Post*, 17 May 1999, B-01.

4. "School Board Meets at W.H.S. May 6," *West Side Recorder* 5, no. 10 (April 1969): 1.

5. "Sidewalk School Drop Out Hit," *West Side Recorder* 7, no. 2 (June 1970): 4.

6. 1930 US Census, Fremont County, Wyoming, Population Schedule, Riverton, p. 10B, dwelling 257, family 263, "Josephine Ornelas," digital image, accessed 24 December 2019, http://ancestry.com; Burt Hubbard, "Living without a Chance

to Learn in a Land of Literacy, Communication Rules, but Some Are Left Out," *Rocky Mountain News*, 13 August 2001, 7A; and Historic Denver, Inc., with Fairhill & Co., *La Alma Lincoln Park*, Historic District Context Draft, 11 April 2019, 39–40, https://historicdenver.org/wp-content/uploads/2019/04/LALP-Historic-Context-draft-2019.04.11.pdf.

7. 155 Cong. Rec. 22803 (2009).

8. Reporter's Transcript, Pre-Trial Conference, 25 November 1969, 22–23, folder 5, box 10, Keyes Records.

9. A number of school desegregation cases were filed in multiracial western cities. See Guadalupe San Miguel Jr., *Brown, Not White: School Integration and the Chicano Movement in Houston* (College Station: Texas A&M University Press, 2005); Brian Behnken, *Fighting Their Own Battles: Mexican Americans, African Americans, and the Struggle for Civil Rights in Texas* (Chapel Hill: University of North Carolina Press, 2010); Daniel Martinez HoSang, "The Changing Valence of White Racial Innocence: Black-Brown Unity in the 1970s Los Angeles School Desegregation Struggles," in *Black and Brown in Los Angeles: Beyond Conflict and Coalition*, ed. Josh Kun and Laura Pulido (Berkeley: University of California Press, 2013), 115–142; and David G. García, *Strategies of Segregation: Race, Residence, and the Struggle for Educational Equality* (Oakland: University of California Press, 2018). On the multiracial history of postwar Denver, see Tom I. Romero Jr., "Of Race and Rights: Legal Culture, Social Change, and the Making of a Multiracial Metropolis, Denver 1940–1975" (PhD diss., University of Michigan, 2004).

10. Tom I. Romero II, "¿La Raza Latina? Multiracial Ambivalence, Color Denial, and the Emergence of a Tri-Ethnic Jurisprudence at the End of the Twentieth Century," *New Mexico Law Review* 37 (Spring 2007): 245–306.

11. Ian Haney López, *White by Law: The Legal Construction of Race*, 10th anniversary ed. (New York: New York University Press, 2006), 86–90, quote on 89.

12. I use the definition of *racial formation* put forth by Michael Omi and Howard Winant in *Racial Formation in the United States*, 3rd ed. (New York: Routledge, 2015). "We define racial formation as the sociohistorical process by which racial identities are created, lived out, transformed, and destroyed" (109).

13. Natalia Molina, *How Race Is Made in America: Immigration, Citizenship, and the Historical Power of Racial Scripts* (Oakland: University of California Press, 2014), 7.

14. Steven H. Wilson, "*Brown* over 'Other White': Mexican Americans' Legal Arguments and Litigation Strategy in School Desegregation Lawsuits," *Law and History Review* 21, no. 1 (Spring 2003): 177–190.

15. Ernesto Vigil, "Rodolfo Gonzales and the Advent of the Crusade for Justice," in *La Gente: Hispano History and Life in Colorado*, ed. Vincent C. de Baca (Denver: Colorado Historical Society, 1998), 162–163; and Ernesto B. Vigil, *The Crusade for Justice: Chicano Militancy and the Government's War on Dissent* (Madison: University of Wisconsin Press, 1999), 23–24.

16. Ariela J. Gross, "'The Caucasian Cloak': Mexicans Americans and the Politics of Whiteness in the Twentieth Century Southwest," *Georgetown Law Journal*

95, no. 2 (January 2007): 337–392; Ariela J. Gross, *What Blood Won't Tell: A History of Race on Trial in America* (Cambridge, MA: Harvard University Press, 2008); and Ignacio M. García, *White but Not Equal: Mexican Americans, Jury Discrimination, and the Supreme Court* (Tucson: University of Arizona Press, 2008).

17. The first case to utilize this new strategy was filed in Corpus Christi, Texas, one year before *Keyes* was filed (*Cisneros v. Corpus Christi Independent School District*). See Guadalupe San Miguel Jr., *"Let All of Them Take Heed": Mexican Americans and the Campaign for Educational Equality in Texas, 1910–1981* (Austin: University of Texas Press, 1987), 177–181.

18. Nancy MacLean, "The Civil Rights Act and the Transformation of Mexican American Identity and Politics," *Berkeley La Raza Law Journal* 18 (2007): 127.

19. Ian F. Haney López, *Racism on Trial: The Chicano Fight for Justice* (Cambridge, MA: Belknap Press of Harvard University Press, 2004); and Carlos Muñoz Jr. *Youth, Identity, Power: The Chicano Movement* (London: Verso, 1989). David G. Gutiérrez shows that the assimilation strategy had a long history of failure. *Walls and Mirrors: Mexican Americans, Mexican Immigrants, and the Politics of Ethnicity* (Berkeley: University of California Press, 1995), esp. 179–205.

20. For a fuller examination of the shift in school desegregation legal strategy see Wilson, "*Brown* over 'Other White.'" On LULAC and its shift from advocating whiteness to promoting brownness, see Craig A. Kaplowitz, *LULAC, Mexican Americans, and National Policy* (College Station: Texas A&M University Press, 2005).

21. *Ross v. Eckels*, Civil Action No. 10-444 (S.D. Tex. 24 May 1971), 7, quoted in Margaret E. Montoya, "A Brief History of Chicana/o School Segregation: One Rationale for Affirmative Action," *Berkeley La Raza Law Journal* 12, no. 2 (Fall 2001): 170.

22. Wilson, "*Brown* over 'Other White,'"181.

23. On Mexican American whiteness, see Hernandez v. Texas, 347 U.S. 475 (1954). On school segregation, see Brown v. Board of Education of Topeka 347 U.S. 483 (1954).

24. Michael A. Olivas, "From a 'Legal Organization of Militants' into a 'Law Firm for the Latino Community': MALDEF and the Purposive Cases of *Keyes*, *Rodriguez*, and *Plyler*," *Denver University Law Review* 90 (2012–2013): 1154.

25. Much of this work was influenced by Latina/o critical theory (LatCrit), a field that developed primarily out of Latina/o scholar critiques of critical race theory (CRT). They challenged CRT scholars on their Black-White focus. See generally Richard Delgado and Jean Stefancic, eds., *The Latino/a Condition: A Critical Reader* (New York: New York University Press, 1998).

26. Juan F. Perea, "The Black/White Paradigm of Race: The 'Normal' Science of American Racial Thought," *California Law Review* 85, no. 5 (October 1997): 1219.

27. Legal scholar Kristi L. Bowman argues that the Supreme Court in *Keyes* helped erect a White-nonwhite paradigm, which was accomplished by allowing the plaintiffs to group Mexican American and Black students into one category. She writes, "The White-Non-White paradigm is injurious to *Brown*'s intent, because

instead of promoting equality, it promotes the dominance of whiteness. 'White' becomes the singular point of reference for all other races; if one is not White, the 'other' race to which one belongs is immaterial." "The New Face of School Desegregation," *Duke Law Journal* 50, no. 6 (April 2001): 1753.

28. Molina, *How Race Is Made*, 43–44, quote on 44. The 1870 Naturalization Act added "persons of African nativity, or African descent" to the list of persons eligible for naturalization. Thus, after 1870 only Whites and Blacks could naturalize. Haney López, *White by Law*, 31.

29. The Civil Rights Act of 1964 provided a plethora of new legal rights, and the Elementary and Secondary Education Act of 1965 gave teeth to the Supreme Court's school desegregation mandate. Essential to the mission to extend equality to Black Americans, moreover, was the creation of bureaucratic institutions from which civil rights advocates could launch their efforts. These included, for example, the Equal Employment Opportunity Commission, the Department of Labor's Office of Federal Contract Compliance, and HEW's office for Civil Rights. John D. Skrentny, *The Minority Rights Revolution* (Cambridge, MA: Harvard University Press, 2004), 8.

30. The 1954 Supreme Court ruling in *Hernandez v. Texas* established that Mexican Americans were "a distinct class" of people who often experienced discrimination based on *"ancestry or national origin"*. 347 U.S. 475, 477–481 (1954) (emphasis added).

31. US Commission on Civil Rights, *Racial Isolation in the Public Schools* (Washington, DC: Government Printing Office, 1967). For more on the EEO-1 form, see Skrentny, *Minority Rights Revolution*, 85–142.

32. Reporter's Transcript, Pre-Trial Conference, 34–35, folder 5, box 10, Keyes Records; and League of Women Voters of Denver, "Composite View of Denver's School Desegregation," September 1976, 2, folder 12, box 1, Rachel Noel Papers.

33. During the trial the plaintiffs focused on Black, White, and Mexican American students. During the remedy stage of the case American Indian and Asian American students were also defined as "minorities."

34. Reporter's Transcript, Pre-Trial Conference, 34–35, folder 5, box 10, Keyes Records.

35. Reporter's Transcript, Pre-Trial Conference, 35, folder 5, box 10, Keyes Records.

36. Robert T. Connery, "*Keyes v. School District No. 1*: A Personal Remembrance of Things Past and Present," *Denver University Law Review* 90, no. 5 (2013): 1092–1096.

37. A 1967 study put the Northeast Park Hill population at about 70 percent Black and 30 percent White. This was a dramatic shift from 1960, when the area was about 97 percent White and 3 percent Black. Jules Mondechein, "The Summer of 1967—Northeast Park Hill," 31 August 1967, 3, folder 3, box 1, Rachel Noel Papers.

38. For a legal perspective on the multiracial realities in the US West, see Romero, "¿La Raza Latina?" More generally, see Mark Brilliant, *The Color of America Has*

Changed: How Racial Diversity Shaped Civil Rights Reform in California, 1941–1978 (Oxford: Oxford University Press, 2010).

39. Guadalupe San Miguel Jr. demonstrates that in Houston, school desegregation efforts were similarly plagued by an inability to represent Mexican American educational interests. *Brown, Not White*.

40. Charles Carter, "Integration Plan Talks Disrupted," *Denver Post*, 27 October 1968, 1.

41. "Chicano 'Socks It' to the School Board," *El Gallo* 2, no. 3 (December 1968): 3. See also Christine Marín, *A Spokesman of the Mexican American Movement: Rodolfo "Corky" Gonzales and the Fight for Chicano Liberation, 1966–1972* (San Francisco: R & E Research Associates, 1977), 9–10.

42. Denver Board of Education, Meeting Minutes, 16 January 1969, 30 January 1969, and 11 March 1969. At community meetings, there was also dissent among Mexican Americans. Alan Cunningham, "Hispano Push for Unity to Effect School Change," *Rocky Mountain News*, 24 March 1969.

43. Reporter's Transcript, Pre-Trial Conference, 58, folder 5, box 10, Keyes Records.

44. Westside Action Ministry, "Supplement," *West Side Recorder*, 5, no. 9 (March 1969): insert. For more on the school walkouts, see "Racist West High Teacher Must Go," *El Gallo* 2, no. 4 (March 1969): 4; Marín, *Spokesman of the Mexican American Movement*; and Vigil, *Crusade for Justice*, 80–95. Chicano school walkouts, also called blowouts, occurred throughout the nation in the late 1960s. See generally Mario T. García and Sal Castro, *Blowout! Sal Castro and the Chicano Struggle for Educational Justice* (Chapel Hill: University of North Carolina Press, 2011).

45. Keyes v. School District No. 1, 439 F. Supp. 393, 418 (D. Colo. 1977).

46. Court Transcript, 2–20 February 1970, 485a-500a. See also Frederick D. Watson, "Removing the Barricades from the Northern Schoolhouse Door: School Desegregation in Denver" (PhD diss., University of Colorado at Boulder, 1993), 13–14.

47. Haney López, *White by Law*, 89.

48. The 1960 census reported Mexican Americans and other Latinas/os as racially White, although there was a separate section that asked the census taker to mark "persons of Spanish surname." Clara E. Rodríguez, *Changing Race: Latinos, the Census and the History of Ethnicity* (New York: New York University Press, 2000), 102.

49. Court Transcript, 2–20 February 1970, 788a.

50. Court Transcript, 2–20 February 1970, 788a.

51. Court Transcript, 2–20 February 1970, 788a–789a.

52. San Miguel, *"Let All of Them Take Heed"*, 175–77; and Wilson, "*Brown* over 'Other White,'" 178.

53. Court Transcript, 2–20 February 1970, 789a.

54. Keyes v. School Dist. No. 1, 313 F. Supp. 61, 69, 82–83 (1970). See also Plessy v. Ferguson, 163 U.S. 537 (1896).

55. Keyes v. School Dist. No. 1, 313 F. Supp. 61, 77 (1970). Judge Doyle specified that "a concentration of either Negro or Hispano students in the general area of 70 to 75 percent is a concentrated school likely to produce the kind of inferiority which we are here concerned with."

56. Keyes v. School Dist. No. 1, 313 F. Supp. 61, 69 (1970).

57. Keyes v. School Dist. No. 1, 313 F. Supp. 61, 69 (1970).

58. Plaintiff's Notice of Appeal (Cross-Appeal), U.S. Court of Appeals for the Tenth Circuit, 24 June 1970, Keyes Records.

59. Keyes v. School Dist. No. 1, 445 F.2d 990 (10th Cir. 1971).

60. Richard A. Shaffer, "Showdown in Denver: School-Integration Case Could Decide How Far North's Cities Must Go," *Wall Street Journal*, 15 June 1972, William E. Doyle Papers, MSS-035, Auraria Library Archives and Special Collections, Denver, Colorado.

61. "Test of Northern Integration: Legality of Neighborhood Schools at Issue in Denver," *Washington Post*, 21 September 1972, E1, William E. Doyle Papers.

62. On New York City, see Sonia Song-Ha Lee, *Building a Latino Civil Rights Movement: Puerto Ricans, African Americans, and the Pursuit of Racial Justice in New York City* (Chapel Hill: University of North Carolina Press, 2014), 165–210. On Boston, see Tatiana M. F. Cruz, "'We Took 'Em On': The Latino Movement for Educational Justice in Boston, 1965–1980," *Journal of Urban History* 43, no. 2 (2017): 235–255.

63. Johnson v. San Francisco USD, 339 F. Supp. 1315 (1971); Brief Amici Curiae, Robert G. Nelson, et al., Supreme Court of the United States, October term 1971, No. 71-507, Keyes v. School Dist. No. 1 (hereafter cited as Brief Amici Curiae, Robert G. Nelson, et al.). For more on the multiracial nature of the *Johnson* case, see Brilliant, *Color of America Has Changed*, 227–245; and Rand Quinn, *Class Action: Desegregation and Diversity in San Francisco Schools* (Minneapolis: University of Minnesota Press, 2020).

64. Brief Amici Curiae, Robert G. Nelson, et al., 64.

65. Brief Amici Curiae, Robert G. Nelson, et al., 75.

66. Daniel T. Valdes, "What You Are," *La Luz* 1 (1972), 56, cited in Brief Amici Curiae, Robert G. Nelson, et al., 78.

67. Brief Amici Curiae, Robert G. Nelson, et al., 79.

68. Lorentz transformations are a complex set of equations in physics that determine the relationship between space and time. Brief Amici Curiae, Robert G. Nelson, et al., 79–80.

69. Justice William Rehnquist dissented, and Justice Byron White did not participate in the decision. Justice William Brennan wrote the majority opinion.

70. Keyes v. School Dist. No. 1, 413 U.S. 189, 213 (1973), citing Green v. County School Board, 391 U.S. 430, 438 (1968).

71. Keyes v. School Dist. No. 1, 413 U.S. 189, 196–198 (1973). The court cited *Hernandez v. Texas* to support its ruling that "Hispanos constitute an identifiable class for purposes of the Fourteenth Amendment." Hernandez v. Texas 347 U.S. 475 (1954).

72. Keyes v. School Dist. No. 1, 413 U.S. 189, 197 (1973).

73. Keyes v. School Dist. No. 1, 413 U.S. 189, 197–198 (1973), citing Keyes v. School Dist. No. 1, 313 F. Supp. 61, 69 (D. Colo. 1970).
74. Cisneros v. Corpus Christi ISD, 324 F. Supp. 599 (S.D. Tex. 1970). For more on the case, see San Miguel, *"Let All of Them Take Heed"*; and Wilson, *"Brown* over 'Other White,'" 181–190.
75. Keyes v. School Dist. No. 1, 413 U.S. 189 (1973).
76. Keyes v. School Dist. No. 1, 413 U.S. 189 (1973).

CHAPTER 5. "NOT WHITE, YET NOT, IN THE OLD-STYLE PARLANCE, 'COLORED'"

1. "Supreme Court Has Spoken," *Denver Post*, 24 June 1973.
2. Sonia Song-Ha Lee, *Building a Latino Civil Rights Movement: Puerto Ricans, African Americans, and the Pursuit of Racial Justice in New York City* (Chapel Hill: University of North Carolina Press, 2014), 171–187, quote on 175. Also see Kwame Ture and Charles V. Hamilton, *Black Power: The Politics of Liberation* (New York: Random House, 1967), 167–171.
3. Luther P. Gerlach and Virginia H. Hine demonstrated this phenomenon in their early examination of the Black power movement. They charted a "conservative—moderate—militant continuum" of Black power organizations. *People, Power, Change: Movements of Social Transformation* (Indianapolis: Bobbs-Merrill Educational Publishing, 1970), 17–32.
4. Juan Gómez-Quiñones, *Mexican Students por La Raza: The Chicano Movement in Southern California, 1967–1977* (Santa Barbara, CA: Editorial La Causa, 1978); Carlos Muñoz Jr., *Youth, Identity, Power: The Chicano Movement* (London: Verso, 1989); Ignacio M. García, *United We Win: The Rise and Fall of La Raza Unida Party* (Tucson: University of Arizona Press, 1989); Armando Navarro, *Mexican American Youth Organization: Avant Garde of the Chicano Movement in Texas* (Austin: University of Texas Press, 1995); Ignacio M. García, *Chicanismo: The Forging of a Militant Ethos among Mexican Americans* (Tucson: University of Arizona Press, 1997); Ernesto B. Vigil, *The Crusade for Justice: Chicano Militancy and the Government's War on Dissent* (Madison: University of Wisconsin Press, 1999); Armando Navarro, *The Cristal Experiment: A Chicano Struggle for Community Control* (Madison: University of Wisconsin Press, 1999); Ernesto Chávez, *¡Mi Raza Primero! Nationalism, Identity, and Insurgency in the Chicano Movement in Los Angeles, 1966–1978* (Berkeley: University of California Press, 2002); George Mariscal, *Brown-Eyed Children of the Sun: Lessons of the Chicano Movement, 1965–1975* (Albuquerque: University of New Mexico Press, 2005); Lorena Oropeza, *¡Raza Sí! ¡Guerra No! Chicano Protest and Patriotism during the Viet Nam Era* (Berkeley: University of California Press, 2005); Ian F. Haney López, *Racism on Trial: The Chicano Fight for Justice* (Cambridge, MA: Belknap Press of Harvard University Press, 2004); Vicki L. Ruiz, *From Out of the Shadows: Mexican Women in Twentieth-Century America*, 10th anniversary ed. (Oxford: Oxford University Press,

2008), 99–126; David Montejano, *Quixote's Soldiers: A Local History of the Chicano Movement, 1966–1981* (Austin: University of Texas Press, 2010); Maylei Blackwell, *¡Chicana Power! Contested Histories of Feminism in the Chicano Movement* (Austin: University of Texas Press, 2011); Matt Garcia, *From the Jaws of Victory: The Triumph and Tragedy of Cesar Chavez and the Farm Worker Movement* (Berkeley: University of California Press, 2012); Mario T. García, ed., *The Chicano Movement: Perspectives from the Twenty-First Century* (New York: Routledge: 2014); Jimmy Patiño, *Raza Sí, Migra No: Chicano Movement Struggles for Immigrant Rights in San Diego* (Chapel Hill: University of North Carolina Press, 2017); Dionne Espinoza, María Eugenia Cotera, and Maylei Blackwell, eds., *Chicana Movidas: New Narratives of Activism and Feminism in the Movement Era* (Austin: University of Texas Press, 2018); Lori A. Flores, *Grounds for Dreaming: Mexican Americans, Mexican Immigrants, and the California Farmworker Movement* (New Haven, CT: Yale University Press, 2016); and Lorena Oropeza, *The King of Adobe: Reies* López Tijerina, *Lost Prophet of the Chicano Movement* (Chapel Hill: University of North Carolina Press, 2019).

5. Edward J. Escobar, *Race, Police, and the Making of a Political Identity: Mexican Americans and the Los Angeles Police Department, 1900–1945* (Berkeley: University of California Press, 1999); Edward J. Escobar, "The Unintended Consequences of the Carceral State: Chicana/o Political Mobilization in Post-World War II America," *Journal of American History* 102, no. 1 (June 2015): 174–184; and Kelly Lytle Hernández, *City of Inmates: Conquest, Rebellion, and the Rise of Human Caging in Los Angeles, 1771–1965* (Chapel Hill: University of North Carolina Press, 2017).

6. Haney López, *Racism on Trial*.

7. For example, see "Editorial," *El Gallo*, 28 July 1967, 2.

8. George Azcarate Macias, "Mexican, Mexican-American, Chicano," *El Gallo*, December 1968, 6.

9. Rosalie Montoya, "Chicano Power," *El Gallo*, April 1972, 6.

10. Jack Gaskie, "Gonzales Views His Poverty Role," *Rocky Mountain News*, 29 September 1965, 5.

11. Alex Johnson claimed a Spanish-American identity in his letter. "Who Shall Speak for Spanish-Descent Minority?," Open Forum, *Denver Post*, n.d., folder 20, box 12, Corky Gonzales Papers.

12. Richard Tucker, "Pueblo Councilman Attacks Prejudice and Bias," *Rocky Mountain News*, 6 May 1966, 56.

13. Richard Tucker, "Awareness Will Increase Aid," *Rocky Mountain News*, 11 May 1966, 36. This was the last in a seven-part series entitled "Our Spanish American Leaders Speak Out." The *Rocky Mountain News* noted that Corky Gonzales was given the opportunity to be a part of the series, but he declined. This provides another example of his rejection of traditional methods. From his viewpoint, both the *Rocky Mountain News* and the *Denver Post* were biased toward his community, a point Crusaders made in every issue of *El Gallo*. Thus, there was no point in participating in the forum.

14. John Haro, "Betterment of Hispanos," letter to the editor, *Denver Post*, 20 December 1966, 17. See also Marie Lujan, "Hispano Politics," letter to the editor, *Denver Post*, 11 December 1966.

15. Jack Gaskie, "Gonzales Views His Poverty Role," *Rocky Mountain News*, 29 September 1965, 5.

16. MALDEF, Motion to Intervene as Parties Plaintiffs, no. 47, book 1, box 25, Keyes Records.

17. MALDEF intervened or tried to intervene in several Texas school desegregation cases between 1970 and 1972, including cases in Corpus Christi, Houston, Dallas, Austin, Uvalde, and Waco, as well as a statewide case against the Texas Education Agency. Guadalupe San Miguel Jr., *"Let All of Them Take Heed": Mexican Americans and the Campaign for Educational Equality in Texas, 1910–1981* (Austin: University of Texas Press, 1987), 180.

When US District Court Judge Ben Connally (S.D. Tex.) approved a desegregation plan submitted by the Houston school district (HISD) that treated Mexican Americans as White for racial balance purposes, community activist Lorenzo P. Díaz insisted that school officials were "using Mexican Americans as 'pawns, puppets, and scapegoats' just to make it appear as if HISD was abiding by the Supreme Court mandate to integrate the schools." Guadalupe San Miguel Jr., *Brown, Not White: School Integration and the Chicano Movement in Houston* (College Station: Texas A&M University Press, 2005), 82. See also Brian D. Behnken, "Pawns, Puppets, and Scapegoats," in *Fighting Their Own Battles: Mexican Americans, African Americans, and the Struggle for Civil Rights in Texas* (Chapel Hill: University of North Carolina Press, 2010).

18. Fernie Baca Moore, "Report on Workshop to Develop Human Resources among Mexican-American Teachers in the Denver Metropolitan Area, June 9–15, 1968," July 1968, box 1, unprocessed, Congress of Hispanic Educators Records, 1963–2014 (hereafter CHE Records), WH2334, WHC-DPL.

19. Baca Moore, "Report on Workshop to Develop Human Resources," 8 (emphasis in original).

20. Congress of Hispanic Educators, "Proposal for Quality Education," 1969, box 1, CHE Records.

21. Congress of Hispanic Educators, "Proposal for Quality Education," 1969, box 1, CHE Records. Also see Congress of Hispanic Educators, "Recommendation for Enhancing the Educational Process for Hispano Students in the Denver Public Schools," 7 January 1969, box 1, CHE Records.

22. Baca Moore, "Report on Workshop to Develop Human Resources," 4.

23. Carey McWilliams, *North from Mexico: The Spanish-Speaking People of the United States* (Philadelphia: J. B. Lippincott, 1949).

24. Baca Moore, "Report on Workshop to Develop Human Resources," 6.

25. Congress of Hispanic Educators, "Viva Congress of Hispanic Educators," pamphlet (Denver, CO, ca. 1968), box 1, CHE Records.

26. *El Plan Espiritual de Aztlán*, March 1969. For more on the development of *El Plan*, see Muñoz, *Youth, Identity, Power*, 75–78; Vigil, *Crusade for Justice*, 97–100;

Lee Bebout, *Mythohistorical Interventions: The Chicano Movement and Its Legacies* (Minneapolis: University of Minnesota Press, 2011), 1–7, 76–79; and Juan Gómez-Quiñones and Irene Vásquez, *Making Aztlán: Ideology and Culture of the Chicana and Chicano Movement, 1966–1977* (Albuquerque: University of New Mexico Press, 2014), 191–192.

27. Cisneros v. Corpus Christi ISD, 324 F. Supp. 599 (S.D. Texas, 1970).

28. MALDEF, Motion to Intervene as Parties Plaintiffs, no. 47, book 1, box 25, Keyes Records.

29. MALDEF, Motion to Intervene as Parties Plaintiffs, no. 47, book 1, box 25, Keyes Records.

30. MALDEF, Memorandum of Law in Support of Motion to Intervene as Parties Plaintiffs, no. 49, book 1, box 25, Keyes Records.

31. Ross v. Eckels, Civil Action No. 10-444 (S.D. Texas, May 24, 1971), 7.

32. MALDEF, Memorandum of Law in Support of Motion to Intervene as Parties Plaintiffs, no 49, book 1, box 25, Keyes Records. For more on the Houston case, see San Miguel, *Brown, Not White*.

33. MALDEF, Memorandum of Law in Support of Motion to Intervene as Parties Plaintiffs, no 49, book 1, box 25, Keyes Records (emphasis in original).

34. MALDEF, Memorandum of Law in Support of Motion to Intervene as Parties Plaintiffs, no 49, book 1, box 25, Keyes Records.

35. MALDEF, Memorandum of Law in Support of Motion to Intervene as Parties Plaintiffs, no 49, book 1, box 25, Keyes Records.

36. Stanley Pottinger, Memorandum to School Districts with More Than Five Percent National Origin-Minority Group Children, 25 May 1970. For a deeper analysis of the factors that distinguished Mexican Americans as an identifiable class, see Richard Delgado and Vicky Palacios, "Mexican Americans as a Legally Cognizable Class under Rule 23 and the Equal Protection Clause," *Notre Dame Law Review* 50, no. 3 (1974–1975): 393–418.

37. MALDEF, Memorandum of Law in Support of Motion to Intervene as Parties Plaintiffs, no. 49, book 1, box 25, Keyes Records; and MALDEF Exhibit 3: HEW Memorandum to School Districts with More Than Five Percent National Origin-Minority Group Children from J. Stanley Pottinger, 25 May 1970, box 55, Records of District Courts of the United States, Denver, Colorado, RG21, National Archives and Records Administration (hereafter NARA), Denver, Colorado, Keyes v. School District No. One, 1969–1981.

38. Vilma Martinez, Gen. Counsel, Mexican American Legal Defense & Educational Fund, Speech at the University of Notre Dame Center for Civil Rights Conference: *Brown v. Board of Education* Twentieth Anniversary, 22 March 1974, cited in Tom I. Romero II, "¿La Raza Latina? Multiracial Ambivalence, Color Denial, and the Emergence of a Tri-Ethnic Jurisprudence at the End of the Twentieth-Century," *New Mexico Law Review* 37 (Spring 2007): 256.

39. Richard Tucker, "Assimilation in U.S. Structure Urged," *Rocky Mountain News*, 5 May 1966, 14.

40. Gene Cooper, "Spanish-Named Told to Change Their Culture," *Rocky Mountain News*, 2 June 1966, folder 26, box 11, Corky Gonzales Papers.

41. James R. Sena, "Hispano Role in U.S. History Corrected," *Register*, Denver Archdiocesan edition, 25 September 1969, 1, 8, cited in Vigil, *Crusade for Justice*, 112–113.

42. Robert L. Perkin, "LULAC Asks Informed Citizenry," *Rocky Mountain News*, 14 April 1954, 48.

43. Tucker, "Assimilation in U.S. Structure Urged," 14. Several of the other Mexican American leaders featured in this series shared similar views. See Richard Tucker, "'Handle for Understanding' Provided: Valdez," *Rocky Mountain News*, 7 May 1966, 42; Richard Tucker, "Education Is Key to Progress: Vigil," *Rocky Mountain News*, n.d., ca. 1966, folder 9, box 12, Corky Gonzales Papers; and Richard Tucker, "Awareness Will Increase Aid," *Rocky Mountain News*, 11 May 1966, 36.

44. "Young Hispanos Feel Sense of Pride," *Rocky Mountain News*, 28 October 1969, 42.

45. "Misled," letter to the editor, *Rocky Mountain News*, 6 November 1970, 70.

46. See, for example, "Denver Spanish-American Unity Talks Set," 24 January 1962, folder 41, box 1, Corky Gonzales Papers; "Spanish Problem Blamed on Lack of Political Unity," 2 December 1965, folder 47, box 1, Corky Gonzales Papers; and Alan Cunningham, "Hispanos Push for Unity to Effect School Change," *Rocky Mountain News*, 24 March 1969, folder 11, box 12, Corky Gonzales Papers.

47. For references to "Spanglos," see "El Gallo Comments," *El Gallo*, May 1968, 2; and "El Gallo Comments," *El Gallo*, September 1968, 2.

48. US Commission on Civil Rights, *Hearing Before the United States Commission on Civil Rights: Hearing Held in Denver, Colorado*, 17–19 February 1976 (Washington, DC: Commission on Civil Rights, 1977), 296.

49. US Commission on Civil Rights, *Hearing Held in Denver, Colorado*, 17–19 February 1976, 295–297.

50. San Miguel, *Brown, Not White*.

51. The Denver school walkouts did not occur until almost a year later.

52. "Crusade News Flashes," *El Gallo*, May 1968, 5.

53. "Albuquerque Students Demand End to Racism," "Brown Berets Get 'Maximum Security,'" and "Who Are the Black Berets?," *El Gallo*, May 1968, 5.

54. Charles Carter, "Integration Plan Talks Disrupted," *Denver Post*, 27 October 1968, 1.

55. Martin Moran, "Corky, Commandos Take Podium at School Parley," *Rocky Mountain News*, 2 November 1968, folder 47, box 1, Corky Gonzales Papers.

56. Moran, "Corky, Commandos Take Podium at School Parley," folder 47, box 1, Corky Gonzales Papers.

57. "Chicano 'Socks It' to the School Board," *El Gallo*, December 1968, 3.

58. For example, Noel was one of the founding board members of LARASA, established in 1964. LARASA Founders Recognition, 13 September 1987, 4, folder 111, box 20, LARASA Collection, MSS1185, History Colorado, Denver, Colorado.

59. On the development of a theory of Chicano internal colonialism, see George Rivera Jr., Aileen F. Lucero, and Richard Castro, "Internal Colonialism in Colorado: The Westside Coalition and Barrio Control," in *La Gente: Hispano History and Life in Colorado*, ed. Vincent C. de Baca (Denver: Colorado Historical Society, 1998), 203–221. More generally, see Muñoz, *Youth, Identity, Power*, 146–148 and 153–154.

60. Manuel Lopez, "How Chicanos Sell Out 'La Raza,'" *Denver Post*, 10 October 1970, 12, folder 14, box 12, Corky Gonzales Papers. On the Colorado LRUP, see Vigil, *Crusade for Justice*, 164–168, 184–200. Generally, see García, *United We Win*.

61. Joseph Sanchez, "La Raza Candidate Concerned with 'Needs of People,'" *Denver Post*, 17 May 1970, 39.

62. "Raza Candidates Oppose Forced Busing," *Rocky Mountain News*, 23 April 1971, 16.

63. Commission on Civil Rights, *Hearing Held in Denver, Colorado*, 17–19 February 1976, 439–440.

64. Germaine Aragon, letter to the editor, *West Side Recorder* 6, no. 2 (June 1969), 2.

65. *West Side Recorder* 6, no. 1 (May 1969), 1.

66. Germaine Aragon, letter to the editor, *West Side Recorder* 7, no. 11 (April 1971), 3.

67. Several schools on the West Side had at least one of these programs, thanks to federal funding under Title I of the Elementary and Secondary Education Act of 1965. Under the rules of Title I, HEW granted federal money to schools based on the number of students whose family incomes fell below a certain income level. If those students were transported to other schools, federal funding for these programs would be lost because it depended on a concentration of poor students.

68. Vigil, *Crusade for Justice*, 103.

69. Tom I. Romero Jr., "Of Race and Rights: Legal Culture, Social Change, and the Making of a Multiracial Metropolis, Denver 1940–1975" (PhD diss., University of Michigan, 2004), 411–412.

70. Allen Gomez and Bert Gallegos were the two non-LRUP candidates. While Gomez was opposed to "busing" for racial balance, he did qualify his opposition by implying he would support it if ordered by the courts. "Allen Gomez Enters School Board Race," *Rocky Mountain News*, 9 April 1971, 48; and "Gallegos Candidate for Board," *Denver Post*, 12 April 1971, 4.

71. Denver Board of Education, Minutes of Meeting, 25 May 1971, 2.

72. Colorado Partido de La Raza Unida 1972 Platform, folder 10, box 6, Corky Gonzales Papers.

73. Denver Board of Education, Minutes of Meeting, 18 December 1969, 19-20.

74. Denver Board of Education, Minutes of Meeting, 26 February 1970, 18.

75. Denver Board of Education, Minutes of Meeting, 17 March 1971, 9.

76. Denver Board of Education, Minutes of Meeting, 17 March 1971, 9–10.

77. "Gallegos Candidate for Board," *Denver Post*, 12 April 1971, 4.

78. "Juvenile Judge Candidates' Report," *Rocky Mountain News*, 27 September 1964, 36.

79. "Juvenile Judge Candidates' Report," 36; and "Rep. Gallegos Announces Switch to GOP," *Rocky Mountain News*, 21 October 1962, 5.

80. Ignacio M. García, *White but Not Equal: Mexican Americans, Jury Discrimination, and the Supreme Court* (Tucson: University of Arizona Press, 2008), 58. See 209 n28. See also Ignacio M. García, *Viva Kennedy: Mexican Americans in Search of Camelot* (College Station: Texas A&M Press, 2000), 26–28.

81. Valdez was first appointed to the Denver Board of Education when Bert Gallegos resigned in 1972 to accept a position in Washington, D.C. In 1973, Valdez won a seat in the school board elections, a position he held until 1978. In 1975 he was elected president of the board. Tom Rees, "Valdez Compromise School Board Head," *Rocky Mountain News*, 29 May 1975, 8.

82. Art Branscombe, "School Board Names Valdez, Blair to Top Positions," *Denver Post*, 29 May 1975, 2.

83. Reporter's Transcript of Trial Proceedings, vol. VIII, 28 February 1974, 1805, folder 2, box 16, Keyes Records.

84. Reporter's Transcript of Trial Proceedings, folder 2, box 16, Keyes Records.

85. Song-Ha Lee, *Building a Latino Civil Rights Movement*, 6.

86. Song-Ha Lee, *Building a Latino Civil Rights Movement*, 165–210.

CHAPTER 6. "AMERICAN," NOT "MINORITY"

1. Denver Board of Education, Meeting Minutes, 14 November 1974, 4.

2. On litigating racial identity, see Ian Haney López, *White by Law: The Legal Construction of Race*, 10th anniversary ed. (New York: New York University Press, 2006); Ariela J. Gross, *What Blood Won't Tell: A History of Race on Trial in America* (Cambridge, MA: Harvard University Press, 2008); and Peggy Pascoe, *What Comes Naturally: Miscegenation Law and the Making of Race in America* (Oxford: Oxford University Press, 2009), pt. 2.

3. Legal institutions included not just courts but various other state bodies as well. See, for example, Peggy Pascoe, "Seeing Like a Racial State," ch. 5 in *What Comes Naturally*; and Natalia Molina, *How Race Is Made in America: Immigration, Citizenship, and the Historical Power of Racial Scripts* (Oakland: University of California Press, 2014). For literature on the US state and its role in regulating citizenship, see Linda Gordon, *Pitied but Not Entitled: Single Mothers and the History of Welfare, 1890–1953* (Cambridge, MA: Harvard University Press, 1994); Mary L. Dudziak, *Cold War Civil Rights: Race and the Image of American Democracy* (Princeton, NJ: Princeton University Press, 2000); Erika Lee, *At America's Gates: Chinese Immigration during the Exclusion Era, 1882–1943* (Chapel Hill: University of North Carolina Press, 2003); Mae M. Ngai, *Impossible Subjects: Illegal Aliens and the Making of Modern America* (Princeton, NJ: Princeton University Press, 2004); Martha Gardner, *The Qualities of a Citizen: Women, Immigration, and Citizenship, 1870–1965* (Princeton, NJ: Princeton University Press, 2005); Natalia Molina, *Fit to Be Citizens? Public Health and Race in Los Angeles, 1879–1939* (Berkeley: University

of California Press, 2006); Pippa Holloway, *Sexuality, Politics, and Social Control in Virginia, 1920–1945* (Chapel Hill: University of North Carolina Press, 2006); Haney López, *White by Law*; Gross, *What Blood Won't Tell*; Kelly Lytle Hernández, *Migra! A History of the U.S. Border Patrol* (Berkeley: University of California Press, 2010); Margot Canaday, *The Straight State: Sexuality and Citizenship in Twentieth-Century America* (Princeton, NJ: Princeton University Press, 2010); Marc Stein, *Sexual Injustice: Supreme Court Decisions from Griswold to Roe* (Chapel Hill: University of North Carolina Press, 2010); Barbara Young Welke, *Law and the Borders of Belonging in the Long Nineteenth Century United States* (Cambridge: Cambridge University Press, 2010); Nayan Shah, *Stranger Intimacy: Contesting Race, Sexuality, and the Law in the North American West* (Berkeley: University of California Press, 2012); Jessica R. Pliley, *Policing Sexuality: The Mann Act and the Making of the FBI* (Cambridge, MA: Harvard University Press, 2014); S. Deborah Kang, *The INS on the Line: Making Immigration Law on the U.S.-Mexico Border, 1917–1954* (New York: Oxford University Press, 2017); and Martha S. Jones, *Birthright Citizens: A History of Race and Rights in Antebellum America* (Cambridge: Cambridge University Press, 2018).

4. See chapter 4.

5. The literature here is voluminous. See, for example, Reginald Horsman, *Race and Manifest Destiny: Origins of American Racial Anglo-Saxonism* (Cambridge, MA: Harvard University Press, 1981); Patricia Nelson Limerick, *The Legacy of Conquest: The Unbroken Past of the American West* (New York: W. W. Norton, 1987); George J. Sánchez, *Becoming Mexican American: Ethnicity, Culture, and Identity in Chicano Los Angeles, 1900–1945* (New York: Oxford University Press, 1993); Tomás Almaguer, *Racial Fault Lines: The Historical Origins of White Supremacy in California* (Berkeley: University of California Press, 1994); David G. Gutiérrez, *Walls and Mirrors: Mexican Americans, Mexican Immigrants, and the Politics of Ethnicity* (Berkeley: University of California Press, 1995); Neil Foley, *The White Scourge: Mexicans, Blacks, and Poor Whites in Texas Cotton Culture* (Berkeley: University of California Press, 1997); Nyan Shah, *Contagious Divides: Epidemics and Race in San Francisco's Chinatown* (Berkeley: University of California Press, 2001); Robert O. Self, *American Babylon: Race and the Struggle for Postwar Oakland* (Princeton, NJ: Princeton University Press, 2003); Lee, *At America's Gates*; Ngai, *Impossible Subjects*; Pablo Mitchell, *Coyote Nation: Sexuality, Race, and Conquest in Modernizing New Mexico, 1880–1920* (Chicago: University of Chicago Press, 2005); Molina, *Fit to Be Citizens?*; Pascoe, *What Comes Naturally*; Mark Brilliant, *The Color of America Has Changed: How Racial Diversity Shaped Civil Rights Reform in California, 1941–1978* (Oxford: Oxford University Press, 2010); Brian D. Behnken, *Fighting Their Own Battles: Mexican Americans, African Americans, and the Struggle for Civil Rights in Texas* (Chapel Hill: University of North Carolina Press, 2010); Shah, *Stranger Intimacy*; Kelly Lytle Hernández, *City of Inmates: Conquest, Rebellion, and the Rise of Human Caging in Los Angeles, 1771–1965* (Chapel Hill: University of North Carolina Press, 2017); and Beth Lew-Williams, *The Chinese Must Go: Violence, Exclusion, and the Making of the Alien* (Cambridge, MA: Harvard University Press, 2018).

6. For a concise discussion of the emergence of colorblind discourse in American politics and its different phases, see Michael Omi and Howard Winant, *Racial Formation in the United States*, 3rd ed. (New York: Routledge, 2015), 211–221. Generally, see Eduardo Bonilla-Silva, *Racism without Racists: Color-Blind Racism and the Persistence of Racial Inequality in America*. 3rd ed. (New York: Rowman & Littlefield, 2009).

7. Matthew D. Lassiter, *The Silent Majority: Suburban Politics in the Sunbelt South* (Princeton, NJ: Princeton University Press, 2006); and Kevin M. Kruse, *White Flight: Atlanta and the Making of Modern Conservatism* (Princeton, NJ: Princeton University Press, 2005), 78–104.

8. See Neil Gotanda, "A Critique of 'Our Constitution Is Color-Blind,'" *Stanford Law Review* 44, no. 1 (November 1991): 1–68; Ian F. Haney López, "'A Nation of Minorities': Race, Ethnicity, and Reactionary Colorblindness," *Stanford Law Review* 59, no. 4 (2007): 985–1064; and Christopher W. Schmidt, "*Brown* and the Colorblind Constitution," *Cornell Law Review* 94, no. 1 (2008): 203–238.

9. Reva B. Siegel shows that "the anticlassification principle as we understand it today is the artifact of political struggles over *Brown*'s implementation." "Equality Talk: Antisubordination and Anticlassification Values in Constitutional Struggles over *Brown*," *Harvard Law Review* 117, no. 5 (March 2004): 1475.

10. Mary L. Dudziak and Leti Volpp, "Introduction: Legal Borderlands: Law and the Construction of Legal Borderlands," *American Quarterly* 57, no. 3 (September 2005): 595 (emphasis original).

11. Supreme Court justices had utilized colorblind logic in several decisions since the late nineteenth century, particularly after the 1954 *Brown* decision. But the adherents of colorblind constitutionalism had not yet developed a sophisticated case for it, nor had a plurality on the matter been reached. The first judicial statement in support of colorblind constitutionalism was in Justice John Marshall Harlan's dissent in *Plessy v. Ferguson* (1896), in which he famously wrote "Our Constitution is colorblind, and neither knows nor tolerates classes among citizens." 163 U.S. 537, 559 (1896) (Harlan, J., dissenting). According to legal scholar Neil Gotanda, "Though aspects of color-blind constitutionalism can be traced to pre-Civil War debates, the modern concept developed after the passage of the Thirteenth, Fourteenth, and Fifteenth Amendments and matured in 1955 in *Brown v. Board of Education*." "Critique of 'Our Constitution Is Color-Blind,'" 2. For a detailed history of the court's rationale in *Brown*, and the justices' thinking on the constitutionality of racial classification, see Schmidt, "*Brown* and the Colorblind Constitution."

12. George Lipsitz, "The Sounds of Silence: How Race Neutrality Preserves White Supremacy," in *Seeing Race Again: Countering Colorblindness across the Disciplines*, ed. Kimberlé Williams Crenshaw, Luke Charles Harris, Daniel Martinez HoSang, and George Lipsitz (Oakland: University of California Press, 2019), 24.

13. Self, *American Babylon*; Kruse, *White Flight*; Lassiter, *Silent Majority*; Joseph E. Lowndes, *From the New Deal to the New Right: Race and the Southern Origins of Modern Conservatism* (New Haven, CT: Yale University Press, 2008); Daniel Martinez HoSang, *Racial Propositions: Ballot Initiatives and the Making of Postwar*

California (Berkeley: University of California Press, 2010); Bonilla-Silva, *Racism without Racists*; Omi and Winant, *Racial Formation in the United States*, 218–219; Ian Haney López, *Dog Whistle Politics: How Coded Racial Appeals Have Reinvented Racism and Wrecked the Middle Class* (Oxford: Oxford University Press, 2014); Matthew F. Delmont, *Why Busing Failed: Race, Media, and the National Resistance to School Desegregation* (Oakland: University of California Press, 2016); and Ariela Gross, "A Grassroots History of Colorblind Conservative Constitutionalism," *Law & Social Inquiry* 44, no. 1 (February 2019): 58–77.

14. Omi and Winant, *Racial Formation in the United States*, 219.

15. Dennis A. Deslippe, "'Do Whites Have Rights?': White Detroit Policemen and 'Reverse Discrimination' Protests in the 1970s," *Journal of American History* 91, no. 3 (December 2004): 932–960. See also *Kaiser Aluminum & Chemical Corporation and United Steelworkers of America, AFL-CIO v. Brian F. Weber*, a case filed in 1974. United Steelworkers of America v. Weber, 443 U.S. 193 (1979); Dennis Deslippe, *Protesting Affirmative Action: The Struggle over Equality after the Civil Rights Revolution* (Baltimore, MD: Johns Hopkins University Press, 2012); and Nancy MacLean, *Freedom Is Not Enough: The Opening of the American Workplace* (Cambridge, MA: Harvard University Press, 2005), 249–257.

16. The legislation was House Joint Resolution 620 (H.J. Res. 620). "Statement of Hon. Norman F. Lent, A Representative in Congress from the State of New York," 165, cited in Delmont, *Why Busing Failed*, 111.

17. US Commission on Civil Rights, *Hearing Before the United States Commission on Civil Rights: Hearing Held in Denver, Colorado*, 17–19 February 1976, 477–478 (Washington, DC: Commission on Civil Rights, 1977).

18. Parents Involved in Community Schools v. Seattle School District No. 1, 551 U.S. 701 (2007). On colorblindness and the law, see Gotanda, "Critique of 'Our Constitution Is Color-Blind'"; Andrew Kull, *The Color-Blind Constitution* (Cambridge, MA: Harvard University Press, 1992); Kimberlé Williams Crenshaw, "Race, Reform, and Retrenchment: Transformation and Legitimization in Antidiscrimination Law," in *Critical Race Theory: The Key Writings That Formed the Movement*, ed. Kimberlé Crenshaw, Neil Gotanda, Gary Peller, and Kendall Thomas (New York: New Press, 1995), 115–116; Siegel, "Equality Talk"; Lani Guiner, "From Racial Liberalism to Racial Literacy: *Brown v. Board of Education* and the Interest-Divergence Dilemma," *Journal of American History* 91, no. 1 (June 2004): 92–118; Haney López, "'A Nation of Minorities'"; Schmidt, "*Brown* and the Colorblind Constitution"; and Michelle Alexander, *The New Jim Crow: Mass Incarceration in the Age of Colorblindness* (New York: New Press, 2010).

19. Gross, "Grassroots History."

20. Omi and Winant, *Racial Formation*, 262.

21. Keyes v. School Dist. No. 1, 380 F. Supp. 673 (D. Colo. 1974).

22. Keyes v. School Dist. No. 1, 380 F. Supp. 673, 695 (D. Colo. 1974).

23. The Cardenas Plan was submitted to the court by the intervenors, CHE, and it was endorsed by the plaintiffs. The CHE also wrote, in consultation with Dr. Cardenas, and submitted, an addendum to the plan, which included several specific

recommendations for implementing the plan in Denver. Reporter's Transcript, Trial Proceedings, vol. V, 25 February 1974, 1032–1033, folder 3, box 15, Keyes Records.

24. Reporter's Transcript, Trial Proceedings, 25 February 1974, 991, folder 3, box 15, Keyes Records.

25. Congress of Hispanic Educators, in consultation with Dr. Jose A. Cardenas, "Addendum to the Intervenor's Education Plan for the Denver Public Schools" (hereafter Cardenas Plan), 5 February 1974, no. 55, book 2, box 25, Keyes Records.

26. Elaine Nathanson, "Winsett: Mr. Anti-Busing Steps Toward the Ballot," *Straight Creek Journal*, 2–9 July 1974, 6. Article IX, Section 8 of the Civil Rights Act of 1964 read: "'Desegregation' means the assignment of students to public schools and within such schools without regard to their race, color, religion, or national origin, but 'desegregation' shall not mean the assignment of students to public schools in order to overcome racial imbalance." Civil Rights Act of 1964, Pub. L. No. 88-352, 78 Stat. 241 (1964).

27. Denver Board of Education, Meeting Minutes, 18 April 1974, 12.
28. Denver Board of Education, Meeting Minutes, 18 April 1974, 9.
29. Denver Board of Education, Meeting Minutes, 14 November 1974, 12.
30. Denver Board of Education, Meeting Minutes, 18 April 1974, 9.

31. On the development and deployment of *mestizaje* in twentieth-century Latin America, see Helen I. Safa, "Introduction: Race and National Identity in the Americas," *Latin American Perspectives* 25, no. 3 (May 1998): 3–20; Lourdes Martínez-Echazábal, "Mestizaje and the Discourse of National/Cultural Identity in Latin America, 1845–1959," *Latin American Perspectives* 25, no. 3 (May 1998): 21–42; Jeffrey L. Gould, *To Die This Way: Nicaraguan Indians and the Myth of Mestizaje, 1880–1965* (Durham, NC: Duke University Press, 1998); Marisol de la Cadena, *Indigenous Mestizos: The Politics of Race and Culture in Cuzco, Peru, 1919–1991* (Durham, NC: Duke University Press, 2000); María Josefina Saldaña-Portillo, *The Revolutionary Imagination in the Americas and the Age of Development* (Durham, NC: Duke University Press, 2003); Nancy A. Appelbaum, Anne S. Macpherson, and Karin Alejandra Rosemblatt, "Introduction: Racial Nations," in *Race and Nation in Modern Latin America*, ed. Nancy A. Appelbaum, Anne S. Macpherson, and Karin Alejandra Rosemblatt (Chapel Hill: University of North Carolina Press, 2003), 7; Jorge Duany, "Neither White nor Black: The Representation of Racial Identity among Puerto Ricans on the Island and in the U.S. Mainland," in *Neither Enemies nor Friends: Latinos, Blacks, Afro-Latinos*, ed. Anani Dzidzienyo and Suzanne Oboler (New York: Palgrave Macmillan, 2005), 173–188; Ilan Stavans, *José Vasconselos: The Prophet of Race* (New Brunswick, NJ: Rutgers University Press, 2011); Deborah Poole, "Mestizaje, Distinction, and Cultural Presence: The View from Oaxaca," in *Histories of Race and Racism: The Andes and Mesoamerica from Colonial Times to the Present*, ed. Laura Gotkowitz (Durham, NC: Duke University Press, 2011), 179–203; Michelle A. McKinley, "The Unbearable Lightness of Being (Black): Legal and Cultural Constructions of Race and Nation in Colonial Latin America," in *Racial Formation in the Twenty-First Century*, ed. Daniel Martinez HoSang, Oneka LaBennett, and Laura Pulido (Berkeley: University of California

Press, 2012), 116–161; Grace Peña Delgado, *Making the Chinese Mexican: Global Migration, Localism, and Exclusion in the U.S.-Mexico Borderlands* (Palo Alto, CA: Stanford University Press, 2013); Tanya Golash-Boza and Eduardo Bonilla-Silva, "Rethinking Race, Racism, Identity and Ideology in Latin America," *Ethnic and Racial Studies* 36, no. 10 (2013): 1485–1489; Christina A. Sue, *Land of the Cosmic Race: Race Mixture, Racism, and Blackness in Mexico* (New York: Oxford University Press, 2013); and Jason Oliver Chang, *Chino: Anti-Chinese Racism in Mexico, 1880–1940* (Champaign: University of Illinois Press, 2017).

32. Reporter's Transcript, Conference, Keyes v. School Dist. No. 1, U.S. District Court for the District of Colorado, 10 June 1974, folder 6, box 17, Keyes Records.

33. Defendants' Motion for Modification and Clarification of Judgment and Decree, Keyes v. School Dist. No. 1, 17 April 1974, no. 32, book 3, box 25, Keyes Records.

34. Reporter's Transcript, Conference, 10 June 1974, folder 6, box 17, Keyes Records.

35. Reporter's Transcript, Conference, 10 June 1974, folder 6, box 17, Keyes Records.

36. Keyes v. Sch. Dist. No. 1, 413 U.S. 189, 217–253 (1973) (Powell, J., concurring in part and dissenting in part). Also see john a. powell, "Living and Learning: Linking Housing and Education," in *In Pursuit of a Dream Deferred: Linking Housing and Education Policy*, ed. john a. powell, Gavin Kearney, and Vina Kay (New York: Peter Lang Publishing, 2001), 15–48; and Drew S. Days III, "The Current State of School Desegregation Law: Why Isn't Anybody Laughing?," in powell, Kearney, and Kay, *In Pursuit of a Dream Deferred*, 164–165.

37. Keyes v. Sch. Dist. No. 1, 413 U.S. 189, 216 (1973) (Douglas, W., concurring).

38. Martha Menchaca, *Recovering History, Constructing Race: The Indian, Black, and White Roots of Mexican Americans* (Austin: University of Texas Press, 2002); and Laura E. Gómez, *Manifest Destinies: The Making of the Mexican American Race* (New York: New York University Press, 2008).

39. W. W. H. Davis, *El Gringo*, 85, cited in Adrian Bustamante, "Los Hispanos: Ethnicity and Social Change in New Mexico" (PhD diss., University of New Mexico, 1982), 103.

40. Order, Judge William E. Doyle, *Keyes v. School Dist. No. 1*, U.S. District Court for the District of Colorado, 19 June 1974, no. 30, book 3, box 25, Keyes Records.

41. Denver Board of Education, Meeting Minutes, 8 August 1974, 26. As of September 1974, the total student population of the district was 79,670. Denver Board of Education, Meeting Minutes, 21 November 1974, 25.

42. Jane Earle, "Denver Indians Protest 'Being Used' by Parents to Avoid Busing," *Denver Post*, 3 October 1974, 2.

43. Philip J. Deloria, *Playing Indian* (New Haven, CT: Yale University Press, 1998), 128–153.

44. Earle, "Denver Indians Protest 'Being Used' by Parents to Avoid Busing," 2.

45. Jane Earle, "New School Affidavits Sought," *Denver Post*, 23 October 1974, 4.

46. "Rockwell, Bradford Win Seats on School Board," *Rocky Mountain News*, 21 May 1975, 5.

47. Bradford explained that her community was "caught in the middle," too poor to own a home and belong to a homeowners' association, but not poor enough to qualify for federal subsidies. Art Branscombe, "Early Poverty Molded Board Member," *Denver Post*, 19 October 1975, 24.

48. Lassiter, *Silent Majority*, 5.

49. "Bradford Solidly Supports 'Neighborhood Schools,'" *Rocky Mountain News*, 14 May 1981, 73.

50. On consumer citizenship and anti-busing politics, see Clarence Y. H. Lo, *Small Property versus Big Government: Social Origins of the Property Tax Revolt* (Berkeley: University of California Press, 1990), 57–60; Lassiter, *Silent Majority*; Delmont, *Why Busing Failed*, 142–167; and Elizabeth Gillespie McRae, *Mothers of Massive Resistance: White Women and the Politics of White Supremacy* (New York: Oxford University Press, 2018), 217–240.

51. While Bradford was a grassroots activist, she positioned herself in opposition to the Chicana/o movement. "I reject the term Chicano," she explained. "To me, that's a political term. The only people who'll call themselves Chicanos are political activists.... I'm not a part of that radical element." Branscombe, "Early Poverty Molded Board Member," 24. On the Silent Majority, race, and the rise of conservatism in the postwar period, see Dan T. Carter, *From George Wallace to Newt Gingrich: Race in the Conservative Counter-Revolution* (Baton Rouge: Louisiana State University Press, 1992); Lisa McGirr, *Suburban Warriors: The Origins of the New American Right* (Princeton, NJ: Princeton University Press, 2001); Donald T. Critchlow, *Phyllis Schlafly and Grassroots Conservatism: A Woman's Crusade* (Princeton, NJ: Princeton University Press, 2005); Kruse, *White Flight*; Lassiter, *Silent Majority*; Joseph Crespino, *In Search of Another Country: Mississippi and the Conservative Counterrevolution* (Princeton, NJ: Princeton University Press, 2007); Lowndes, *From the New Deal to the New Right*; Nancy MacLean, "Neo-Confederacy versus the New Deal: The Regional Utopia of the Modern American Right," in *The Myth of Southern Exceptionalism*, ed. Matthew D. Lassiter and Joseph Crespino (New York: Oxford University Press, 2009), 308–329; Michelle M. Nickerson, *Mothers of Conservatism: Women and the Postwar Right* (Princeton, NJ: Princeton University Press, 2012); and Nancy MacLean, *Democracy in Chains: The Deep History of the Radical Right's Stealth Plan for America* (New York: Penguin Books, 2017). On Latina/o conservatism, see Geraldo Cadava, *The Hispanic Republican: The Shaping of an American Political Identity, from Nixon to Trump* (New York: Echo, 2020).

52. According to school board member Omar Blair, Bradford used racist language in public forums on more than one occasion, calling Blair "a black s.o.b." and Bernard Valdez (another board member) "a wetback." Mitch Geller, "The Real Naomi Bradford," *Denver Magazine* 7, no. 1 (December 1976): 44–45, quote on 44.

53. Bradford's firm rejection of bilingual-bicultural education often made her the target of Mexican American educational organizations and activists. Tom Rees,

"Chicanos Angered by Bilingual Criticism," *Rocky Mountain News*, 16 July 1975, 6; and "Bradford Solidly Supports 'Neighborhood Schools,'" 73.

54. "Bradford Solidly Supports 'Neighborhood Schools,'" 73. In another interview she told the *Denver Post*'s education editor, "I've been called a Mexican all my life." Branscombe, "Early Poverty Molded Board Member," 24.

55. Jane Earle, "School, Indian Impasse Declared," *Denver Post*, 10 November 1974, 51.

56. Earle, "Denver Indians Protest 'Being Used' by Parents to Avoid Busing," 2. In the United States there is a long history of federal imposition on the Indigenous right to name the members of their own communities. See Alexandra Harmon, *Indians in the Making: Ethnic Relations and Indian Identities around Puget Sound* (Berkeley: University of California Press, 1998); Alexandra Harmon, "Tribal Enrollment Councils: Lessons on Law and Indian Identity," *Western Historical Quarterly* 32, no 2 (2001): 175–201; Eva Marie Garroutte, "The Racial Formation of American Indians: Negotiating Legitimate Identities within Tribal and Federal Law," *American Indian Quarterly* 25, no. 2 (2001): 224–239; Circe Strum, *Blood Politics: Race, Culture, and Identity in the Cherokee Nation of Oklahoma* (Berkeley: University of California Press, 2002); and Mark Edwin Miller, *Claiming Tribal Identity: The Five Tribes and the Politics of Federal Acknowledgement* (Norman: University of Oklahoma Press, 2013). Examining the conflict between civil rights and sovereignty is beyond the scope of this chapter. For an excellent starting place, see Circe Strum, "Race, Sovereignty, and Civil Rights: Understanding the Cherokee Freedman Controversy," *Cultural Anthropology* 29, no. 3 (2014): 575–598; and Alaina E. Roberts, *I've Been Here All the While: Black Freedom on Native Land* (Philadelphia: University of Pennsylvania Press, 2021).

57. In his order, Judge Doyle wrote, "An Indian means any individual who 1. Is a member of a tribe, band, or other organized group of Indians, including those tribes, bands, or groups terminated since 1940 and those recognized now or in the future by the State in which they reside, or who is a descendant, in the first or second degree, of any such member, or 2. Is considered by the Secretary of the Interior to be an Indian for any purpose or 3. Is an Eskimo or Aleut or other Alaskan Native, or 4. Is determined to be an Indian under regulations promulgated by the Commissioner [of education], after consultation with the National Advisory Council on Indian Education." Order, *Keyes v. School Dist. No. 1*, 4 October 1974, no. 52, book 1, box 26, Keyes Records.

This continued to be a problem for the school district and the court. In April 1975 the court had to go even further to establish rules for the "American Indian" classification. Judge Doyle ordered that any parent who filed an affidavit claiming their child was American Indian would undergo an investigation that would be conducted by the Parents Committee formed under the Indian Education Act of Title IV. Judge William E. Doyle, Supplemental Order, *Keyes v. School Dist. No. 1*, 25 April 1975, no. 68, book 1, box 26, Keyes Records.

58. Earle, "School, Indian Impasse Declared," 51.

59. Scholarship on the one-drop rule and "passing" is voluminous. See Gross, *What Blood Won't Tell*; Allyson Hobbs, *A Chosen Exile: A History of Racial Passing in American Life* (Cambridge, MA: Harvard University Press, 2014); and Tyina L. Steptoe, *Houston Bound: Culture and Color in a Jim Crow City* (Oakland: University of California Press, 2015), esp. 120–151.

60. Denver Board of Education, Meeting Minutes, 14 November 1974, 13.

61. Denver Board of Education, Meeting Minutes, 14 November 1974, 13–14.

62. Denver Board of Education, Meeting Minutes, 14 November 1974, 13–14.

63. Richard Lewis Jr. and Joanne Ford-Robertson, "Understanding the Occurrence of Interracial Marriage in the United States through Differential Assimilation," *Journal of Black Studies* 41, no. 2 (2010): 405–420; and Zhenchao Qian, "Breaking the Racial Barriers: Variations in Interracial Marriage Between 1980 and 1990," *Demography* 34, no. 2 (May 1997): 263–276.

64. Earle, "Denver Indians Protest 'Being Used' by Parents to Avoid Busing," 2.

65. Pascoe, *What Comes Naturally*, 301–306. Tanya Katerí Hernández argues that the contemporary mixed category movement's fixation on a mixed-race category for the US Census and its use of multiracial discourse supports colorblind jurisprudence by inadvertently implying that race is an individual, cultural category, rather than a sociopolitical one. "Multiracial Discourse: Racial Classifications in an Era of Color-Blind Jurisprudence," *Maryland Law Review* 57, no. 1 (1998): 97–173. George J. Sanchez similarly critiques the mixed-race movement and mixed-race scholars who posit that an increasing population of mixed-race individuals will lead to the end of race as a meaningful social category in US life. The Latin American history of race and racism reveals the fallacies of such claims. "'Y tú, ¿qué?' (Y2K): Latino History in the New Millennium," in *Latinos Remaking America*, ed. Marcelo M. Suárez-Orozco and Mariela M. Páez (Berkeley: University of California Press, 2008), 45–58. See also Joel Perlmann and Mary C. Waters, eds., *The New Race Question: How the Census Counts Multiracial Individuals* (New York: Russell Sage Foundation, 2005).

66. Denver Board of Education, Meeting Minutes, 12 February 1976, 12–13.

67. Keyes v. School Dist. No. One, 521 F.2d 465 (10th Cir. 1975).

68. Order, *Keyes v. School Dist. No. 1*, U.S. District Court for the District of Colorado, 10 February 1976, box 33, U.S. District Court of the U.S., Denver, Colorado, Keyes v. Sch. Dist. No. One, Civil Case File C-1499, RG21, NARA, Denver, Colorado.

69. Denver Board of Education, Meeting Minutes, 11 March 1976, 10.

70. School Board President Bernard Valdez surveyed Mexican American teachers at the five predominantly Mexican American schools to determine if they supported desegregating. Almost all of them did. At Swansea, they were unanimous in their support for desegregation. Art Branscombe, "Valdez Puts Hispano Goals on Scales," *Denver Post*, 4 April 1976, 20.

71. Denver Board of Education, Meeting Minutes, 11 March 1976, 9–11.

72. On the Pontiac mothers' march, see Delmont, *Why Busing Failed*, 157–164.

73. David Jenkins, "38 School Buses Bombed," *Denver Post*, 6 February 1970, 1, 4.

74. "Jim Perrill Home Firebombed," *Denver Post*, 22 February 1970, 1; "Explosive Rips Denver Home," *Denver Post*, 25 February 1970, 3; Harry Gessing, "Task Force to Aim at Bombings," *Denver Post*, 25 February 1970, 1; and "FBI Probes Bombings in Denver," *Denver Post*, 27 February 1970, 2.

75. Sharon Ruth Brown-Bailey, "Journey Full Circle: A Historical Analysis of *Keyes v. School District No. 1*" (PhD diss., University of Colorado at Denver, 1998), 94.

76. Delmont, *Why Busing Failed*, 190-212.

77. Neil Foley, "Becoming Hispanic: Mexican Americans and the Faustian Pact with Whiteness," in *Reflexiones 1997: New Directions in Mexican American Studies*, ed. Neil Foley (Austin: Center for Mexican American Studies, University of Texas, 1998), 53–70.

78. Stipulation, *Keyes v. School Dist. No. 1*, 17 March 1976, DPS Resolution 1897 attached, box 33, RG21, NARA-Denver.

79. Complaint, *Susan Anita Garcia, et al. v. The Board of Education, School Dist. No. 1, et al.*, Civil Action 76-M-292, U.S. District Court for the District of Colorado, 16 March 1976, folder 10, box 1, Omar Blair Papers, ARL2, BCAARL, Denver Public Library, Denver, Colorado. See also Art Branscombe, "Hispanos Appeal School Suit," *Denver Post*, 8 April 1976, 18.

80. Denver Board of Education, Meeting Minutes, 29 April 1976, 28–29.

81. For example, at a March 4, 1974, school board meeting Bradford said that she had spoken with "mostly Spanish" people at the Southwest Action Center on the Westside, most of whom were opposed to "busing." Denver Board of Education, Meeting Minutes, 4 March 1974, 10.

82. Judge Matsch applied the principle of res judicata in making this determination. Res judicata translates to "a matter judged" or "a thing decided" and means that once a court has litigated a lawsuit and reached a decision, a separate lawsuit dealing with essentially the same issues cannot be relitigated. The decision of the initial court must be applied in the second instance. Memorandum Opinion and Order, *Garcia v. The Board of Education*, Civil Action 76-M-292, U.S. District Court for the District of Colorado, 1 June 1976, cited in Brief of Appellants, *Garcia v. The Board of Education*, No. 76-1575, United States Court of Appeals for the Tenth Circuit, 30 August 1976, 20–21, box 151, RG276, NARA-Denver.

83. Memorandum Opinion and Order, *Garcia v. The Board of Education*, Civil Action 76-M-292, U.S. District Court for the District of Colorado, 1 June 1976, cited in Brief of Appellants, *Garcia v. The Board of Education*, No. 76-1575, United States Court of Appeals for the Tenth Circuit, 30 August 1976, 59–60, box 151, RG276, NARA-Denver.

84. Brief of Appellants, *Garcia v. The Board of Education*, No. 76-1575, United States Court of Appeals for the Tenth Circuit, 30 August 1976, 2, box 151, RG276, NARA-Denver.

85. Brief of Appellants, *Garcia v. The Board of Education*, No. 76-1575, United States Court of Appeals for the Tenth Circuit, 30 August 1976, 2–5, box 151, RG276,

NARA-Denver. Lawyers stated several times in the brief that Swansea children were receiving "superior" education at that school. See, for example, p. 12.

86. Keyes v. School Dist. No. 1, 413 U.S. 189, 203 (1973).

87. Keyes v. School Dist. No. 1, 368 F. Supp. 207 (D. Colo. 1973).

88. Brief of Appellants, *Garcia v. The Board of Education*, No. 76-1575, United States Court of Appeals for the Tenth Circuit, 30 August 1976, 2, box 151, RG276, NARA-Denver.

89. Brief of Appellants, *Garcia v. The Board of Education*, No. 76-1575, United States Court of Appeals for the Tenth Circuit, 30 August 1976, 13, box 151, RG276, NARA-Denver.

90. *Blanqueamiento*, the belief in and practice of whitening over time, was and is common in Latin American nations dedicated to the racial politics of *mestizaje*. See Tanya Katerí Hernández, "Spanish America Whitening the Race—The Un(written) Laws of Blanqueamiento and Mestizaje," in *Racial Subordination in Latin America: The Role of the State, Customary Law, and the New Civil Rights Response* (New York: Cambridge University Press, 2013), 19-46.

91. Brief of Appellants, *Garcia v. The Board of Education*, No. 76-1575, United States Court of Appeals for the Tenth Circuit, 30 August 1976, 13 (note 4), box 151, RG276, NARA-Denver (emphasis added).

92. José Martí, *Nuestra América* (1891), as translated and cited in McKinley, "Unbearable Lightness of Being (Black)," 117.

93. McKinley, "Unbearable Lightness of Being (Black),"117.

94. Martínez-Echazábal, "Mestizaje and the Discourse," 21–42; Gould, *To Die This Way*; de la Cadena, *Indigenous Mestizos*; Saldaña-Portillo, *Revolutionary Imagination*; Nancy A. Appelbaum, Anne S. Macpherson, and Karin Alejandra Rosemblatt, eds., *Race and Nation in Modern Latin America*; Duany, "Neither White nor Black," 173–188; Helen I. Safa, "Challenging Mestizaje: A Gender Perspective on Indigenous and Afrodescendant Movements in Latin America," *Critique of Anthropology* 25, no. 3 (2005): 307–330; Stavans, *José Vasconselos*; Poole, "Mestizaje, Distinction, and Cultural Presence"; McKinley, "Unbearable Lightness of Being (Black)"; Delgado, *Making the Chinese Mexican*; Hernández, *Racial Subordination in Latin America*; Sue, *Land of the Cosmic Race*; and Chang, *Chino*.

95. Brief of Appellants, *Garcia v. The Board of Education*, No. 76-1575, United States Court of Appeals for the Tenth Circuit, 30 August 1976, 14, box 151, RG276, NARA-Denver.

96. Reply Brief of Appellants, *Garcia v. The Board of Education*, No. 76-1575, United States Court of Appeals for the Tenth Circuit, 14 October 1976, 6, box 151, RG276, NARA-Denver.

97. Reply Brief of Appellants, *Garcia v. The Board of Education*, No. 76-1575, United States Court of Appeals for the Tenth Circuit, 14 October 1976, 6, box 151, RG276, NARA-Denver.

98. Keyes v. School Dist. No. One, 521 F.2d 465, 475-6 (10th Cir. 1975).

99. Brief of Appellants, *Garcia v. The Board of Education*, No. 76-1575, United States Court of Appeals for the Tenth Circuit, 30 August 1976, 15 (note 5), box 151, RG276, NARA-Denver.

100. Brief of Appellants, *Garcia v. The Board of Education*, No. 76-1575, United States Court of Appeals for the Tenth Circuit, 30 August 1976, 15 (note 5), box 151, RG276, NARA-Denver.

101. Brief of Appellants, *Garcia v. The Board of Education*, No. 76-1575, United States Court of Appeals for the Tenth Circuit, 30 August 1976, 17, box 151, RG276, NARA-Denver.

102. Brief of Appellants, *Garcia v. The Board of Education*, No. 76-1575, United States Court of Appeals for the Tenth Circuit, 30 August 1976, 19, box 151, RG276, NARA-Denver.

103. Brief of Appellants, *Garcia v. The Board of Education*, No. 76-1575, United States Court of Appeals for the Tenth Circuit, 30 August 1976, 5, box 151, RG276, NARA-Denver.

104. Brief of Appellants, *Garcia v. The Board of Education*, No. 76-1575, United States Court of Appeals for the Tenth Circuit, 30 August 1976, 2, box 151, RG276, NARA-Denver.

105. Brief of Appellants, *Garcia v. The Board of Education*, No. 76-1575, United States Court of Appeals for the Tenth Circuit, 30 August 1976, 11, box 151, RG276, NARA-Denver. The brief argues that Swansea was separate from the original focus of *Keyes* several times. See pp. 12–14.

106. Brief of Appellants, *Garcia v. The Board of Education*, No. 76-1575, United States Court of Appeals for the Tenth Circuit, 30 August 1976, 2, box 151, RG276, NARA-Denver.

107. Brief of Appellants, *Garcia v. The Board of Education*, No. 76-1575, United States Court of Appeals for the Tenth Circuit, 30 August 1976, 2, box 151, RG276, NARA-Denver.

108. Brief of Appellants, *Garcia v. The Board of Education*, No. 76-1575, United States Court of Appeals for the Tenth Circuit, 30 August 1976, 5, box 151, RG276, NARA-Denver.

109. Brief of Appellants, *Garcia v. The Board of Education*, No. 76-1575, United States Court of Appeals for the Tenth Circuit, 30 August 1976, 12, box 151, RG276, NARA-Denver.

110. Brief of Appellants, *Garcia v. The Board of Education*, No. 76-1575, United States Court of Appeals for the Tenth Circuit, 30 August 1976, 20, box 151, RG276, NARA-Denver.

111. Office of Policy Planning and Research, United States Department of Labor, *The Negro Family: The Case for National Action* (Washington, DC: Government Printing Office, 1965). See also Oscar Lewis, *La Vida: A Puerto Rican Family in the Culture of Poverty—San Juan and New York* (New York: Random House, 1966); Michael B. Katz, ed., *The Underclass Debate: Views from History* (Princeton, NJ: Princeton University Press, 1993); Daryl Michael Scott, *Contempt and Pity: Social Policy and the Image of the Damaged Black Psyche, 1880-1996* (Chapel Hill: University

of North Carolina Press, 1997); Alice O'Connor, *Poverty Knowledge: Social Science, Social Policy, and the Poor in Twentieth-Century U.S. History* (Princeton, NJ: Princeton University Press, 2001), 196-210; James T. Patterson, *Freedom Is Not Enough: The Moynihan Report and America's Struggle over Black Family Life—from LBJ to Obama* (New York: Basic Books, 2010); Michael B. Katz, *The Un-Deserving Poor: America's Enduring Confrontation with Poverty*, 2nd ed. (New York: Oxford University Press, 2013); and Sonia Song-Ha Lee, *Building a Latino Civil Rights Movement: Puerto Ricans, African Americans, and the Pursuit of Racial Justice in New York City* (Chapel Hill: University of North Carolina Press, 2014), 41–55.

112. Crenshaw, "Race, Reform, and Retrenchment," 115–116.

113. Brief of Appellants, *Garcia v. The Board of Education*, No. 76-1575, United States Court of Appeals for the Tenth Circuit, 30 August 1976, 12, box 151, RG276, NARA-Denver.

114. Ellen D. Wu, *The Color of Succuss: Asian Americans and the Origins of the Model Minority* (Princeton, NJ: Princeton University Press, 2014), 2 (emphasis in original). See also Scott Kurashige, *The Shifting Grounds of Race: Black and Japanese Americans in the Making of Multiracial Los Angeles* (Princeton, NJ: Princeton University Press, 2008), 186–204; Diane C. Fujino, "Black Militants and Asian American Model Minorities: Contesting Oppositional Representations; or, On Afro-Asian Solidarities," *Kalfou: A Journal of Comparative and Relational Ethnic Studies* 2, no. 1 (2015): 97–116; and Madeline Y. Hsu, *The Good Immigrants: How the Yellow Peril Became the Model Minority* (Princeton, NJ: Princeton University Press, 2017).

115. Wu, *Color of Success*.

116. Brief of Appellants, *Garcia v. The Board of Education*, No. 76-1575, United States Court of Appeals for the Tenth Circuit, 30 August 1976, 4–5, box 151, RG276, NARA-Denver.

117. Brief of Appellants, *Garcia v. The Board of Education*, No. 76-1575, United States Court of Appeals for the Tenth Circuit, 30 August 1976, 14, box 151, RG276, NARA-Denver.

118. Brief of Appellants, *Garcia v. The Board of Education*, No. 76-1575, United States Court of Appeals for the Tenth Circuit, 30 August 1976, 14–15, box 151, RG276, NARA-Denver.

119. Garcia v. The Board of Education, School Dist. No. 1, 573 F.2d 676 (10th Cir. 1978).

CONCLUSION

1. US Commission on Civil Rights, *Hearing Before the United States Commission on Civil Rights: Hearing Held in Denver, Colorado*, 17–19 February 1976 (Washington, DC: Commission on Civil Rights, 1977), 1; *Civil Rights Commission Authorization Act of 1978, Hearings on S. 2300, Day 3, Before the Subcomm. on the Constitution of the Comm. on the Judiciary*, 95th Cong. 144 (1978) (testimony of

Naomi L. Bradford, Member, Board of Education, Denver, CO, and Member, National Association for Neighborhood Schools).

2. US Commission on Civil Rights, *Fulfilling the Letter and Spirit of the Law: Desegregation of the Nation's Public Schools* (Washington, DC: Government Printing Office, 1976), i, 43–47, 49–50.

3. US Commission on Civil Rights, *Fulfilling the Letter and Spirit of the Law*, 49.

4. See, for example, Tom Rees, "Citizens' Group Reports Bilingual Program Lagging," *Rocky Mountain News*, 25 September 1974; and Tom Rees, "Committee Says School Board Drags Feet on Desegregation," *Rocky Mountain News*, 15 February 1975.

5. Garcia v. The Board of Education, School Dist. No. 1, 573 F.2d 676 (10th Cir. 1978).

6. Gene Amole, "Anybody Listening to Foes of Busing?," *Rocky Mountain News*, 28 November 1991, 8.

BIBLIOGRAPHY

PRIMARY SOURCES

Archival Collections

Baca, Polly. Papers. WH1793. Western History Collection. Denver Public Library, Denver, Colorado. Unprocessed.

Blair, Omar. Papers. ARL2. Blair-Caldwell African-American Research Library. Denver Public Library, Denver, Colorado.

Congress of Hispanic Educators. Records, 1963–2014. WH2334. Western History Collection. Denver Public Library, Denver, Colorado. Unprocessed.

Denver Commission on Community Relations. Papers. WH903. Western History Collection. Denver Public Library, Denver, Colorado.

District Courts of the United States, Denver, Colorado. Records. RG21. National Archives and Records Administration, Denver, Colorado.

Doyle, William E. Papers. MSS-035. Auraria Library Archives and Special Collections, Denver, Colorado.

Etter, Don, and Carolyn Etter. Papers. WH1974. Western History Collection. Denver Public Library, Denver, Colorado. Unprocessed.

Gonzales, Rodolfo "Corky." Papers. WH1971. Western History Collection. Denver Public Library, Denver, Colorado

Keyes (Wilfred) v. Denver School District. Records, 1969–1986. Accession 1. COU: 931. University of Colorado Boulder Libraries. Special Collection. Archives and Preservation Department, Boulder, Colorado.

Latin American Research and Service Agency. Collection. MSS1185. History Colorado, Denver, Colorado.

Latin American Research and Service Agency. Records. WH1842. Western History Collection. Denver Public Library, Denver, Colorado.

Lucero, Helen. Papers. WH2029. Western History Collection. Denver Public Library, Denver, Colorado. Unprocessed.

McNichols, William. Papers. WH1015. Western History Collection. Denver Public Library, Denver, Colorado.
Noel, Rachel. Papers. ARL117. Blair-Caldwell African American Research Library. Denver Public Library, Denver, Colorado.
United States Court of Appeals for the Tenth Circuit. Records. RG276. National Archives and Records Administration, Denver, Colorado.
Valdez, Bernard. Papers. WH1839. Western History Collection. Denver Public Library, Denver, Colorado. Unprocessed.
Yasui, Minoru. Papers. MSS-033. Auraria Library Archives and Special Collections, Denver, Colorado.

Newspapers and Magazines

The Atlantic
Denver Blade
Denver Inquirer
The Denver Magazine
Denver Post
Denver Post Empire Magazine
El Gallo (Denver). This locally run newspaper was dated inconsistently; some issues have a volume and number, others do not. Some include a full date and some only a month/year.
El Tiempo (Denver)
Harper's Weekly
Horizon
Intermountain Jewish Jews (Denver)
La Luz
The Nation
New Republic
The New Yorker
Rocky Mountain News (Denver)
The Straight Creek Journal (Denver)
Washington Post
West Side Recorder (Denver)

Denver School District No. 1 Administration Records

Advisory Council on Equality of Educational Opportunity. *Final Report and Recommendations to the Board of Education School District Number One, Denver, Colorado*. Denver: Denver Public Schools, 1967.
Atkins, James A. *Human Relations in Colorado: A Historical Record*. Denver: Colorado Department of Education, Division of Elementary and Secondary Education, Office of Instructional Services, 1968.
Denver Board of Education. Minutes of Meetings, 1962–1976.

Department of General Curriculum Services, Division of Instructional Services. "The Heritage and Contributions of the Hispanic American." Denver Public Schools, 1968.

Report... a Study of Pupil Population, School Boundaries, Pupil Transportation and School Buildings. Denver: Denver Public Schools, 1962.

Special Study Committee on Equality of Educational Opportunity in the Denver Public Schools. *Report and Recommendations to the Board of Education, School District No. 1*. Denver: Denver Public Schools, 1964.

Published Reports

Civil Rights Commission Authorization Act of 1978, Hearings on S. 2300, Day 3, Before the Subcomm. on the Constitution of the Comm. on the Judiciary. 95th Congress (1978).

Crow, Eleanor G. *A Time for Change and Challenge: Civil Rights in Colorado, 1966–1969*. Colorado Civil Rights Commission, December 1969.

Denver Commission on Human Relations. *Inventory of Human Relations: Summaries and Recommendations*. In Cooperation with the Anti-Defamation League of B'Nai B'Rith, The Denver Urban League, Japanese American Citizens League, Adult Education Council, Anti-Discrimination Division of the State Industrial Commission, Western District of the National Conference of Christians and Jews, State Employment Service, League of United Latin American Citizens, and the United Packinghouse Workers of America. 1955.

Historic Denver, Inc., with Fairhill & Co. *La Alma Lincoln Park*. Historic District Context Draft. April 11, 2019. https://historicdenver.org/wp-content/uploads/2019/04/LALP-Historic-Context-draft-2019.04.11.pdf.

Lee, Chungmei. *Denver Public Schools: Resegregation, Latino Style*. The Civil Rights Project. Harvard University, January 2006.

National Education Association. *The Invisible Minority: Report of the NEA-Tucson Survey on the Teaching of Spanish to the Spanish-Speaking*. Washington, DC: Department of Rural Education, National Education Association, 1966.

Office of Policy Planning and Research. United States Department of Labor. *The Negro Family: The Case for National Action*. Washington, DC: Government Printing Office, 1965.

Orfield, Gary, and Erica Frankenberg, with Jongyeon Ee and John Kuscera. *Brown at 60: Great Progress, a Long Retreat and an Uncertain Future*. The Civil Rights Project/Proyecto Derechos Civiles, 15 May 2014.

US Bureau of the Census. *Census of Population and Housing: 1970, Census Tracts, Final Report*. PHC (1)—56. Denver Colorado SMSA.

US Commission on Civil Rights. *Fulfilling the Letter and Spirit of the Law: Desegregation of the Nation's Public Schools*. Washington, DC: Government Printing Office, 1976.

———. *Hearing before the United States Commission on Civil Rights: Hearing Held in Denver, Colorado*, 17–19 February 1976. Washington, DC: Commission on Civil Rights, 1977.

———. *1961 Commission on Civil Rights Report: Housing.* Washington, DC: Government Printing Office, 1961.

———. *Racial Isolation in the Public Schools.* Vol. 1. Washington, DC: Government Printing Office, 1967.

Court Records

Appendix, vol. 1, Supreme Court of the United States, October Term 1971, No. 71-507, *Keyes et. al., Petitioners v. School District No. 1, Denver, Colorado, et. al.*

Appendix, vol. 2, Supreme Court of the United States, October Term 1971, No. 71-507, *Keyes et. al., Petitioners v. School District No. 1, Denver, Colorado, et. al.*

Appendix, vol. 3, Supreme Court of the United States, October Term 1971, No. 71-507, *Keyes et. al., Petitioners v. School District No. 1, Denver, Colorado, et. al.*

Appendix, vol. 4, Supreme Court of the United States, October Term 1971, No. 71-507, *Keyes et. al., Petitioners v. School District No. 1, Denver, Colorado, et. al.*

Appendix, vol. 5, Supreme Court of the United States, October Term 1971, No. 71-507, *Keyes et. al., Petitioners v. School District No. 1, Denver, Colorado, et. al.*

Websites

Ancestry.com

SECONDARY SOURCES

Acuña, Rodolfo. *Occupied America: The Chicano Struggle toward Liberation.* New York: Harper and Row, 1972.

Alexander, Michelle. *The New Jim Crow: Mass Incarceration in the Age of Colorblindness.* New York: New Press, 2010.

Almaguer, Tomás. "Race, Racialization, and Latino Populations in the United States." In *Racial Formation in the Twenty-First Century*, edited by Daniel Martinez HoSang, Oneka LaBennett, and Laura Pulido, 143–161. Berkeley: University of California Press, 2012.

———. *Racial Fault Lines: The Historical Origins of White Supremacy in California.* Berkeley: University of California Press, 1994.

Alvarez, Robert R., Jr. "The Lemon Grove Incident: The Nation's First Successful Desegregation Court Case." *Journal of San Diego History* 32, no. 2 (Spring 1986). https://sandiegohistory.org/journal/1986/april/lemongrove/.

Appelbaum, Nancy A., Anne S. Macpherson, and Karin Alejandra Rosemblatt. "Introduction: Racial Nations." In *Race and Nation in Modern Latin America*, edited by Nancy A. Appelbaum, Anne S. Macpherson, and Karin Alejandra Rosemblatt, 1–31. Chapel Hill: University of North Carolina Press, 2003.

Arnesen, Eric. "Whiteness and the Historian's Imagination." *International Labor and Working-Class History*, no. 60 (Fall 2001): 3–32.

Arredondo, Gabriela. *Mexican Chicago: Race, Identity, and Nation, 1919–1936*. Urbana: University of Illinois Press, 2008.

Barrett, James R. and David Roediger. "Inbetween Peoples: Race, Nationality, and the 'New Immigrant' Working Class." *Journal of American Ethnic History* 16, no. 3 (Spring 1997): 3–44.

Bebout, Lee. *Mythohistorical Interventions: The Chicano Movement and Its Legacies*. Minneapolis: University of Minnesota Press, 2011.

Behnken, Brian D. *Fighting Their Own Battles: Mexican Americans, African Americans, and the Struggle for Civil Rights in Texas*. Chapel Hill: University of North Carolina Press, 2010.

Bell, Derrick A. *Race, Racism and American Law*. New York: Little Brown & Co., 1973.

Blackwell, Maylei. *¡Chicana Power! Contested Histories of Feminism in the Chicano Movement*. Austin, TX: University of Texas Press, 2011.

Blanton, Carlos K. "George I. Sánchez, Ideology, and Whiteness in the Making of the Mexican American Civil Rights Movement, 1930–1960." *Journal of Southern History* 72, no. 3 (August 2006): 569–604.

Blanton, Carlos Kevin. *George I. Sánchez: The Long Fight for Mexican American Integration*. New Haven, CT: Yale University Press, 2014.

Blaut, J. M., and Antonio Ríos-Bustamante. "Commentary on Nostrand's 'Hispanos and their Homeland.'" *Annals of the Association of American Geographers* 74, no. 1 (1984): 157–163.

Bonilla-Silva, Eduardo. *Racism without Racists: Color-Blind Racism and the Persistence of Racial Inequality in America*. 3rd ed. New York: Rowman & Littlefield, 2009.

Bowman, Kristi L. "The New Face of School Desegregation." *Duke Law Journal* 50, no. 6 (April 2001): 1751–1808.

Brilliant, Mark. *The Color of America Has Changed: How Racial Diversity Shaped Civil Rights Reform in California, 1941–1978*. Oxford: Oxford University Press, 2010.

Brodkin, Karen. *How Jews Became White Folks and What That Says about Race in America*. New Brunswick, NJ: Rutgers University Press, 1998.

Brown-Bailey, Sharon Ruth. "Journey Full Circle: A Historical Analysis of *Keyes v. School District No. 1*." PhD diss., University of Colorado at Denver, 1998.

Burgos, Adrian, Jr. *Playing America's Game: Baseball, Latinos, and the Color Line*. Berkeley: University of California Press, 2007.

Bustamante, Adrian. "Los Hispanos: Ethnicity and Social Change in New Mexico." PhD diss., University of New Mexico, 1982.

Cadava, Geraldo. *The Hispanic Republican: The Shaping of an American Political Identity, from Nixon to Trump*. New York: Echo, 2020.

Camarillo, Albert. *Chicanos in a Changing Society: From Mexican Pueblos to American Barrios in Santa Barbara and Southern California, 1848–1930*. Cambridge, MA: Harvard University Press, 1979.

Canaday, Margot. *The Straight State: Sexuality and Citizenship in Twentieth-Century America*. Princeton, NJ: Princeton University Press, 2010.

Carter, Dan T. *From George Wallace to Newt Gingrich: Race in the Conservative Counter-Revolution*. Baton Rouge: Louisiana State University Press, 1992.

Chang, Jason Oliver. *Chino: Anti-Chinese Racism in Mexico, 1880–1940*. Champaign: University of Illinois Press, 2017.

Chávez, Ernesto. *¡Mi Raza Primero! Nationalism, Identity, and Insurgency in the Chicano Movement in Los Angeles, 1966–1978*. Berkeley: University of California Press, 2002.

Chávez, John R. *The Lost Land: The Chicano Image of the Southwest*. Albuquerque: University of New Mexico Press, 1984.

Chávez-García, Miroslava. *Negotiating Conquest: Gender and Power in California, 1770s to 1880s*. Tucson: University of Arizona Press, 2004.

Cohen, Lizabeth. *A Consumer's Republic: The Politics of Mass Consumption in Postwar America*. New York: Vintage, 2003.

"Comment: The Courts, HEW, and Southern School Desegregation." *Yale Law Journal* 77, no. 2 (December 1967): 321–365.

Connery, Robert T. "*Keyes v. School District No. 1*: A Personal Remembrance of Things Past and Present." *Denver University Law Review* 90, no. 5 (2013): 1092–1096.

Crenshaw, Kimberlé Williams. "Race, Reform, and Retrenchment: Transformation and Legitimization in Antidiscrimination Law." In *Critical Race Theory: The Key Writings that Formed the Movement*, edited by Kimberlé Crenshaw, Neil Gotanda, Gary Peller, and Kendall Thomas, 103–122. New York: New Press, 1995.

Crespino, Joseph. *In Search of Another Country: Mississippi and the Conservative Counterrevolution*. Princeton, NJ: Princeton University Press, 2007.

Critchlow, Donald T. *Phyllis Schlafly and Grassroots Conservatism: A Woman's Crusade*. Princeton, NJ: Princeton University Press, 2005.

Cruz, Tatiana M. F. "'We Took 'Em On': The Latino Movement for Educational Justice in Boston, 1965–1980." *Journal of Urban History* 43, no. 2 (2017): 235–255.

Days, Drew S., III. "The Current State of School Desegregation Law: Why Isn't Anybody Laughing?" In *In Pursuit of a Dream Deferred: Linking Housing and Education Policy*, edited by john a. powell, Gavin Kearney, and Vina Kay, 159–182. New York: Peter Lang, 2001.

de la Cadena, Marisol. *Indigenous Mestizos: The Politics of Race and Culture in Cuzco, Peru, 1919–1991*. Durham, NC: Duke University Press, 2000.

Delgado, Grace Peña. *Making the Chinese Mexican: Global Migration, Localism, and Exclusion in the U.S.-Mexico Borderlands*. Palo Alto, CA: Stanford University Press, 2013.

Delgado, Richard, and Vicky Palacios. "Mexican Americans as a Legally Cognizable Class under Rule 23 and the Equal Protection Clause." *Notre Dame Law Review* 50, no. 3 (1974–1975): 393–418.

Delgado, Richard, and Jean Stefancic, eds. *Critical White Studies: Looking behind the Mirror*. Philadelphia: Temple University Press, 1997.

———. *The Latino/a Condition: A Critical Reader*. New York: New York University Press, 1998.

Delmont, Matthew F. *Why Busing Failed: Race, Media, and the National Resistance to School Desegregation*. Oakland: University of California Press, 2016.
Deloria, Philip J. *Playing Indian*. New Haven, CT: Yale University Press, 1998.
Deslippe, Dennis A. "'Do Whites Have Rights?': White Detroit Policemen and 'Reverse Discrimination' Protests in the 1970s." *Journal of American History* 91, no. 3 (December 2004): 932–960.

———. *Protesting Affirmative Action: The Struggle over Equality after the Civil Rights Revolution*. Baltimore, MD: Johns Hopkins University Press, 2012.
Deutsch, Sarah. *No Separate Refuge: Culture, Class, and Gender on an Anglo-Hispanic Frontier in the American Southwest, 1880–1940*. New York: Oxford University Press, 1987.
Dimond, Paul R. *Beyond Busing: Reflections on Urban Segregation, the Courts, and Equal Opportunity*. Ann Arbor: University of Michigan Press, 2005.
Donato, Ruben. *Mexicans and Hispanos in Colorado Schools and Communities, 1920–1960*. Albany: State University of New York Press, 2007.

———. *The Other Struggle for Equal Schools: Mexican Americans During the Civil Rights Era*. Albany: State University of New York Press, 1997.
Dorsett, Lyle. *The Queen City: A History of Denver*. 2nd ed. Boulder, CO: Pruett Publishing, 1985.
Dowling, Julie A. *Mexican Americans and the Question of Race*. Austin: University of Texas Press, 2014.
Duany, Jorge. "Neither White nor Black: The Representation of Racial Identity among Puerto Ricans on the Island and in the U.S. Mainland." In *Neither Enemies nor Friends: Latinos, Blacks, Afro-Latinos*, edited by Anani Dzidzienyo and Suzanne Oboler, 173–188. New York: Palgrave Macmillan, 2005.
DuBois, W. E. Burghardt. *Black Reconstruction in America: 1860–1880*. New York: Free Press, 1998.
Dudziak, Mary L. *Cold War Civil Rights: Race and the Image of American Democracy*. Princeton, NJ: Princeton University Press, 2000.
Dudziak Mary L., and Leti Volpp. "Introduction: Legal Borderlands; Law and the Construction of Legal Borderlands." *American Quarterly* 57, no. 3 (September 2005): 593–610.
Erickson, Ansley T. *Making the Unequal Metropolis: School Desegregation and Its Limits*. Chicago: University of Chicago Press, 2016.
Escobar, Edward J. *Race, Police, and the Making of Political Identity: Mexican Americans and the Los Angeles Police Department, 1900–1945*. Berkeley: University of California Press, 1999.

———. "The Unintended Consequences of the Carceral State: Chicana/o Political Mobilization in Post-World War II America." *Journal of American History* 102, no. 1 (June 2015): 174–184.
Escobedo, Elizabeth. *From Coveralls to Zoot Suits: The Lives of Mexican American Women on the World War II Homefront*. Chapel Hill: University of North Carolina Press, 2013.

Espinoza, Dionne, María Eugenia Cotera, and Maylei Blackwell, eds. *Chicana Movidas: New Narratives of Activism and Feminism in the Movement Era*. Austin: University of Texas Press, 2018.

Fernández, Lilia. *Brown in the Windy City: Mexicans and Puerto Ricans in Postwar Chicago*. Chicago: University of Chicago Press, 2012.

Fields, Barbara. "Ideology and Race in American History." In *Region, Race, and Reconstruction: Essays in Honor of C. Vann Woodward*, edited by J. Morgan Kousser and James M. McPherson, 143–177. New York: Oxford University Press, 1982.

Fine, Michelle, Lois Weis, Linda C. Powell, and L. Mun Mong, eds., *Off White: Readings on Race, Power and Society*. New York: Routledge, 1997.

Flores, Lori A. *Grounds for Dreaming: Mexican Americans, Mexican Immigrants, and the California Farmworker Movement*. New Haven, CT: Yale University Press, 2016.

Foley, Neil. "Becoming Hispanic: Mexican Americans and the Faustian Pact with Whiteness." In *Reflexiones 1997: New Directions in Mexican American Studies*, edited by Neil Foley, 53–70. Austin: Center for Mexican American Studies, University of Texas, 1998.

———. "Over the Rainbow: *Hernandez v. Texas, Brown v. Board of Education*, and Black v. Brown." In *"Colored Men" and "Hombres Aquí": Hernandez v. Texas and the Emergence of Mexican-American Lawyering*, edited by Michael A. Olivas, 111–122. Houston: Arte Público Press, University of Houston Press, 2006.

———. "Partly Colored or Other White: Mexican Americans and Their Problem with the Color Line." In *Beyond Black and White: Race, Ethnicity, and Gender in the U.S. South and Southwest*, edited by Stephanie Cole and Alison M. Parker, 123–144. College Station: Texas A&M University Press, 2004.

———. *Quest for Equality: The Failed Promise of Black-Brown Solidarity*. Cambridge, MA: Harvard University Press, 2010.

———. "Straddling the Color Line: The Legal Construction of Hispanic Identity in Texas." In *Not Just Black and White: Historical and Contemporary Perspectives on Immigration, Race, and Ethnicity in the United States*, edited by Nancy Foner and George M. Fredrickson, 341–357. New York: Russell Sage Foundation, 2004.

———. *The White Scourge: Mexicans, Blacks, and Poor Whites in Texas Cotton Culture*. Berkeley: University of California Press, 1997.

Fonseca-Chávez, Vanessa. "Contested Querencia in *The Last Conquistador* (2008) by John J. Valdez and Cristina Ibarra." In *Querencia: Reflections on the New Mexico Homeland*, edited by Vanessa Fonseca-Chávez, Levi Romero, and Spencer R. Herrera, 79–97. Albuquerque: University of New Mexico Press, 2020.

Freund, David. *Property: State Policy and White Racial Politics in Suburban America*. Chicago: University of Chicago Press, 2007.

Fujino, Diane C. "Black Militants and Asian American Model Minorities: Contesting Oppositional Representations; or, On Afro-Asian Solidarities." *Kalfou: A Journal of Comparative and Relational Ethnic Studies* 2, no. 1 (2015): 97–116.

Gadsden, Brett. *Between North and South: Delaware, Desegregation, and the Myth of American Sectionalism*. Philadelphia: University of Pennsylvania Press, 2012.

Gaillard, Frye. *The Dream Long Deferred*. Chapel Hill: University of North Carolina Press, 1988.

Gallegos, Magdalena. "The Forgotten Community: Hispanic Auraria in the Twentieth Century." *Colorado Heritage* 2 (1985): 5–20.

García, David G. *Strategies of Segregation: Race, Residence, and the Struggle for Educational Equality*. Oakland: University of California Press, 2018.

García, Ignacio M. *Chicanismo: The Forging of a Militant Ethos among Mexican Americans*. Tucson: University of Arizona Press, 1997.

———. *United We Win: The Rise and Fall of La Raza Unida Party*. Tucson: University of Arizona Press, 1989.

———. *Viva Kennedy: Mexican Americans in Search of Camelot*. College Station: Texas A&M Press, 2000.

———. *White but Not Equal: Mexican Americans, Jury Discrimination, and the Supreme Court*. Tucson: University of Arizona Press, 2008.

García, Mario T. "Americans All: The Mexican-American Generation and the Politics of Wartime Los Angeles, 1941–1949." *Social Science Quarterly* 65 (June 1984): 278–289.

———, ed., *The Chicano Movement: Perspectives from the Twenty-First Century*. New York: Routledge, 2014.

———. *Mexican Americans: Leadership, Ideology, and Identity: 1930–1960*. New Haven, CT: Yale University Press, 1989.

García, Mario T., and Sal Castro, *Blowout! Sal Castro and the Chicano Struggle for Educational Justice*. Chapel Hill: University of North Carolina Press, 2011.

Garcia, Matt. *From the Jaws of Victory: The Triumph and Tragedy of Cesar Chavez and the Farm Worker Movement*. Berkeley: University of California Press, 2012.

Gardner, Martha. *The Qualities of a Citizen: Women, Immigration and Citizenship, 1870–1965*. Princeton, NJ: Princeton University Press, 2006.

Garroutte, Eva Marie. "The Racial Formation of American Indians: Negotiating Legitimate Identities within Tribal and Federal Law." *American Indian Quarterly* 25, no. 2 (2001): 224–239.

Gerlach, Luther P., and Virginia H. Hine. *People, Power, Change: Movements of Social Transformation*. Indianapolis: Bobbs-Merrill Educational Publishing, 1970.

Golash-Boza, Tanya, and Eduardo Bonilla-Silva. "Rethinking Race, Racism, Identity and Ideology in Latin America." *Ethnic and Racial Studies* 36, no. 10 (2013): 1485–1489.

Gómez, Laura E. *Manifest Destinies: The Making of the Mexican American Race*. New York: New York University Press, 2008.

Gómez-Quiñones, Juan. *Mexican Students por La Raza: The Chicano Movement in Southern California, 1967–1977*. Santa Barbara, CA: Editorial La Causa, 1978.

Gómez-Quiñones, Juan, and Irene Vásquez. *Making Aztlán: Ideology and Culture of the Chicana and Chicano Movement, 1966–1977*. Albuquerque: University of New Mexico Press, 2014.

González, Deena J. *Refusing the Favor: The Spanish-Mexican Women of Santa Fe, 1820–1880*. New York: Oxford University Press, 1999.

González, Gabriela. *Redeeming La Raza: Transborder Modernity, Race, Respectability, and Rights*. New York: Oxford University Press, 2018.

Gonzalez, Gilbert G. *Chicano Education in the Era of Segregation*. Philadelphia: Balch Institute Press, 1990.

———. "The 'Mexican Problem': Empire, Public Policy, and the Education of Mexican Immigrants, 1880–1930." *Aztlán* 26, no. 2 (Fall 2001): 199–207.

Gonzales, Phillip B. "History Hits the Heart: Albuquerque's Great Cuartocentenario Controversy, 1997–2005." In *Expressing New Mexico: Nuevomexicano Creativity, Ritual, and Memory*, edited by Phillip B. Gonzales, 207–232. Tucson: University of Arizona Press, 2007.

———. "'La Junta de Indignación': Hispano Repertoire of Collective Protest in New Mexico, 1884–1933." *Western Historical Quarterly* 31, no. 2 (Summer 2000): 161–186.

Goodstein, Phil. *Big Money in the Big City: A People's History of the Modern Mile High City*. Vol. 1 of *Denver in Our Time*. Denver: New Social Publications, 1999.

———. *DIA and Other Scams*. Vol. 2 of *Denver in Our Time: A People's History of the Modern Mile High City*. Denver: New Social Publications, 2000.

Gordon, Leah N. *From Power to Prejudice: The Rise of Racial Individualism in Midcentury America*. Chicago: University of Chicago Press, 2015.

Gordon, Linda. *The Great Arizona Orphan Abduction*. Cambridge, MA: Harvard University Press, 1999.

———. *Pitied but Not Entitled: Single Mothers and the History of Welfare, 1890–1935*. Cambridge, MA: Harvard University Press, 1994.

Gotanda, Neil. "A Critique of 'Our Constitution Is Color-Blind.'" *Stanford Law Review* 44, no. 1 (November 1991): 1–68.

Gould, Jeffrey L. *To Die This Way: Nicaraguan Indians and the Myth of Mestizaje, 1880–1965*. Durham, NC: Duke University Press, 1998.

Gould, Richard. *The Life and Times of Richard Castro: Bridging the Cultural Divide*. Denver: Colorado Historical Society, 2007.

Gross, Ariela. "A Grassroots History of Colorblind Conservative Constitutionalism." *Law & Social Inquiry* 44, no. 1 (February 2019): 58–77.

Gross, Ariela J. "'The Caucasian Cloak': Mexicans Americans and the Politics of Whiteness in the Twentieth Century Southwest." *Georgetown Law Journal* 95, no. 2 (January 2007): 337–392.

———. "Texas Mexicans and the Politics of Whiteness." *Law and History Review* 21, no. 1 (Spring 2003): 195–205.

———. *What Blood Won't Tell: A History of Race on Trial in America*. Cambridge, MA: Harvard University Press, 2008.

Guberman, Rachel. "The Real Silent Majority: Denver and the Realignment of American Politics after the Sixties." PhD diss., University of Pennsylvania, 2015.

Guglielmo, Thomas A. "Fighting for Caucasian Rights: Mexicans, Mexican Americans, and the Transnational Struggle for Civil Rights in World War II Texas." *Journal of American History* 92, no. 4 (March 2006): 1212–1237.

———. *White on Arrival: Italians, Race, Color, and Power in Chicago, 1890–1945*. Oxford: Oxford University Press, 2004.

Guiner, Lani. "From Racial Liberalism to Racial Literacy: *Brown v. Board of Education* and the Interest-Divergence Dilemma." *Journal of American History* 91, no. 1 (June 2004): 92–118.
Gutiérrez, David G. *Walls and Mirrors: Mexican Americans, Mexican Immigrants, and the Politics of Ethnicity*. Berkeley: University of California Press, 1995.
Gutiérrez, Ramón A. *When Jesus Came, the Corn Mothers Went Away: Marriage, Sexuality, and Power in New Mexico, 1500–1846*. Stanford, CA: Stanford University Press, 1991.
Hall, Thomas. "Comment on the Nostrand, Hansen, Nostrand, Blaut and Ríos-Bustamante, Nostrand Debate." Paper presented at the Annual Meeting of the Western Social Science Association, Fort Worth, Texas, 1985.
Haney López, Ian. *Dog Whistle Politics: How Coded Racial Appeals Have Reinvented Racism and Wrecked the Middle Class*. Oxford: Oxford University Press, 2014.
———. *White by Law: The Legal Construction of Race*. 10th anniversary ed. New York: New York University Press, 2006.
Haney López, Ian F. "'A Nation of Minorities': Race, Ethnicity, and Reactionary Colorblindness." *Stanford Law Review* 59, no. 4 (2007): 985–1064.
———. "Race and Colorblindness after *Hernandez* and *Brown*." In *"Colored Men" and "Hombres Aquí": Hernandez v. Texas and the Emergence of Mexican-American Lawyering*, edited by Michael A. Olivas, 41–52. Houston: Arte Público Press, University of Houston Press, 2006.
———. "Race, Ethnicity, Erasure: The Salience of Race to LatCrit Theory." *University of California Law Review* 85 (1997): 1143–1211.
———. *Racism on Trial: The Chicano Fight for Justice*. Cambridge, MA: Belknap Press of Harvard University Press, 2004.
———. "The Social Construction of Race: Some Observations on Illusion, Fabrication, and Choice." *Harvard Civil Rights-Civil Liberties Law Review* 29 (1994): 1–62.
———. "White Latinos." *Harvard Latino Law Review* 6 (2003): 1–7.
Hansen, Niles. "Commentary: The Hispano Homeland in 1900." *Annals of the Association of American Geographers* 71, no. 2 (1981): 280–282.
Harmon, Alexandra. *Indians in the Making: Ethnic Relations and Indian Identities around Puget Sound*. Berkeley: University of California Press, 1998.
———. "Tribal Enrollment Councils: Lessons on Law and Indian Identity." *Western Historical Quarterly* 32, no 2 (2001): 175–201.
Harris, Cheryl. "Whiteness as Property." *Harvard Law Review* 106, no. 8 (June 1993): 1707–1791.
Harvey, James. "Negroes in Colorado." MA thesis, University of Denver, 1941.
Harvey, Robert. *Amache: The Story of Japanese Internment in Colorado during World War II*. Dallas, TX: Taylor Trade Publishing, 2004.
Hernández, Kelly Lytle. *City of Inmates: Conquest, Rebellion, and the Rise of Human Caging in Los Angeles, 1771–1965*. Chapel Hill: University of North Carolina Press, 2017.
———. *Migra! A History of the U.S. Border Patrol*. Berkeley: University of California Press, 2010.

Hernández, Tanya Katerí. "Multiracial Discourse: Racial Classifications in an Era of Color-Blind Jurisprudence." *Maryland Law Review* 57, no. 1 (1998): 97–173.

———. *Racial Subordination in Latin America: The Role of the State, Customary Law, and the New Civil Rights Response.* New York: Cambridge University Press, 2013.

Hirsch, Arnold R. *Making the Second Ghetto: Race and Housing in Chicago, 1940–1960.* Chicago: University of Chicago Press, 1998.

"History of Escuela Tlatelolco." Escuela Tlatelolco. 2003. www.escuelatlatelolco.org/Escuela_2013/History.html.

Hobbs, Allyson. *A Chosen Exile: A History of Racial Passing in American Life.* Cambridge, MA: Harvard University Press, 2014.

Hobbs, Gregory J., Jr. "Personal Memoir: Judge William E. Doyle and Governor Ralph L. Carr; Peers for Equal Justice." *Denver University Law Review* 90, no. 5 (2013): 1121–1137.

Holloway, Pippa. *Sexuality, Politics, and Social Control in Virginia, 1920–1945.* Chapel Hill: University of North Carolina Press, 2006.

hooks, bell. *Black Looks: Race and Representation.* 1st ed. Boston, MA: South End Press, 1992.

Horsman, Reginald. *Race and Manifest Destiny: Origins of American Racial Anglo-Saxonism.* Cambridge, MA: Harvard University Press, 1981.

Horton, Sarah. "New Mexico's Cuarto Centenario and Spanish-American Nationalism: Collapsing Past Conquests and Present Dispossession." *Journal of the Southwest* 44, no. 1 (2002): 49–60.

Hsu, Madeline Y. *The Good Immigrants: How the Yellow Peril Became the Model Minority.* Princeton, NJ: Princeton University Press, 2017.

Ignatiev, Noel. *How the Irish Became White.* New York: Routledge, 2008.

Jackson, Kenneth T. *Crabgrass Frontier: The Suburbanization of the United States.* New York: Oxford University Press, 1987.

Jacobson, Matthew Frye. *Whiteness of a Different Color: Immigrants and the Alchemy of Race.* Cambridge, MA: Harvard University Press, 1999.

James, Franklin J., and Christopher B. Gerboth. "A Camp Divided: Annexation Battles, the Poundstone Amendment, and Their Impact on Metropolitan Denver, 1941–1988." *Colorado History*, no. 5 (2001): 129–174.

Johnson, Benjamin H. "The Cosmic Race in Texas: Racial Fusion, White Supremacy, and Civil Rights Politics in Texas." *Journal of American History* 98, no. 2 (September 2011): 404–419.

Johnson, Kevin R. Review of *The Minority Rights Revolution*, by John D. Skrentny. *American Journal of Legal History* 47, no. 3 (July 2005): 315–317.

Jones, Martha S. *Birthright Citizens: A History of Race and Rights in Antebellum America.* Cambridge: Cambridge University Press, 2018.

Kang, S. Deborah. *The INS on the Line: Making Immigration Law on the U.S.-Mexico Border, 1917–1954.* New York: Oxford University Press, 2017.

Kaplowitz, Craig A. *LULAC, Mexican Americans, and National Policy.* College Station: Texas A&M University Press, 2005.

Katz, Michael B., ed. *The Underclass Debate: Views from History*. Princeton: Princeton University Press, 1993.

———. *The Un-Deserving Poor: America's Enduring Confrontation with Poverty*. 2nd ed. New York: Oxford University Press, 2013.

Katznelson, Ira. *When Affirmative Action Was White: An Untold History of Racial Inequality in Twentieth-Century America*. New York: W. W. Norton, 2005.

Kim, Claire Jean. *Bitter Fruit: The Politics of Black-Korean Conflict in New York City*. New Haven, CT: Yale University Press, 2000.

———. "The Racial Triangulation of Asian Americans." *Politics and Society* 27, no. 1 (1999): 105–138.

Klarman, Michael J. *From Jim Crow to Civil Rights: The Supreme Court and the Struggle for Racial Equality*. New York: Oxford University Press, 2004.

Kluger, Richard. *Simple Justice: The History of* Brown v. Board of Education *and Black America's Struggle for Equality*. Rev. ed. New York: Vintage Books, 2004.

Kolchin, Peter. "Whiteness Studies: The New History of Race in America." *Journal of American History* 89, no. 1 (June 2002): 154–173.

Kruse, Kevin M. *White Flight: Atlanta and the Making of Modern Conservatism*. Princeton, NJ: Princeton University Press, 2005.

Kull, Andrew. *The Color-Blind Constitution*. Cambridge, MA: Harvard University Press, 1992.

Kurashige, Scott. *The Shifting Grounds of Race: Black and Japanese Americans in the Making of Multiracial Los Angeles*. Princeton, NJ: Princeton University Press, 2008.

Lassiter, Matthew D. "De Jure/De Facto Segregation: The Long Shadow of a National Myth." In *The Myth of Southern Exceptionalism*, edited by Matthew D. Lassiter and Joseph Crespino, 25–48. Oxford: Oxford University Press, 2009.

———. *The Silent Majority: Suburban Politics in the Sunbelt South*. Princeton, NJ: Princeton University Press, 2006.

Lee, Erika. *At America's Gates: Chinese Immigration during the Exclusion Era, 1882–1943*. Chapel Hill: University of North Carolina Press, 2003.

Lee, Michael. "Dirty Jew-Dirty Mexican: Denver's 1949 Lake Junior High School Gang Battle and Jewish Racial Identity in Colorado." *Ethnic Studies Review* 35 (2012): 135–155.

Leonard, Stephen J., and Thomas J. Noel. *Denver: Mining Camp to Metropolis*. Boulder: University Press of Colorado, 1990.

Lew-Williams, Beth. *The Chinese Must Go: Violence, Exclusion, and the Making of the Alien*. Cambridge, MA: Harvard University Press, 2018.

Lewis, Oscar. *La Vida: A Puerto Rican Family in the Culture of Poverty—San Juan and New York*. New York: Random House, 1966.

Lewis, Richard, Jr., and Joanne Ford-Robertson. "Understanding the Occurrence of Interracial Marriage in the United States through Differential Assimilation." *Journal of Black Studies* 41, no. 2 (2010): 405–420.

Limerick, Patricia Nelson. *The Legacy of Conquest: The Unbroken Past of the American West*. New York: W. W. Norton, 1987.

Linden, Glen. *Desegregating Schools in Dallas: Four Decades in the Federal Courts.* Dallas, TX: Three Forks Press, 1995.

Lipschütz, Alejandro. *El Indoamericanismo y el Problema Racial en las Americas.* Santiago, Chile: Editorial Nascimento, 1944.

Lipsitz, George. *The Possessive Investment in Whiteness: How White People Profit from Identity Politics.* Rev. and exp. ed. Philadelphia: Temple University Press, 2006.

———. "The Sounds of Silence: How Race Neutrality Preserves White Supremacy." In *Seeing Race Again: Countering Colorblindness across the Disciplines*, edited by Kimberlé Williams Crenshaw, Luke Charles Harris, Daniel Martinez HoSang, and George Lipsitz, 23–51. Oakland: University of California Press, 2019.

Lo, Clarence Y. H. *Small Property versus Big Government: Social Origins of the Property Tax Revolt.* Berkeley: University of California Press, 1990.

Locke, Joseph L. "The Heathen at Our Door: Missionaries, Moral Reformers, and the Making of the 'Mexican Problem.'" *Western Historical Quarterly* 49 (Summer 2018): 127–153.

López Pulido, Alberto, Barbara Driscoll de Alvarado, and Carmen Samora, eds. *Moving beyond Borders: Julian Samora and the Establishment of Latino Studies.* Urbana: University of Illinois Press, 2009.

Lowndes, Joseph E. *From the New Deal to the New Right: Race and the Southern Origins of Modern Conservatism.* New Haven, CT: Yale University Press, 2008.

Lyles, Lionel Dean "An Historical-Urban Geographical Analysis of Black Neighborhood Development in Denver." PhD diss., University of Colorado, 1977.

MacLean, Nancy. "The Civil Rights Act and the Transformation of Mexican American Identity and Politics." *Berkeley La Raza Law Journal* 18 (2007): 123–133.

———. *Democracy in Chains: The Deep History of the Radical Right's Stealth Plan for America.* New York: Penguin Books, 2017.

———. *Freedom Is Not Enough: The Opening of the American Workplace.* Cambridge, MA: Harvard University Press, 2005.

———. "Neo-Confederacy versus the New Deal: The Regional Utopia of the Modern American Right." In *The Myth of Southern Exceptionalism*, edited by Matthew D. Lassiter and Joseph Crespino, 308–329. New York: Oxford University Press, 2009.

Marín, Christine. *A Spokesman of the Mexican American Movement: Rodolfo "Corky" Gonzales and the Fight for Chicano Liberation, 1966–1972.* San Francisco: R & E Research Associates, 1977.

Mariscal, George. *Brown-Eyed Children of the Sun: Lessons of the Chicano Movement, 1965–1975.* Albuquerque: University of New Mexico Press, 2005.

Márquez, Benjamin. *LULAC: The Evolution of a Mexican American Political Organization.* Austin: University of Texas Press, 1993.

Martinez HoSang, Daniel. "The Changing Valence of White Racial Innocence: Black-Brown Unity in the 1970s Los Angeles School Desegregation Struggles." In *Black and Brown in Los Angeles: Beyond Conflict and Coalition*, edited by Josh Kun and Laura Pulido, 115–142. Berkeley: University of California Press, 2013.

———. *Racial Propositions: Ballot Initiatives and the Making of Postwar California.* Berkeley: University of California Press, 2010.

Martínez, María Elena. *Genealogical Fictions: Limpieza De Sangre, Religion, and Gender in Colonial Mexico*. Stanford, CA: Stanford University Press, 2008.

Martínez-Echazábal, Lourdes. "Mestizaje and the Discourse of National/Cultural Identity in Latin America, 1845–1959." *Latin American Perspectives* 25, no. 3 (May 1998): 21–42.

McGirr, Lisa. *Suburban Warriors: The Origins of the New American Right*. Princeton, NJ: Princeton University Press, 2001.

McKinley, Michelle A. "The Unbearable Lightness of Being (Black): Legal and Cultural Constructions of Race and Nation in Colonial Latin America." In *Racial Formation in the Twenty-First Century*, edited by Daniel Martinez HoSang, Oneka LaBennett, and Laura Pulido, 116–161 Berkeley: University of California Press, 2012.

McRae, Elizabeth Gillespie. *Mothers of Massive Resistance: White Women and the Politics of White Supremacy*. New York: Oxford University Press, 2018.

McWilliams, Carey. *North from Mexico: The Spanish-Speaking People of the United States*. Philadelphia: J. B. Lippincott, 1949.

Menchaca, Martha. *Naturalizing Mexican Immigrants: A Texas History*. Austin: University of Texas Press, 2011.

———. *Recovering History, Constructing Race: The Indian, Black, and White Roots of Mexican Americans*. Austin: University of Texas Press, 2002.

Michney, Todd M. "Constrained Communities: Black Cleveland's Experience with World War II Public Housing." *Journal of Social History* 40, no. 4 (Summer 2007): 933–956.

Mile High Chapter 7. "Bernard Valdez." *Colorado Civilian Conservation Core* (blog). Accessed September 15, 2017. https://coloradoccc.org/people/bernard-valdez/.

Miller, Mark Edwin. *Claiming Tribal Identity: The Five Tribes and the Politics of Federal Acknowledgement*. Norman: University of Oklahoma Press, 2013.

Mitchell, Pablo. *Coyote Nation: Sexuality, Race, and Conquest in Modernizing New Mexico, 1880–1920*. Chicago: University of Chicago Press, 2005.

Molina, Natalia. *Fit to Be Citizens? Public Health and Race in Los Angeles, 1879–1939*. Berkeley: University of California Press, 2006.

———. *How Race Is Made in America: Immigration, Citizenship, and the Historical Power of Racial Scripts*. Oakland: University of California Press, 2014.

Monroy, Douglas. *Thrown among Strangers: The Making of Mexican Culture in Frontier California*. Berkeley: University of California Press, 1990.

Montejano, David. *Anglos and Mexicans in the Making of Texas, 1836–1986*. Austin: University of Texas Press, 1987.

———. *Quixote's Soldiers: A Local History of the Chicano Movement, 1966–1981*. Austin: University of Texas Press, 2010.

Montgomery, Charles. *The Spanish Redemption: Heritage, Power, and Loss on New Mexico's Upper Rio Grande*. Berkeley: University of California Press, 2002.

Montoya, Margaret E. "A Brief History of Chicana/o School Segregation: One Rationale for Affirmative Action." *Berkeley La Raza Law Journal* 12, no. 2 (Fall 2001): 159–172.

Montoya, María E. *Translating Property: The Maxwell Land Grant and the Conflict Over Land in the American West, 1840–1900*. Berkeley: University of California Press, 2002.

Mora, Anthony. *Border Dilemmas: Racial and National Uncertainties in New Mexico, 1848–1912*. Durham, NC: Duke University Press, 2011.

Moran, Rachel F. "Courts and the Construction of Racial and Ethnic Identity: Public Law Litigation in the Public Schools." *Bulletin of the American Academy of Arts and Sciences* 50, no. 6 (April 1997): 19–39.

———. "Foreword—The Lessons of *Keyes:* How Do You Translate 'The American Dream'?" *La Raza Law Journal* 1, no. 3 (1986): 195–212.

———. "Getting a Foot in the Door: The Hispanic Push for Equal Educational Opportunity in Denver." *Kansas Journal of Law & Public Policy* 2, no. 2 (Summer 1992): 35–47.

Muñoz, Carlos, Jr. *Youth, Identity, Power: The Chicano Movement*. London: Verso, 1989.

Murch, Donna Jean. *Living for the City: Migration, Education, and the Rise of the Black Panther Party in Oakland, California*. Chapel Hill: University of North Carolina Press, 2010.

Myrdal, Gunnar. *An American Dilemma: The Negro Problem and American Democracy*. New York: Harper and Row, 1944.

Navarro, Armando. *The Cristal Experiment: A Chicano Struggle for Community Control*. Madison: University of Wisconsin Press, 1999.

———. *Mexican American Youth Organization: Avant Garde of the Chicano Movement in Texas*. Austin: University of Texas Press, 1995.

Ngai, Mae M. *Impossible Subjects: Illegal Aliens and the Making of Modern America*. Princeton, NJ: Princeton University Press, 2004.

Nickerson, Michelle M. *Mothers of Conservatism: Women and the Postwar Right*. Princeton, NJ: Princeton University Press, 2012.

Nicolaides, Becky M. *My Blue Heaven: Life and Politics in the Working-Class Suburbs of Los Angeles, 1920–1965*. Chicago: University of Chicago Press, 2002.

Nieto-Phillips, John M. *The Language of Blood: The Making of Spanish-American Identity in New Mexico, 1880s–1930s*. Albuquerque: University of New Mexico Press, 2004.

Nightingale, Carl. *Segregation: A Global History of Divided Cities*. Chicago: University of Chicago Press, 2012.

Noel, Linda C. "'I Am an American': Anglos, Mexicans, *Nativos*, and the National Debate over Arizona and New Mexico Statehood." *Pacific Historical Review* 80, no. 3 (August 2011): 430–467.

Nostrand, Richard. "The Hispano Homeland in 1900." *Annals of the Association of American Geographers* 70, no. 3 (1980): 382–396.

Nostrand, Richard L. "The Hispanic-American Borderland: Delimitation of an American Culture Region." *Annals of the Association of American Geographers* 60, no. 4 (1970): 638–661.

———. *The Hispano Homeland*. Norman: University of Oklahoma Press, 1992.

———. "Mexican Americans circa 1850." *Annals of the Association of American Geographers* 65, no. 3 (1975): 378–390.
O'Connor, Alice. *Poverty Knowledge: Social Science, Social Policy, and the Poor in Twentieth-Century U.S. History*. Princeton, NJ: Princeton University Press, 2001.
Olivas, Michael A., ed. *"Colored Men" and "Hombres Aquí"*: Hernandez v. Texas *and the Emergence of Mexican-American Lawyering*. Houston: Arte Público Press, University of Houston Press, 2006.
———. "From a 'Legal Organization of Militants' into a 'Law Firm for the Latino Community': MALDEF and the Purposive Cases of *Keyes, Rodriguez*, and *Plyer*." *Denver University Law Review* 90 (2012–2013): 1151–1208.
Omi, Michael, and Howard Winant, *Racial Formation in the United States*. 3rd ed. New York: Routledge, 2015.
Ono, Azusa. "The Relocation and Employment Assistance Programs, 1948–1970: Federal Indian Policy and the Early Development of the Denver Indian Community." *Indigenous Nations Studies Journal* 5, no. 1 (Spring 2004): 27–50.
Orfield, Gary. *Must We Bus? Segregated Schools and National Policy*. Washington, DC: Brookings Institution, 1978.
Orfield, Gary, and Susan E. Eaton. *Dismantling Desegregation: The Quiet Reversal of Brown v. Board of Education*. New York: New Press, 1996.
Oropeza, Lorena. *The King of Adobe: Reies López Tijerina; Lost Prophet of the Chicano Movement*. Chapel Hill: University of North Carolina Press, 2019.
———. *¡Raza Sí! ¡Guerra No! Chicano Protest and Patriotism during the Viet Nam Era*. Berkeley: University of California Press, 2005.
Orozco, Cynthia. *No Mexicans, Women, or Dogs Allowed: The Rise of the Mexican American Civil Rights Movement*. Austin: University of Texas Press, 2009.
Page, Brian, and Eric Ross. "Envisioning the Urban Past: GIS Reconstruction of a Lost Denver District." *Frontiers in Digital Humanities* 2 (August 2015). https://doi.org/10.3389/fdigh.2015.00003.
Park, Robert E. *Race and Culture*. New York: Free Press, 1950.
Pascoe, Peggy. *What Comes Naturally: Miscegenation Law and the Making of Race in America*. Oxford: Oxford University Press, 2009.
Patiño, Jimmy. *Raza Sí, Migra No: Chicano Movement Struggles for Immigrant Rights in San Diego*. Chapel Hill: University of North Carolina Press, 2017.
Patterson, James T. Brown v. Board of Education: *A Civil Rights Milestone and Its Troubled Legacy*. New York: Oxford University Press, 2001.
———. *Freedom Is Not Enough: The Moynihan Report and America's Struggle over Black Family Life—from LBJ to Obama*. New York: Basic Books, 2010.
Pearl, Sharrona. *About Faces: Physiognomy in Nineteenth-Century Britain*. Cambridge, MA: Harvard University Press, 2010.
Pearson, Jessica, and Jeffrey Pearson. "Keyes v. School District No. 1." In *Limits of Justice: The Courts' Role in School Desegregation*, edited by Howard I. Kalodner and James F. Fishman, 167–222. Cambridge, MA: Ballinger, 1978.

Perea, Juan F. "The Black/White Paradigm of Race: The 'Normal' Science of American Racial Thought." *California Law Review* 85, no. 5 (October 1997): 1213–1258.

Perkin, Robert L. *The First Hundred Years: An Informal History of Denver and the Rocky Mountain News*. Garden City, NY: Doubleday, 1959.

Perlmann, Joel, and Mary C. Waters, eds. *The New Race Question: How the Census Counts Multiracial Individual*s. New York: Russell Sage Foundation, 2005.

Phillips, Michael. *White Metropolis: Race, Ethnicity, and Religion in Dallas, 1841– 2001*. Austin: University of Texas Press, 2006.

Pitti, Stephen J. *The Devil in Silicon Valley: Northern California, Race, and Mexican Americans*. Princeton, NJ: Princeton University Press, 2003.

Pliley, Jessica R. *Policing Sexuality: The Mann Act and the Making of the FBI*. Cambridge, MA: Harvard University Press, 2014.

Poole, Deborah. "Mestizaje, Distinction, and Cultural Presence: The View from Oaxaca." In *Histories of Race and Racism: The Andes and Mesoamerica from Colonial Times to the Present*, edited by Laura Gotkowitz, 179–203. Durham, NC: Duke University Press, 2011.

powell, john a. "Living and Learning: Linking Housing and Education." In *In Pursuit of a Dream Deferred: Linking Housing and Education Policy*, edited by john a. powell, Gavin Kearney, and Vina Kay, 15–48. New York: Peter Lang, 2001.

Powers, Jeanne M., and Lirio Patton. "Between *Mendez* and *Brown*: Gonzales v. Sheely (1951) and the Legal Campaign against Segregation." *Law and Social Inquiry* 33, no. 1 (Winter 2008): 127–171.

Pulido, Laura *Black, Brown, Yellow and Left: Radical Activism in Los Angeles*. Berkeley: University of California Press, 2006.

Qian, Zhenchao. "Breaking the Racial Barriers: Variations in Interracial Marriage Between 1980 and 1990." *Demography* 34, no. 2 (May 1997): 263–276.

Quinn, Rand. *Class Action: Desegregation and Diversity in San Francisco Schools*. Minneapolis: University of Minnesota Press, 2020.

"Rachel Noel (1918–2007)." Denver Public Library. Accessed September 15, 2017. https://history.denverlibrary.org/rachel-noel-1918-2008.

Rangel, Jorge C., and Carlos M. Alcala. "Project Report: De Jure Segregation of Chicanos in Texas Schools." *Harvard Civil Rights-Civil Liberties Law Review* 7, no. 2 (March 1972): 307–391.

Rivera, George, Jr., Aileen F. Lucero, and Richard Castro. "Internal Colonialism in Colorado: The Westside Coalition and Barrio Control." In *La Gente: Hispano History and Life in Colorado*, edited by Vincent C. de Baca, 203–221. Denver: Colorado Historical Society, 1998.

Robbins, William. "Language and Cultural Diversity: Monroe Sweetland, Adalberto Guerrero and the Bilingual Education Act of 1968." Paper presented at the Annual Meeting of the Western History Association, Tucson, AZ, October 12, 2013.

Roberts, Alaina E. *I've Been Here All the While: Black Freedom on Native Land*. Philadelphia: University of Pennsylvania Press, 2021.

Rodriguez, Alex. "Introduction." *Inequality in Education*, no. 19 (February 1975): 4.
Rodríguez, Clara E. *Changing Race: Latinos, the Census and the History of Ethnicity*. New York: New York University Press, 2000.
Rodríguez, Sylvia. "The Hispano Homeland Debate Revisited." *Perspectives in Mexican American Studies* 3 (1992): 95–116.
Roediger, David. *The Wages of Whiteness: Race and the American Working Class*. New York: Verso Books, 1991.
———. *Working toward Whiteness: How America's Immigrants Became White; The Strange Journey from Ellis Island to the Suburbs*. New York: Basic Books, 2005.
Romero, Levi. "Following the Manito Trail: A Tale of Two Querencias." In *Querencia: Reflections on the New Mexico Homeland*, edited by Vanessa Fonseca-Chávez, Levi Romero, and Spencer R. Herrera, 308–324. Albuquerque: University of New Mexico Press, 2020.
Romero, Tom I., Jr. "Of Race and Rights: Legal Culture, Social Change, and the Making of a Multiracial Metropolis, Denver 1940–1975." PhD diss., University of Michigan, 2004.
Romero, Tom I., II. "*Kelo*, *Parents* and the Spatialization of Color (Blindness) in the *Berman-Brown* Metropolitan Heterotopia." *Utah Law Review* 3 (2008): 947–1018.
———. "La Raza Latina? Multiracial Ambivalence, Color Denial, and the Emergence of a Tri-Ethnic Jurisprudence at the End of the Twentieth-Century." *New Mexico Law Review* 37 (Spring 2007): 245–306.
———. "Our Selma Is Here: The Political and Legal Struggle for Educational Equality in Denver, Colorado, and Multiracial Conundrums in American Jurisprudence." *Seattle Journal for Social Justice* 3, no. 1 (Fall/Winter 2004): 73–142.
———. "The Tri-Ethnic Dilemma: Race, Equality, and the Fourteenth Amendment in the American West." *Temple Political & Civil Rights Law Review* (Spring 2004): 817–856.
Rothstein, Richard. *The Color of Law: A Forgotten History of How Our Government Segregated America*. New York: Liveright, 2017.
Ruiz, Vicki L. *From Out of the Shadows: Mexican Women in Twentieth-Century America*. 10th anniversary ed. Oxford: Oxford University Press, 2008.
———. "South by Southwest: Mexican Americans and Segregated Schooling, 1900–1950." *OAH Magazine of History* 15, no. 2 (Winter 2001): 23–27.
Safa, Helen I. "Challenging Mestizaje: A Gender Perspective on Indigenous and Afrodescendant Movements in Latin America." *Critique of Anthropology* 25, no. 3 (2005): 307–330.
———. "Introduction: Race and National Identity in the Americas." *Latin American Perspectives* 25, no. 3 (May 1998): 3–20.
Saldaña-Portillo, María Josefina. "'How Many Mexicans [Is] a Horse Worth?' The League of United Latin American Citizens, Desegregation Cases, and Chicano Historiography." *South Atlantic Quarterly* 107, no. 4 (Fall 2008): 809–831.
———. *The Revolutionary Imagination in the Americas and the Age of Development*. Durham, NC: Duke University Press, 2003.

San Miguel, Guadalupe, Jr. *Brown, Not White: School Integration and the Chicano Movement in Houston.* College Station: Texas A&M University Press, 2005.

———. *Contested Policy: The Rise and Fall of Federal Bilingual Education in the United States, 1960–2001.* Denton, TX: Al Filo: Mexican American Studies Series, University of North Texas Press, 2004.

———. *"Let All of Them Take Heed": Mexican Americans and the Campaign for Educational Equality in Texas, 1910–1981.* Austin: University of Texas Press, 1987.

Sánchez, George J. *Becoming Mexican American: Ethnicity, Culture, and Identity in Chicano Los Angeles, 1900–1945.* New York: Oxford University Press, 1993.

———. "'Y tú, ¿qué?' (Y2K): Latino History in the New Millennium." In *Latinos Remaking America,* edited by Marcelo M. Suárez-Orozco and Mariela M. Páez, 45–58. Berkeley: University of California Press, 2008.

Schmidt, Christopher W. "*Brown* and the Colorblind Constitution." *Cornell Law Review* 94, no. 1 (2008): 203–238.

Schrecker, Ellen. *Many Are the Crimes: McCarthyism in America.* New York: Little Brown, 1998.

Schwartz, Bernard. *Swann's Way: The School Busing Case and the Supreme Court.* New York: Oxford University Press, 1986.

Scott, Daryl Michael. *Contempt and Pity: Social Policy and the Image of the Damaged Black Psyche, 1880–1996.* Chapel Hill: University of North Carolina Press, 1997.

———. "Postwar Pluralism, *Brown v. Board of Education,* and the Origins of Multicultural Education." *Journal of American History* (June 2004): 69–82.

Self, Robert O. *American Babylon: Race and the Struggle for Postwar Oakland.* Princeton, NJ: Princeton University Press, 2003.

Shah, Nyan. *Contagious Divides: Epidemics and Race in San Francisco's Chinatown.* Berkeley: University of California Press, 2001.

———. *Stranger Intimacy: Contesting Race, Sexuality, and the Law in the North American West.* Berkeley: University of California Press, 2012.

Sharif, Rana. "The Right to Education: From La Frontera to Gaza; A Brief Communication." *American Quarterly* 62, no. 4 (December 2010): 855–860.

Sheridan, Claire. "'Another White Race': Mexican Americans and the Paradox of Whiteness in Jury Selection." *Law and History Review* 21, no. 1 (Spring 2003): 109–144.

———. "Peremptory Challenges: Lessons from *Hernandez v. Texas.*" In *"Colored Men" and "Hombres Aquí":* Hernandez v. Texas *and the Emergence of Mexican-American Lawyering,* edited by Michael Olivas, 143–160. Houston: Arte Público Press, University of Houston Press, 2006.

Siegel, Reva B. "Equality Talk: Antisubordination and Anticlassification Values in Constitutional Struggles over *Brown.*" *Harvard Law Review* 117, no. 5 (March 2004): 1470–1547.

Skrentny, John D. *The Minority Rights Revolution.* Cambridge, MA: Harvard University Press, 2004.

Smith, Robert C. *Racism in the Post-Civil Rights Era: Now You See It, Now You Don't.* Albany: State University of New York Press, 1995.

Song-Ha Lee, Sonia. *Building a Latino Civil Rights Movement: Puerto Ricans, African Americans, and the Pursuit of Racial Justice in New York City*. Chapel Hill: University of North Carolina Press, 2014.

Stavans, Ilan. *José Vasconselos: The Prophet of Race*. New Brunswick, NJ: Rutgers University Press, 2011.

Stein, Marc. *Sexual Injustice: Supreme Court Decisions from Griswold to Roe*. Chapel Hill: University of North Carolina Press, 2010.

Steptoe, Tyina L. *Houston Bound: Culture and Color in a Jim Crow City*. Oakland: University of California Press, 2015.

Strum, Circe. *Blood Politics: Race, Culture, and Identity in the Cherokee Nation of Oklahoma*. Berkeley: University of California Press, 2002.

———. "Race, Sovereignty, and Civil Rights: Understanding the Cherokee Freedman Controversy." *Cultural Anthropology* 29, no. 3 (2014): 575–598.

Strum, Philippa. *Mendez v. Westminster: School Desegregation and Mexican-American Rights*. Lawrence: University Press of Kansas, 2010.

Sue, Christina A. *Land of the Cosmic Race: Race Mixture, Racism, and Blackness in Mexico*. New York: Oxford University Press, 2013.

Sugrue, Thomas J. *The Origins of the Urban Crisis: Race and Inequality in Postwar Detroit*. Princeton, NJ: Princeton University Press, 1996.

———. *Sweet Land of Liberty: The Forgotten Struggle for Civil Rights in the North*. New York: Random House, 2009.

Takaki, Ronald. *Strangers from a Different Shore: A History of Asian Americans*. Boston: Little, Brown, 1989.

Taylor, Clarence. "Hurricane Katrina and the Myth of the Post-Civil Rights Era." *Journal of Urban History* 35, no. 5 (2009): 640–655.

Taylor, Keeanga-Yamahtta. *Race for Profit: How Banks and the Real Estate Industry Undermined Black Homeownership*. Chapel Hill: University of North Carolina Press, 2019.

Taylor, Mary. "Leadership Responses to Desegregation in the Denver Public Schools." PhD diss., University of Denver, 1990.

Taylor, Paul S. *Mexican Labor in the United States, Valley of the South Platte, Colorado*. University of California Publications in Economics vol. 6, no. 2. Berkeley: University of California Press, 1929.

Thompson, Cooper, Emmett Robert Schaefer, and Harry Brod. *White Men Challenging Racism: 35 Stories*. Durham, NC: Duke University Press, 2003.

Treviño, Robert L. "Facing Jim Crow: Catholic Sisters and the 'Mexican Problem' in Texas." *Western Historical Quarterly* 34 (Summer 2003): 139–164.

Trujillo, Michael L. *Land of Disenchantment: Latina/o Identities and Transformations in Northern New Mexico*. Albuquerque: University of New Mexico Press, 2009.

Ture, Kwame, and Charles V. Hamilton. *Black Power: The Politics of Liberation*. New York: Random House, 1967.

Valencia, Richard. *Chicano Students and the Courts: The Mexican American Legal Struggle for Educational Equality*. New York: New York University Press, 2010.

Vigil, Ernesto. "Rodolfo Gonzales and the Advent of the Crusade for Justice." In *La Gente: Hispano History and Life in Colorado*, edited by Vincent C. de Baca, 155–202. Denver: Colorado Historical Society, 1998.

Vigil, Ernesto B. *The Crusade for Justice: Chicano Militancy and the Government's War on Dissent*. Madison: University of Wisconsin Press, 1999.

Vinson, Ben, III. *Before Mestizaje: The Frontiers of Race and Caste in Colonial Mexico*. New York: Cambridge University Press, 2018.

Walsh, James Patrick. "Young and Latino in a Cold War Barrio: Survival, the Search for Identity, and the Formation of Street Gangs in Denver, 1945–1955." MA thesis, University of Colorado at Denver, 1996.

Waters, Mary C. *Ethnic Options: Choosing Identities in America*. Berkeley: University of California Press, 1990.

Watson, Frederick D. "Removing the Barricades from the Northern Schoolhouse Door: School Desegregation in Denver." PhD diss., University of Colorado at Boulder, 1993.

Wayne, George H. "Negro Migration and Colonization in Colorado, 1870–1930." *Journal of the West* 15, no. 1 (January 1976): 102–120.

Weise, Julie M. *Corazón de Dixie: Mexicanos in the U.S. South since 1910*. Chapel Hill: University of North Carolina Press, 2015.

Welke, Barbara Young. *Law and the Borders of Belonging in the Long Nineteenth Century United States*. Cambridge: Cambridge University Press, 2010.

Wildman, Stephanie M. "Reflections on Whiteness and Latina/o Critical Theory." *Harvard Latino Law Review* 2 (1997): 307–316.

Wilkinson, J. Harvie, III. *From* Brown *to* Bakke: *The Supreme Court and School Integration: 1954–1978*. New York: Oxford University Press, 1979.

Wilson, Steven H. "*Brown* over 'Other White': Mexican Americans' Legal Arguments and Litigation Strategy in School Desegregation Lawsuits." *Law and History Review* 21, no. 1 (Spring 2003): 145–194.

Winant, Howard. "Racism Today: Continuity and Change in the Post-Civil Rights Era." *Ethnic and Racial Studies* 21, no. 4 (1998): 755–766.

Wu, Ellen D. *The Color of Success: Asian Americans and the Origins of the Model Minority*. Princeton, NJ: Princeton University Press, 2014.

Zamora, Emilio. *Claiming Rights and Righting Wrongs in Texas: Mexican Workers and Job Politics during World War II*. College Station: Texas A&M University Press, 2008.

INDEX

Advisory Council on Equality of Educational Opportunity, 83–84
affirmative action, 13; Denver school district resistance to, 189; as reverse racism, 150–151; Richard Matsch on need for, 175
African Americans: achievement, disparities by race and ethnicity, 76; Advisory Council on Equality of Educational Opportunity study, 83–84; antiblackness, Mexican Americans and, 11, 41–42, 43, 143, 174, 180, 181; "antibusing" sentiment among, 142–143; creating meaning out of difference, 142–143; Denver, demographics of, 53–60; Denver, housing segregation, 56–58, 60–67; Denver, job discrimination, 58–60; Denver, poverty rates, 59–60; Denver schools, segregation of, 69, 72; discrimination, roots of, 33; dropout rates, 76; educational equality, conceptions of, 3, 4, 114; equal protection clause, Fourteenth Amendment, 14; model minorities as different than, 183–184; *The Negro Family: A Case for National Action* (1965) (Moynihan), 183; Noel resolution, 79*fig*, 98, 136, 137; post–civil rights politics, 17–18; Rachel Noel, 50–53, 52*fig*, 78, 133, 135, 172; racial blackness, markers of, 164–165; school desegregation, court monitoring of, 191; school integration demands, 77–80, 79*fig*; social and legal construction of race, 18–21; use of term, 25. See also *Garcia, et al. v. The Board of Education, School District No. I, et al.* (1976); *Wilfred Keyes v. School District No.1, Denver, Colorado*
AGIF. *See* American G.I. Forum (AGIF)
Aid to Families with Dependent Children (ADC), 59
Air Force Finance Center, 53
Albuquerque, NM, 133–134
American G.I. Forum (AGIF), 9–10, 116–117, 121
American-Statesman, 45
Anaya, Frank, 121
Anglo, use of term, 25
Anglo-Hispanic frontier, 35–36
Anglo/minority binary, 23–24, 87–90, 93–106, 127–130, 170
annexations, city and suburban areas, 12–13
"antibusing" movement, 11, 13, 16–17, 31–32, 135–144, 149–150, 170–187, 172*fig*, 188, 191–192
Anti-Defamation League (ADL): Advisory Council on Equality of Educational Opportunity, 83–84
Apaches, 35–36
Aragon, Germaine, 136, 137
Arapaho, 56
Armour, 58
Asian Americans, 3, 54, 61, 63–64, 102, 108, 158; *(David) Johnson, et al. v. San Francisco Unified School District, et al.*, 108–109; as model minority, 184;

265

Asian Americans (*continued*)
  naturalization of, 93–94. *See also* Japanese Americans; Chinese Americans; Oriental
assimilation: assimilationist Mexican Americans in Denver, 119, 121, 130, 141, 184; barrio Americanism, 48, 141–142; Chicana/o movement, goals of, 92, 116–117, 119, 134; confronting desegregation in Denver, 130–144; cultural *vs.* racial differences, 32–33; culture talk, 40, 41; Denver, demographic changes in, 55; Denver Public Schools, integration via assimilation, 72, 81; the "Spanish American Problem," 55, 69–71
Atkins, James, 80
Atlantic, 82
Auraria neighborhood, 56, 57–58, 59, 70
Aztlán, 126

Baker Junior High, 73–75
Baker Junior High Extension Center, 87
banks, housing discrimination and, 62
Bardwell, George, 85, 102–103, 104
barrio Americanism, 48, 141–142
Benavidez, Waldo, 77
Berge, William, 83
bias: of media, 117; standardized testing, 76
bilingual-bicultural education, 3, 215n25; activism in districts other than Denver, 3–4, 107–108; Congress of Hispanic Educators (CHE) and, 122–130, 125*fig*; challenges to, 168, 235n53; Denver Board of Education elections of 1971, 138–142, 139*fig*; Denver Public Schools, programs in, 168–171; Denver school district resistance to, 189–190; Denver schools, final order and decree 1974, 152–153, 167–168; Denver's desegregation plan, 93, 133–135; local educational issues and, 55; as priority of Mexican American activists and parents, 75–76, 75*fig*, 80–84, 93, 98–99, 114–116, 191–192; US Commission on Civil Rights report, 189–190
biological characteristics, racial identity and, 34, 37, 42, 154
Black, use of term, 25. *See also* African Americans

Black Berets, 133–134
Black-White Paradigm, 93
Blanton, Carlos, 43
Boston, MA, 56, 107–108, 172, 188
Bradford, Naomi, 145–146, 148, 160–164, 161*fig*, 163*fig*, 168, 171, 175, 235n47, 235n51, 235n52, 235n53, 238n81
Bradford, Ronald, 160, 163*fig*
Brennan, William, 110–111
Brown, George, 78
Brown Berets, 133–134
Brown v. Board of Education Topeka (1954), 2, 11–17, 78, 80, 84, 89, 91, 92, 96, 103, 104–105, 108, 138, 147, 149, 188, 192
"busing," 99, 166*fig*, 196n22; "antibusing" movement, 11, 13, 16–17, 135–144, 149–150, 170–187, 172*fig*, 191–192; colorblind racial ideology and, 149–150; Denver Board of Education elections of 1971, 138–142, 139*fig*; Denver's desegregation plan, 134, 135–137; Naomi Bradford and the fight against forced busing, 160–164, 161*fig*, 163*fig*; racial differences in, 69; *Swann v. Charlotte-Mecklenburg Board of Education* (1970), 12. *See also Garcia, et al. v. The Board of Education, School District No. 1, et al.* (1976)
Byers Junior High, 102

California: Fiesta de Coronado: A Pageant of the Peoples of the Southwest, 30–31, 31*fig*; Los Angeles school district, 3–4; police and Mexican Americans, 117; race and social position, 34; San Francisco, school integration, 109; school walkouts, 133, 221n44; zoot suit riots, 65–66
Campa, Arthur, 31*fig*
Canales, Blas, 171
CANS (Citizens Association for Neighborhood Schools), 154, 160, 167, 186
Cardenas, Jose, 76, 152–153
Cardenas Plan, 152–153, 167–168, 169
Caucasian, use of term, 25
Caucasian cloak, 47
Census Bureau, US, 20, 40–41, 102–103, 104, 221n48
Chacón, Eusebio, 36–37

Charlotte-Mecklenburg school district, 12
Chavez, Everett, 132
Chavez, Uvaldo "Sam," 130
CHE. *See* Congress of Hispanic Educators (CHE)
Cheltenham school, 152
Cheyenne, 56
Chicana/o, use of term, 25, 129
Chicana/o movement, 4–5, 91; confronting desegregation in Denver, community divisions, 130–144; in Denver, history of, 116–122, 118*fig*, 120*fig*; Denver Board of Education elections of 1971 and, 138–142, 139*fig*; goals of, 3, 99, 114–116, 134; history of, 7–11; Mexican Americans, embrace or rejection of movement, 7–8, 9, 20–21; political landscape created by, 92; tactics used by, 121
"Chicano Power" (Montoya), 119
Chicano Youth Liberation Conference, 126
Chinese Americans, 63, 108; (*David) Johnson, et al. v. San Francisco Unified School District, et al.*, 108–109; as model minority, 184. *See also* Asian Americans; Oriental
Cisneros, Roger, 130–131
Cisneros v. Corpus Christi Independent School District (1970), 111, 219n17
Citizens Association for Neighborhood Schools (CANS), 154, 160, 167, 186
citizenship, 205n46, 220n28; assimilation and, 33; "nonwhite" category for naturalizing citizens, 93–94, 184; "other White" category, benefits of, 8, 36, 43, 146; racial scripts as barriers to full citizenship, 89–90; social and legal construction of race, 19; Spanish colonial identity and, 29–30, 36–37; Treaty of Guadalupe Hidalgo (1848), 44, 134
Civil Rights Act (1875), 14
Civil Rights Act (1964), 8–9, 17–18, 92, 103–104, 146–149, 220n29
Civil Rights Cases (1883), 14
civil rights movements: 1930s through 1950s, 8; 1960s through 1970s, 8–11; colorblind racial ideology, overview of, 147–149, 190–192; conservative resistance to, 160–164, 167–168; the "other White" legal strategy, 43–48, 92, 94–95, 103–104, 110–112, 129–130; violent responses to, 117; White American anxieties about, 42
class. *See* socioeconomic class
Cole Junior High, 102
colonialism, 21–22; double colonization, 7; Hispanophilic cultural movement, 37; Indigenous peoples, taking of land from, 34; Latin American Educational Foundation (LAEF), 28; Mexican American racial identity formation, 28–31; New Mexico, colonial history of, 33–37; settling of the Anglo-Hispanic frontier, 35–36; Spanish fantasy heritage, 34, 117, 124; in US Southwest, history of, 33
Colorado: Fiesta de Coronado: A Pageant of the Peoples of the Southwest, 30–31, 31*fig*; Hispano Homeland, 34–35; housing segregation, 60–67; Mexican Americans, history of, 6–7, 22; migrant labor in, 57; Poundstone Amendment, 12–13
Colorado Fair Housing Law (1959), 65
Colorado Federation of Latin American Groups, 81
Colorado La Raza Unida Party (LRUP), 135–136, 139–142, 139*fig*
colorblind racial ideology, 145–149, 190–192; colorblind legal language, 13, 16–17, 18, 41, 87–89, 231n11; colorblindness in modern America, 149–152; Denver School Board, racial classification challenges, 153–168; *Garcia, et al. v. The Board of Education, School District No. 1, et al.* (1976), 173–187; racial classification, court challenges, 168–187
colored, use of term, 25
Commission on Civil Rights, US, 12, 95, 151, 188–190
Community Education Council, 189
Congress of Hispanic Educators (CHE), 122–130, 125*fig*, 132, 136, 144, 152–153, 170, 173, 174, 176, 180, 186
Congress on Racial Equality (CORE): Advisory Council on Equality of Educational Opportunity, 83–84

Connery, Robert, 98
conservative resistance to the civil rights movement, 160–164, 167–168
Constitution, US: civil rights, the "other White" legal strategy, 43–48, 92, 94–95, 103–104, 110–112, 129–130; colorblind racial ideology, 147–152, 190–192; Fourteenth Amendment, 2, 14–17, 43–44, 47–48, 102, 105, 108, 111, 126–127, 129–130, 147, 153, 173, 185, 205n46, 222n71
Cordova, Marguerite, 154
covenants, housing discrimination and, 56, 61
Creighton, Thomas, 97
Crenshaw, Kimberlé, 183
Crider, Robert, 139*fig*
Crusade for Justice, 8, 100, 115, 130, 131, 191; desegregation of Denver schools, response to, 133–144; history of, Denver, 117–122, 118*fig*, 120*fig*
Crystal City, TX, 135
Cudahy, 58
culturally relevant education: Denver schools, Mexican American teachers in, 73–74; Latin American Educational Foundation (LAEF), 27–30, 28*fig*. See also bilingual-bicultural education
cultural pluralism, 71–72
culture: creating meaning out of difference, 142–143; cultural *vs.* racial differences, 32; culture talk, 40; Mexican Americans, diverse perspective about culture, 131–133; Spanish fantasy heritage, 34, 117, 124. See also Mexican Americans
Curtis Park, Denver, 59

Davis, W. W. H., 157
de facto segregation, 80, 185, 198n30
de jure segregation, 185, 198n30
Deline Box Company, 58
Deloria, Philip, 159
Del Pueblo school, 152. See also Elmwood school
Democratic party, 119
Denver: annexations, city and suburban areas, 12–13; Chicana/o movement, history of, 116–122, 118*fig*, 120*fig*; Curtis Park riots, 38; demographic changes in, 53–55; desegregation of schools, 3; Fiesta de Coronado: A Pageant of the Peoples of the Southwest, 30–31, 31*fig*; growth and development of, 53–60; housing segregation, 60–67, 180–181; Latin American Educational Foundation (LAEF), 27–30, 28*fig*; Mexican Americans, categories of, 33; neighborhood map (1960s, 1970s), iii*map*; neighborhoods, segregation and, 56–60; population of, 53–54; post-World War II growth in, 53–55, 54*fig*; racialized urban geography, 68–84; racial migrations (1945–1969), 49–55, 51*fig*, 52*fig*, 54*fig*; school boundaries, drawing of, 69; segregation, history of, 56–60; Spanish American identity formation, 37–43
Denver Area Welfare Council, 33, 59–60, 69–71
Denver Blade, 1–2, 66
Denver Board of Education: Bernard Valdez and, 49–50, 51*fig*, 142, 229n81, 235n52, 237n70; demands for local neighborhood control of schools, 134–136; elections of 1971, 138–142, 139*fig*; Naomi Bradford and, 160–162, 161*fig*, 171, 175, 235n52, 235n53; Rachel Noel and, 52–53, 52*fig*, 78, 133, 135, 172; racial classification, court challenges, 168–187; racial classification challenges of, 153–168; school overcrowding, 1950s, responses to, 68–69. See also *Garcia, et al. v. The Board of Education, School District No. I, et al.* (1976); *Wilfred Keyes v. School District No.1, Denver, Colorado*
Denver Commission on Community Relations (CCR), 57, 63
Denver Housing Authority, 50
Denver Indian Center, 159
Denver Planning Office, 65
Denver Post, 31*fig*, 75*fig*, 113–114, 115, 135, 139*fig*, 167, 172*fig*
Denver Public Schools (DPS), 22–24; Advisory Council on Equality of Educational Opportunity, 83–84; Bernard Valdez and, 49–50, 51*fig*, 142, 229n81,

235n52, 237n70; Black students, segregation of, 69; "busing" practices, 69, 99; Cardenas Plan, 152–153; Congress of Hispanic Educators (CHE), 122–130, 125*fig*; cultural pluralism, policy of, 71–72; Denver Board of Education elections of 1971, 138–142, 139*fig*; desegregation, court monitoring of, 191; desegregation plan, 3, 133–137, 145–146; facilities, inequality of, 77; final court order and decree 1974, 152–153; Finger Plan, 152–153; Joint City-Schools Program, 74–75; Lake Junior High School, student conflicts in, 70–71; Mexican American community confronting desegregation, 130–144; overcrowding, response in 1950s, 68–70; Rachel Noel and, 52–53, 52*fig*, 78, 133, 135, 172; racial imbalance as evidence of segregation, 95–97; Resolution 1490, integration and, 53; "Spanish American Problem," 69–71; student demographics, 13; student demonstrations (1969), 1–2, 2*fig*; US Commission on Civil Rights report, 188–190. *See also Garcia, et al. v. The Board of Education, School District No. I, et al.* (1976); *Wilfred Keyes v. School District No.1, Denver, Colorado*
Denver Unity Council, 54
Department of Health Education and Welfare (HEW), US, 103–104, 128, 190, 220n29, 228n67
De Pinedo, Andres, 133
desegregation, schools, 3, 22–24; Advisory Council on Equality of Educational Opportunity study, 83–84; African American integration demands, 77–80, 79*fig*; "antibusing" movement, 11, 13, 135–144, 149–150, 170–187, 172*fig*, 191–192; civil rights, the "other White" legal strategy, 43–48, 92, 94–95, 103–104, 110–112, 129–130; colorblind racial discourse and, 13, 16–17; Congress of Hispanic Educators (CHE) and, 122–130, 125*fig*; Denver, Finger Plan and Cardenas Plan, 152–153; Denver, housing segregation and, 65; Denver, Mexican American community divisions, 130–144; Denver, Resolution 1490 and, 53; Denver Board of Education elections of 1971, 138–142, 139*fig*; Denver Public Schools plan for, 133–137, 145–146; Denver school desegregation, court monitoring of, 191; Mexican American civil rights movements 1930s to 1950s, 8; Mexican Americans, differing opinions on desegregation, 114–116, 191–192; *Milliken v. Bradley* (1974), 12–13; in postwar U.S., 11–17; racial classification, challenges of, 145–149, 153–168; racial classification, court challenges, 168–187; racial differences in approaches to, 55; racial identity of Mexican Americans and, 4–6; space and place factors, 56–60; suburbs, growth of, 12–17; timeline for, "with all deliberate speed," 15–16. *See also Garcia, et al. v. The Board of Education, School District No. I, et al.* (1976); *Wilfred Keyes v. School District No.1, Denver, Colorado*
Deutsch, Sarah, 35
discrimination: civil rights, the "other White" legal strategy, 43–48, 92, 94–95, 103–104, 110–112, 129–130; Denver, housing segregation, 56–67; Denver, labor market, 58–59; Mexican Americans downplaying of race in daily life, 39–43; reverse discrimination, 16–17, 150–151, 185
double colonization, 7
Douglas, William O., 157
Dowling, Julie, 40–41
Doyle, William, 98, 99, 100, 103, 104, 105–106, 110, 136, 141, 152–153, 155–156, 158, 164, 169, 172
dropout rates, 76, 77, 82, 84
Dudziak, Mary, 148

East-Manual Complex, 169
Eaton Metal Products Company, 58
education, quality of: access to high-quality education, 29, 100; achievement, disparities by race and ethnicity, 76; demands for improvements, Denver, 115, 117, 122–123; different ideas about, Mexican Americans and African

education (*continued*)
  Americans, 3–4, 22, 50, 52, 87, 123, 135, 136, 137, 174, 192; facilities, inequality of, 77, 105, 106; lack of Mexican American teachers, 73–74; Latin American Educational Foundation (LAEF), 27–30, 28*fig*; non-English speakers and, 45; opportunity, limitations due to segregation, 96; the "Spanish American Problem," 69–71. *See also* desegregation, schools; *Wilfred Keyes v. School District No.1, Denver, Colorado*
El Gallo, 117, 133–134
elites, settling of the Anglo-Hispanic frontier, 35–36
Elmwood school, 77, 152. *See also* Del Pueblo school
El Plan Espirtual de Aztlán (The spiritual plan of Aztlán), 126
English language skills: Denver schools, cultural pluralism policy, 72–73; job opportunities and, 59; parental involvement and, 74–75. *See also* bilingual-bicultural education
entremetido (intruder), 118
Equal Employment Opportunity Commission (EEOC): Spanish American minority classification, 95, 220n29
equal protection clause, Fourteenth Amendment, 14–17, 108; civil rights, the "other White" legal strategy, 43–48, 92, 94–95, 102, 103–104, 110–112, 129–130
Espinoza, Eloy, 133, 136, 137
Esquibel, James, 136
ethnicity: civil rights, the "other White" legal strategy, 46–48, 92, 94–95, 103–104, 110–112, 129–130; culture talk, 40; discrimination and, 95; *Garcia, et al. v. The Board of Education, School District No. I, et al.* (1976)6, 173–187; Hispano as ethnic identity, 7–8; identity formation, 40–46; jury selection and, 15; minority classification and, 110–111, 170; political whiteness, 10–11

Fairmont Elementary School, West Denver, 136

Fiesta de Coronado: A Pageant of the Peoples of the Southwest, 30–31, 31*fig*
Finger, John A., 152–153
Finger Plan, 152–153
Fitzsimmons Army Hospital, 53
Five Points neighborhood, 56, 59, 65, 66, 101, 180
Foley, Neil, 72, 173
Ford, Gerald, 171
Foster and Barnard, 62
Fourteenth Amendment, US Constitution, 14–17, 105, 126–127; civil rights, the "other White" legal strategy, 43–48, 92, 94–95, 103–104, 110–112, 129–130; colorblind racial ideology and, 147–152, 190–192; due process clause, 47–48, 108, 185; equal protection clause, 14–15, 43–44, 47–48, 102, 108, 111
freedom of association, 13, 16–17, 149–150
freedom of choice, 13, 16–17, 149–150
Fulfilling the Letter and Spirit of the Law: Desegregation of the Nation's Public Schools (Commission on Civil Rights, 1976 report), 188–190

Gallegos, Bert, 31*fig*, 138, 139*fig*, 140–142, 228n70, 229n81
gangs, conflicts at Lake Junior High School, 70–71
Garcia, et al. v. The Board of Education, School District No. I, et al. (1976), 173–187, 190
Garcia, John, 170
Garcia, Lena, 74
Garden Place school, 152
Gardner Denver, 58
Garreaux, Manson, 159
Garza, Vincent, 82
gentrification, 132
Gilberts, Robert D., 76, 134
Glenn L. Martin Company, 53
Gómez, Laura, 35
Gonzales, Manuel, 171
Gonzales, Rodolfo "Corky," 99, 117–122, 118*fig*, 130, 134–135, 224n13
government jobs, Denver, 58–59
Great Society, 9, 20, 120, 146
Great Western Sugar Company, 57

Greeley, Colorado, 45–46
Greiner, Gordon, 88, 89, 96, 100–101, 105, 107, 156, 157–158
Gross, Ariela, 44
Gutiérrez, David, 40, 41

Hackworth, Theodore, 139*fig*, 175
Hamilton, Charles, 18
Haney López, Ian, 19, 89
Haro, John, 121
Harper's Weekly, 37
Harris, Cheryl, 9
Hernández, Pete, 14–15, 47–48
Hernandez v. Texas (1954), 14–15, 47–48, 90–91, 111, 220n30, 222n71
Hispano Homeland, 7, 34–35
Hispano Lay Advisory Committee, 138, 140
Hispanophilic cultural movement, 37
Hispanos: Anglo/minority binary legal strategy, 95–112, 113; Bert Gallegos as, 141–142; colorblind racial ideology, use of, 148–149, 177; as ethnic identity, 5, 7–8, 17, 46, 48, 108–109, 129, 130, 132, 141, 187; *Garcia, et al. v. The Board of Education, School District No. 1, et al.* (1976), 175–187; identity formation, 32, 34–37, 116, 190; Judge Doyle's list of racial categories for Denver Public Schools, 158; Mexican Americans downplaying of race in daily life, 39–43; Naomi Bradford as, 145, 162; racial mixing and racial classification, 154, 157, 158, 165; Spanish fantasy heritage, abandoning of, 124–126, 129; at Swansea Elementary School, 168, 169, 173–174, 176–177, 178, 179; use of term, 25, 113–114
Hodges, Paul, 139*fig*
Holm Elementary School, 173
Honeywell, 53
HoSang, Daniel Martinez, 10
housing: Denver, segregation and, 56–67; gentrification debates, 132; neighborhood schools and segregation, 100; quality of, 65; segregation in, 156–157, 180–181; the "Spanish American Problem," 69–71; suburbs and school segregation, 12–17

Houston, Texas, 88, 92–93, 127–128, 132–133, 207n11, 221n39, 225n17
Howell, Duane, 139*fig*

identity formation: ambiguities of, Mexican Americans, 4–6, 21–22, 27–32; creating meaning out of difference, 142–143; culture talk, 40; Hispanos as ethnic identity, 7–8, 32, 34–37, 116, 190; Mexican Americans downplaying of race in daily life, 39–43; Spanish American identity, 37–43. *See also* Hispanos
"illiterate Chicanos," use of term, 131
immigration / immigrants: politics of whiteness, 10; social and legal construction of race, 19; White hostility toward, 39. *See also* assimilation
Indians, 54–55, 236n57; in Anglo-Hispanic frontier, 35–36; Chicana/o movement and, 117–118; Denver population data, 54–55; Hispano identity and, 35–36, 157; Mexican-Indian identity formation, 124, 157; minority classification and, 109, 157; Naomi Bradford's claim for her children, 162–164; playing Indian, 159; racial classification, Denver schools and, 157–160, 164, 166*fig*; requirement to prove Indian heritage, 164–168
Indigenous peoples: colonialism, taking of land, 34; Denver, history of, 56; Mexican American identity formation and, 32; settling of the Anglo-Hispanic frontier, 35–36. *See also* Indians
In re Rodriguez (1897), 90, 206n57
institutional racism, 18
Inter-Agency Committee on Mexican American Affairs, 91
Invisible Minority, The (National Education Association), 81–82
IQ tests, 76

Jackson, Michael, 101
Japanese Americans, 54, 61, 63–64, 93–94, 109, 208n17; as model minority, 184. *See also* Asian Americans; Oriental
Jewish students: conflict at Lake Junior High School, 70–71

Jim Crow, 10, 17–18, 42, 48; Jim Crowism in reverse, 150–151; racial formation post-Jim Crow, 178
The Jim Crow School—North and West: Facts for Action, 80
Johnson, Alex, 120
Johnson, Lyndon, 91, 120
(David) Johnson, et al. v. San Francisco Unified School District, et al., 108–109
Johnson Elementary school, 158–164
Joint City-Schools Program, 74–75
judicial fiat, 140
jury of peers, right to, 14–15, 47
juvenile delinquency: the "Spanish American Problem," 69–71

Kahn, Stirling, 62
Kaman Corporation, 53
Keyes. See Wilfred Keyes v. School District No.1, Denver, Colorado
Keyes, Wilfred, 85–86, 172. *See also Wilfred Keyes v. School District No.1, Denver, Colorado*
King, Martin Luther Jr., 52–53, 52*fig*, 149
Klite, Paul, 100–101

labor, migrant, 57
la junta de indignación (mass meeting of indignation), 36–37
Lake Junior High School, 70–71
land ownership, social position and, 34
la raza, 118, 126, 129
Lassiter, Matthew, 160
Latin American Educational Foundation (LAEF), 27–30, 28*fig*, 31*fig*, 80–81
Latin American Research and Service Agency (LARASA), 74, 82; Advisory Council on Equality of Educational Opportunity, 83–84; creation of, 81; Mexican Americans, country of origins data, 32; Mexican Americans downplaying of race in daily life, 39–40, 41
Latin American student clubs, 81
Latinas/os: Census Bureau racial categories, 20, 40–41, 53, 91, 102–104, 221n48
League of United Latin American Citizens (LULAC), 8, 116–117; on divide between Spanish Americans and Mexicans, 38–39; politics of whiteness and, 9–10; school segregation, challenges to, 46–47
legal construction of race, 18–21, 147–149, 190–192. *See also* colorblind racial ideology
legal strategy: Black activists and school integration, 78–80, 79*fig*; *Garcia, et al. v. The Board of Education, School District No. I, et al.* (1976), 175–187; multiracial student populations, challenge of, 90. *See also Wilfred Keyes v. School District No.1, Denver, Colorado*
Lent, Norman, 150–151
Leonard, Stephen J., 56
Lewis, Lila, 154, 155, 165, 167
Limited Enrollment plans, 101
Lipsitz, George, 149
Liss, Samuel, 57
little brothers (manitos), 38
Litton Industries, 53
loans, housing discrimination and, 62
Lockheed Martin, 53
Lopez, Hank, 38
Lopez, Manuel, 135
Los Angeles, 133; police and Mexican Americans, 117; zoot suit riots, 65–66
Los Angeles School District, 3–4
Love, John, 28
Loving v. Virginia (1967), 167
Lowry Air Force Base, 53–55, 54*fig*
LRUP (Colorado La Raza Unida Party), 135–136, 139–142, 139*fig*
LULAC. *See* League of United Latin American Citizens (LULAC)
Lyles, Lionel Dean, 59

MacLean, Nancy, 92
MALDEF. *See* Mexican American Legal Defense and Educational Fund (MALDEF)
manitos (little brothers), 38
Manual High School, 101
Martí, José, 177–178
Martinez, Soledad, 135–136
Martinez, Vilma, 129
mass meeting of indignation *(la junta de indignación),* 36–37

Matsch, Richard, 175, 238n82
McClain, Betty, 164–165
McKinley, Michelle, 178
McWilliams, Carey, 34, 46, 124
meat packing plants, 58
media bias, 117
Memorandum to School Districts with More Than Five Percent National Origin-Minority Group Children (HEW), 128
meritocracy, 183
mestizaje, 126, 155, 162–163, 177–178
Metro Denver Fair Housing Center, 65
Mexican American Legal Defense and Educational Fund (MALDEF), 4, 90, 225n17; Congress of Hispanic Educators (CHE) and, 122–130, 125*fig*; Finger Plan and, 152–153; school desegregation case in Houston, Texas, 92–93
Mexican American Racial Ideology Continuum, 41
Mexican Americans: achievement, disparities by race and ethnicity, 76; Advisory Council on Equality of Educational Opportunity study, 83–84; antiblackness and, 11, 41–42, 43, 143, 174, 180, 181; bicultural and bilingual schools, strategy of, 80–84; Census Bureau racial categories, 20, 40–41, 53, 91, 102–104, 221n48; civil rights, the "other White" legal strategy, 43–48, 92, 94–95, 103–104, 110–112, 129–130; conflicts at Lake Junior High School, 70–71; confronting desegregation, Denver, 130–144; cultural and political divisions among, 113–114, 119, 121–122, 130–144, 191–192; Denver, housing segregation, 57–67; Denver, job discrimination, 58–60; Denver, poverty rates, 59–60; Denver schools, racialization of students, 69–84; Denver schools, segregation of, 72–73; Denver schools, "Spanish American Problem," 69–71; discrimination, roots of, 32–33; double colonization, 7; downplaying of race in daily life, 39–43; dropout rates, 76; educational equality, conceptions of, 3, 4, 114, 191–192; equal protection clause, Fourteenth Amendment, 14–17;

Hispano Homeland, 34–35; as invisible minority, 81–82; Latin American Educational Foundation (LAEF), 27–30, 28*fig*; as minority group, 5, 127–130, 170; opposition to "busing" by, 11, 13, 16–17, 135–144, 149–150, 170–187, 191–192; political whiteness, 10–11; post–civil rights politics, 17–18; racial identity, ambiguities of, 4–6, 21–22, 27–32; school desegregation, court monitoring of, 191; social and legal construction of race, 18–21; Spanish American identity and, 37–43; Spanish fantasy heritage, 34, 117, 124; in special education classes, 76; tenuous whiteness of, 32–43, 91–95; use of term, 25; whiteness, contention over, 4–6, 6–11, 40–43, 115–116, 119, 130–133. *See also* Chicana/o movement; colorblind racial ideology; Hispanos; *Wilfred Keyes v. School District No.1, Denver, Colorado;* individual names
Mexican-American War (1846–48), 35
Mexicans: settling of the Anglo-Hispanic frontier, 35–36; Spanish Americans, tensions between, 37–43
migrant labor, 57
Milliken v. Bradley (1974), 12–13
minority classification, 9, 87–89, 170; *Garcia, et al. v. The Board of Education, School District No. I, et al.* (1976), 173–187; importance in legal challenges, 92, 126–130; minority as synonymous with blackness, 112; multiracial student populations, as challenge for lawsuits, 90; racial classification, challenges of, 145–149, 153–168; racial classification, court challenges, 168–187; "Spanish Americans," EEOC classification, 95; Supreme Court ruling on, 110–112. *See also Wilfred Keyes v. School District No.1, Denver, Colorado*
Mitchell elementary school, 86
mixed race, racial classification challenges and, 145–149, 153–168, 237n65; court challenges, 168–187
model minority, 184
Molina, Natalia, 71, 89–90
Montclair Improvement Association, 64

INDEX · 273

Montoya, Rosalie, 119
Moon Realty Company, 64
Moore, Fernie Baca, 123
Moore Elementary School, Denver, 136
Morey Junior High, 102, 105, 106
Moynihan, Daniel P., 183

NAACP (National Association for the Advancement of Colored People), 78–80, 79*fig*, 107; Advisory Council on Equality of Educational Opportunity, 83–84
Nabrit, James M. III, 107
National Education Association (NEA): *The Invisible Minority* report, 81–82
Native Americans. *See* Indians
Navajos, 35–36
Negro, use of term, 25
The Negro Family: A Case for National Action (1965) (Moynihan), 183
neighborhood schools, segregation and, 12, 14, 65, 100, 106, 107, 108, 154, 160. *See also* Denver Public Schools (DPS); desegregation, schools
New Mexico, 6–7, 22; colonial history of, 33–37; Hispano Homeland, 34–35; settler colonialism, 28–31
New Rochelle, New York, 80
New York City, NY, 107–108, 114
Nixon, Richard, 160, 171
Noel, Rachel, 50–53, 52*fig*, 78, 79*fig*, 133, 135, 172
Noel, Thomas J., 56
Noel Resolution, 79*fig*, 98, 136, 137
non-English speakers, school segregation and, 45
non-White, use of term, 25
North Carolina, 12
North High School, Denver, 138, 140
Nostrand, Richard, 34–35
Nuestra América (Our America) (Martí), 177
nuevomexicanos, 31, 48

Oberholtzer, Kenneth E., 76
O'Hara, James, 159
Olivas, Michael, 93
Omi, Michael, 4, 150, 205n48

Oñate, Juan de, 33, 37
Oriental, 63, 102, 158. *See also* Asian Americans; Japanese Americans; Chinese Americans
Ozawa v. United States (1922), 94, 147

pan-Latin American identity, 177–178
Park Hill Action Committee (PHAC), 67, 83–84, 98
Park Hill neighborhood, Denver, 59, 66, 67, 128, 141, 180–181, 220n37
Pascoe, Peggy, 167
Perea, Juan, 93
Perez, Josephine, 86–87, 86*fig*, 99, 180
Perrill, James, 136, 137, 140, 172
physiognomic traits, 37, 42
pigmentocracy, 34
Plessy v. Ferguson, 105, 231n11
police, Mexican Americans and, 117, 132
political whiteness, 9–10. *See also* whiteness / White identity
Pontiac, MI, 171
post-civil rights politics, 17–18
post-racial society, 191
Poundstone Amendment, 12–13
poverty: Denver, demographics of, 59–60; the "Spanish American Problem," 69–71
Powell, Lewis F., 157
President's Commission on Migratory Labor, 57
Proficiency and Review (PAR) test, 76
protest tactics, 121
Pueblos, 35–36

race / racism: ambiguities of Mexican American racial identity, 4–6; Anglo/minority binary, 88–89, 93–95, 100–112, 127–130, 170; antiblackness, Mexican Americans and, 11, 41–42, 43, 143, 174, 180, 181; Census Bureau racial categories, 20, 40–41, 53, 91, 102–104, 221n48; Chicana/o movement and, 4–5, 116–119; civil rights, the "other White" legal strategy, 43–48, 92, 94–95, 103–104, 110–112, 129–130; colorblind racial discourse, 13, 16–17, 87–89; culture talk, 40; Denver, housing segregation, 60–67; Denver schools, "Spanish American Problem," 69–71; *El Plan Espiritual de Aztlán* (The spiritual plan of Aztlán), 126; jury selection and, 15; mass meeting of indignation *(la junta de indignación)*, 36–37; Mexican Americans, contention over whiteness, 4–11, 32–43, 91–95, 115–116, 119, 130–133; Mexican Americans, downplaying of race in daily life, 39–43; minority classifications and, 9, 127–130, 170; physiognomic traits, 37; pigmentocracy, 34; post-civil rights politics, 17–18; post-racial society, 191; segregated schools, opinion polls on, 45; social and legal construction of, 18–21; social position and, 34; structural racism, colorblind reframing of, 182; terminology used in text, 25; US Bureau of Naturalization categories, 94; White-Non-White paradigm, 219–220n27. *See also* colorblind racial ideology; *Wilfred Keyes v. School District No. 1, Denver, Colorado*

racial balance. *See* desegregation, schools

racial classification, challenges of: court challenges, 168–187; Denver Board of Education, 145–149, 153–168; *Garcia, et al. v. The Board of Education, School District No. I, et al.* (1976), 173–187

racial formation, 9–10, 199n39, 200n43, 218n12; creating meaning out of difference, 142–143; *El Plan Espiritual de Aztlán* (The spiritual plan of Aztlán), 126; of Mexican Americans, 2–11, 18–21, 32–43, 48, 55, 89–90, 111, 145–149, 174–175, 178; racial identity, determination of, 145–149; racial identity and politics, 119; school desegregation as lens for, 11–17; social and legal construction of race, 4–11, 18–21, 23, 43–48, 88–90, 91–112, 127–130, 145–187, 190, 212n3

racial individualism, 71–72

racial migrations, 49–55, 51*fig*, 52*fig*, 54*fig*

racial politics, 4–7, 9–11, 17–18, 40–43, 116–122, 126, 130–144, 149–152, 155, 190–192

racial projects, 4–5, 20–21, 44, 47, 55, 89–91, 205n48

racial scripts, 71, 72, 89–90, 212n3

railroad, settling of Southwest, 35, 56

raza conquistadora, 37

Reagan, Ronald, 3–4

relational racialization, 89–90, 93–95, 109–112, 129–130

reverse discrimination, 16–17, 150–151, 165, 185–186

reverse racism, 150–151

riots, 1–2, 38, 65–66, 117. *See also* urban rebellions

Ris, William, 102–103, 104

Roberts, Bill, 164

Rockwell International, 53

Rocky Flats, 53

Rocky Mountain Arsenal, 53

Rocky Mountain News, 66, 70, 120, 131, 224n13

Romero, Tom, 61, 72, 137

Rosales, John, 120–121

Ross v. Eckels, 92, 127–128, 225n17

Russell Stover Candies, 58

Samora, Julian, 29–30, 200n4

Sanchez, Aniceto, 47

Sánchez, George I, 43

Sandoval, David, 136

Sandoval, Paul, 62–63

San Francisco, CA, 109

San Miguel, Guadalupe Jr., 132–133

school board. *See* Denver Board of Education

schools: facilities, inequality of, 77, 100, 105, 106; segregated schools definition, *Keyes,* 107. *See also* Denver Public Schools (DPS); desegregation, schools

segregation: Black-White color line, 44; civil rights, the "other White" legal strategy, 43–48, 92, 94–95, 103–104, 110–112, 129–130; colorblind legal language and resegregation, 13–14; Denver housing and, 56–67; Denver Public Schools, process for school segregation, 100–101; Greeley, CO, school segregation in, 45–46; housing in Denver, 60–67, 180–181; patterns of,

segregation (*continued*)
44–48; racial imbalance in DPS, 95–97; reverse discrimination and, 185–186; schools, definition of in *Keyes,* 107. *See also* Denver Public Schools (DPS); desegregation, schools
"separate but equal" doctrine, 105
Settler colonialism, 22, 28–31, 48, 75–76, 158. *See also* colonialism
Shaffer, Harry, 1–2, *2fig*
Shagaloff, June, 80
Sharif, Rana, 76
Silent Majority, 160
skin color, race and, 34, 42, 48
Snyder, Nellie, 36
Social construction: of ethnicity and race, 4–11, 18–21, 23, 35, 43–48, 88–112, 127–130, 145–187, 190, 212n3; of the law, 19, 88–89, 174–175. *See also* racial formation
socioeconomic class: confronting desegregation in Denver, 130–144, 192; creating meaning out of difference, 142–143; Denver, demographics of, 58–60; Denver, housing segregation, 64–65; housing segregation and, 156–157; pigmentocracy, 34; whiteness, benefits of, 9–10, 11, 16–17, 30
Song-Ha Lee, Sonia, 143
southerners (surumatos), 38
South High School, 74
Southwest, US: Anglo-Hispanic frontier, 35–36; colonial history of, 33; Hispano Homeland, 34–35; Mexican Americans, history of, 22; settler colonialism, 28–31
Southworth, Frank, 136, 137
Spain: colonial history in US Southwest, 33; Latin American Educational Foundation (LAEF), 27–28, *28fig*; Mexican American racial identity formation, 28–31; New Mexico, colonial history of, 33–37
"Spanglos," use of term, 131–132
Spanish, use of term, 25
"Spanish American Problem," 69–71
Spanish Americans: Denver, housing segregation and, 63–64; distinguishing themselves from Mexicans, 37–43; as EEOC minority classification, 95;

Hispano Homeland, 34–35; identity formation and, 32, 35–43; Mexican Americans downplaying of race in daily life, 39–43; settler colonialism and, 31; settling of the Anglo-Hispanic frontier, 35–36; use of term, 7–8, 25. *See also* Hispanos
Spanish colonization, 7; Hispanophilic cultural movement, 37
Spanish fantasy heritage, 34, 124. *See also* Spanish fantasy past
Spanish fantasy past, 117, 124. *See also* Spanish fantasy heritage
Spanish-speaking, use of term, 25
Spanish-surnamed, use of term, 25
special education classes, 76
Squire, J. E., 64
standardized tests, 76
Stapleton Airfield, 53
Steptoe, Tyina, 33
student protests, Denver schools, 1–2, *2fig*, *75fig*, 100, 133, 140
suburbs: colorblind racial ideology, justification for moving, 147, 160; Denver, housing segregation and, 58; Denver, population growth of, 53, 59, 74; school desegregation and, 11–17, 18
sugar beet industry, 57
Supreme Court, U.S., 231n11; on causes of segregated housing, 156–157; *Civil Rights Cases* (1883), 14; *Hernandez v. Texas* (1954), 14–15, 47–48, 91, 111, 220n30, 222n71; Mexican Americans as a "distinct class" of Whites, 8; *Milliken v. Bradley* (1974), 12–13; *Swann v. Charlotte-Mecklenburg Board of Education* (1970), 12; White-Non-White paradigm, 219–220n27; *Wilfred Keyes v. School District No.1, Denver, Colorado,* 2, 3, 4, 5, 85–112
surumatos (southerners), 38
Swann v. Charlotte-Mecklenburg Board of Education (1970), 12
Swansea school, 152, 168, 169, 170–173, 181. *See also Garcia, et al. v. The Board of Education, School District No. I, et al.* (1976)
Swift, 58

Tafoya, Charles, 124
teachers: Congress of Hispanic Educators (CHE), 122–130, 125*fig*; experience levels of, 105; at Lake Junior High School, 70–71; Mexican American teachers, lack of, 73–74, 75, 75*fig*, 81; racism of, 69–70; school desegregation, court monitoring of, 191; teaching experience by school, 96, 97*fig*
Texas, 45; *Cisneros v. Corpus Christi Independent School District* (1970), 111, 219n17; *Hernandez v. Texas* (1954), 14–15, 47–48, 90–91, 111, 220n30, 222n71; school segregation in, 8, 46; use of "the other White" strategy, 103–104
Texas Court of Criminal Appeals, 15
Thorberg, Donna, 165
Treaty of Guadalupe Hidalgo (1848), 44, 134
Trevor, John P., 166*fig*
Trujillo, Cheri, 73–74
Trujillo, Cindy, 73–74
Ture, Kwame, 18

Union Pacific railroad, 56
United Farm Workers, 116–117
United States v. Bhagat Singh Thind (1923), 94, 147
Urban League, 39, 42, 78
Urban rebellions, 18
US Bureau of Naturalization, 93–94
US Commission on Civil Rights, 12, 95, 151, 188–190
US Constitution. *See* Constitution, US
US Department of Health, Education, and Welfare (HEW), 103–104, 128, 190, 220n29, 228n67
US District Court, Colorado, 5–6, 20, 23, 24, 48, 90, 95–106, 113, 126–130, 140, 145, 152–153, 163, 169, 173–175, 176, 191
US District Court, Texas, 126–127, 190
Utes, 35–36, 56

Valdes, Daniel T., 7, 42–43, 109, 130–131
Valdez, Bernard, 31*fig*, 49–50, 51*fig*, 53, 57, 83, 142, 229n81, 235n52, 237n70
value system, use of term, 142
Van Schoick, Loisa (Sanchez), 168, 169–171, 173

Villa, Pancho, 38
violence, conflicts at Lake Junior High School, 70–71
¡Viva Kennedy! campaign, 119
Volpp, Leti, 148
Voting Rights Act (1965), 8–9, 17–18

Wall Street Journal, 107
Warren, Earl, 47–48
Washington Post, 107
Weaver, Robert, 154
West High School, Denver, 1–2, 2*fig*, 87, 137, 138
West Side elementary schools, 77
West Side Recorder, 136
White Americans: achievement, disparities by race and ethnicity, 76; "antibusing" movement and, 171–187, 172*fig*
whiteness / White identity: Anglo/minority binary, 23–24, 87–90, 93–95, 100–112, 127–130, 170; as an ideology, 119, 190–192; benefits of, 9–10, 11, 16–17, 30; Census Bureau racial categories, 20, 40–41, 91, 102–104, 221n48; Chicana/o movement and, 4–11, 117–121; civil rights, the "other White" legal strategy, 43–48, 92, 94–95, 103–104, 110–112, 129–130; conservative resistance to civil rights movement, 160–164, 167–168; creating meaning out of difference, 142–143; Denver, housing segregation, 60–67; *Garcia, et al. v. The Board of Education, School District No. 1, et al.* (1976), 173–187; *Hernandez v. Texas* (1954), 15, 47–48, 91, 111; Mexican Americans, contention over whiteness, 4–11, 40–43, 115–116, 119, 130–133; Mexican Americans, tenuous whiteness of, 6–11, 32–43, 91–95; Mexican Americans as a "distinct class" of Whites, 8, 15, 47–48, 91, 220n30; physiognomic traits, 37; pigmentocracy, 34, 239; political whiteness, 9–11; racial categorization and White supremacy, 147–149; social and legal construction of race, 18–21; terminology used in text, 25; US Bureau of Naturalization categories, 93–94; White-Non-White paradigm,

whiteness / White identity *(continued)* 219–220n27. *See also* colorblind racial ideology

Whittier neighborhood, Denver, 66–67

Wildman, Stephanie, 25–26

Wilfred Keyes v. School District No. 1, Denver, Colorado, 2, 3, 4, 157, 190; Anglo/minority binary, argument of, 87–89, 93–95, 100–112; Anglo/minority binary, specific use of term during trial, 96, 97–98, 97*fig*, 101, 102–103; appeal of decision, 106–112; bilingual and bicultural education, goals of, 98–99; *Brown* decision, influence of, 14–17; Census Bureau racial categories, discussions about, 102–103, 104; Congress of Hispanic Educators (CHE) and, 122–130, 125*fig*; Denver Public Schools, legal arguments and strategy, 96–98; differing goals of Mexican American community, 99–100, 130–144, 191–192; DPS process of systemic segregation, 100–101; final order and decree 1974, 152–153; final order and decree 1974, appeals to, 169; *Garcia, et al. v. The Board of Education, School District No. 1, et al.* (1976), 173–187; limited enrollment plans, 101; Mexican Americans as minority group, 5, 127–130, 170; minority classifications and, 9, 127–130, 170; plaintiffs in, 85; racial imbalance in schools as evidence of segregation, 95–97; ruling in case, lower courts, 105–106; ruling in case, Supreme Court, 110–112; school boundaries, shifting of, 101, 102

Wilson, 58

Winant, Howard, 4, 150, 205n48

Winsett, Nolan, 154

Workshop to Develop Human Resources, 122–123, 124

Wormwood, Kenneth, 99–100

Wu, Ellen, 184

Zamora, Sofie, 82

Zapata, Emiliano, 130

Ziegler, Edward, 61

Ziegler, Mable, 61

zoot suit riots, 65–66

Zunis, 35–36

AMERICAN CROSSROADS

Edited by Earl Lewis, George Lipsitz, George Sánchez, Dana Takagi, Laura Briggs, and Nikhil Pal Singh

1. *Border Matters: Remapping American Cultural Studies,* by José David Saldívar
2. *The White Scourge: Mexicans, Blacks, and Poor Whites in Texas Cotton Culture,* by Neil Foley
3. *Indians in the Making: Ethnic Relations and Indian Identities around Puget Sound,* by Alexandra Harmon
4. *Aztlán and Viet Nam: Chicano and Chicana Experiences of the War,* edited by George Mariscal
5. *Immigration and the Political Economy of Home: West Indian Brooklyn and American Indian Minneapolis, 1945–1992,* by Rachel Buff
6. *Epic Encounters: Culture, Media, and U.S. Interests in the Middle East since 1945,* by Melani McAlister
7. *Contagious Divides: Epidemics and Race in San Francisco's Chinatown,* by Nayan Shah
8. *Japanese American Celebration and Conflict: A History of Ethnic Identity and Festival, 1934–1990,* by Lon Kurashige
9. *American Sensations: Class, Empire, and the Production of Popular Culture,* by Shelley Streeby
10. *Colored White: Transcending the Racial Past,* by David R. Roediger
11. *Reproducing Empire: Race, Sex, Science, and U.S. Imperialism in Puerto Rico,* by Laura Briggs
12. *meXicana Encounters: The Making of Social Identities on the Borderlands,* by Rosa Linda Fregoso
13. *Popular Culture in the Age of White Flight: Fear and Fantasy in Suburban Los Angeles,* by Eric Avila
14. *Ties That Bind: The Story of an Afro-Cherokee Family in Slavery and Freedom,* by Tiya Miles
15. *Cultural Moves: African Americans and the Politics of Representation,* by Herman S. Gray
16. *Emancipation Betrayed: The Hidden History of Black Organizing and White Violence in Florida from Reconstruction to the Bloody Election of 1920,* by Paul Ortiz

17. *Eugenic Nation: Faults and Frontiers of Better Breeding in Modern America*, by Alexandra Stern
18. *Audiotopia: Music, Race, and America*, by Josh Kun
19. *Black, Brown, Yellow, and Left: Radical Activism in Los Angeles*, by Laura Pulido
20. *Fit to Be Citizens? Public Health and Race in Los Angeles, 1879–1939*, by Natalia Molina
21. *Golden Gulag: Prisons, Surplus, Crisis, and Opposition in Globalizing California*, by Ruth Wilson Gilmore
22. *Proud to Be an Okie: Cultural Politics, Country Music, and Migration to Southern California*, by Peter La Chapelle
23. *Playing America's Game: Baseball, Latinos, and the Color Line*, by Adrian Burgos, Jr.
24. *The Power of the Zoot: Youth Culture and Resistance during World War II*, by Luis Alvarez
25. *Guantánamo: A Working-Class History between Empire and Revolution*, by Jana K. Lipman
26. *Between Arab and White: Race and Ethnicity in the Early Syrian-American Diaspora*, by Sarah M. A. Gualtieri
27. *Mean Streets: Chicago Youths and the Everyday Struggle for Empowerment in the Multiracial City, 1908–1969*, by Andrew J. Diamond
28. *In Sight of America: Photography and the Development of U.S. Immigration Policy*, by Anna Pegler-Gordon
29. *Migra! A History of the U.S. Border Patrol*, by Kelly Lytle Hernández
30. *Racial Propositions: Ballot Initiatives and the Making of Postwar California*, by Daniel Martinez HoSang
31. *Stranger Intimacy: Contesting Race, Sexuality, and the Law in the North American West*, by Nayan Shah
32. *The Nicest Kids in Town: American Bandstand, Rock 'n' Roll, and the Struggle for Civil Rights in 1950s Philadelphia*, by Matthew F. Delmont
33. *Jack Johnson, Rebel Sojourner: Boxing in the Shadow of the Global Color Line*, by Theresa Rundstedler
34. *Pacific Connections: The Making of the US-Canadian Borderlands*, by Kornel Chang

35. *States of Delinquency: Race and Science in the Making of California's Juvenile Justice System,* by Miroslava Chávez-García

36. *Spaces of Conflict, Sounds of Solidarity: Music, Race, and Spatial Entitlement in Los Angeles,* by Gaye Theresa Johnson

37. *Covert Capital: Landscapes of Denial and the Making of U.S. Empire in the Suburbs of Northern Virginia,* by Andrew Friedman

38. *How Race Is Made in America: Immigration, Citizenship, and the Historical Power of Racial Scripts,* by Natalia Molina

39. *We Sell Drugs: The Alchemy of US Empire,* by Suzanna Reiss

40. *Abrazando el Espíritu: Bracero Families Confront the US-Mexico Border,* by Ana Elizabeth Rosas

41. *Houston Bound: Culture and Color in a Jim Crow City,* by Tyina L. Steptoe

42. *Why Busing Failed: Race, Media, and the National Resistance to School Desegregation,* by Matthew F. Delmont

43. *Incarcerating the Crisis: Freedom Struggles and the Rise of the Neoliberal State,* by Jordan T. Camp

44. *Lavender and Red: Liberation and Solidarity in the Gay and Lesbian Left,* by Emily K. Hobson

45. *Flavors of Empire: Food and the Making of Thai America,* by Mark Padoongpatt

46. *The Life of Paper: Letters and a Poetics of Living Beyond Captivity,* by Sharon Luk

47. *Strategies of Segregation: Race, Residence, and the Struggle for Educational Equality,* by David G. García

48. *Soldiering through Empire: Race and the Making of the Decolonizing Pacific,* by Simeon Man

49. *An American Language: The History of Spanish in the United States,* by Rosina Lozano

50. *The Color Line and the Assembly Line: Managing Race in the Ford Empire,* by Elizabeth D. Esch

51. *Confessions of a Radical Chicano Doo-Wop Singer,* by Rubén Funkahuatl Guevara

52. *Empire's Tracks: Indigenous Peoples, Racial Aliens, and the Transcontinental Railroad,* by Manu Karuka
53. *Collisions at the Crossroads: How Place and Mobility Make Race,* by Genevieve Carpio
54. *Charros: How Mexican Cowboys are Remapping Race and American Identity,* by Laura R. Barraclough
55. *Louder and Faster: Pain, Joy, and the Body Politic in Asian American Taiko,* by Deborah Wong
56. *Badges without Borders: How Global Counterinsurgency Transformed American Policing,* by Stuart Schrader
57. *Colonial Migrants at the Heart of Empire: Puerto Rican Workers on U.S. Farms,* by Ismael García Colón
58. *Assimilation: An Alternative History,* by Catherine S. Ramírez
59. *Boyle Heights: How a Los Angeles Neighborhood Became the Future of American Democracy,* by George J. Sánchez
60. *Not Yo' Butterfly: My Long Song of Relocation, Race, Love, and Revolution,* by Nobuko Miyamoto
61. *The Deportation Express: A History of America through Mass Removal,* by Ethan Blue
62. *An Archive of Skin, An Archive of Kin: Disability and Life-Making during Medical Incarceration,* by Adria L. Imada
63. *Menace to Empire: Anticolonial Solidarities and the Transpacific Origins of the US Security State,* by Moon-Ho Jung
64. *Suburban Empire: Cold War Militarization in the US Pacific,* by Lauren Hirshberg
65. *Archipelago of Resettlement: Vietnamese Refugee Settlers across Guam and Israel-Palestine,* by Evyn Lê Espiritu Gandhi
66. *Arise! Global Radicalism in the Era of the Mexican Revolution,* by Christina Heatherton
67. *Resisting Change in Suburbia: Asian Immigrants and Frontier Nostalgia in L.A.,* by James Zarsadiaz
68. *Racial Uncertainties: Mexican Americans, School Desegregation, and the Making of Race in Post–Civil Rights America,* by Danielle R. Olden

Founded in 1893,
UNIVERSITY OF CALIFORNIA PRESS
publishes bold, progressive books and journals
on topics in the arts, humanities, social sciences,
and natural sciences—with a focus on social
justice issues—that inspire thought and action
among readers worldwide.

The UC PRESS FOUNDATION
raises funds to uphold the press's vital role
as an independent, nonprofit publisher, and
receives philanthropic support from a wide
range of individuals and institutions—and from
committed readers like you. To learn more, visit
ucpress.edu/supportus.